INSIDE TRACK

INSIDE TRACK

*How to Get Into
and Succeed in
America's
Prestige
Companies*

Ross and Kathryn Petras

VINTAGE BOOKS

A Division of Random House   *New York*

LIBRARY OF CONGRESS CATALOGUING-IN-PUBLICATION DATA
Petras, Ross.
Inside track.

1. Vocational guidance—United States.   2. Business
enterprises—United States—Case studies.   3. Young
adults—Employment—United States.   4. Success in
business—United States.   I. Petras, Kathryn.   II. Title.
HF5382.U5P44   1986   650.1′4′0973   85-40868
ISBN 0-394-74339-3

Manufactured in the United States of America

Designed by Beth Tondreau

To James Petras, our uncle,
and Marika Leopold, our grandmother—
for encouragement and support.

E Tan E Epi Tas.

ACKNOWLEDGMENTS

Putting this book together in only six months would have been impossible if not for the help and support of quite a few key people. So we want to give our thanks to them all: to our agent, Kris Dahl of the Andrew Wylie Agency, for dealing with our proposal at the same time as hers and negotiating both successfully (of course . . .); to our editor, Derek Johns, for remaining calmly British and expertly editorial while working with hyperactive Americans; to Sly Lovegren and John Russell, not only for strong reporting, but for putting up with us; Louise Cherkis, Jane and Matt De Lorenzo, Kathy Hamilton and Bill Harlow for all of their contributions; Mike Geylin and R. B. Plunkett, Jr., for last-minute help; to Ed Kenna for many sambucas, Shawn Foley for free therapy, Laura Wessner for sympathizing, L.C. for living next door, Mona Reiser for believing we had it in us; to Guy Albertini and Karl Pincus for keeping the Tandy running; and, naturally, to our parents, George and Beki, for, well, being our parents.

And, most importantly, we want to thank the people who let us into their companies, the people we interviewed who talked frankly with us and infected us with their enthusiasm—we couldn't have done this without each of them.

CONTENTS

INTRODUCTION

It's not easy finding a job. And there are hundreds of books out there that try to make it easier, by telling you how to write the perfect resumé, how to hone your interviewing techniques, how to sell yourself. This isn't one of them.

First of all, we're not you. How can we tell you what to do? That's your job, not ours. And we mean it. Virtually every recruiter we talked to in the course of writing this book told us about the "clone" problem in interviews—people reading the same books and saying the same things in their attempts to get the job. In the words of a Wall Street investment banking partner, "They all have the same educational background, they all have the same blah, blah, blah. They all kind of look alike . . ." Blue suits, yellow ties, and rehearsed interview answers are just not enough.

Today, you have to want more than just a job. You have to want a specific job or career, and you have to think very carefully about it before you go on the interview circuit.

Finding the right career in the right company can be tough. That's what we discovered when we got out of school. We also discovered that, short of having a friend on the inside, it's almost impossible to get the real story on what the prestige companies—the companies where most people *really* want to work—are like. Read an annual report and you'll learn about the company's earnings, but not much more. Pore over a recruitment booklet and you'll find out what training programs a company offers. You'll also learn that they're "dedicated to excellence," that they hire "highly motivated self-starters with strong interpersonal skills," and that they create an "atmosphere of success."

What does all that mean? Not very much.

There's a big difference between the carefully posed pictures and carefully crafted sentences in a recruitment book and the actual working environment. Yes, it's great to know a company's earnings, its organizational setup, and its benefits package. But what about all the other things, the things you can't ask a recruiter? What are the people like? How long would it take to be promoted? Is it a conservative environment or a flexible one? Is this place heavy on politics? Would I *really* fit in?

We decided to write this book to answer these and many other questions.

The only way to find out what a company is really like is to ask people who work there. Young people, people who have just landed entry-level positions and those who are moving up the ladder. And that's exactly what *Inside Track* is—the result of over four hundred interviews with employees in the companies that most people are interested in.

We selected the companies for this book based upon surveys of friends and acquaintances, college students, graduate students and fellow workers. These are the brand-name companies, the best names to have on your resumé. It's tough getting jobs at them, and it's tough to find out what it's like working for them.

We got behind the public relations puff and asked people straight questions. What's it like there? What does it take to succeed? How was the interview?

We got some very straight answers. We wanted to find success stories, but we got a fair dose of negatives as well. Some we used, others we didn't. Because, to be frank, we wanted to find out how you succeed, not how you fail. And one thing kept on coming up again and again—if you want to succeed you'd better like what you are doing. It sounds obvious, but many people are unhappy because they're in the wrong field, for the wrong reasons. So we talked with success stories, with people who are toughing it out because they like the field they're in. And they like the companies. If enough people didn't like a firm, we didn't include it. We're not judging these companies; we're reporting what we saw and heard as objectively as possible. Because what's right for one person may be completely wrong for someone else.

We included some statistics, a little history and information on co-workers, job tracks, salaries, life, and getting in. We *didn't* include the names of specific people to call or places to write.

One thing we learned in writing this book is that the corporate world changes daily. And the right person to contact today may well be at another company tomorrow. We also didn't include our interview subjects' names. They were straightforward with us; we didn't want to hurt anyone's career. Not that this book would. We focused on people who were genuinely pleased with their jobs and companies. Sure, they had complaints. No company is perfect. But these are good places to work. *For the right people*. That's what this book is all about.

That's also why there's such a diversity in the book. It's one thing, for example, to be a loan officer at a bank, another thing to be a financial analyst for a high tech firm. *Inside Track* points out the differences.

No matter how well prepared you may be, you're probably interested in more than one possible career track. In advertising *or* public relations, retailing *or* the record industry, banking *or* accounting. So *Inside Track* isn't only a look at specific companies; it's also designed to give people a view of different industries, and the different jobs within each industry.

One more thing. We worked hard, but we had fun. And as we have said, most of the people we talked with were also having fun. They were working hard, but enjoying the challenge or just plain enjoying the work. Enthusiastic people get jobs! We got a few offers and we weren't even looking. So quit worrying and get a job—one that you'll like and do well.

As Robert Townsend wrote in *Up the Organization*: "If you can't do it excellently, don't do it at all. Because if it's not excellent it won't be profitable or fun, and if you're not in business for fun or profit, what the hell are you doing here?"

INSIDE TRACK

ACCOUNTING

Accountants try to make sense out of the sloppy human world of business. They analyze, measure, and report business information in clear, standardized accounting language. And then the trouble begins.

Why? Because accounting is a lot more than bookkeeping, green ledger sheets, and calculators. It's systems analysis and accounting theory—the whys and why nots of business financial organization. It gets to the heart of business—the flow of money through and out of a corporation—to government, tax collectors, and shareholders. It's not an easy profession, and whatever people say, it's not for dull, retiring types. Accountants have been called everything from bean counters to . . . well, forget it, but don't forget that it is a dynamic service industry that defines the bottom line. And that's what business is all about.

Accounting is a profession, and like law or medicine, it has professional organizations, rule-makers, and rules. The professional organization is the American Institution of Certified Public Accountants (AICPA). AICPA selects members to serve on the Financial Accounting Standards Board (FASB—pronounced fasbee), which outlines accounting rules, called Generally Accepted Accounting Principles (GAAP). Accountants work wherever money exists—in government, in corporations, in public organizations, and as private practitioners. They keep the books, develop internal financial systems, pay the bills and taxes, write the budgets, and rewrite the budgets.

But big-time accounting is public accounting. Public accounting firms are usually private partnerships of accountants who serve corporate clients. They prepare and audit financial statements and tax returns and offer financial consulting services—all in accordance with GAAP (and GAAS, or Generally Accepted Accounting Standards). The "Big Eight" are the biggest and most prestigious of the public accountants, eight multinational giants that audit most of the *Fortune* 500 companies and a host of smaller ones as well. Even their names sound blue-chip—Arthur Andersen, Coopers & Lybrand, Deloitte Haskins & Sells, Ernst & Whinney, Peat Marwick Mitchell, Price Waterhouse, Touche Ross, and Arthur Young.

Because accounting is a more organized, more conservative profession than most, the differences between these giants seem slight—until you visit the firms. Then the differences in style, in people, and in management become a bit more apparent. Firms differ, and regional offices of the same firm differ. When choosing a job in public accounting, its important to get an idea of the firm and the office you'll be working out of.

But wherever you are, be prepared for a grind. Virtually every partner in every Big Eight firm speaks of the early years in accounting as grueling. Many wanted to quit and go somewhere else—anywhere else. But those who stick it out may make big money (salaries for partners usually begin at well over $100,000). And because public accounting is one of the fastest growing professions, it can be a fast five to fifteen years to make partner. Beginning salaries of $24,000–$30,000 (a bit higher for MBAs) aren't so bad either. But it's hard work and usually up or out. Only 3 percent or so make partner. If you don't, headhunters are calling and private industry loves accountants trained by the Big Eight.

So what do accountants do? Public accounting firms are usually divided into three broad areas—auditing, tax, and consulting. **Auditing** is the bread and butter of accounting, and it brings in perhaps two thirds of most firms' revenue. Auditors check a client company's financial statements for accuracy and issue an opinion. Usually it's a standard paragraph to the effect that the company's statement is in accordance with GAAP. In other words, the company has reported its financial operations fairly, accurately, and consistently. This is more important than it sounds. If a company wishes to issue equity (stock) or debt (bonds), the Securities and Exchange Commission requires audited financial statements. And, of course, investors want them too. Audits are conducted like military campaigns. Usually a partner heads the "engagement," supervising a team of more junior employees—managers, supervisors, seniors, and staff accountants. With the partner, they plan what should be done, how long it will take, and who will do what. The lower levels do most of the verifying—making certain serial numbers match, bank balances are accurate, and inventories are actually there. Auditors "test" certain areas. In a limited amount of time they must verify that what the company reports is true. So they spot-check certain areas, talk with management, learn about the industry, and "tick" the numbers— check the company's reported figures with their own. If they find errors or discrepancies, management is alerted and solutions are suggested. At the end, if all goes well, an unqualified audit report is made. And the auditors go to another company and another engagement and more long hours.

Tax is an even more complex area of public accounting. If the tax laws are complex, tax accounting is even more so. Usually tax specialists have MBAs or law degrees in addition to CPAs. Or they have years of experience. Tax CPAs prepare corporate returns, but more important, advise corporations of the tax consequences of business activities before the IRS comes calling.

Consulting is the newest area in public accounting, and in many ways the most exciting. Big Eight firms usually call what they do "management consulting," but unlike the big consulting firms, more of the work is strictly financial. As computers become even more important and financial systems more complex, who better to sort out the mess than financial specialists from public accounting firms? They advise corporations on the financial systems they need, then help select and install the best system.

That's public accounting. And even more changes are coming. Computers are naturally becoming the most valuable tool in this still very labor-intensive business, and young computer experts and systems analysts can advance quite quickly. Some problems are in the air, however. Some firms have been criticized for being a bit too competitive and either careless with auditing, or plain wrong. Lawsuits and controversy have surrounded certain audits of the Big Eight, and right now it's a very sore point for most firms.

As accounting becomes more competitive, people skills become more important. Firms may lose clients simply because management didn't like the auditors. So people skills and communications skills count—in addition to the numbers.

ARTHUR ANDERSEN

VITAL STATISTICS

- locations: Chicago, IL and Geneva, Switzerland (head-quarters); 215 offices in 49 countries
- revenues: $1.5 billion (1985)
- rank: 1st
- employees: 30,000 (worldwide total); 14,450 (U.S.)

AS SEEN FROM THE OUTSIDE

The name says it all. One man's name, and one firm. Arthur Andersen offices may differ, and people may differ, but Arthur Andersen is not as much divided as united. It's a centralized firm with two centers, U.S. headquarters in Chicago, and world headquarters in Geneva.

And one main training center in St. Charles, Illinois, called the Center for Professional Education. Everybody has gone, is going, or will go to St. Charles to study or teach the Arthur Andersen way of tax accounting, auditing, or consulting.

Arthur Andersen's "one firm" approach and extensive attention to training has helped push it to the top. It's the largest U.S. firm in fee income, number of staff, and in consulting services.

But it started very small, and relatively late. In 1913, Arthur Andersen, an assistant professor at Northwestern University, opened a small partnership with an associate, Clarence Delaney, and eight staff members. Fees increased rapidly, from $1,000 in December 1913, to $45,000 in 1914, to $322,000 in 1930. By 1920, Arthur Andersen had left Northwestern to devote his full energies to his firm.

And they've been hustling ever since. Andersen is known as one of the more aggressive accounting firms, redefining itself and in the process redefining the profession of public accounting as well. It was among the first to use microcomputers, and the biggest booster of information consulting as part of the public accounting profession.

Being the biggest has its problems as well. Andersen has been hit with a number of lawsuits over its audits of several failed financial companies, settling in and out of court. Similar, though smaller, claims against other Big Eight firms have prompted a fair amount of controversy within the profession and the financial community.

Andersen is big and getting bigger. It audits more public companies in the U.S. than any other firm, and is already far more than just an accounting firm: its tax consulting and management information consulting comprised over half of fee income in 1985.

A long way from when a professor sat in a small office in downtown Chicago . . .

HEARD AT THE WATER COOLER—
WHAT IT'S REALLY LIKE TO WORK HERE

Everything is "by the book" at Arthur Andersen. Innovative, yes, but innovative the Arthur Andersen way. At other firms you hear more about the *similarities* among the Big Eight; at Andersen, you hear about Andersen. "I think there's a distinct culture. And there certainly is an Arthur Andersen way of doing things," commented one staffer.

A consultant spoke of the advantages in his own field, which is information consulting, an Andersen speciality.

"The point is there is a specific method, it's documented, and it's used. No matter which office you happen to be in, you all speak the same language."

The same language, and it's not just in info-systems. It's the Andersen way, whether in tax, audit, or management information consulting. And it starts at St. Charles, the training center forty-five miles from the firm's headquarters in Chicago. "We've all been to St. Charles, we've all been to the classes, and it creates a cohesiveness, a culture within the firm," said one young staffer.

So what is that culture? "It's shared experience in terms of education, methodology, the way you do work; and shared values," summed up another employee.

Well, the shared experience is St. Charles. The shared methodology and the way you do work is *taught* at St. Charles, and the shared values are basic—belief in client service, self-motivation, and hard work. Just like the other firms, but with an Andersen touch.

PEOPLE

"The kind of person we attract is very much internally motivated," said one go-getter. "Someone who wants to do the job
right, not because if he or she doesn't they're going to be beaten
up for it, but because they want to see it work, they want to see
it get done on time."

That dedication to work seems to be the key to Arthur Andersen people. Sure, they differ a bit from office to office. But
they don't seem to differ all that much. One consultant described
driving in a limousine to St. Charles with staffers from the Oslo
office and realizing that "they knew what you knew. The other
side of the coin is that it may seem like a cookie cutter thing."

Actually, it's all part of the "one firm" thinking, a serious-
minded attitude toward work and Andersen that most people
share. And no wonder. As a young man stated, "This is very
much an up or out organization."

So Andersen people learn to move up. And they learn to be
pretty tough in the process.

"You learn to accept constructive criticism or you don't stay
around," noted a manager. "People just want to get on with the
job."

Naturally. After all, that's the Andersen way.

JOBS

The jobs here are similar to those at any Big Eight firm, but
there is one distinction—at Andersen, most jobs take you to St.
Charles. And that's something everyone at Andersen talks about.

"St. Charles frankly is intended to be boot camp," a young
man said. "It's intended to inculcate a set of values."

Others disagreed with the "boot camp" analogy, but all agreed
on the essentials: "It's intensive, it's informative, and it's a lot of
fun," said a graduate. And it's intended to give new hirees education in Andersen's approach to auditing, tax consulting, and
management information consulting.

Generally, staffers starting out in the **audit** area begin with a
three week course called FASTS—Firmwide Audit Staff Training
School. The first week, it's orientation held at regional offices.
Then it's off to St. Charles for the next two weeks. At St. Charles,
new employees meet staffers from both the U.S. and worldwide
offices. "It's quite an intensive experience, both professionally

and personally," said a manager. "You make friendships there you keep for a long, long time."

The social aspect is only part of it. It's also a lot of work, capped off by a complete audit of a case company. Trainees feel prepared (or should feel prepared) for real audits back at the office.

Andersen differs a bit from some other firms in terms of audit team assignments. Sometimes junior staffers work in a staff pool—where they are assigned to various engagements as needed. In some offices, audit staff are assigned to a specific division within their office, and their engagements are within that specific sector. The New York office is divided into three: Financial Services, Commercial, and Small Business. The Los Angeles office is divided into seven: Oil and Gas, Real Estate, Financial Services, Entertainment and Hospitality, Commercial, Small Business, and Health Care. Some people we talked to outside the firm chose not to accept an Andersen offer because of this: they wanted to play the field in their early years as staff auditors, and get to know many industries.

"I think that's what scares a lot of college students about Arthur Andersen, having to choose a division; they think it's so limiting," commented one staffer. But he then went on to describe the range of companies within his division (the Commercial Division) in Chicago. "We do large manufacturing companies, publishers, printers, advertising companies, as well as hospitals and health care organizations."

It depends on what you view as limiting. The work itself certainly isn't limiting. Although Andersen uses its own audit approach, called TFA—Transaction Flow Analysis—junior staffers describe the work in much the same way as those at other firms. "The work is about the same, you're going to do xeroxing, cash, accounts payable—it's basic to public accounting," explained one experienced person. "Cash is cash," commented another. "It's things where not a lot of judgment is involved." The next year does get more involved with things that do require judgment—like bad debt review and obsolescence review. "They let you think, when you're not ticking or tying."

But there are differences within the firm. "It's very different depending on the size of the office," said one manager in L.A. "If you go down to our San Diego office, which has forty-five people, you'll be on shorter engagements. You may get responsibility a little faster. But you may not get exposure to more sophisticated areas such as heavy duty taxes or SEC reporting."

And within the firm itself there are differences by division. The Small Business divisions are the more entrepreneurial areas. "You get a lot of responsibility, you get your feet wet early in the game," one person said. Another added that college left him "totally unprepared; in school, everyone talks theory, not how to look at cancelled checks." One staffer categorized the work as half audit, and half "fun stuff." The fun stuff includes tax-consulting work, talking with top management, and generally acting as an accounting consultant.

Arthur Andersen's **Management Information Consulting** area is the largest of the Big Eight. That's something employees find attractive, as it offers them a broad scope of projects and the chance to expand the practice into specific industry areas. According to one staffer, the bulk of the consulting practice is "mainstream" projects—the development and installation of large computer systems.

While projects tend to be mainstream and people have common experiences, there is something about consulting here that isn't run-of-the-mill—the work itself.

"It took me a couple of years to adjust to situations where every client was different, with a different set of problems," a six-year vet said. "After a while, though, you begin seeing the common thread between industries."

The fact that the projects are mainstream means that employees get the opportunity to see direct results from their work. And the results aren't peripheral; they're as mainstream as the systems themselves. One employee mentioned a project he worked on for a financial services company. "We helped them save $50 million the first year. We had a big mainstream impact on their operations. And we take a lot of pride in that."

Newly hired staffers in consulting begin with three weeks of training in the office. Then it's to St. Charles for three weeks, where new hirees receive orientation to consulting the Andersen way, and courses in computer fundamentals. The course work involves a series of projects, in which employees design and code programs in COBOL, and make sure their projects work.

"The twenty-one days they're there are twenty-one days of work," a manager said. "I think one Sunday afternoon there's a break, as I recall."

But the intensive training pays off. For one thing, new hirees quickly get immersed in the type of work they're going to be handling. And they get immersed in the Andersen way of approaching work. "As important as St. Charles is to get the computer fundamentals, it's equally important that it serves as a vehicle for instilling a sense of culture, of the shared values, and the spirit of cooperation. That's such a key factor when they get out on the job."

So teamwork is heavily stressed during the first training period, as recruits break into small groups for assignments in and out of the classroom. "There's a very clear emphasis on not so much coming up with your own solution, but rather sharing and pulling other members of the team along," a manager noted. "It's important to us, because in the real world, on your first job, that's what happens. You're put out in an environment that could be very stressful if not for the fact that you were working as part of a team."

Once people conclude their initial training, they begin working as staff members in consulting. At that level, the focus is on technical skills, getting the foundations down. Then it's a matter of rising through the ranks, taking on more responsibility, managing people, and eventually selling the firm to clients.

And people are expected to rise through the ranks. As one young man noted, "We don't have people who are professional programmers, we don't have people who are forever systems analysts. And I think that's a strength."

One of the reasons for that could be Andersen's organization. While it is a partnership, individual partners aren't profit centers. So employees say there's more interaction between offices and less competition.

"What struck me as a first-year staff person was how I could call up a partner from another office and the guy would spend a lot of time with me," an old hand recalled.

Open interaction, a one-firm philosophy, and a mainstream project focus leads to people from different offices working together on projects. "I'm managing a project that we have to have twenty-five consultants on," said a manager. "And I've got seven from Houston, a person from New Orleans, a person from Oslo. Sight unseen I can take a staff person from any office and know what that person can do."

Finally, there's **Andersen's tax division**, which begins with tax courses at St. Charles, and concludes with on-the-job training.

Andersen hires BAs directly into tax, and helps them obtain CPAs, which are required for advancement. Like the rest of Andersen, this is a huge division. And like the rest of the Big Eight, work here includes tax compliance engagements as well as tax consulting.

LIFE

As at other Big Eight firms, life here can differ some from office to office. But since this is Andersen and offices don't differ too much, there are some common aspects.

For one thing, dedication to work. Virtually everyone we talked to at the firm, as well as former employees, categorized Andersen offices as "serious." Life at Andersen to a great extent means giving your all to the firm—whenever necessary.

"Friday, we had a Christmas party scheduled for five. But we had to get a proposal out. So we had a team—a partner, myself, another manager, and a staff person, plus our typing department stay until three in the morning," a manager said. "That's kind of accepted here. We had to do it. No one likes doing that. You know, I didn't like calling my wife who's going to meet me at the cocktail party. No one *likes* doing that, but it's the sense that we want to get this done."

But shared values and experience don't just mean work. There is a lighter side to life at Andersen. Like St. Charles. Sure, it's a place where people are trained. But it's also a place where people meet other people, at the beginning and throughout their careers here.

DOLLARS AND SENSE

No one would mention specific salary levels except to say they were within industry ranges (see industry profile). As one person summed it up, "The profession pays, I'd say, a mediocre B until you're a partner, and Andersen is no exception." But everyone cites the benefits of learning at St. Charles as a definite plus.

GETTING IN—TRICKS OF THE TRADE

Everyone recommends relaxing during interviews on campus— no one wants to hire nervous wrecks. And Andersen *does* want to hire people with interests and experiences that go beyond public accounting.

A partner advised candidates to study the local office in the city where they want to work, and to ask questions. "What is your growth rate? How many partners have you promoted? How long have people been in various positions. What are the significant clients in your local office? Are you gaining market share?"

Staff people recommended applying for summer internships before graduation, through campus placement or by going directly to the firm. It all adds up to one thing. Get to know the profession (not just the theory), the firm, and the office before the interviews.

THE BOTTOM LINE

Big, serious, and great training.

COOPERS & LYBRAND

VITAL STATISTICS

- **locations:** New York (headquarters); 95 offices nation-wide; 226 offices worldwide
- **revenues:** $760 million (approximate; exact figures not available)
- **rank:** 4th in U.S.
- **employees:** 23,700 (worldwide total); 9,400 (U.S.)

AS SEEN FROM THE OUTSIDE

Coopers does well on the campus recruiting circuit, and that's no surprise, since the firm audits or services five Ivy League colleges (Columbia, Cornell, Harvard, Penn, and Yale) as well as Stanford, USC, MIT, and Ohio State.

It does a lot more than just pore over academic ledgers, however. Coopers is in the big league of the Big Eight, moving toward international yearly revenues of a billion dollars. In Britain, it's the largest and most innovative firm of the bunch, with an advertisement playing off the TV show "Dallas," and an aggressive move into the nonaudit side of public accounting.

In the U.S., Coopers isn't on TV, but it does audit CBS. Like its British partner firm, it sees movement away from traditional bread-and-butter auditing into a broader role as a financial services–public accounting firm. It's a "multidisciplinary" approach. Coopers is divided into the traditional three sections of Audit, Tax, and Consulting, but also has a separate Actuarial, Benefits, and Compensation Group. Unlike some other firms, its Computer Audit Assistance Group is a separate group as well.

Coopers sees itself as a market leader when it comes to computerized audits. It was one of the first firms to realize and use computer power, and it takes great pride in that fact. And in its move into the middle market. And in its consulting. And in specialties like state and local taxation. Coopers can be aggressive when it comes to talking about Coopers' place in public accounting.

And it's not a bad place to be. Unlike some other firms, Coopers has faced few problems or embarrassments with lawsuits over negligent auditing procedures. Its decentralized partnership structure allows for a bit more partner control and, thus, a bit more flexibility.

HEARD AT THE WATER COOLER— WHAT IT'S REALLY LIKE TO WORK HERE

Ask a Coopers person why they chose Coopers and you almost always hear the same answer. "I felt most comfortable at Coopers" said one junior staff accountant in New York. "I felt like I could be myself."

"It's very, very informal," said a go-getting partner. "Everyone's on a first name basis. I haven't heard a 'Mr.' yet."

Almost everyone we talked to said it. Yes, offices differ and people differ, and Coopers *is* Big Eight accounting, but there is a casual feel about most Coopers offices. Not as preppie and blue-blooded as Price Waterhouse, not as hungry and aggressive as Arthur Andersen, Coopers is a comfortable haven for people who like public accounting but aren't stuffy about it.

It's an in-between firm in that sense, "not too strict and not too lax," in the words of a junior staffer. Maybe that's why it has a reputation for being a bit more creative than some other firms. Others say they're more aggressive and competitive, fighting the rest for a bigger slice of the pie. But however they act in the marketplace, in their offices there's a casual feel.

Walk into a Coopers office and you don't feel intimidated by dark paneling, dark walls, and hushed voices, as at some other firms. Here light colors, beige rugs, and friendly attitudes are more the norm. Coffee? Have some—in a styrofoam cup.

PEOPLE
"Some firms are a little more stuffy," said a manager cautiously, trying to explain what makes Coopers people different. "Certainly we're professional," she quickly added.

Well, so is everybody in the Big Eight. You've got to be. And certainly Coopers is not casual when it comes to work. But everyone talks about the "relaxed and friendly atmosphere," and the "good mix of professionalism and friendliness."

One person who interviewed with and was accepted by all of

the Big Eight thought that Price Waterhouse had "the most intelligent people I spoke to," but that Coopers people were, you guessed it, friendlier. She chose Coopers. Enough said.

JOBS

Coopers prides itself on its personalized staffing approach. And most staffers are pretty happy with it. Unlike at some other firms, new hirees aren't expected to join one team for one specific industry; they get a chance to see them all.

Auditors start with two weeks of training—the Staff Accountant Courses I and II—where they learn about Coopers and its auditing approach. Training is held at regional centers, including New York, L.A. and Chicago. The approach, in the words of one trainee, is "middle of the road." But not easy.

One person felt "overwhelmed. Here I was coming in thinking I was a fairly bright person, and then these people were rambling on and on. At times I'd say 'I'm not absorbing this. How am I going to deal with it?' "

But it's only two weeks for Staff Bs—Coopers' entry-level auditors—and they then start out with the grunt work of public accounting.

"Normally, they'll send you out to do an audit, say in the payroll department, or in the cash disbursements department," explained one Staff B. "My first job was a cash account. Regional disbursements and receipts, for cash. We sort of took the controls over. We were checking invoices, and seeing what type of controls there were. Were supervisors signing the things they should have signed and for the right amounts? Did they have invoices to back up different purchases?"

And of course, there's "xeroxing, that dreaded Staff B chore," added a person with experience.

The jobs vary in quality. One senior person advised entry-level auditors to be prepared "for a little junk work, a little good work, and a lot in between."

"A lot of it depends on fate," commented a Staff B. And on your scheduler. These are the people who decide what jobs the auditors will get. New hirees are assigned one and told to list their preferences in terms of type of work and availability for travel. And the scheduler assigns you on that basis, and according to the needs of the firm.

Staff Bs all talk about the other major aspect of public accounting: getting along with different types of people. "You meet everyone from the file clerk to the controller," said one personable Staff B, "and you have to get along with them all."

Why? Because as an auditor, you need people to give you the right information. And, of course, sometimes they might not want to. "People get nervous when the auditors come in," explained a staffer. "They think, 'the auditors are here to find out my mistakes and I'll lose my job.' "

One person described one audit where she was allowed to talk with only three people in a client's department. In cases like this, "you have to figure out how to finagle people to give you the information you need without overstepping limits." And without annoying the clients.

Public accounting is not a cut-and-dried profession. And diplomacy can be as important as technical brilliance. One staffer explained the difficulties: "Here you are, telling this total stranger, 'You made a mistake. You have to correct it.' You're right out of college, and you're telling this guy whose been in the industry for ten years he doesn't know what he's doing." So you do it as tactfully as possible. "You get them to kind of find their own mistakes," one Staff B said.

Like their counterparts at the other firms, Staff Bs are evaluated after forty hours of work and each audit engagement. But unlike the others, Coopers promotes quarterly. A young Coopers recruiter reported the reality of that policy.

"Everyone says 'Wow! Does that mean I get promoted quarterly?' " She laughed and answered the question. "No!" What it *does* mean is that people are given four chances for one promotion. If you miss it once, you don't have to wait until next year. It has its advantages, although one person complained that the ten to twelve evaluations employees receive each year are "not as timely as they could be." Spoken like a true Coopers diplomat.

Training continues throughout Coopers. Staff Bs promoted to Staff As get more advanced training; overall, people are expected to meet a requirement of 120 hours of training a year. "It's extremely easy to meet," reported one manager. "In fact, it's almost impossible not to meet."

Higher level training may be more technical, focusing on auditing strategies and specific industries; or more general, focusing on supervision. The job changes, too. Staff As are "still working, cranking out papers," but in more technically difficult and more interesting areas.

After Staff A comes senior, and then manager. As you go up the ladder there's "more behind the scenes work," supervising and developing auditing strategies, in addition to auditing work. "I don't have a calculator on my desk," a partner said. "I'm a manager of people and resources."

The reward for all those hard years of number-crunching is a partnership. As elsewhere, few are chosen. But by that time many will have left Coopers. Turnover is high in all the firms, and Coopers is no exception. One Coopers partner recommended postponing the decision whether to stay until senior or manager level: "One of the things I tell people who leave after one or two years is 'You don't know enough yet!' "

But those who know enough not to like auditing have an option. Coopers is flexible enough to allow people to switch into **tax accounting** or **Management Consulting Services** (MCS). That's what one disenchanted auditor did, and he now works in the Minneapolis office as a consultant. Here, the work is more entrepreneurial and market research oriented. Coopers is very big in health care consulting, real estate consulting, and something just a little bit different: consulting for public assembly facilities, including the Miami Dolphins stadium and Kansas City domes.

Public accounting isn't just number-crunching.

LIFE
"During the day it's pretty intense," said one young Staff B. "There's a lot of work. There is not a lot of time for fooling around. I think it differs from engagement to engagement. I've heard people at other jobs who were only in there 9 to 5, with a good hour for lunch, and a little bit of joking around."

It all depends. One thing for sure is that while Coopers' offices may be nice, you don't have to expect to spend any time in them. One person spent four days in the office during a three month engagement, and the rest of the time at the client's office. That's typical. Nevertheless, those who request less traveling do get it.

There are some complaints. The work load is heavy, and usually concentrated in heavy doses around Christmas; the job can be boring and uninspiring. "It was too much historical information," complained one ex-auditor. "I just don't like looking backwards." That was the first year. "I thought, well, I'll spend another year. It didn't get better, it got worse."

But there are fun times as well: parties after each training session, get-togethers with other junior employees for drinks on Friday nights.

And then there's the exposure, the chance to see different businesses and how they operate. "I barely knew what a brokerage firm did," explained one staffer. "Now, I know them inside and out."

DOLLARS AND SENSE

Salaries are competitive but vary with location. New Yorkers get more because of the high cost of living. Expect something in the low twenties for BAs. Benefits include health and life insurance, and an overtime policy that allows you to credit overtime work for extra vacation.

GETTING IN—TRICKS OF THE TRADE

"We're usually competing for the same student," said one recruiter. Coopers looks for the same things that all the Big Eight look for. A recruiter listed the six traits she sees as essential: motivation, communications skills, executive presence, intellectual skills, judgment, and leadership ability. So what else is new?

Well, for one thing, try to sound new. "I hate standard questions like 'Do you have a training program?' " the recruiter said.

Otherwise, interviews are like all Big Eight interviews: campus interviews in September with recruiters, and office interviews for a day in midwinter, meeting with a recruiter, then a manager, a partner, and other employees. "Then a staff person will take you to lunch. It's supposed to be where you can ask things like 'can I wear black stockings or do I have to wear beige all the time,' " reported a (female) recruit.

All in all, in the words of a recruit who interviewed at six of the Big Eight, "The interviews were all boring, the offices were all the same." But, of course, Coopers seemed a bit friendlier, and "more personal."

It's also a good idea to check individual offices for advancement possibilities. Whatever firms may say about corporate culture, offices may vary considerably.

THE BOTTOM LINE

Computers and a little hustle in shirtsleeves.

ERNST & WHINNEY

VITAL STATISTICS

- **locations:** Cleveland, OH (headquarters); 119 offices nationwide; 226 worldwide
- **revenues:** $800 + million (approximate 1985 fee income)
- **rank:** 3rd
- **employees:** over 23,000 (worldwide total), over 12,000 (U.S.)

AS SEEN FROM THE OUTSIDE

The Los Angeles Summer Olympics of 1984 made history, and Ernst and Whinney was there. The firm's management consulting section designed, implemented, and operated the computerized system that reported the results. It was fitting that the Olympic Committee chose an American firm that early on realized the importance of consulting as an integral part of public accounting.

Ernst and Whinney was founded in Cleveland in 1903, by A.C. Ernst, an early advocate of the idea that accounting should be far more than record-keeping. By 1908, limited consulting services were offered, and by 1913, with the enactment of the U.S. Federal Income Tax, a separate tax department was formed.

Today, E&W's Tax Services department is one of the largest of the Big Eight, and widely regarded as one of the best. While the company has a reputation for conservatism and caution, lately it has become a bit more aggressive. Management consulting has now received a strong emphasis, highlighted by E&W's consulting work on Chrysler for the Federal Government. But audit is still the bread and butter of the firm, bringing in well over half the company's income in 1985.

Ernst & Whinney is a "one firm" firm, operating as a worldwide partnership with standardized accounting procedures. In the U.S., it's the third largest firm, but it operates everywhere from Akron to Zimbabwe.

HEARD AT THE WATER COOLER—
WHAT IT'S REALLY LIKE TO WORK HERE

First of all, Ernst & Whinney is a Big Eight firm, right? And you know what that means . . .

As a senior manager here said, "When you're looking at a Big Eight firm, you should look more toward the office than the firm overall. Every Big Eight firm, from top to bottom, is probably just as good as Ernst & Whinney."

"Some offices are structured, some aren't, some are in-between," one employee summed up. As for his office? "I think we've got one of the better offices Ernst & Whinney has."

But the more employees talk about how wonderful their office is and how individual, the more you start noticing similarities.

Yes, offices do differ, but they also seem to have an E&W feel to them—more laid-back than super-polished (like Price Waterhouse) or super-hustling (like Arthur Andersen). As one staffer commented, describing his office in South Carolina, "if the job gets done, there's no riding herd every minute. The office is run loose, and as long as everybody keeps acting professional, they'll keep it that way."

PEOPLE

"It's the people who make the firm," said a senior manager, "and every office is different."

Here we go again . . . but not exactly. Ernst & Whinney staffers might see differences from office to office, but there are a few similarities. For one thing, just like E&W itself, most employees here seem rather low-keyed. Sure, they're professional, they hustle to get their jobs done. But they do it in a relaxed sort of way.

"People are under a lot of pressure just being in this profession," a tax manager said, "so it's nice when you can come to the office and spend a few minutes joking around, keeping it as loose as possible."

Even the larger, more structured offices have that kind of "loose" camaraderie among the workers.

"You don't feel as if you have to put on a lot of airs here," an audit staff person said. "We don't have that stuffiness that puts other people on the defensive."

But still, lack of stuffiness *doesn't* mean lack of drive. That's something E&W staffers have in common with people at the other Big Eight firms. They know they're in the big leagues and they're going to push to make it to the top.

"When I was in school, I thought, 'Ernst & Whinney, wow! To be a partner! What more in life could you want?,' " a six-year vet remembered. "And it's a lot of hard work, but you just take it one step at a time and you'll eventually get there."

Well, maybe.

JOBS

There might be a somewhat relaxed atmosphere at Ernst & Whinney, but that's not because the jobs here are easy. Not by a long shot. As at the other Big Eight firms, working here means long hours, lots of pressure, dealing with a variety of clients, and constant learning. And whether you're in audit, tax, or consulting, the learning generally begins on the job. Initial on-the-job training, before classroom training, is something Ernst & Whinney feels strongly about.

An **audit** staffer explained that usually a new audit person works from four weeks to two months before having the first week of core training. "What they want you to do is get a feeling what it's like out there," said a young man. "And, of course you're going to struggle a little bit," admitted a young man. "Because they're kind of just sending you out . . ." Not alone, though. New hirees are sent out with one or two people a year or two ahead of them to serve as trainers.

Still, that first audit can be quite an experience. "It was kind of scary," a new hiree said. "It was just a senior and me and the area I worked on is usually done by a person with one year of experience. I was in an area that was over my head—it was challenging."

To say the least. But many staffers find the work first, train later experience helpful. An audit staffer described what it's like dealing with clients on an engagement thus: "There's an awful lot of massaging you have to do and a lot of gentle pressure here and there. It's tough, but you're forced to pick it up quickly. No one's going to hold your hand." He added that, in core training, he went through a course on working with people, complete with videotapes and instruction on how to work with a difficult client. "But nothing can train you like getting out there and doing it," he concluded. And that's just what Ernst & Whinney thinks.

The first core training is a week of classroom work led by a manager or supervisor. Then it's back out in the field, dealing with the headaches of being a first-year staff accountant: "the things you weren't trained for—like copying and going on pop runs, stuff like that," as an audit staffer explained. "But it's part of the business. Somebody's got to do that stuff."

As a person gets more experience, there's work with more responsibility. To prepare staffers, core training continues each year, with at least a week of level training. Courses covered over the initial two-year period are basic—communications skills, audit sampling, microcomputer training, various accounting systems and techniques. Later on, training continues in a more specific way. Staffers can take courses applicable to a particular industry, such as health care or manufacturing. It's all designed to fit in with what E&W calls "The Ernst & Whinney Audit Approach," an operations-oriented approach to auditing. And it's all part of typical Big Eight accounting.

E&W's **tax** practice is another area where you learn by doing at the start. But the actual classroom training in tax is considered more extensive than at most other firms. There are four training levels. At levels 1 and 2, new hires are taught the basics in taxation. "Anything from individuals to corporations to partnerships to tax-exempt organizations, so you get a broad overview of the various tax areas," explained a senior manager. Levels 3 and 4 are more specialized, offering courses in such things as consolidated returns, family financial planning, and then going into specific industries. Most classes involve a combination of homework, small group discussions, and case studies.

As for the on-the-job training, it's largely a matter of getting involved very quickly with the work at hand. "You're coming out of school and they throw you in the fire and see what you can do," explained a successful tax employee. He added that tax is a great area in which to move ahead quickly. "On the audit staff, it might take a little longer to really tell if a person knows what he's doing because there's so much compliance work. But in tax there's so much individualism that you can tell pretty quickly how fast a person's progressing, where he's weak, that type of thing."

Getting ahead in tax is largely based on the old standbys of working hard, having a good attitude, and putting in those long hours. And those hours are most definitely long. When asked when he worked overtime, one young man answered, "during the busy season—which is January 1 to December 31!"

The usual busy season in tax actually runs from January to April 15 (for obvious reasons). Then there's supposedly a lull till the fall, when clients want tax planning done for the year-end. Essentially, the work done in the tax area is of two kinds: recurring, such as when a client's tax return is prepared year after year; and nonrecurring, the special one-shot projects that require special skills and command higher billings. This work may range from working with a company going through reorganization, putting together a tax shelter, or going through a bankruptcy.

According to one tax employee, about 60 percent of his work is of the nonrecurring kind—and that's what keeps the job interesting. "You're always getting calls from clients wanting you to research this, that, or the other. So if you don't like what you're doing today, it's not that bad. Tomorrow you'll be doing something else. It's not as if you're tied up for six months."

Not only is the nonrecurring work interesting, it's also a way to begin specializing. Generally, people begin moving toward an area of specialization here after two years, when they've moved up to levels 3 and 4 in training. And specializing in a particular tax area is a great way to get noticed and move ahead, according to some staffers. "If I didn't have expertise in real estate or in something, I'd just be another run-of-the-mill guy," said a senior manager. "Whereas if you have a special niche, if you know how to do computers or pension plans or be a corporate expert, then you're needed and you can grow with that."

Creating a niche for yourself means moving on to the areas of tax work that are most interesting, acting more as a consultant.

"I do a lot of structuring, putting real estate deals together, coming up with the best tax angles, ways to get faster write-offs," said the senior manager who specializes in real estate. "The planning part is what it's all about, being able to show someone that you've saved him 15, 20, 50, or even 100 thousand dollars. There's a lot of satisfaction in that."

The kind of satisfaction that comes from planning and advising clients is one aspect of consulting at Ernst & Whinney also. E&W's **Management Consulting Service** is an area that's growing fast—the staff has increased over 60 percent during the last five years. As with audit and tax, there's an emphasis on the importance of working out in the field to learn the job. And that emphasis even extends to interns.

"They bring you right in and treat you as if you're a real consultant," an former intern explained. "You're not asked to do the xeroxing and run errands for the partners."

Staffers in consulting get an ongoing education, with training courses both on the national and regional level. According to one staffer, the initial training (called a "consultants' workshop") takes place after a new hiree has been in the field about six months. Given at the education center in Cleveland, it usually lasts about four days and covers a general orientation to consulting, writing skills, and more. Employees continue to go back for training at the national level for about a week once a year, taking courses in such things as financial modeling and different specialized industries in the second year with the firm, recruiting, marketing, and supervisory skills in the third year. On the regional level, courses are offered in a variety of subjects, including technical systems, accounting updates, and communications skills.

Essentially, the courses are designed to parallel a person's move upward in rank: from staff consultant, doing the more basic technical work such as financial analyses and initial report preparation; to senior consultant, dealing more with client interviews and sales calling; to manager, doing product management functions; to senior manager, where "you're heavily into the project director mode and marketing"; then finally, to partner.

After a new staffer has been here a year or two, he or she begins specializing, either in a functional area, such as financial planning and control, information systems or human resources management; or into an industry-specific area, like health care, manufacturing, banking, insurance, or utilities. But even with a specialization, consultants deal with a variety of projects. One young woman in information systems reeled off the type of clients she's dealt with: "I've worked with everything from TV stations to churches, law firms, record companies, government agencies, hair salons, racetracks, restaurants . . ." But while the client and the project constantly change, the basics of consulting don't.

After staffers begin moving up and reach the senior consultant level, they start getting involved in client interviews and sales calls. According to one staffer, just as Ernst & Whinney believes in getting employees immediately out in the field, it also believes in getting them into face-to-face meetings with clients. And while that first sales call can be "nervewracking," as one staffer recalled, it's a great way to learn the business quickly.

Moving up in consulting requires self-motivation to a great extent. "A lot of it depends on your own initiative," remarked a fast-tracker. "You can't rely on somebody up the corporate ladder to bring you a bunch of work and say 'Do this.' A lot of it is hustling. You have to be out there, almost soliciting work for yourself."

And you have to listen well. A three-year vet explained that clients are good teachers. "After a while, you start picking up things that are basic ingredients to any successful organization. You also find out about a lot of pitfalls. You really do see companies that make incredible blunders; then you look at other companies and say, 'Wait a minute. You're heading down the same path.'"

LIFE
Working at a Big Eight firm eats up a lot of time. "People tend to put in quite a few hours here, but it's not a sweatshop by any means," said a young woman. "It's a fun kind of environment, in that we work hard and play hard."

Playing hard in her office includes things like having a social outing every quarter. She's gone to a resort for the day, sailed around a marina at sunset, and more. "There's a real emphasis on social activities here," she added. "Making sure if people work hard, they're rewarded for it."

DOLLARS AND SENSE
Average for the Big Eight. As one young man summed it up, "Don't get into this, at least in the opening stages, expecting it to make you extremely wealthy. Public accounting on the whole pays well, but no one at my level is getting rich from working."

GETTING IN—TRICKS OF THE TRADE
Numbers, those ubiquitous "people skills," and technical ability will get you everywhere.

Like the other Big Eight firms, Ernst & Whinney is looking for someone who'll put in the hours without too much complaining, someone who'll be dedicated.

"People think when you get into the Big Eight firm, all you

do is crunch numbers. *Wrong!* Really wrong! To keep the business moving forward you have to be out there selling, selling, selling—particularly on the consulting side," stressed one manager.

Consulting also usually requires an MBA. And sales ability aside, interviewers are looking for good listeners more than great talkers. "Do they listen to questions that we're asking or just go right ahead and say what they want to say?" a consultant on the interview circuit asks. "Some people will just charge right ahead without listening to the question. And that's not good, because you have to listen to the client."

A lot of young people here say the interview process is relatively painless, whether you're going for audit, tax, or consulting. Few technical questions, no putting you on the defensive. And remember, Ernst & Whinney is competing for the cream of the crop with the rest of the Big Eight. So a lot of it comes down to whether you will fit in.

THE BOTTOM LINE

Good, middle-of-the-road public accounting.

PRICE WATERHOUSE

VITAL STATISTICS

- **locations:** New York (headquarters); 98 offices nationwide, 330 offices worldwide
- **revenues:** $645 million (1985 fee income)
- **rank:** 5th
- **employees:** 22,000 (worldwide total); 10,844 (U.S.)

AS SEEN FROM THE OUTSIDE

Price Waterhouse has been called many names over the years. The Tiffany's of accounting. The Brooks Brothers accounting firm. The blue chip partnership.

It adds up to one thing. Price Waterhouse (PW) is known as *the* quality accounting firm—not the biggest, but the best. More *Fortune* 500 clients than the other Big Eight firms. More *Forbes* 100 U.S. multinational corporations than the others. The only accounting firm that handles the Academy Awards. At PW, there's a top quality image to uphold; a tradition of being the best—and knowing it.

Part of that tradition was decentralized management. Partners in the field shared PW values but made the business decisions themselves. More than other Big Eight firms, partners at PW felt like owners of the firm, not just employees with nice titles (and a direct phone line to headquarters).

It made a difference and gave PW an edge on personalized auditing and accounting services when those were the growth places to be. Now the emphasis has changed. Tax, management consulting, and small business accounting services are the faster growth areas, and traditional PW is gradually changing to meet new needs of the profession. Auditing partners still dominate the firm, however, and consulting lags behind.

But tradition has its virtues. While the accounting profession has recently had its share of auditing errors, lawsuits, and out-of-court settlements, traditional PW has remained pretty clean. Integrity counts for a lot in accounting, and PW does its best to maintain a balance between aggressive growth and top quality service.

And changes and innovation certainly have occurred. Of PW's revenues in the U.S., 37 percent are now nonaccounting and audit-related. Management Consulting Services (MCS) accounts for 16 percent of U.S. revenues, and is staffed with younger professionals eager to increase that revenue share. Moreover, PW is hardly traditional when it comes to new technology. Computerized auditing, including two sophisticated software systems, PW Analyzer and PW Base, are just two state-of-the-art systems that PW uses—and teaches.

PW training is among the best of the Big Eight. The National Office–Continuing Education offers over one hundred courses in all areas of accounting, including topics like Advanced Petroleum Accounting—not found in most college catalogues—and a wealth of courses related to Comprehensive Professional Services (CPS), PW's program designed to meet the needs of small and medium-size businesses.

Smaller business is where Price Waterhouse got its start in the U.S. Like many accounting firms, PW was founded in London in the mid-1800s. Then in 1865, Samuel Lowell Price, the religiously minded founder, joined forces with the aptly named William Hopkins Holyland and Edwin Waterhouse to form Price Holyland Waterhouse. And not too long after, Price Waterhouse entered the U.S. market, auditing U.S. breweries. Beer led to bigger things, and in 1890, PW opened its first branch in downtown New York. Today, the U.S. firm is the largest in the international PW network.

So that's Price Waterhouse. But whatever happened to Holyland?

HEARD AT THE WATER COOLER— WHAT IT'S REALLY LIKE TO WORK HERE

It all depends on which water cooler. Like the other Big Eight firms, Price Waterhouse is everywhere—different offices, different states, and different types of clients. People talk about *their* PW office, *their* clients. There's really not as much difference between PW and other firms as among PW offices or PW positions.

Okay, maybe there are a few more differences, like PW's top-down approach to auditing and its reputation for conservatism.

And there's one other thing—a trait that all of Price Water-house seems to have, whoever the staffer, wherever the office, and whatever the position—something that ties it all together: Pride.

"We know where we are; we're not selling you on it," summed up an eager young staffer. "When I interviewed, it always seemed the other firms were selling, selling, pounding the numbers . . ."

Well, not *all* accountants can appear at the Academy Awards.

PEOPLE

Price Waterhouse people are like people anywhere who also happen to be Big Eight accountants. And that means a well-organized accounting major who has a large dose of self-confidence, a lot of extracurricular activities on the resumé, and an ability to work hard, very hard.

"Price Waterhouse is without a doubt the toughest partnership to get into. They have the highest earnings of any partner in the Big Eight," said a young manager in hushed tones. "I've seen people not make it and I say 'Wow! If they can't make it, how will I?' "

One way is to start working hard. Price Waterhouse is big-time public accounting, and all staffers share a deep commitment to hard, hands-on work. "There's a feeling of camaraderie," said one man who made partner. "From day one you do work in the trenches. There are clean audits and messy audits—and you remember the messy ones."

And laugh about them after they're over. That's the fun part—the shared professionalism that makes accounting more than just a job. Particularly at PW.

Forget stereotypes of green eyeshades and shy retiring personalities. What makes a good Price Waterhouse accountant? "Self-confidence," said a thirty-year-old partner. "An outgoing personality is essential," said a mid-forties partner. "Lively, dynamic people," said a soft-spoken young manager.

They're not kidding. PW people are smart, sharp, a bit conservative, good with numbers, and not so bad with words. They have to be. "I think a lot of clients fear the auditor," said a smooth young manager.

And its a PW staffer's job to change all that. Or try to.

JOBS

Lots of them. Accounting is a growth profession. In the past fifteen years, the number of PW offices has increased by half, and the professional staff has doubled.

Most people start fresh out of college in **auditing**, but some begin a year earlier as Price Waterhouse interns. The jobs are essentially the same—staff accountant work along with classroom instruction in PW auditing philosophies and techniques. The philosophy? "Top-down auditing," which means learning the big picture before doing the nitty-gritty. There's a three-week in-house training program, mock situations where you learn how to deal with clients; then "ticking and turning," checking inventories and cash balances—the drudge work of accounting.

But as you become more experienced, "you get into judgmental areas like A/R," said an enthusiastic staffer. "Is this account going to be fully collected or not?" And PW people can wax enthusiastic about the theoretical aspects of their work, even at low levels. While partners, managers, and senior staff plan the audit engagement and have the ultimate responsibility, there's a real effort to involve staff in the overall picture.

There's another side to life for entry-level people, though. "It's a very demeaning situation in the beginning," said one young employee. "They say go get me coffee, go get me a taxi."

Young auditors seem happiest in CPS—Price Waterhouse's small business program. It's like regular auditing in that there's an audit team (partner, manager, and two or three staffers), but usually there are more clients and a broader scope of work. "In your first two years, your learning curve is a lot greater," said a hard-charging staffer. And responsibility comes quickly. "Here, after two years, I was running some smaller engagements," a very young partner said. "I was pulling the whole thing together."

The auditing promotion tracks are typical, three years on staff— the first year, you're called "light," the second year "medium," and the third year "heavy." Then, three years as a junior accountant, light, medium, and heavy, then three years as a manager, light, medium, and heavy, then senior manager and the push to become partner.

At the lower levels, the work is hard but competition hasn't heated up yet. Some auditing teams have parties after each major audit, but what motivates most is learning more and rising through the ranks. "If you're good, they'll give you all the more," said a staffer who takes on as much work as he can. PW is not a coddling organization, and it stresses professionalism and "value-added work."

As one person put it, "In the beginning you really have to prove yourself here. That means a willingness to do whatever. If it's two hours of xeroxing you make it the best set of copies anyone's ever seen."

Tax is quieter, more research oriented. Junior people begin with audit training, then move into the tax department. What makes a good tax accountant? "The combination of being very good in accounting and also enjoying law," said a staffer who enjoys both. Some of the work is audit-related, a lot deals with tax compliance research and planning. One good thing—departments are smaller, and junior people get more exposure. And PW hires some right out of college.

"I like it here . . . If only we could broaden our market," said one manager in MCS, Price Waterhouse's **consulting** section. That about sums up the best and worst of PW consulting. It gets many of its clients through the audit side, so much of the work is accounting and financial related. But it wants more . . .

"We have the talent and the desire, but especially to outsiders, we are an accounting firm," said one employee.

Things are changing, though, as auditors learn to hustle and pass on problems to this group. It's a great place for young, technically minded types—researching and implementing financial and information systems, and sometimes doing good old-fashioned consulting as well. Exposure is better—at higher levels there's a great deal of autonomy and good people "can fly through the ranks."

"We get solicited constantly," said one manager. "I get phone calls from headhunters at least four times a week, for salaries 25 percent to 40 percent more." But he's definitely staying.

LIFE
"There are probably very few skiers who are public accountants," said one staffer, who described himself as an ex-skier. Everyone talks of the long hours at the end of the fiscal year—usually in the winter.

"Like any business, it has a crummy side," explained a partner. "The client comes first. You have to put your client's needs above your personal life," explained another. And younger people describe the high work pressure and turnover at the lower ranks for different jobs outside.

But there's a lot of enthusiasm at PW as well. Public accounting is changing rapidly, becoming more technical, more sophisticated—and more fun. One staff member waxed eloquent on how his computerized auditing changed his client's operation. There's a lot of gratification in servicing clients, and many cited it as the best part of public accounting. And Price Waterhouse takes client service very seriously.

DOLLARS AND SENSE
Price Waterhouse may be blue chip, but it's Big Eight, and that means relatively standardized entry level salaries, with some variation for regional differences, background, and ability. Overtime is paid up to the senior level. Partners supposedly are among the best compensated in the Big Eight.

GETTING IN—TRICKS OF THE TRADE

"To be honest with you, what they went for the most were my extracurricular activities," said a young staff accountant.

"When I interviewed at this firm, no one even asked me a technical question," said a slightly older manager. "We talked about the weather, the latest current events."

Price Waterhouse can trust your GPA and accounting background, so they're looking at poise, self-confidence, and communications skills.

"The interview is like going out with a client," explained another manager. "They're checking. 'Can you handle yourself with a client?' "

Others stressed background research on what you want to do in accounting. "If you want tax, express it," commented a tax accountant who did just that. And if you don't know, PW is a great place to get exposure to all businesses. Some described PW as an "up or out organization" in a positive sense. The training is great, and there's an excellent name to put on your resumé.

"It's a long hard pull to partner," a staffer asserted. "And there's a great 'resumé value' to Price Waterhouse jobs."

THE BOTTOM LINE

The price is right, but the work is hard.

ADVERTISING

Advertising's purpose is to sell products and make money for the client. It *can* be creative, it *can* be glamorous, it *can* be exciting—it should always sell the product. It isn't easy. Over 1,000 ads pass by the average American every day. And it's the advertiser's job to make sure that his ad is the one that stands out.

An ad agency is a collection of experts who dream up, produce and place ads for its clients. About 10,000 ad agencies are out there competing for their piece of the action. The good part is that over $96 billion is spent by companies to promote their business, and advertising itself is growing at a heart-stopping rate of $10 billion a year.

Advertising is a field where struggling artists and writers can stop struggling and buy condos instead. But creative people aren't the only ones who make it. Advertising is really two worlds—one populated by the creative staff and the other by the business staff. There is an overlap, though: advertising people are either business-minded creative types or creative-minded business types. And they're all after one thing—making a product sell.

The **creative** staff members are called simply the "creatives." They are either writers or artists. The various jobs are copywriter, art director, staff artist, and staff photographer (starting salary range is $15,000–$25,000.

A copywriter writes the copy of an ad. The catchy slogans, the compelling prose in a print ad, the radio spot or TV script—they're all the copywriter's work. Copywriters are usually English majors who decided not to be Hemingway and go for the money instead. But they haven't necessarily sold out. Many consider copywriting an art. (Hemingway himself tried to be a copywriter and failed. He had to write famous books instead.)

Working in tandem with the copywriter is the art director, who comes up with the look of an ad, the visual "feel." Staff artists, illustrators and photographers then make the art director's ideas come to life.

Members of the creative team often work their way up the ladder if they consistently produce winners. And that's when the big money comes. Top copywriters can earn well over $60,000 and creative directors, who oversee the entire creative team, over $80,000. It's possible to move from senior copywriter to copy chief, creative director, even chief executive, with the right blend of ingenuity, creativity and luck.

And it's that blend that can get your foot in the door in the first place. There is no such thing as a truly typical creative—the one common requisite is (you guessed it) creativity. One thing every agency likes to see is a "book"—a portfolio of advertisements you've done that can give them an idea of your work. It doesn't matter if they're real ads or fake ones—at least when you're going for an entry-level spot. The key is standing out from the crowd and showing a fresh outlook. This isn't the time to figure out whether the commercial you've dreamed up could actually be produced. Many creative directors say they would rather see something really different that *wouldn't* work, than something tried, true and typical.

You want to be a creative? Then dare to be different.

Working closely with the creatives is the **production** staff. They're the people who take the copywriter's text and the art director's layout plan and convert it into a finished product. It's the hands-on work, pens and ink, cameras and celluloid, less talk and more action. The jobs are production manager, production assistant and layout artist, and the starting salary range is $13,000–$25,000.

As one would guess, if you want to break into production work, it's best to have technical skills. Many people are hired with art backgrounds or video expertise.

Then there's the business side of advertising—one step away from creativity and conceptual thinking to the reality of numbers and profit. Here the jobs are **account** supervisor, account executive and assistant account executive, and the starting salary range is $16,000–$25,000; MBAs, $20,000–$35,000. Key to the advertising business are the account managers. They're the MBAs (or economics and marketing majors) who talk about budgets and billings. There is a more distinct hierarchy here, clear career paths and carefully delineated duties. But first and foremost, account managers are diplomats. They have the task of acting as go-betweens—between agency and clients, upper management and account group, and business staff and creatives.

An account executive draws up a plan, often gives the creatives the general thrust of an ad campaign, and then leaves it up to them to make it sing. That's because account executives work hand in hand with the client and know (or try to know) what the client wants. The account exec is usually the one who sold the client on the agency in the first place, and he's the one who makes sure that the client will be pleased with the end result.

A lot of account executives got their foot in the door by knowing as much as possible about an agency's clients. And having a business background certainly doesn't hurt. As an account exec at a large agency, you'll be dealing with a variety of clients in different industries, so the more you know about business in general, the better off you'll be.

Beyond that, it's a combination of energy, selling skills and the ability to present well. If you've got that package, you just might have what it takes.

In this insecure business, **researchers** are always there to back up ideas. They do the consumer surveys, the data gathering and the checkups on the client's products. Is the product in tune with the agency? What types of people will buy it? What's the major competition doing? The research staff can answer all that and more. They're the ones with their fingers on the public's pulse. While the creatives get the glory and the account managers the money, the researchers have the knowledge. Here the jobs are research director, research analyst and research assistant, and the starting salary range is $15,000–$35,000.

This is an area that demands an ability to work with statistics day in and day out. But it's not all numbers. A working knowledge of psychology or sociology can help get you in, as well as an ability to translate data into clear, readable reports. But the bottom line is quantitative skills—plus a genuine love for research. Most people on research staffs seem crazy about their work, and they have to be. They're working with numbers and stats, they're tracking audience group responses and analyzing sample group surveys. And, not the least of their job, they're trying to inject a bit of science into a speculative industry.

And there's the **media** staff. Here the jobs are media director, media buyer, media planner and media assistant, and the starting salary range is $11,000–$18,000. Perpetually on the phone surrounded with Arbitron rating guides, publication rate cards and broadcasting yearbooks, or punching numbers into a calculator and scanning computer readouts, media personnel spend the money the agency brings in. They control time and space— purchasing a minute of prime time during the Super Bowl or three inches in the local paper. They play the numbers day after day after day. And the agency expects them to hit the jackpot every time.

The media department at an agency speaks a different language. Its lingo revolves around things like GRPs (gross rating points), psychographics (the psychological factors of a target audience), effective frequency (how many times a person has to see an ad before it has impact) and net reach. There's even a special way to do math, a formula to plan a media program that involves manipulating factors like Homes Using Television (HUTs) and Viewers per Viewing Household.

At least that's what a media planner has to contend with. Media planners devise programs for ads, choosing those TV shows, newspapers, magazines or radio time slots that will reach potential buyers of a product. Then media buyers buy the times and spaces that the media planner has decided are best.

It sounds a little confusing, and it is. That's why you need strong analytical and mathematical skills, as well as a cool head under pressure, to be a good media person. But it's not too bad. In fact, many people use the media side as a way of getting into account management. Because once you've mastered the numbers, you know more than you ever did about effectively marketing a product.

Finally, there's the **traffic** department, where a lot of account executives start out. Traffic people work on production schedules, coordinate between departments and keep track of deadlines. It's a lot of paperwork, a lot of running around, and not too much money—salaries start at about $15,000. But it's a good way to learn all aspects of the business.

Put these varied jobs together and you have an advertising agency. A crazy mixture of numbers-crunchers, artists, writers and business people. Does it work? Wrong question. Does it *sell*?

N.W. AYER

VITAL STATISTICS

- **locations:** New York (headquarters); Chicago; Detroit; Los Angeles; London; 13 international partners
- **billings:** $751.7 million 1984 worldwide billings
- **rank:** 18th (in worldwide billings)
- **employees:** 3,500

AS SEEN FROM THE OUTSIDE

"Reach out and touch someone" made the large impersonal AT&T sound *human*. And that's just what Ayer does for all of its clients. Ayer is proud to say it's different from all those other backstabbing, fear-driven, hard-charging ad agencies over on Madison Avenue. The difference? "Human Contact"—Ayer's soft-sell approach to advertising everything from Avon cosmetics to the U.S. Army. From the chairman on down, everyone lives, breathes and eats "human contact." It's their corporate slogan and more. It's a creed, almost a religion. They can get pretty preachy about it.

Maybe that's because NW Ayer began as a one-man agency representing religious weekly newspapers way back in 1869— which makes Ayer the oldest advertising agency in the United States. Advertising was very different then. Ayer's motto was a not-so-catchy "keeping everlastingly at it brings success." But they did keep at it. It was the first agency to hire an artist, the first to intiate corporate advertising, the first to use radio, the first to produce TV ads, and, of course, the first to push the humanistic soft-sell approach. *Advertising Age* gave Ayer the "Agency of the Year" award for that in 1979, and since then Ayer has kept on smiling and peddling its softly emotional advertising style. Fuzzy commercials, smiling faces, Mom and apple pie? That's Ayer, that's Human Contact—at least on the surface.

HEARD AT THE WATER COOLER—
WHAT IT'S REALLY LIKE TO WORK HERE

"No caffeine. Never had it, never will." Ayer came up with that famous tag line for 7Up, the UnCola. No wonder it was able to come up with such a winner. Ayer seems to be the Unadvertising agency. It's not at all the typical image of the high-pressure advertising world. No crazy people running up and down the halls, no frenzied hustle and bustle, no superaggressive feel. Here, it's quieter, more laid back, and a bit more thoughtful.

The distinct personality of Ayer is a lot like the ads it produces—soft focused and unabrasive. Even the offices—whether an account executive's or a copywriter's—look alike: two plants, one hanging, the other on the vents; one funny cartoon or poster; a few tear sheets of ads pinned to the wall; one ashtray that appears to be rarely used; a cluttered but organized desk. These offices are arranged over seven labyrinthine floors. And each floor looks the same as the one under or over it: the same reception area, the same handsome woven tapestry, the same tasteful prints and photographs lining the walls.

And, incidentally, there really *is* no caffeine here. Not a single coffee or Coke machine on the premises. Nope. Ayer personnel are too full of the milk of human kindness—or is it Human Contact?

PEOPLE
One guy at Ayer swears he can stand inside the door at the annual Christmas party and pick out the Ayer employees from the gate-crashers without a single mistake. How? "Ayer people have well-scrubbed shiny faces and look like they all came from Ohio."

He's right. Ayer people look like anyone, only more so. And their personalities match. The traditional advertising distinction between account management people and creative people is blurred here. Sure, they dress differently. Creatives might wear jeans while "account management people are three-piece suits, oxford shoes, suspenders, vests, the whole schtick. But it's Barney's as opposed to Brooks Brothers," said a self-described preppie group assistant.

That's about the only difference between the two groups. It must be the Human Contact approach. Everyone's contacting everyone else so much that they've all become the same person—

"smart, talented, and a little more subdued than you might find at another agency," according to a two-year copywriter who did stints at many other shops.

JOBS

According to an Ayer ad, "a diamond is forever." So are the jobs here. People simply don't get fired. Get a job at Ayer and you're virtually guaranteed one for life. There might be occasional weedings out, but no all-out purges. People here can sit back and relax.

But you've got to pay your dues first. Just talk with a **Group Assistant**, Ayer's lowest of the low—a combination advertising assistant, secretary and gofer. Group assistants are sent to work with their group (account, creative, media or research) and suddenly they realize that it's not the glamorous introduction to advertising they imagined.

"It begins to filter down that what you're doing is gofer jobs—getting coffee, (from the downstairs coffee shop, that is), typing, taking messages. You want something more challenging intellectually, but you realize you weren't hired for that," said a creative group assistant who is proud of his ability to speak French, German and Latin.

And group assistants find out another shocker. As one frustrated young woman put it, "You could work in your entry-level position until you drop dead and never get promoted."

But those who stick it out learn to play the game and show whatever initiative they can. And slowly they work their way up.

An account group assistant summed up management's position: "If you want to be with us, you'll have to suffer a little bit. Eventually it will pay off."

There are those people at Ayer who don't pay the group assistant's dues. MBAs come in as assistant account executives—three steps above group assistants. There, the rewards are greater and the advancement much quicker. Ayer account people are much like any agency's **account staff**. But add a dose of Human Contact, of course . . .

Chameleon-like, Ayer people will act in whatever way necessary to keep business going smoothly. "Management made me grow this mustache," an AT&T senior account supervisor said, fondling the hair beneath his nose. "They thought I looked too young and the AT&T people were in their 50s. We didn't want them to think a kid was handling their account. So management said, 'Do something. Put gray streaks in your hair. Anything . . .' "

Like account management, Ayer **creatives** do all they can *not* to rock the boat. Most of them are experienced, and having paid their dues at other agencies, they know they've got it good—so they get along with each other, no matter what. It's not easy all the time. At Ayer, creatives work one-on-one for long periods. It's one art director and one copywriter and there's not much shifting of teams.

"Sure, you get on each other's nerves," said an open-faced copywriter. "You can't help it."

Still, it works. Maybe because there's no need for prima donnas here; maybe it's the friendly, uncrazy atmosphere. There's simply no room for crazy at Ayer. While Ayer creatives describe themselves as "a little offbeat and a little eccentric," they don't push that description. Maybe they are just a *little* bit of both—but for Philadelphia as opposed to New York. Philly is where Ayer started and that's obviously where its roots remain.

LIFE

"Everybody's happy here," a young woman said. "Not necessarily as happy as they can be, but happy under the circumstances."

Ayer people are advertising pros and they know not to expect paradise at any agency. Still, they do wind up praising Ayer—even though it's often in low-key terms.

The one thing they're *not* usually low-key about is how much less pleasant life was at other agencies and how comfortable they are now. "I think they do a pretty good job," said one employee of Ayer. "I don't go home anymore thinking, "Where else can I work?" I don't think it's going to be any better than I have it now."

Sure, there's a little glamour—"I was over to Loni Anderson's house for lunch, worked out with Arnold Schwarzeneggar, rollerskated with Flip Wilson and watched TV with Margaux Hemingway," an account supervisor boasted.

But no one's here for the glitzy side of advertising. What you've got is a friendly, nonaggressive haven in the fast-paced advertising world at Ayer. And that's the way Ayer people want it.

"I wanted to find a home," a veteran creative said. "And that's how I feel right now."

DOLLARS AND SENSE

When it comes to money, Ayer is like everywhere else—only less so. Especally at the entry levels. Group assistants begin at a mind-numbing $200 a week. There's a joke among these people: "My father put me through college; now he's putting me through Ayer."

Salaries aside, the benefits and perks are good. Beyond the basic traditional benefits and profit-sharing plans, Ayer adds that Human Contact touch. For example, every employee got at least $900 as a Christmas bonus in 1984—even the people who had been hired only a few days before.

"They go out of their way to help people," said an employee at the group assistant level. "If someone has a drinking problem, they'll literally go out of their way to help—even pay for a rehabilitation program."

GETTING IN—TRICKS OF THE TRADE

Geniuses and superstars need not apply. Ayer wants that well-rounded type who will get along with everyone. And what type is that? Upper management is a little bit vague—there's a lot of talk about the right chemistry, the right feel. The key is (sorry) that old Human Contact again.

"I can interview a hundred people with a perfect background and all the right answers," a well-groomed VP explained. "So many are too aggressive, too know-it-all."

The perfect Ayer employee is a sort of humble eager beaver who knows something about advertising and a lot about getting along with others. But that doesn't mean you have to be completely sincere. One account executive who interviews potential employees said with a smile, "I want someone who shows some commitment and enthusiasm, whether it's a real feeling or a snow job."

THE BOTTOM LINE

Human Contact.

OGILVY & MATHER

VITAL STATISTICS

- **locations:** New York (headquarters); 194 offices world-wide
- **revenues:** $2.88 billion (1984 worldwide billings)
- **rank:** 2nd (in worldwide billings)
- **employees:** 7,428

AS SEEN FROM THE OUTSIDE

> We have succeeded in getting big without becoming a bureaucratic sausage machine. —David Ogilvy

So they say and so they did. From a one-man shop with no clients to one of the largest advertising agencies in the world—and hardly a sausage in sight. Great ads, first-class clients, happy employees and straight A's on *Adweek*'s Agency Report Card for 1984.

Ogilvy & Mather was founded in one man's image—David Ogilvy's. The Scottish-born founder and former CEO is now in active retirement in a chateau in France's Loire Valley—successful advertising has its rewards. He has an opinion on everything and a way of imposing those opinions on others. There's an old-fashioned word for that—leadership—and it hasn't disappeared here. A leader sets the tone, motivates people to go in the right direction—and that direction is the one David Ogilvy wants.

Even if the leader has retired from active management. Good leaders (sometimes) pick good successors, and the distinctive, classy Ogilvy feel remains. Maybe because it's so hard to forget David Ogilvy and $500 million in billings and a witty saying for everything under the sun.

And some top-notch advertising. From the old Hathaway shirt ads (remember the guy with the eyepatch?) to the American Express Travelers Cheques ads ("Don't leave home without them"), there's a creative flair at Ogilvy that is blended with strong research and some very hard work. It's a creative place—but it's also a very disciplined place. David Ogilvy likes it that way.

And his successors at the helm aren't sleeping. A few more maxims, another great year and a new name for the company. The Ogilvy Group, Inc. is now the parent, overseeing three separate parts. Ogilvy & Mather Worldwide is the international advertising network, with Ogilvy & Mather New York as the U.S.-based advertising agency. The SMS Group (Scali, McCabe, Sloves) offers specialized creative services, and the third part includes a group of independent associate agencies. The company as a whole is represented in 41 countries, 220 offices in 93 cities, and almost 2,000 clients. But whether in Auckland or Oslo, there's still an earnest striving for that Ogilvy feel. Slightly British, a little clubby—but unlike the British Empire, the sun isn't setting on this one.

HEARD AT THE WATER COOLER— WHAT IT'S REALLY LIKE TO WORK HERE

". . . I am proud to be with Ogilvy & Mather," said David Ogilvy at a 1984 Chairman's Dinner. "First, because it is now better than any other agency on the face of the earth. Second, because I like the atmosphere."

Of course he does. Ogilvy & Mather *is* David Ogilvy. The two are inseparable. The man is classy, clever, creative and civil. So is the agency. And like its founder, the agency is also very personable.

There's a warm feeling about the place, coupled with a sense of polite restraint. And that's echoed in the physical appearance—white and tan couches and carpets are offset by a bright red wall. "Ogilvy Red" it's sometimes called, and insiders say it matches David's trademark suspenders.

That's not the only reminder of D.O. that you get here. Wherever you go at O&M, you hear Ogilvy's maxims quoted, his theories and philosophies discussed. It's like stepping into a private club, where all the members share a common bond.

People say "we," "us" and "our" all the time. It's never "my campaign," it's "ours." You sense a pride in being part of a bigger whole here. And there's a camaraderie in belonging—people chat with one another, they encourage, joke, laugh and, yes, complain—but always with a sense of gentility. That's the way David would want it. There's a Britishness about O&M, making it civilized, friendly and very proper, yet accessible. And this in the high-pressured world of advertising.

As a creative director said, "Ogilvy proves you can be a human being *and* work in advertising at the same time."

PEOPLE
In a letter describing O&M's corporate culture, David Ogilvy said, "We despise office politicians, toadies, bullies and pompous asses."

And if David Ogilvy said it, you know it had better be true. So what you've got here instead are people who are "extremely intelligent, extremely well educated and well bred," according to an assistant account executive.

Well bred? That counts a lot here.

"It's the Ivy League advertising agency," a recent hiree said with a grin. "Squash is a big sport here."

Well, it's not only that. Breeding at O&M doesn't mean being a blueblood. It simply means that courtesy and civility are the norm.

"Everyone here is well mannered," said a young woman. "One of David's lines in the training program was 'Charm will get you everywhere.' "

At O&M, that's not far from the truth. Winners of the annual Jules Fine award get an all-expenses-paid trip to anywhere in the world. Why? For having the qualities O&M admires—strong professional skills *plus* goodwill and good manners.

Still, it's not a bunch of Pollyanna clones running around the halls. While they are all people your mother would love, there is variety. Well, sort of.

"It's a very large organization and the people aren't off a cookie cutter," explained a research staffer.

"We try not to be all alike," confirmed an account executive. "We don't need cookie cutters of each other."

Well stated, both of you.

"There is a certain commonality," confessed one young man. Of course there is. And its initials are D.O.

JOBS
"We pursue knowledge the way a pig pursues truffles."

And how! David Ogilvy hit the mark again. O&M sticks to the letter of this particular maxim—offering twenty-seven official training courses in creative, research, media and account management skills. Beyond that, it also holds special presentation technique workshops and a trainer's training program when needed.

Training is a way of life here. It begins when a person joins O&M and continues all the way to senior management levels. New hirees quickly learn that, although they've left school behind, their education is just beginning.

"You just teach them and teach them and teach them—and they don't come up for air for six months," stated an account executive involved in the training process.

She's not exaggerating. All assistant account executives participate in the **account management** program—kicked off by a four-day weekend and followed by thirty two-hour sessions. All facets of advertising are examined, including media, creative and research from the account manager's perspective, in a series of lectures and interactive sessions.

And during the formal training, there's informal training, too. Assistants go on a rotation system, to learn about advertising on the job. They first work on a service account, then spend nine months on a package goods account. Designed to give new hirees hands-on experience, the system does slow down chances for quick promotion. But some trainees don't mind that.

"At a lot of other agencies, I would have been promoted the first year," a recently hired assistant cheerfully commented. "But I wouldn't have had the exposure."

O&M stresses that exposure to all facets of the advertising process and all departments. There's a careful emphasis on the advertising team—not just account and creative people, but media and research staffs, too.

"We're part of the team, rather than a support function," a research manager said. And that expanded research role is probably why staffers are expected to have "some talents that are not always found in researchers—creativity, imagination, flair."

The people who have to have that flair, the **creatives**, are particularly happy about working at Ogilvy & Mather. It stems in part from having two creatives in charge of the company.

"There's a lot less competitiveness here—intentionally," stated a refugee from another large agency.

Fewer bureaucratic layers and a freer atmosphere. Not that it's laid back, though. Dues must be paid, and junior copywriters and art directors serve an apprenticeship, in effect.

"I can't stand a kid who gets out of school and expects to be a full art director," a creative supervisor said. "You have to learn your craft. You know, earn money the old-fashioned way."

But that's the way it is at any Ogilvy & Mather job. You must earn and learn your way up the ladder, according to the pre-scribed theories.

"The word I'd use instead of structure is guidelines," said one account executive. "In terms of advertising itself, there are very few rules that are set in stone. But there are the principles of Ogilvy & Mather. Those *are* set in stone. Like 'First class business in a first class way.' "

D.O. said it. And that's what O&M people are dedicated to.

LIFE

"Some of our people devote their entire working lives to our agency," David Ogilvy wrote. "We do our damnedest to make working here a happy experience. I put this first, at the top of our priorities . . ."

Yet again David Ogilvy lays down the law. And it apparently works. Part of making working here a happy experience is the O&M Christmas party, not the usual yawn-yawn affair, but a real blowout. In 1984, the agency rented Carnegie Hall and put on a musical with office talent.

There's also an in-house bar, the Central File, a place people can go to relax, socialize and complain. But there is much more life at Ogilvy than parties and booze.

"It's a very devoted company," a quiet research staffer said. "People have to identify with the company. There are very few cynics—and they don't tend to be happy if they're here."

That's almost an understatement. The key to being happy at O&M is accepting the O&M beliefs hook, line and sinker. There's a strong corporate culture here that people *must* absorb.

Ask an Ogilvy person a question and he'll read some of the sayings of David Ogilvy. Ask him to use his own words, and he'll *recite* some of those sayings. In short, the Ogilvy life is great, but only if you're a true believer.

"Most people quickly develop a sense of allegiance," said a young man. Well, kind of . . . "People poke fun at it all the time, really," confessed one staffer. "David is called God . . ."

But that's just what makes life here pleasant. At O&M, people manage to deal with the long hours, the grueling assignments and the hard work that come with working at a major agency by feeling that they belong. Besides, it's those things that make O&M so successful.

"It's a real positive atmosphere," summed up an eager assistant. "This company is doing great. It's on a roll and it keeps getting real quality accounts. You're not going to come to work here and get put on some discount department store or some shlocky cigarette account."

DOLLARS AND SENSE

"You have to understand that you may get paid better at some other place, but the standards here will probably make you the best."

No, David Ogilvy *didn't* say that. An account executive did. And that seems to be the prevalent feeling here. Money isn't fabulous, but there are compensations, not the least of which is being part of O&M.

GETTING IN—TRICKS OF THE TRADE

Getting into Ogilvy & Mather is much the same as getting into other agencies—it's that old combination of brains, talent, creativity and perseverance.

"Be prepared to know campaigns and who's doing what," warned a recently hired O&M staffer. "And talk about plays or books."

Huh? Yes, here, they're after that loosely defined well-rounded person. They want to be sure "that you won't just be a jacket—empty, lame looking, one dimensional," as one account person put it.

Beyond that, one account executive says, they look for "a great sense of fun, great sense of humor, great stick-to-it-iveness—and someone who can eat lunch very fast."

"A person who wouldn't make it here?" a senior member of the creative staff asked rhetorically. "A, not a team player, and B, not a nice person."

And that's really the key to O&M. To join this particular club, you'd better be a plain old nice guy (and it wouldn't hurt if you could spout some David Ogilvy sayings, either). That's the way D.O. would want it. And that's the way it is.

THE BOTTOM LINE

Father knows best.

J. WALTER THOMPSON

VITAL STATISTICS

- **locations:** New York (headquarters) and offices worldwide
- **revenues:** $2.70 billion (1984 worldwide billings)
- **rank:** 4th (in worldwide billings)
- **employees:** 8,174

AS SEEN FROM THE OUTSIDE

The Commodore would be very happy. He was the bearded gentleman and supersalesman who gave the agency its name, and its unofficial logos—a beard and an owl.

J. Walter Thompson (also called J. Walter, Thompson and JWT) is a strong force in advertising again—bigger, better and younger. No more talk of impending doom, a syndication scandal, lawsuits and defecting clients. That's what was happening a long time ago in the early 1980s. Instead of abandoning ship, Thompson management closed ranks, kept on offering better and better client services, and kept up with a reorganization plan that emphasized creativity as well. Not so unusual, but until recently Thompson was known as somewhat stuffy, a bit dowdy and huge.

But management is strong, and the creative steam is rising. The agency won the Miller High Life account in 1984, and is becoming known as a pretty creative place—a creative *driven* place.

That probably wouldn't have made the other founder of JWT all that happy. Stanley Resor bought JWT in 1916, married Helen Landsdowne, a JWT copywriter, in 1917, and spent the next forty-three years at the helm. He loved research and scientific advertising, hired Ph.D.'s, and presided over a loosely organized but very correct agency. Ivy League account executives (at JWT, they're called account representatives) were king. Helen Resor encouraged employees to furnish their offices with antiques, while Stanley encouraged researchers to study every facet of American life, and to base advertising on the research results. It wasn't a bad way of doing things—JWT became the undisputed leader of advertising.

Except that younger, "hotter" shops were nipping at JWT's heels. Resor didn't have as much respect for creatives as he did for research—and that hurt JWT.

Until recently. Change is in the air, even though a strong sense of tradition is present. Research is still big, as it should be. And international is very strong. And growth and being the best is still the goal, of course.

JWT Group Inc. is the holding company that owns J. Walter Thompson Company, with 192 offices around the world. It also owns Hill & Knowlton (see separate profile), the second largest public relations firm, Simmons Market Research Bureau Inc., and Lord, Geller, Federico, Einstein Inc., a large U.S. ad agency. And JWT still prides itself on its international excellence. It won 576 awards worldwide in 1984. Not all that bad.

HEARD AT THE WATER COOLER— WHAT IT'S REALLY LIKE TO WORK HERE

"We don't believe in hard sell. Just a little friendly persuasion."

No fooling. That little slogan is how JWT sells itself to clients. But it could just as well be its corporate motto. Everything about JWT is insidiously persuasive. If you're not careful, you can easily become a convert to its way of thinking.

The first thing that strikes you about JWT is its headquarters. The building is a showcase—a gleaming glass tower with escalators leading to the main floor and an atrium behind the elevators. Go upstairs and you find marble floors and reception desks, walls covered with nubby, expensive-looking fabric and carpets with a sleek geometric design. That's the look on each of the floors; the only difference among them is the color scheme—which is always tasteful, naturally.

And how many offices do you know that have impressive art work on the walls, items like original Picassos, Lautrecs and other masters? Wait, there's more . . . JWT doesn't just stop with the artwork; it has an art curator on staff (something its PR department is quick to boast about) who takes the part of the budget allotted him and buys major pieces by "important young artists" and pencil and pen drawings by others.

Still not dazzled? Well, the executive dining room is an Ipswich,

Connecticut farmhouse kitchen that was moved "peg by peg, board by board" from the 1627 house it was once in. And this room, used primarily by senior management for real big "do's" (including the chairman's personal Christmas party), boasts an authentic Revere lamp.

Phew! This place is enough to impress anybody. And that's the problem. People can be so caught up with the externals that they don't notice anything else. Which just *might* be the way JWT likes it.

Walking off the beaten track, you get the feeling that it's actually a rather friendly company. But it's difficult to get past the slick, ultra-modern, ultra-*ultra* appearance.

So what's the real JWT behind that facade? Even the people who work here aren't quite sure.

As one young account supervisor put it, "The one thing that distinguishes this place from others is that it's very heterogeneous. It's always what struck me about this place, that I *couldn't* put my finger on it. Name any stereotype—it wasn't stuffy, it wasn't 'hot,' and it wasn't this wildly creative environment by appearance, it wasn't Ivy League, it wasn't anything."

No, it's not anything but J. Walter Thompson—which isn't a bad thing to be. Or so they say.

PEOPLE

As one might imagine, JWT people are quick to tell you there is no such thing as a JWT person. Instead you hear talk about JWT's standards and principles.

One of these is a belief that the company is humanistic—that it truly respects the individual. Maybe that's why everyone says everyone else here is so diverse. "There are very few people who *wouldn't* fit into JWT," according to an easy-going creative.

"It's easy to come in here and be accepted,"said a creative director. "I think it's one of those places where young people easily find their peer group."

That's another thing about JWT employees. They're getting younger and younger. You still have a lot of people who've been here upward of twenty years at the upper management levels, but at lower and middle levels, it's mostly young people. And upper management seems to be getting younger, too.

"Recently there's a more aggressive young management," a

recently hired account rep said. "Less concerned with image—there's a little less weight on the suits."

Maybe. But there's still a corporate feeling. People are very careful and cautious about what they say. You can't *completely* escape a stodgy past.

JOBS

JWT has been called the "University of Advertising" because there's a great belief in training and research here.

"To say that we produce the most effective advertising doesn't differentiate us from any other agency," said a senior VP to a group of management trainees. "What differentiates us is our knowledge of how advertising works."

JWT is big on knowledge—adding to it, changing it, shaping it and passing it on, as new hirees are told. And JWT is rightly proud of its training program. This combines actual hands-on work in an assistant's job with lectures, seminars and casework. But the main thing both management and trainees like about the program is its "cross-curricular approach." What that means in plain English is that trainees from all the different departments—account management, creative, media and research—go through the same program together.

"The idea is to work as a team with all the different departments," said a research trainee.

Right. And the idea behind *that*—"Young people are 'I' and 'me' oriented," a senior VP pontificated. "They have to unlearn that and become group motivated. "I succeed when the group succeeds, not despite the group . . ."

Apparently it works. "I've been through two of the training programs and each time I come out amazed at how little importance I've placed on the collaborative process," marveled an account manager. "You're learning about how to get along with people."

"Old pros of five years in the business are supportive of people who've been here five weeks," a creative said. "It's a very mutually supportive atmosphere here. People like the way we work."

If you produce.

That's the general consensus among **creatives**. At JWT, there are six creative groups, and as with most agencies, there are groups within groups within those six groups. Unlike most agencies, JWT fought against a bad industry image and has emerged victorious. And that's something the creatives in particular are enjoying.

"A friend of mine is a writer here," an account rep cautiously explained. "A year and a half ago, she was very negative. Now she says there's no better agency in New York, creatively, to be in."

"There's a very charged-up atmosphere," says a high level creative. "It's exciting for old pros like me. It keeps me constantly on my toes."

Another thing most JWT creatives like about working here is the focus on television. While lower-level creatives still often do print, there's not as long a wait to do TV as there is at other shops. But it's not as though you can walk into JWT and end up producing big ads the first day. There's the typical dues-paying you find anywhere.

Account managers here are called account representatives, ostensibly (according to a rah-rah trainee program speech) because "we believe in a humanist philosophy—account representatives *represent* consumers. And we treat consumers adult to adult. We don't condescend."

Huh? Well, whatever *that* really means, account representatives do what account executives do at any other agency. And, like others, the competition is tough. Of every ten to twelve new employees, JWT hopes to promote two or three. So evaluations and accountability are the name of the game. People are rated by their supervisors and a senior account manager who tracks, evaluates and then reevaluates your performance.

"We're bringing in good new people, *young* good people," a senior VP said. "It's not just long tenures anymore. People know this is what's going to happen and will have even greater pride that they're the chosen."

LIFE

The shift in morale is the key thing about life at Thompson. It's riding a crest now.

"There's that move from *not* being on the leading edge of creativity to being on it," summed up one staffer. "There's a feel to a winning team here now." And people like each other when they win. And they like Thompson when it's winning too.

"It's becoming a little less formal and structured," an account rep stated. "People also are generally less caught up in formality, stuffiness."

One thing that's decidedly unstuffy about JWT is the on-premises bar, the Company Store. Here, people hang out, chat with their co-workers and maybe, just maybe, there's something else going on.

Explaining how easy it is to "belong" at JWT, a creative director added by way of proof, "Just go down to the bar. It's like a singles bar on Second Avenue."

Hmm . . . Might be more to this team spirit than meets the eye.

DOLLARS AND SENSE

Nice, but nothing out of the ordinary.

GETTING IN—TRICKS OF THE TRADE

Given JWT's assertion that the individual is important, there are no strict guidelines governing hiring. Still, there are those little touches that they seem to prefer.

On the account side: JWT used to be big on MBAs, but that's changing. "We have been going between MBAs and BAs—an intelligent BA who's proven himself in college. After that, it's personality. Honesty, integrity, willing to work hard," summarized a senior VP.

You also need a dash of humility. "Regardless of all the skills and aptitudes and functions you have to perform, you have to perform a service. Some people can't accept that service orientation."

A creative director who hires entry-level people explains that he wants to see "a new way of looking at something you've been looking at forever—if I see something I wish I had done, I'm sort of disposed to that person."

One other suggestion—a research director summing up the majority of people he's hired came up with a common denominator. "They had all read David Ogilvy's book. It's a few extra little points."

And that from a competitor.

THE BOTTOM LINE

A *little* friendly persuasion? Try a lot.

YOUNG & RUBICAM

VITAL STATISTICS

- **locations:** New York (headquarters); offices worldwide
- **revenues:** $3.20 billion (1984 worldwide billings)
- **rank:** 1st (in worldwide billings)
- **employees:** 8,418

AS SEEN FROM THE OUTSIDE

Young & Rubicam is an ad agency that can best be described as a supermarket. A supermarket? That's the Y&R plan—to be the biggest, broadest-based marketing communications company in the world. One-stop shopping for all advertising and marketing needs. Y&R calls this comprehensive approach "the whole egg."

In 1970, Y&R was a troubled giant in danger of becoming a dwarf. Then, Edward N. Ney came up as chairman and CEO, and the whole egg was hatched. Billings went from $507 million to $3.2 billion and Y&R became the largest advertising agency in the world. A supermarket of corporate services—organized into four giant divisions: Y&R USA; Y&R International; Marsteller Inc.; and the world's largest PR firm, Burson Marsteller. In 1981, Y&R joined its largest international rival, Dentsu Inc. of Japan, to form DYR, a joint venture serving both Japanese and Western clients. If you can't beat 'em, join 'em.

Now Y&R has a new CEO, Alex Kroll, and talk has drifted away from Y&R as a supermarket to Y&R as a superpower, "a superpower of talent, brains and mainly spirit." Offices are everywhere, from New York to San Francisco, Australia to Tokyo. And like the superpowers, strategy is all important. Y&R's corporate credo, "Understand through discipline. Compel through imagination," could easily be blazoned on a Washington or Moscow monument.

But as with any giant bureaucracy, red tape can get in the way of imagination and movement. Y&R's multidisciplinary approach, with integrated services, layers of executives and rotational assignments, can be bewildering to clients and frustrating to its employees. And many of Y&R's big-spender clients are the packaged goods producers like General Foods and Proctor & Gamble. Profitable, yes, but also boring. Cookies instead of creativity. But changes are in the air. Y&R New York has a new creative director, who, by most accounts, is zanier than the Y&R corporate norm.

In fact, Y&R began as a noncorporate, nonbuttoned-down agency. An account manager and a copywriter at Ayer, Mr. Young and Mr. Rubicam (who else?), went for a walk on a spring day in 1923 and decided to start out on their own. They snagged the Postum account from General Foods, moved on to Grape Nuts, and kept on growing.

Y&R was unusual in that it gave copywriters and art directors creative control—and, more important, stocks and partnerships. This creative drive took it to the No. 2 spot by the 1940s. Now it's a giant No. 1, facing the problems all superpowers face: cutting the red tape and staying on top.

HEARD AT THE WATER COOLER— WHAT IT'S REALLY LIKE TO WORK HERE

Y&R is big. That's the main thing about it. It's a huge, lumpy mass that's a little of this, a little of that, and a lot of everything else.

But while it *is* a huge corporation, there isn't a supertraditional feel in the air. Maybe it's the nature of the business. Whatever it is, it's what makes Y&R like a creative person's concept of a corporation. Even the corporate headquarters is comfortable. Hundreds of offices are crammed together in a building that seems a few sizes too small and a few years too old to belong to a corporate giant. It's homey. There's a warm, lived-in atmosphere that's different from the high-tech steel and glass towers of Y&R's slicker, younger competitors.

Not that Y&R isn't slick when it has to be. You don't become No. 1 without savvy and style. It's just that Y&R doesn't force slickness down your throat. It's large enough to be slick sometimes and middle-of-the-road at others. There's something for everyone here.

Everything about Y&R reflects that diversity. Offices range from old-maid-neat to creatively sloppy. Even the reception areas on each floor have a personality all their own—from wood paneling and ancient urns to modular furniture and chrome ashtrays. But on all floors, there's something unifying. It's like the home of a rich old bachelor uncle, someone who's sure of himself and isn't out to make any statements. Except, instead of Old Masters on the walls, there are giant, lucited posters of Irish Spring and potato chips.

That's because Y&R is a giant amoeba that has swallowed thousands of every type of advertising executive and creative that ever 'graced the planet. Or to put it in the words of a Y&R copywriter, "It's a big one."

PEOPLE

It figures that Y&R once called itself a supermarket. The people working here are like the people you'd run into at your local Pathmark, especially if you're living in a major metropolitan suburb. Just regular folks here. Different types, some more creative and some more corporate, but they're all like your next door neighbors.

And like a neighbor in a middle-class suburban town, no one keeps much hidden here. There's an openness in the way people speak, a willingness to share advice, experiences and even frustrations.

"Everyone bitches here. That's the nature of the business," a suave account manager said. "You're always under pressure, so people complain—sometimes with a smile."

That smile makes all the difference. Sure, there's competition here and a great deal of pressure. But everyone takes it in stride. Maybe it's because Y&R is so big. There's room for everybody. And everybody at Y&R ranges from a typically arty creative to a typically businesslike account exec. There's also room for your typically average person—which is the norm at Y&R.

JOBS

Lots of them. That's the key thing about jobs in Y&R. It's so big that it's had to make itself small. That's why Y&R is organized into product groups—clusters of creatives and account executives all trying to make their product sell like crazy.

That arrangement is supposed to make people feel as if they're working at a small agency. But it doesn't quite work. People still complain about the layers of bureaucracy they're stuck with, the "six to ten levels of corporate America here."

"You get a little tired of selling five times before you leave the agency to go to the client," said a harried account executive. "And *then* you have to go through the five layers at the client."

Despite all the complaining, though, few seem sorry they came to this advertising Harvard. **Account** people, in particular, rave about the training. Many come up through traffic, where on-the-job training quickly gives them a real sense of advertising the Y&R way. They like the gradual imposition of responsibility and the overview of all of Y&R that traffic gives. Not that it's all sunshine and roses though. Seeing all of Y&R in its vastness can be kind of frightening.

"My first day of work here, I was just floored," said a now-confident account executive. "They gave me this huge book, the Traffic Manual, and I said, 'There's not enough hours in a day to do all this stuff.' I saw form after form after form after form . . ."

The trick is to cut through the red tape and learn which forms to throw away. And above all, ask for help. The sooner you know your stuff and toot your own horn, the sooner you can move quickly. That's something you have to do fast because it's easy to get lost in the shuffle. Horror stories abound about being stuck in traffic for the rest of one's natural life and never making it to the account side. Creatives, too, talk about having to push ahead and get noticed quickly.

It can be a little difficult. The formal training program for entry-level **creatives** is a mini-course in creativity, and no one thinks too highly of it. After a few weeks of learning what creativity is, there's no hand-holding. You know what creativity is now, or so Y&R management thinks, so, by gum, you're going to go out there and be creative!

That's sometimes not so easy. First of all, many accounts are package goods—usually not the hottest property for a fertile imagination. And, beyond that, an entry-level creative trainee is tossed into a group without having any assignments. You do a lot of practice work and hope that a real project will come your way. It's catch as catch can. If you're lucky, you'll land something that will lead to something else. If not . . .

Then there's the other side of the tracks—**media**. At least that's what a lot of other agencies think about *their* media department. But it's not the case at Y&R. Media isn't treated like a wallflower at the senior prom here. Y&R actually pays attention to the nitty-gritty of buying time and ad space. Media people all say Y&R has the best training program in the industry. And yet, many still dream wistfully of switching over to account executive positions.

Nevertheless, wherever you work at Y&R, you're still part of the over-extended family.

LIFE

"Most of the people I'm friends with here are 'drinks after work,' 'once a week for dinner . . .' "

It's back to the suburbs once again—with a sort of team spirit and drinks and dinner before the train ride home. Life in the medium-fast lane. You go above 55 mph, but not all the time.

"I work till 11 now and then, until 9 occasionally, and until 7 usually," a copywriter explained in his empty office at 5:30 P.M.

Account people seem more harried—particularly those who service Y&R's more distant accounts. "We're stretched thin. Some of us are working on three different accounts. You can't be in three different places at once," explained an a/e between phone calls.

But for all that, there's a certain feeling of security. Y&R formally assigns mentors to its incoming trainees, but most staffers scoff at the program if they mention it at all. So maybe it's the bigness that breeds this security. There are so many people, so many accounts, that it's not too difficult to find your particular niche.

It can be lonely, though, when your product group is changed.

"You may never see those guys you've worked with for months. That's how big we are—all of a sudden, gone! And you've got a whole new frame of reference," said a three-year veteran.

It can be difficult to adjust, because a Y&R product group becomes a lot like a family—always bickering, always complaining, but always loyal.

Virtually every a/e complains about the creatives and every creative complains about the account people. But when the dust has settled, there's a camaraderie. Each creative swears that his product group has great account people and vice versa.

And most like Y&R. "The atmosphere is great. It's very relaxed here. It's relaxed and it's frantic, but it's always relaxed."

Huh? Well, that's what it's like. A commitment to work, a little boredom with the packaged goods advertising, a little fun with the glitzier stuff—and there's always juicy gossip about the *other* product group. It's Y&R, a suburban superpower.

DOLLARS AND SENSE

Low pay at the beginning, but most feel the training and the prestige of a Y&R degree are worth it all. Add a savings plan and excellent benefits—it's a package many find hard to leave, despite outside offers.

"I call them the golden handcuffs," one a/e explained. "Y&R will load you up. The longer you stay, the better it gets."

And for those in trouble, Y&R is ready and waiting with a paternal hand. There's an on-site Alcoholics Anonymous program and a friendly dose of understanding for temporary burn-outs.

One account exec who sat and stared vacantly at his desk for weeks was shocked at upper management's attitude. "They never let me go. They said, 'Stick with us. We'll deal with it.' It was tremendous."

GETTING IN—TRICKS OF THE TRADE

Every Y&R person has some sort of special trick, one that they know is *the* one to break down the entry-level barriers.

One person researched the agency for weeks, wrote pages on Y&R marketing strategy and casually handed it over to the interviewer, just to show he knew his stuff. A copywriter prepared a slick ad campaign; another just bubbled enthusiasm.

All agree on the old adage: "Get contacts in the business first." And remember Y&R's conservative clients. Buttoned-down oxford shirts, dark silk ties and half windsor knot—optional for creatives *after* the interview.

THE BOTTOM LINE

A suburban supermarket that's pushing its eggs.

AUCTION HOUSES

Auction houses demonstrate that art can be business. Big business. Totals in 1984 for the top auction houses, Christie's and Sotheby's, prove it. Combined, their worldwide operations brought in over $1 billion in sales. Their United States operations alone brought in $400+ million.

Lately the media and the public have begun to pay more attention to the auction houses. Some of this attention was negative (both Christie's and Sotheby's were involved in scandals—Christie's for reportedly announcing the sale of two paintings in 1981 that didn't sell, and Sotheby's for putting up for sale in 1984 Hebrew manuscripts and rare books to which the consignor had no clear title).

But most of the attention Christie's and Sotheby's are getting is positive. It's difficult not to be interested when sixty Impressionist paintings are put up for sale, some of them with price tags of well over a million dollars. That's what the Florence Gould Collection sale was all about. Both Sotheby's and Christie's battled over that collection, and Sotheby's won.

These are the two auction houses that count, and for all the competition between them, there appears to be no antagonism. There are other, smaller houses in the United States, but Christie's and Sotheby's are the firms that win the most impressive collections and ring up the most impressive sales figures.

That combination of fine art and big money is what makes auction houses so intriguing to would-be employees. Long considered *the* place of employment for the offspring of wealthy collectors with artistic aspirations, auction houses are becoming more and more desirable to the average Joe. Well, the average Joe who majored in art history or studio art, that is.

That's the key to landing a job at an auction house and liking a job at an auction house—you've got to love art. And you've also got to love a touch of glamour and a lot of work.

Auction house employees generally work in one of two main areas—specialist or administrative. The **specialist** side is broken into "expert" departments, each responsible for a particular area, such as 19th-century Paintings and Drawings, Chinese Art, or English Furniture, to name a few. Basically, people working in the specialist field are directly involved with the artwork and collectibles that will be sold. Expert departments acquire goods from a consignor, evaluate them, catalog them, and put them up for sale.

The **administrative** side is a support staff. People in administration take care of such things as accounting, personnel, press and public relations, and so on. To some extent, working in auction house administration is much like working for any corporation but with one main difference—at an auction house, staffers are surrounded by Rembrandt paintings, Chippendale furniture, and Ming vases. And that adds a certain tone to the most tedious of job assignments.

The chance to work amid works of art attracts quite a few people. And it's pretty tough breaking in. No one denies that it helps to be from a wealthy family that happens to be an auction house customer. But what counts much more than that is a proven interest in art, a strong academic record with a major in art, and a lot of enthusiasm. And if you want to work in auction houses, don't turn your nose up at entry-level jobs. *Very* entry-level jobs. A lot of people get their foot in the door by working as receptionists, secretaries, and clerks.

One final word about working at auction houses—you won't get rich. Especially not at the beginning. Starting salaries usually hover around the $15,000 mark, if not a bit lower. But most auction house employees and would-be employees don't care about the money. It's not because they're rich, since many aren't. It's because auction houses combine a fast-paced business environment with the rarefied art world. And for a lot of people, that's the perfect blend.

CHRISTIE'S

VITAL STATISTICS

- locations: London (headquarters); New York (U.S. headquarters); offices worldwide
- revenues: $475.9 million (1984–1985 net sales)
- rank: tied for 1st
- employees: 1,100

AS SEEN FROM THE OUTSIDE

You never know. For two hundred years, Christie's has opened its doors for free verbal appraisals on attic treasures, high-quality kickknacks, and heirlooms. And sometimes people leave very happy. Like a Scottish couple who had inherited a lamp with a dull-looking red Chinese vase as its base. Christie's dated the lamp to the 14th century and sold it for about $500,000.

Happy Scottish couples aside, Christie's is one of the two premier auction companies in the world (the other is Sotheby's, profiled separately) auctioning art and fine collectibles. Of the two companies, Christie's is known as the more traditional and the more gentlemanly—auctioneers of the Chatsworth Collection of the Dukes of Devonshire, for example.

The Christie's link to polite society began in 1766, when James Christie opened his London auction house next door to his artist friend, Thomas Gainsborough. In an era before most museums had been established, Christie's became a place to view, as well as purchase, fine paintings. It still is—although the scope has widened considerably. Christie's today has over forty offices in fourteen countries under the umbrella group of Christie's International, with subsidiaries named Christie's UK, Christie's Europe, and Christie's USA. Christie's USA operates primarily out of the salesrooms in New York, with representatives across the United States. It has the highest sales of the group—$178 million in 1984.

The first New York salesroom opened on Park Avenue in 1977, and in 1979 Christie's East opened to handle cheaper (or, in

Christie's words, "more modestly priced") items. In these few years, many landmark sales have occurred, including ten paintings from Henry Ford II's collection. And a touch of scandal—when Christie's New York reported that certain paintings had been sold for a certain price when actually they hadn't. This was a serious matter, since auction house prices dictate prices at galleries around the world.

But the problems seem to be over now, and Christie's experts and salespeople are still doing what they do best—evaluating, cataloging, and selling art treasures and fine collectibles with that Christie's class.

HEARD AT THE WATER COOLER— WHAT IT'S REALLY LIKE TO WORK HERE

Being at Christie's is like automatically becoming part of the upper class. You don't have to be a blueblood to fit in, but, once you are in, you'll begin feeling like one. That's because Christie's is tasteful from the word go.

The galleries and salesrooms have a sleek, elegant air that's a bit intimidating. Particularly the spacious new saleroom (Christie's lingo for the more mundane "salesroom") at 502 Park Avenue. It's a blend of traditional and modern, with cherrywood wainscotting, shiny brass rails, herringbone oak floors, and comfortable modern chairs of dollar green. High-tech projectors display objects to be sold and an electronic currency converter displays the price in British pounds, francs, lire, and yen. And dominating everything is James Christie's old rostrum (designed by Thomas Chippendale) where the auctioneer hammers down prices that extend into the millions. The lighting is tastefully subdued, the acoustics are wonderful, and the entire effect is one of hushed elegance. This is no place to wear sneakers . . .

It's cheerful, crowded, and politely bustling behind those public rooms. Offices have been remodeled and expanded, but they're cluttered with art catalogs, videotapes, and books piled high on desks and tables. Some people say that cluttered office look is Christie's USA's British inheritance. As one person maintained, an ideal Englishman's office is "a little corner somewhere; it doesn't matter if it's piled high with books."

And Christie's offices fit that mold. The clutter extends to the back hallway—mazes that can get very confusing. Everyone uses shortcuts—up back room stairs, across the new saleroom, through galleries in the process of redecoration, past offices of friends and acquaintances . . .

From outside, Christie's may be formal, but inside, it's a slightly casual, definitely clubby, haven.

PEOPLE

Americans are in the majority . . . but you couldn't tell from their accents. Even the staffers from Brooklyn sound British. And while most Christie's people talk about the great variety of different types of people here, it's uncanny how many Ivy League and Seven Sisters graduates you find roaming the halls. It's somehow hard to meet someone from Montana . . .

But Ivy League or not, there's too much work for a lot of stuffiness. And to succeed at that work *and* to fit in, what you should know (or get to know) is art. That's what really counts to Christie's people, and that's what binds them together.

"Christie's is still a small enough organization where one is in contact with every department, everybody," said one staffer.

Christie's USA has far more women employees than most companies, and many young people. Even management are mostly in their 40s—so there's a zest in the air. Restrained, yes, but still exuberant.

JOBS

"It's like being in a rotating museum," maveled a recently promoted department head. "A new exhibit every two to three days."

Everybody loves that aspect of their jobs. Who wouldn't get a kick out of sharing work space with a Rembrandt or Van Gogh? And the **specialists** get to work with these masterpieces every day. They're the "technical staff" at Christie's—the art experts or historians who appraise, evaluate, research, and consign collectibles for auction.

It's not just paintings. Christie's has thirty-one different expert departments, ranging from American furniture and decorative arts to wine. Technical staff head every one, aided by one or two assistants and a secretary. It's rare to meet anyone who dislikes the job. There's the excitement of actually touching works of art, the pleasures of research, and the thrill of seeing them through a major sale.

But it's not all glamour by any means, partcularly at the lower levels. As an intern or an assistant, your connection to that Rembrandt may be typing information about it, filing research materials, or even dusting the frame. So advanced degrees aren't necessarily a necessity.

"There's a large technical staff, particularly in London, people who worked their way up from being porters," said a former department head.

But times are changing, jobs are harder to get, and advanced degrees are now very common. That's why so many people enter Christie's through the **administrative** side—which runs the gamut from personnel to publicity to Special Customers Services.

Special Customers Services people are the personal shoppers of Christie's. They search out and even bid for specific objects for clients who don't have the time to spend every day at the galleries. Publicity people put out the famous Christie's newsletters, and the print department prints them and the more famous Christie's catalogs, which describe those items the art experts have evaluated. The Estates and Appraisals staff try to get those items, keeping in close contact with estate lawyers and bankers, traveling in order to appraise and obtain new consignments.

Whatever the specific job, the business of selling art demands a lot of contact with everybody in every job. Problems tend to be the same, regardless of job title, and the biggest one is the outside world. Not all customers are wonderful, not all consignments are found in clean houses, not all art lovers are gentle and polite.

"You have to be sort of a diplomatic type," said one staffer.

Right. Add patience, an outgoing personality, and an ability to handle long hours and stress.

"I've worked now for four weeks straight," said one department head. "Without a day off. And twelve-hour days."

Christie's has a wonderful policy of promoting from within. It's a young place and no one is going anywhere else. But that creates problems of its own.

"There's a lot of turnover at the lower end," said a young staffer, describing the clogged channels to the top.

Above those lower rungs, it's hard work, but it's home. So people stay here, "inside" as they call it.

One department head who had worked in galleries between jobs at Christie's summed it up for them all. "I've seen the outside world as well as the inside world. And I must say, I was awfully glad to come back."

LIFE

"Your whole life can be taken up by Christie's if you want," said one young woman.

And that's the way most Christie's people like it. The whirl of fine art, sales, "walkabouts" (in-house tours conducted by Christie's experts), and above all, work, can be exhausting, but it's always exhilarating.

DOLLARS AND SENSE

"Far from generous," a staffer said drily.

But that's nothing new. "The art world is notorious for being low paid, so you have to love it," added an employee who does.

Pay does become survivable after internships are over and true responsibility begins. But what really matters to these people is getting paid for looking at, dealing with, and being around art. Another plus—because Christie's is at the center of things, just having worked here can help later on.

GETTING IN—TRICKS OF THE TRADE

It's tough.

"You have to be terribly lucky. It's timing," said one department staffer.

But a little preparation can help. Since almost everyone has a fine arts degree (or two or three), many take the Christie's or Sotheby's Fine Arts Course in London, to give themselves an edge. You should apply first to the New York offices for these courses. The course covers fine and decorative arts over the past three hundred years, for about fifty full-time and twenty-five part-time students of all ages and backgrounds.

Students visit museums and country homes and learn those things that college didn't teach them. As one former student put it, "It's very difficult to get a good course on furniture or silver or ceramics."

Not too many colleges offer Silver 101 . . .

Of course, competition for the course is tough and jobs after completion are far from guaranteed. "They spent the whole time on the course saying, 'You probably will not get a job at Christie's,' " said someone who was lucky and did. Of the seventy-five in her course, she estimates that five were employed by Christie's.

So many people apply for Christie's internships—helping department staffers and administrators do their jobs, and in the process, maybe getting jobs themselves. Initially, "you get the jobs nobody else wants to do"—two to three months of fun stuff like filing, typing, and cleaning. And that at a "salary" of $5.00 a day.

Insiders recommend avoiding the all too common summer rush and instead opting for fall, winter or spring. "There are fewer interns and your chance of finding an interesting job is better. And, there are no auctions in the summer," said a successful former intern.

One final tip. If you want a job at Christie's, it certainly won't hurt to brush up that British accent of yours.

THE BOTTOM LINE

Art-lovers go business.

SOTHEBY'S

VITAL STATISTICS

- **locations:** New York (headquarters); offices and sales-rooms worldwide.
- **revenues:** $642.25 million (1984–1985 net sales)
- **rank:** tied for 1st
- **employees:** 1,350

AS SEEN FROM THE OUTSIDE

The art auction world has changed quite a bit since Sotheby's opened its doors in 1744. Today, it's flashier, trendier, and very concerned with the bottom line. That means attracting clients who might not normally have attended an auction, and that means promotion and advertising.

Some say that when it comes to the *business* of art, Sotheby's started the trend. Under chairman Peter Cecil Wilson, Sotheby's made the transition from staid, stuffy art auction house into the power it is today. He found that the right type of promotions could sell paintings at very high prices. In 1961 Sotheby's set the record for an auction house sale of a painting—$2,300,000 for a Rembrandt. That's since been surpassed, again by Sotheby's. In 1983 it sold a 12th-century manuscript for $11,925,000, setting the record for all works sold at auction. All this talk of record prices and value annoys purists in the art world, who rightly contend that price doesn't necessarily correspond to value. But it does draw attention to art.

And that's what Sotheby's does best. It was founded in 1744 by a bookseller, Samuel Baker, who discovered that auctions were a lucrative way to sell books. Under his nephew, John Sotheby, and his successors, the firm expanded into paintings and other art.

In 1964 it got its American connection, merging with the Parke-Bernet Galleries in New York. And now it's an American firm, owned by Alfred Taubman, a developer from Detroit.

HEARD AT THE WATER COOLER—
WHAT IT'S REALLY LIKE TO WORK HERE

One thing employees at both Christie's and Sotheby's will tell you is that an auction house is an auction house is an auction house. And there are only two major houses based in the United States. So they aren't all that much different. They're both dealing with fine art and collectibles and they're both catering to a pretty upscale customer.

Sotheby's is known as the more business-oriented of the two, and that may be the case. But one thing is certain—business as usual at an auction house is unlike business at any other company.

Just walk around the Sotheby's offices, away from the public exhibition rooms and salesrooms, and you know you're not at just any corporation's headquarters. No careful corporate decoration, sleek modern furniture, or corner offices with windows here. Once you get past the reception desk, you feel as though you've stepped into an overcrowded attic—one that happens to have Dali paintings and Ming vases stored in it. And while the offices are on floors the size of a square city block, there doesn't seem to be a spare square inch of space in sight.

Staffers look as if they're working in the middle of a hectic, classy garage sale. Long tables covered with antique lamps, vases, paintings—every form of decorative and fine art imaginable—fill the large work areas. Rows of tall shelves holding prints and paintings serve as dividers. And in spare corners, groups of desks are clustered together, covered with Sotheby's catalogs, clippings, and photographs.

But despite the displayed works, this is far from being a museum. There's an energy and exuberance in the air. Maybe it's because so many staffers are young. Or maybe it's just the nature of the business.

"If you're interested in art, you're going to be lured here by the incredible amount you're going to see," commented one young woman. "And the business side of it keeps it exciting."

Said a senior employee in his thirties, "I like to think of Sotheby's as a cross between the Metropolitan Museum and Brown Brothers—because we're the best in the business just like both of them. We have the incredible connoisseurship and appreciation of art a museum has, but at the same time we are a commercial institution."

PEOPLE

"There's no question there's a Sotheby's type," one employee stated. "Less so, I think, than in the days of the requisite Hermès scarf and Gucci loafers—everybody was right to the mold then. That's a little less so now, but not *that* much less so."

Just what is that Sotheby's type, then? Well, some Sotheby's staffers do wear single strands of pearls, expensive suits, and so on. But others are more arty looking, even trendy.

Some people do come from "very, very big families, big collectors," as one staffer put it. But not everyone. So being a Sotheby's person seems to have less to do with pedigree and more to do with loving the art business and enduring the fast pace.

"People here are extremely energetic, very civilized, very bright and enthusiastic about art," one expert asserted.

One thing that probably helps deal with the commotion is that most Sotheby's staffers are pretty young. "Between right out of college and mid-thirties," a young woman said. "Even all our senior executives are in their early to mid-thirties for the most part."

"There's also a lot of temperaments here," a young man noted. "It goes with the art world—a lot of big egos, among both consignors and experts working here."

Another staffer put it a bit more diplomatically: "I think you can exhibit a lot more of your personality at a Sotheby's than you can at a different type of corporation. Everybody here is a bit of a character."

Whether they're wearing Gucci loafers or not . . .

JOBS

There are two sides to working for Sotheby's.

"A place like this is perceived as very glamorous and in many ways it absolutely is," said a vet of five years. "There's a lot of glamour, a lot of drama. An evening auction is as good as a Broadway show—there are receptions, there are benefits and parties." Experts deal with important clients, travel to their homes. Employees are surrounded by fine works of art.

"But there's the other side of the fence," an expert warned. "It's extremely high pressured, extremely exhausting."

Employees often begin at Sotheby's by breaking into the competitive summer intern program. According to former interns, the program now is much more sophisticated than in past years, "when daughters and sons of collectors would just pop in."

Now the program has been formalized, with interns serving an eight- or ten-week stint (more or less—it varies.) Each week, interns attend classes given by experts, and go on field trips to museums and galleries, in addition to their hands-on work. And the combination of study and day-to-day duties is what attracts so many people.

"In addition to the grunt work that you just expect—answering the phones, getting coffee, whatever," said one department head, "we try to give the intern an ongoing project that he or she can point to at the end of his period and say, 'I did this and I learned something.'"

Typical intern work involves research. One intern in the Press Relations Department spent her summer collecting every clipping she could find on the Impressionistic Paintings of Florence Gould, organizing them by categories and cataloging them. Another project involves working with the card cataloging and updating all the information on the year's sales at both Christie's and Sotheby's. "It seems like a rather tedious project for the intern," confessed the department head, "but he or she will come across the best of everything that sold during a given year." Interns in the expert departments often do similar work in the archives.

Some lucky interns who prove they're eager to learn and willing to work hard wind up on the Sotheby's staff. Yet again, there are two sides to working here—the administrative, which includes the financial, public relations, and other support areas, and the expert side, which is directly concerned with getting, evaluating, and selling artwork and collectibles.

On the **expert** side, new hirees can end up in the Arcade or in a specialist department. The Arcade is known throughout Sotheby's as the traditional training ground for the experts areas. It handles the moderately valued furniture, decorative art, jewelry, and paintings that complement the upstairs sales that are "a bit pricier."

Since Arcade staffers deal with a wide variety of products, they have to answer to the experts in the specialist departments. And since they're handling such a high volume they also have to answer to the managerial side. But the busy environment is considered an ideal place to learn all about the auction business.

"There's a different atmosphere here," explained the Arcade director. "One of the reasons it's fun for young people is that you're given a lot of responsibility. Instead of being an apprentice to a prima donna—which many of the experts are entitled to be—they can follow a consignment through the entire phase."

That means that Arcade employees get to appraise a piece, do the research on it, and see it through the sale. "On top of that, they get involved with all the functions of Sotheby's—the marketing and advertising, having parties, that sort of thing."

In the specialist departments there's a definite hierarchy: department administrator, cataloger trainee, cataloger, assistant vice president, then vice president (also the department head). But some of those positions are non-existent in smaller departments.

Each department is responsible for its own sales, from getting the art work to selling it. Experts oversee the whole auction process and are primarily responsible for getting the consignments for the sale. But at the lower levels, it's more nuts-and-bolts business.

For example, a department administrator deals more with paperwork and less with the art itself. And there's a lot of paperwork—each consignment generates at least 10 to 12 pieces of mail. But administrators don't handle only clerical work.

"The experts travel a lot, and the administrator in the department really handles the whole office when the expert isn't there," a young woman commented. "They're expected to make decisions on their own, not wait ten days until the expert comes back from Buenos Aires or London."

After you've been an administrator for a while, you get to know the material the department handles. So you move up to cataloger trainee and actually begin to catalog some of the works. At the next step up, full-fledged catalogers do even more assessment and cataloging. Then, finally, it's a move to being an expert (at the assistant vice president or vice president level). This is the glamorous part of working for Sotheby's. And it's also where the pressure mounts and the already hectic pace quickens.

"You're constantly up against deadlines," said one staffer. "When one sale is over, you can't think about that sale, you have to think about the next one. And before you know that's over with, the deadline for your May sale is on."

A typical entry-level position on the **administrative** side of Sotheby's is customer service representative. Customer service reps work in the accounting department. But they're not doing numbers crunching or statistical analyses.

After an auction, purchasers are told to go to the accounting department to pick up their invoices. And that's when the customer service rep steps into action. "You look up their bills on the computer, process them, say, 'here's your invoice, do you want to have it shipped, where's it going, let us help you suggest a mover,' that sort of thing," explained a former customer service rep.

Other entry-level staffers on Sotheby's administrative staff begin as receptionists or assistants to executives. And most staffers say that there's definitely movement from the lower level positions on up. There's no distinct job track on the administrative side as there is in the expert departments, but the pace is the same—hectic.

And that's the way it is at Sotheby's—whether you're on the administrative staff or in the 19th-century Furniture or Chinese Paintings. As one young woman said, "For anybody who really likes a fast-paced, hectic, unpredictable atmosphere, this is the place to be. This or a race car drive."

LIFE

As you'd expect, life at Sotheby's revolves around work. Even after hours.

"You're sitting at a dinner table. Someone asks, 'What do you do?' 'Oh, I work at Sotheby's.' Then everyone has an art question or an art story, a grandmother's locket or something," one man explained with a laugh. "So you're like an ambassador for the company. Always, wherever you go, on vacations even, Sotheby's has that allure that people are interested in."

Most staffers agree that Sotheby's becomes a large part of their life. And they point to the camaraderie that develops among employees through the common bonds of an interest in art and long hours.

And there's one thing most Sotheby's staffers agree upon. Once you've worked here, they say, it's tough to work anywhere else.

"I've entertained the thought of going to work for a gallery, then I think, 'What would I do?'," a young woman asked rhetorically.

"You'd go nuts, you'd be bored stiff," a co-worker answered for her.

DOLLARS AND SENSE

People working here might appreciate the artwork they deal with, but they certainly couldn't afford to buy it on their salaries. Entry-level employees start at about $15,000. But most people are aware that the art business doesn't pay much. And they recognize that there's a trade-off.

"The remuneration *is* on the low end of the scale," said one staffer. "But what you get in exchange is an incredible hands-on education."

"And that touch of glamour," added another.

GETTING IN—TRICKS OF THE TRADE

It's not easy breaking into Sotheby's.

"Six or seven years ago, intern programs meant jobs, or if you went to the London Works of Art course it meant jobs. It doesn't mean that any more," an expert said. "The attrition rate is not what it was. Also the mobility to move from one department to another is practically at a standstill."

Add to that slow job turnover an increasing number of job applicants with high degrees, a heightened public interest in the art business, and you can see why one staffer said Sotheby's wasn't "an easy nut to crack."

So how do you do it? Connections do help; employees don't make any bones about it. But connections aren't everything by any means.

"I look for what they've done summers and in extracurricular activities," said a director. "I'm not that impressed with people who give me a resumé that has every course they took in art history. What I look for is, are they involved in other kinds of projects? Did they go to Nantucket for the summer and bus dishes at a restaurant? That to me is a better kind of social connection."

And there's more. For one thing, entry-level applicants are expected to type about fifty-five words a minute. And attitude is important—most employees say Sotheby's wants people with lots of energy and flexibility.

"If you can't do three things at once, and if you get upset if you can't finish something, forget it," a department head stated. "Go someplace else."

Would-be Sotheby's staffers also should be flexible about the type of job they expect. Entry-level jobs here might not be exactly what they want, but they're better off accepting them and showing they can do the work. Many staffers here began as receptionists or assistants and ended up as either experts or administrative heads. It's all a question of working hard, staying patient, and keeping up your enthusiasm.

"If you can jump into a really hectic, very strong personality situation, juggle a lot of things and get a kick out of it," summed up a department head. "If you like the commotion and get a thrill when something new comes along and ten things get rolled at you, then you're perfect. Because that's the sort of company it is."

THE BOTTOM LINE

Less British, more business, but still art.

AUTOMOBILES

It's only a hundred years since Karl Benz and Gottleib Daimler decided to marry an internal combustion engine to a carriage. Now, to a great degree, the auto industry is the bellwether of economies throughout the world. Car sales are an important economic indicator in this country and, inside the business, "moving iron" is the byword. If the iron doesn't move, well, the losses will be calculated in the billions of dollars.

In the U.S., the auto industry is strong (over ten million sales in 1984). And while it is heavy manufacturing, it is also fashion, image, high technology, and innovation. With four domestic automakers, twenty-two importers (of which four actually build here), there are a lot of job opportunities. And the auto industry's needs are diversified. Whatever your specialization, chances are the industry has a place for you.

Every job focuses on the product. And usually companies are organized into design and engineering functions, manufacturing, marketing, and sales. Of course, because they're massive companies, they have to have their share of massive company jobs—accountants, lawyers, economists, and labor relations and personnel specialists.

But the key to the auto industry is cars. So it's best to focus on the product functions. It all starts with **design and engineering**. Here, new cars have their birth (or rather, conception). Of course, before the design staff gets a project, extensive market research is conducted. So it's not a bunch of creative types going hog-wild in a design studio. Rather, the approach is very controlled to meet market needs. The engineering process takes several years. All new models go through various stages up to running prototypes. Decisions are made about materials, options, etc. The industry runs on three- to five-year lead times with new models.

Once the go-ahead is given, **sales and marketing** come into play. Plans have to be developed to reach the market. Advertising programs must be created in conjunction with advertising agencies and launch dates established. Support material for dealers is created. When that car comes off the line, the whole package must be ready to go. And because of the investment, mistakes are costly.

While the marketing and sales staffs are developing their plans, the **manufacturing** staffs are programming plants. Today, most plants are computerized. Orders have to be placed with suppliers. Manufacturing engineers must be concerned with gearing the plans for a new model. This is the nitty-gritty of the business from weld points down to the exact number of cars coming off the line every hour. And there can be slight changes from model to model within a car family, so these differences have to be worked into the assembly line.

For someone trying to get into the industry, all this means jobs. But no matter what staff a person works for, he usually starts at the bottom. No one is thrown into the fray and told to design a car. Instead, each function of the industry has extensive training programs. New employees are gradually given more responsibility after they have gone though the training programs, which can last from several months to a year or more. The name of the game is to eliminate mistakes. Mistakes are costly and the competition is fierce. After all, there were 502 models offered in 1985 by both domestic manufacturers and importers in this country. With sales running into the ten million range, that's a lot of iron.

It is the domestic manufacturers that employ the major engineering and manufacturing staffs in this country. Importers are geared primarily to sales and marketing. Engineering staffs working for importers are involved more in product quality and testing of products to be offered in this market. But as more and more overseas companies start manufacturing operations here, the situation will change. For our present purposes we have focused on the domestic companies.

As for pay, the term used in the industry is "competitive." They do pay well—which translates into $25,000–$30,000 starting salary. And these companies traditionlly promote from within. The reason is simple. No one walks into the auto industry and begins to manage. It takes too much training and knowledge. If there is movement, it is usually from a domestic manufacturer to an importer. You don't find a person who marketed toothpaste all of a sudden holding a management position in a car company.

One final aspect to the business—you'd better like cars. It's your life.

CHRYSLER

VITAL STATISTICS

■ locations: Detroit and suburbs; sales, service, and financing operations in major cities in the U.S. and Canada; plants in New York, Midwest, Alabama, Georgia, Canada, Mexico
■ revenues: $19,572,700,000 (1984)
■ rank: No. 3 automaker in the U.S.; no. 7 worldwide
■ employees: 100,500 (1984)

AS SEEN FROM THE OUTSIDE

America loves an underdog, America loves a winner, and America loves Lee Iacocca and his Chrysler Corporation—once an underdog, now a winner.

Only at Chrysler will workers rip the CEO's picture from the pages of a magazine and tack it to the wall above their desks. Only at Chrysler will workers unabashedly talk about being proud to be part of their leader's team. For that matter, Chrysler may be the only corporation in America where workers talk at all about their CEO.

Iacocca's charisma might be a novelty in today's industrial world, but Chrysler Corporation has been blessed with charismatic leaders before. While Cadillac's founders were reading the Bible to workers during lunch breaks in a factory across town, Walter P. Chrysler was drinking beer with his immigrant workers at Dodge Main in Hamtramck, a Detroit neighborhood. Like Iacocca today, Chrysler wasn't a buddy, but he was human. Like Iacocca, he was respected—in his case, as a railroad engineer who fell in love with cars, paid his dues, and built a better automobile.

In the years since Walter P. Chrysler, the company earned and then lost a reputation for building Detroit's best-engineered automobiles. It's regaining some of its lost glory these days by its daring moves into new product territories—convertibles, minivans, and turbochargers were all popularized or repopularized by Chrysler Corp. Today, Chrysler is acknowledged as the country's lowest-cost auto producer. But Chrysler Corp. is still an underdog, just by virtue of its size. General Motors produces four times the number of vehicles, Ford more than double. While the big guys build a wide range of cars, Chrysler has to make do with fewer models, use the same components more frequently in the cars it does build, and most of all, not make mistakes. A mistake that Ford or GM could shrug off could be devastating to their smaller competitor.

Whether by luck or genius or a combination of the two, Chrysler has avoided mistakes lately. It has pulled itself out of its Red Sea of debt to become enormously profitable—so profitable that it has acquired a string of financial units and aerospace maker Gulfstream, added an assembly plant, formed a new corporation with Japanese automaker Mitsubishi to build cars in Illinois, and is openly shopping for more acquisitions.

HEARD AT THE WATER COOLER— WHAT IT'S REALLY LIKE TO WORK HERE

Corporate headquarters could have been made for a Hollywood set—the perfect Detroit/smokestack industrial look. Right off the freeway, ten minutes from downtown Detroit, it's nearly in the shadow of the General Motors building. But it's very different— Chrysler's offices are generally old, overcrowded, and industrial looking. And there are reminders of the bailout days—there's no receptionist guarding the modern styling and marketing headquarters here; visitors sign themselves in and out and phone their contacts.

But things are changing with Chrysler's new-found profitability. Some buildings have been redecorated. Leasing, realty, and finance operations have moved to skyscrapers in the suburbs; a new technical center in a far-northern suburb is in the late planning stages. Until it opens, corporate, divisional, and engineering operations share the massive compound in an old city within Detroit, Highland Park.

Once you're inside the gates, the atmosphere changes almost immediately. It's not only the modern marketing and engineering building named after the company founder, the landscaping, or the well-maintained exteriors. There's a sense of community here, of family. People from different parts of the company know each other, share information, and eat lunch together. And they work wherever there's space: temporary walls have been put up to create new offices; desks share what were single-person offices in the days when Chrysler was shrinking.

But there's another big factor to the Chrysler team spirit. It's not where they work, it's who they work for. As one staffer put it, "Iacocca is so famous, so well-known—to be a part of his crew is something I'm proud of. Everyone's proud to be here."

As long as they keep making money. . . .

PEOPLE

Chrysler people are not the entrepreneurial trendsetters you might think they'd be. There aren't many loners here, but a lot of team players. There are few innovators, and many solid conservative business people. (And a lot of these staffers are really *Ford* people.)

In the grim days, Iacocca brought over a slew of Ford managers to fill upper- and middle-management positions. But only a gambler would have left solid Ford to join Chrysler in its time of misery. And only a believer would have bothered to stay.

They're still coming over in dribs and drabs, but nothing like the flood there once was. And that means new hirees don't feel their chances for advancement are blocked.

"I think there's definitely opportunity here," said a young woman who has been carefully weighing her chances. "I think the Ford thing exists, but I don't think it's a threat for people."

Another fear is gone, too—that "knotted feeling in the stomach" employees got as they watched co-workers being laid off and wondered if they'd be next. Staffers are more confident now; they see Chrysler planning for the future. Sure, they know that lean times are inevitably ahead in the cyclical auto industry, but they say Chrysler will use attrition, not the meat cleaver, to cut its work force the next time.

There's another thing about Chrysler that affects its workers. There's little rigid structure, less formalized rotation of jobs than at GM and Ford, less mandatory training and more interaction between its two car divisions. The result is a corporation full of people who have learned the ropes pretty much on their own or with the informal help of co-workers or bosses. But for all the family feel and team spirit, Chrysler feels pretty big to a lot of new workers. So they'd better be self-secure types.

"I felt I was really in over my head for a while," stated one now-confident staffer. "I didn't know the corporation, nor did I know the particular group I was servicing. But like anything else, you learn it."

And it helps to know where you want to go at Chrysler.

"Things aren't as formal as I expected," one woman said. "It's a little more relaxed, and I can pretty much run my own show now that I know what to do. Sometimes I wish I had to really search to find the answers instead of somebody directing me. That has its advantages too. Once you learn something that way, you're never going to forget it."

JOBS

In its dark days, when one Chrysler person would have to do the work of three or four at a larger, healthier company, the hours were as dreary as the morning paper's report of Chrysler's struggle for survival. The hours are better now—so good in many cases that it's possible actually to go home after eight hours. But again, you never know. . . .

"I've been in four jobs in three and a half years here," said a fast-tracker. "I have worked in certain jobs a tremendous amount of overtime and long hours; other jobs have been what I consider lots of work but manageable work. And one of the jobs was pretty much a normal, full day, but not much outside of that."

In many cases, Chrysler is still understaffed. But that can be a positive challenge, some say. "We don't have a lot of folks; by comparison we're small in numbers," a recruiter pointed out. "So what you wind up doing is you stretch yourself."

Like everywhere else, the **financial department** is the crusher, but it's also the heart of the company. Long hours and lots of pressure are the norm, but there's also a sense of mission here. For some people, that helps offset the six- and seven-day work weeks.

"I don't know of anybody who sits and looks at the clock and says, 'Gee, three more hours until I get to go home.' The question is really, 'How am I going to get all this work done that's in front of me?' " said one staffer.

It's long hours for the **sales** force, too—plus lots of traveling, motels, and cross-country transfers. Sales is definitely the place for young employees. And excitement comes with the turf. Those who work here know they're in the front line.

In general, though, the pace is a little more relaxed at Chrysler compared to the other car companies. Maybe that's because there aren't so many young employees driving hard to succeed in their first years. And because it's a manageable size, you know who your competition is for promotions and transfers.

"Chrysler is more of a family of people," one staffer explained. "I mean, General Motors is so massive—I don't know how a person would move within that company or within divisions. You don't get overlooked here. The competition is tough within Chrysler, but I think it's a little bit harder at General Motors."

That's not to say Chrysler isn't a bureaucracy.

"I think the thing that surprises me still every day is that Chrysler is supposedly lean. To me, it's incredibly slow in getting things done," one employee said. "And there's a tremendous amount of politics. That's almost stating the obvious when you describe a large corporation, but I guess I never envisioned it."

That's why some staffers say that it's easier to get ahead "if you've got someone of any power or any stature in the organization who has an eye on you."

As far as formal training goes, it's determined more often by the department than by corporate managers. Classes and seminars are encouraged as needed. Chrysler Institute, a few miles down the street, offers advanced management and engineering degrees. Tuition reimbursement is one of the perks here and the ambitious, both young and old, lately have turned to school with renewed interest. Advanced degrees are now de rigueur for those on the way up. It's all part of making Chrysler more competitive, and it is a mission (and technique) shared by the other domestic automakers.

"I'm not going to be able to move at all very easily without my master's," commented an employee. "So I'm limited. And that goes for everything—as far as money and as far as promotions."

Chrysler takes special care of its MBAs, frequently rotating them into new jobs. This kind of on-the-job training had slipped by the wayside when Chrysler was struggling for survival. Still, rotation across functional areas—from marketing into personnel, for instance—isn't commonplace yet, although it's becoming somewhat more frequent. And staffers say you've got to be self-directed to deal with the frequent job changes.

"While I've been very happy with this bouncing around," said a young man who came to Chrysler because of the variety of jobs it offered, "I think a lot of people became very frustrated at not being directed at one particular thing. I think if they know what they want when they start, they can plan a more precise path through the corporation."

But he and others have discovered that the lateral moves can sometimes be just as important as the upward ones. They not only look good on your record, but also help you learn your way around this relatively unstructured corporation. Also, because it's loosely organized, jobs are flexible enough to be fit to the people who fill them—not the other way around.

"They try now at Chrysler to rotate people within groups, to round you out at the lower level so you have a feel for everything," said one of the company's MBAs. "Then, when a lower-level managerial job comes up, you have a certain scope of the company." Her strategy is to grab at the opportunities at the lower levels, because the chances for lateral moves decrease as you go up the ladder.

"They do have a development committee . . . that will handle all the new employees, to keep an eye on them as they're moving up, with their school and everything else," a young personnel specialist said of her department. "It's comfortable to know you're not going to be stuck in a corner and forgotten, regardless of who you end up working for."

And if you're lucky, you just might end up working in a different country. Just keep hoping that the rumors are true, that Chrysler is indeed shopping for a European presence to replace the operations it had to sell off in the late 1970s. Or that you would be chosen to work with Maserati in Italy on the new Chrysler luxury sports car. . . .

LIFE
You'd think Chrysler wouldn't bother reinforcing team spirit. After all, here's a group of people who pulled a company through financial crisis, who listened to a nation debate whether their company should die with dignity, and who still have to band together against the economy and government decisions. How close can you get?

Yet Chrysler keeps pushing team spirit. There are social events that include families, management clubs that bring together young people from different areas of the company, tickets to hear Iacocca speak, company lunches and breakfasts to hear other top executives speak, and a novel new summer internship program for product development that quickly makes young, out-of-state engineers part of the Chrysler team through mentors, job assignments, after-work baseball games, and after-game stops at the local pizza-and-beer parlor. Walter P. Chrysler would be proud.

Other departments don't use socializing quite so heavily in their initiation of new hires and interns, but most do have some form of what they call "mother hen committees" and sponsors to help in the transition from school-to-work environment.

But it's not social club here. Life at Chrysler is still work at Chrysler—and keeping Lee Iacocca proud.

DOLLARS AND SENSE
Salaries and benefits are comparable to those at Ford and GM. And that certainly isn't shabby. The U.S. auto industry, after all, has earned a reputation for high salaries, cost-of-living increases and strong health benefits. And it doesn't hurt to be headquartered in a metropolitan area where housing costs are low.

Chrysler also offers employee discounts on cars and, for management, low-cost and no-cost auto leases. Then there's the department car, filled with gas and ready to borrow for company business and personal emergencies, and competitor's cars to drive for a lucky few.

GETTING IN—TRICKS OF THE TRADE

If you graduated with honors with an electrical, mechanical, or manufacturing engineering degree from a prestigious university, then Chrysler has probably already interviewed the dean at your school in its search to find you. Everybody else looking for one of the five hundred posts filled each year by recent graduates will have to get in line with the MBA graduates the company is so strong on these days.

But there are other good ways in. Chrysler hires summer interns from undergraduate and graduate schools, and many of them ultimately find permanent employment under the sign of the pentastar. Sometimes, though, it's no easier getting into an internship program than into a permanent job. A prime example was the new product-engineering internship program—in its first year, it took only 24 of 600 candidates. But 60 to 70 percent of those who made it will be hired by Chrysler upon graduation.

Even when Chrysler is interviewing for summer interns, experience counts. "In the marketing area, they're looking for people who are strong academically, but who have had some work experience, too," said one of the people responsible for hiring. "Most of ours this summer had some experience. And they're involved in a lot of things at school—extracurricular organizations and activities. Probably most important is just how they come across in an interview, how personable they are, how well they communicate."

Sales is one of the few operations in Chrysler that regularly has openings for generalists—those with degrees in something besides business and engineering. The Chrysler Finance operation is another.

Co-operative programs, run in conjunction with nearby universities, also provide a chance to show Chrysler your stuff. And although it isn't unknown for a clerical worker to rise into management, it's only with the help of the old sheepskin. There are also openings each year for those with computer skills, as management information specialists.

Chrysler sends its recruiters out to fifty-four campuses, mostly in the East and Midwest, and a handful in the South, near its facilities there. But 60 percent of the recent graduates it hires never saw a recruiter—they mailed in resumés.

"All the opportunities now are for people in their late 20s, early 30s, who have one to two years of experience in a work-related field, like in marketing or sales or finance—then you come into Chrysler with your MBA," said a management trainee. Her assessment was repeated over and over again.

"If I were to do it all over again, I definitely would have stayed up at Michigan State another year and gotten my MA, then come here. Now it's going to take me three years going to night school, meanwhile encountering limited opportunities," said a new hiree in the marketing division. She was one of the few who are hired at all in that department, much less with just an undergraduate degree. She remembers looking at the desk of the man interviewing her. Resumés from her competitors for that single job were stacked sixteen inches high. Her advice: "Follow through on every contact. Get involved in everything you can. Research the corporation. Try to make some fun of it, too. To me it was so frightening. You've got to get any edge you can to compete over other people. Also be persistent—keep calling. I would call once a month. They remembered me, by name. After a couple of times, it was, 'Hi, how are you doing? Nothing's happening yet, we still have you in mind. Keep working, get a little bit more experience . . ."

THE BOTTOM LINE

And the last shall be first: Chrysler made more profit than Ford this last quarter and made more than GM on its auto operations (third quarter, 1985).

FORD MOTOR COMPANY

VITAL STATISTICS

- **locations:** Dearborn, MI (headquarters); group headquarters in downtown Detroit and surrounding areas; car manufacturing plants in eight cities; offices nationwide and overseas
- **revenues:** $52,366.4 billion (1984)
- **rank:** World's second largest auto manufacturer
- **employees:** 173,700 U.S.; 383,700 worldwide

AS SEEN FROM THE OUTSIDE

Nerve and guts aren't usually bywords in the auto industry. It's conservative, frustratingly provincial, and more important, it's big. A typical auto company is a lot like a whale—when it's beached, it doesn't usually get back into deep water without a tow.

But that's not the Ford Motor Company. It has guts. It takes gambles that would make a Las Vegas high roller cringe with terror. And it wins.

Look at the record for proof—between 1980 and 1982, Ford lost $3.3 billion (more than the now-fabled losses of the Chrysler Corporation). But instead of battening down the hatches and weathering the auto sales slump by doing nothing, Ford fought back.

During the final year of that slump, it introduced a radical new approach to auto design—aerodynamic styling. Ford management didn't play safe. They abandoned the traditional boxy-looking cars and decided that Ford cars would have rounded, smooth lines. This product would stand out from the crowd, they decreed. But don't think the executives at headquarters weren't sweating. Especially when the cars *didn't* take off at the start. If they lost this gamble, well . . . they could always melt everything down for scrap iron. But the cars finally did take off. And Ford is making record before-tax profits now—$4.3 billion in 1984.

Innovation and risk-taking are nothing new to the Ford Motor Company. Founded in 1903 by Henry Ford, the company began producing Model As, boxy-looking cars that were far from aero-dynamically styled. Five years and nineteen letters of the alphabet later, Ford decided the key to success was to produce cars for every man, and came out with the not too expensive Model T. The Model T came in "any color as long as it's black," as Henry Ford reportedly said. Lack of color selection didn't dissuade buyers, however—the Model T sold like mad; too well, in fact. By 1913, there were more would-be Model T owners than Model Ts. So Henry came up with another new idea—assembly-line production. And he didn't stop with innovation there. In 1914, Ford announced he was going to pay his workers $5 a day, over double the existing minimum wage. Employees were pleased and, with the extra money, they could afford to buy Ford cars. And that made Henry Ford very pleased. Over fifteen million Model Ts were sold during its nineteen years of production.

The market has changed a lot lately. Fifteen million sales in nineteen years is peanuts nowadays. So Ford has kept pace. Due in part to its newly styled models, Ford sold 5.58 million cars and trucks worldwide in 1984; 2.214 million in the U.S. alone. That's a lot of iron.

While Ford touts "it wants to be your car company," however, it's more than just automobiles. Ford North American Automotive Operations controls the building and marketing of cars and trucks in the U.S. and Canada. These products are marketed through the Ford and Lincoln-Mercury Divisions. The Diversified Products Operations includes Ford Aerospace & Communications Corp., Rouge Steel Company, and Ford Motor Land Development Company. It also has the second largest finance company in the world, Ford Motor Credit, which had earnings of $310 million in 1984.

Overseas, Ford has built a veritable empire. Ford Europe, the fourth largest automaker on that continent, usually is in heated battle with other European manufacturers for the sales lead there. And there are extensive Ford operations in Mexico, Brazil, and other Latin American countries, as well as in Asia and the Pacific. The company has backed up its overseas commitment to the tune of $5.4 billion in investments.

Ford is continuing to look for diversification opportunities and ties with other manufacturers, proving that a conglomerate can move. But then again, Ford is probably going back to its roots. After all, Henry Ford didn't exactly build his empire by doing business in the conventional way. And the family name is still on the building.

HEARD AT THE WATER COOLER—
WHAT IT'S REALLY LIKE TO WORK HERE

The tough times in the auto industry are over—for the time being. And Ford is going through a big transition. Yes, it's still big, it's still manufacturing, and cars are the name of the game. But just as Ford came up with a new twist in car design, it's coming up with a new twist in management style.

In the past, management was "hard-nosed, they'd hammer down all the time, yell and scream . . ." as one young man put it.

And now? It's changed, staffers say, and most seem to like it that way. Employees talk about the new team approach, bosses who are open to suggestions, a "participatory management philosophy," to put it in bureaucratese. That's not to say there's no supervision here. Participatory management simply means input into a final decision.

There's one thing that's not changing about Ford, though. For all the fresh new ideas, the innovative managing, and the new car designs, there's still a distinctly un-modern look to the place. Corporate headquarters, called the "Glass House," has been over-shadowed in the skyline by newer buildings. Inside, it's basic 50s decor—looking at the furniture and carpeting, you feel as though you've walked into a time warp. Some lucky marketing types start in the decade-old Renaissance Center, Henry Ford's monument to downtown Detroit. It's new, it's the business address to have— and locals consider it an architectural blunder.

But few new hirees wind up in either the Glass House or Ren Cen. More often than not they're in plants and district sales offices throughout the country. But that fits with Ford's distinct shirt-sleeves mentality. After all, this *is* heavy manufacturing, and that means employees are expected to get their hands dirty.

It also means that employees know they're expected to work and work hard. And with Ford's new progressive attitude toward employee involvement and developing products, most staffers— especially the young ones—feel as if they're part of a team that's going to start winning.

One staffer cheerfully summed up the feeling at Ford these days. "The sky's the limit."

And maybe it is . . .

PEOPLE

First of all, young staffers say there aren't enough young staffers at Ford. The recession and the consequent layoffs (done largely in reverse order of seniority) cut down on the under-30 set. But since there *aren't* a lot of young staffers here, those there are have found out that Ford is a great place for fast-tracking.

"Opportunities have opened up for younger people to advance more quickly," explained one young woman. "Normally you put your time in, X amount of years at each level up the ladder." "But now . . ."

Now it's a different story. So Ford people seem serious about business—deadly serious. After all, they all want the next promotion. But it's not a shark tank. And personalities vary from division to division and department to department.

In sales and marketing, staffers are typical sales and marketing staffers—social, personable, and aggressive. A Lincoln-Mercury staffer described his work atmosphere as "friendly—they reach out here." In the Ford Division district offices, according to one staffer, "everyone's striving, but people are more personal and flexible."

But the Ford division staffers are also big on getting ahead. "Here, people are *very* aggressive," said one employee. "Competition is much more intense." And since people working in those district offices are out on the road working alone more often than not, there's less of a focus on team spirit. "You have to watch what you say and do," a Ford Division staffer said, "because it can be used against you."

On the corporate side, staffers are very professional, much more inward, because they don't deal with the public as much," said one young man.

But for all the differences among Ford people, there's one overriding similarity. Whether they're in engineering, purchasing, sales and marketing, whatever, they usually like cars.

As a staffer noted, "Basically, you *have* to like cars in this business. That's all you ever see—cars."

JOBS

If you like to work, you'll get your chance at Ford. This is not the place for someone looking to make an easy dollar and coast through life. Ford demands hustle, and once on the job, responsibility comes quickly. Those who can't cut it are out. Putting it simply, Ford is competitive.

Yet with all the pressure to produce, there's enthusiasm at Ford. No matter which department or division, people approach their work with a vigor. Ford promotes from within, and rarely hires from the outside to fill management positions.

So there's a lot of movement at Ford. Assignments change and with those assignments comes more responsibility. When you stop moving, "that's the sign you're not going to go far at Ford," as one staffer stated. Many people singled out the promotional opportunities at Ford. As one woman said, "I feel there's an environment here that's trying to encourage it."

Jobs at Ford are as diversified as the company. But no matter where you are, whether it's sales and marketing, engineering, manufacturing, purchasing, or financial, you start in the training programs.

The training can last for several months to two years if you have limited work experience and are selected for the company's College Graduate Program. But don't get the idea that this is classrooms and theory. No. It's on the job training, pure and simple. And the major difference among the programs is the length of time a person spends making the rounds. For newly hired staffers, Ford believes in giving them solid exposure to most facets of the auto business. And there's one common denominator at Ford—everyone starts at the bottom and works his way up. And that includes MBAs.

The positions all tend to be demanding. There's no such thing as a forty-hour week for the new employee. So much has to be done—and a good portion of it is paperwork. "You need a super amount of organization," said one young employee. "They throw so much at you."

Sales staffers start with on-the-job training in a district office. Then there's a fifteen-week program at the Ford Institute involving training in dealer operations, credit, and zone management. And staffers also put in a few weeks at a dealership, learning about the dealers' needs. Then it's to work, real work, as a "field manager," calling on dealers and working with them to sell cars.

One thing new sales employees learn quickly is that Ford's customers are its dealers, not the general public. So sales reps have to develop strong relationships with the dealers. "If they're not getting along with you, you'll have a hard time," explained one young man. "And it takes time for them to get to know you. If they don't like you, they can make your life miserable."

The biggest gauge of performance is improved market penetration. For each employee there's a series of objectives, and those who meet them move up to larger, more prestigious zones. Then, it may be transfer time to another district. Staffers spend three to five years in the field manager position, moving from a training zone to a metro zone—which means more money. After that, it's a move up the ladder to department manager within a district. Then it may be headquarters or "you can stay in the district forever," as one staffer noted.

What happens if you don't move up? Well, the Japanese manufacturers have their eye out for experienced Ford employees who've been through those training programs . . .

The supply side (not as in economics), which includes purchasing, transportation, and traffic, is another area young employees in the College Graduate Program go into. "It's not the only way to get into Ford Purchasing, but it's the primary avenue," commented a young woman.

Basically, **purchasing** is buying the supplies Ford needs to build its cars. New hires in purchasing combine training courses with hands-on "development assignments," designed to give staffers exposure to the different aspects of purchasing.

"When I joined Ford, I bought sun visors. That was a training assignment," a staffer related. "In fact, that's the toughest training assignment they've got. It doesn't sound tough, but it really is. I never even looked at the darn things until I started buying." It's not *all* sun visors, though. As purchasers move up, they're responsible for things like seats. And that's not as easy as it sounds. Those who thrive on the negotiating with suppliers, the dealing with sticky situations, and the efficient handling of their budget, move up the ladder. It's still purchasing, but the amount of money a buyer can spend increases. So can the variety of work.

"I really like what I do," said an enthusiastic old hand. "I'm involved with the design center a lot, all the guys with the Gucci shoes, with the colors, the shapes, what do they like in seats, and what do we want to do down the road, and new technology. It's dynamic!"

And that's the way Ford wants to be these days.

LIFE
Life at Ford is Ford.

Sorry about that, but if you're working fifty to sixty hours a week, you really don't have much time for anything else. And don't forget the travel schedule, which can really put a crimp in your social life.

But it's not all that grim. Ford does offer continuing education programs that can help you with that advanced degree. And the amount you associate with fellow workers really depends on whether you're in town or not.

Another part of the social side of things at Ford, especially where sales staffers are concerned, is dinners and trips held for dealers. Meeting and greeting and just keeping dealers happy is "a big part of the job, especially in the districts," one zone manager said. "A shy person would have a hard time."

DOLLARS AND SENSE
Pay at Ford is competitive with other companies in the domestic auto industry and other industries. Don't forget, the company is fighting to obtain good recruits—so it *has* to pay on par. And Ford gives frequent merit increases as a reward for hard work.

Gross salary isn't the entire picture, of course. Ford also offers fairly extensive bennies—medical, dental, vision, and life insurance, naturally, but that's just the tip of the iceberg. There are substantial discounts on new cars (Fords, of course), a savings and investment plan through which, with Ford matching contributions, you can buy a share of the company.

Then there's the continuing education program, as well as in-house training programs, which cover everything from technical and business skills to personal skills courses.

GETTING IN—TRICKS OF THE TRADE

"An MBA is like a union card," said one Ford employee.

At Ford, there's a definite trend to hire those with advanced degrees for all positions. While today only about 25 percent of the 1,200 to 1,500 Ford recruits straight from college campuses have advanced degrees, Ford pushes them to get Master's degrees once they're hired. And in some areas, a Master's is a requisite, particularly in employee relations.

But fear not. There is still a place for you in the Ford picture— mainly because there are a lot of jobs to fill. Like most companies, Ford says it looks for people in the top percentile of their class. Grades aren't all, though. Ford recruiters say they're also looking for "the indicators of leadership." That's a fancy way of saying they like people who have served as military officers, held key positions in sororities or fraternities, and most impressive to them, had "meaningful" work experiences.

That work experience can be part-time jobs during the school year and full-time during the summer. Ford recruiters look at this carefully, especially if the student was promoted in that job position. Said one man on the interview circuit, "That's a pretty impressive thing for an employer, because it tells you that you've got a student who is probably earning his own way while going to school at the same time." Ford does offer a few co-op programs, primarily in technical fields, so the work-school record is important.

What else do you need? Several employees stressed the importance of a business degree rather than a liberal arts. While Ford doesn't insist on this, many say that life will be easier during those training programs if you already understand the basics. As one employee said, "Ford will train you, but if you have a business background, it's easier."

THE BOTTOM LINE

Young people can really move at Ford—if they have drive.

GENERAL MOTORS

VITAL STATISTICS

- **locations:** Detroit, MI (headquarters); divisional and group headquarters mostly in southeast Michigan; plants in 90 U.S. cities; international offices in 37 countries outside the U.S.
- **revenues:** $84 billion (1984)
- **rank:** World's largest auto manufacturer
- **employees:** 748,000

AS SEEN FROM THE OUTSIDE

In Detroit—actually, throughout the automotive world—GM's nickname is The General. And even though some of the regimentation is gone from the corporation these days, it still fits: The General gives the marching orders.

It's not only the world's largest automaker, half again the size of its next-largest competitor, it's also one of the country's largest financial institutions. It owns half of this country's largest robot maker, it has bought stakes in machine vision and artificial intelligence companies, and it now owns what is arguably the preeminent computer-services firm, Ross Perot's Electronic Data Systems. Its latest headline-grabbing acquisition was Hughes Aircraft, the nation's seventh largest defense contractor.

But when people think about GM, they think about cars. And no wonder. The General sets car prices; everyone else follows the leader. The General decides how many cars it will sell. Its competitors may scoff, but General Motors will sell those cars, even if it has to cut prices. And the other automakers will follow, kicking and screaming, into the price war that no one but the oh-so-profitable General can win. When The General decided it had just about enough of the computer industry's myriad computer languages and protocols, it ordered up a single protocol. And the industrial computer industry fell into line. When The General decided it wanted to issue stock separately for Electronic

Data, even though S.E.C. rules forbade it, it was the stock exchange that gave way, not GM.

And its influence doesn't stop with the barons of industry. When General Motors went to the United Auto Workers union for Japanese-style work rules for its forthcoming revolutionary small car, Saturn, the union granted them. When The General wanted to form a joint venture to produce cars in California with Toyota, Chrysler's Lee Iacocca cried "Antitrust!" But the Federal Trade Commission said, "Go ahead." Whether it's trade policy, energy policy, or safety regulations, The General and the government frequently speak with one voice. Now it may be that conservative General Motors has simply found a soulmate in Ronald Reagan.

But one thing is certain, the President's brown suits would never wash at General Motors.

HEARD AT THE WATER COOLER— WHAT IT'S REALLY LIKE TO WORK HERE

Times *have* changed at the auto giant. There may not yet be any brown suits, but the guys in gray pinstripes are free to wear colored shirts and to grow mustaches. And the club is no longer just for guys; women have made significant inroads. There may not be any at the top yet, but they're on the way. Most significantly, the old management style is changing—slowly but surely.

"The authoritarian 'I am the boss and I tell you what to do; now go do it,' is being replaced with a participative style of management," explained one young executive.

A big part of the shift is due to the company's massive reorganization—probably the biggest in the history of corporate America. Corporate structure has changed, jobs have changed, even the location of people's jobs has changed since Chairman Roger B. Smith announced the reorganization in January 1984. At first, apprehension filled GM's halls. This has since been replaced by a sense of urgency—"Let's get this company turned around *NOW*"—and energy.

The halls of General Motors are scattered and varied. Now that the company has sold its Manhattan skyscraper and only leases space there for its treasurer's office, there is just one General Motors Building, built of marble and steel by company founder Billy Durant in the old GM style—high-powered, controlled, conservative, and wealthy.

Down the highway in a suburb that GM (figuratively) built, there's the Tech Center (never mind that every automaker and major supplier in town has a technical center; in Detroit, there's only one Tech Center). Built in the 1950s, the mile-square center is where engineering research is conducted, and it is the daytime home to 23,000 employees. Buildings are low and cluster around a massive fountain and pool where workers stroll during lunch and feed the ducks. Hallways are made of glass, adding visibility to the frenetic pace. For this is where the corporate changes are *really* taking place, in the new super-groups, each of which alone is large enough to be near the top of the Fortune 500. They now share space here with the engineers.

It's the same sort of feverish pace in the corporate halls of the car divisions, which are scattered throughout southeast Michigan. Offices are what you'd expect at The Biggest. But the attitudes here make you think that GM workers aren't quite as sure whether they're still The Best. Like everyone else in the U.S. auto industry, they're playing catch-up with the Japanese. And that's tough when you're used to being in charge.

PEOPLE
"The Puritan work ethic is alive and well and living at General Motors," said a young manager who admitted to six-day work weeks ("not counting the paperwork you take home on Sunday.").

These are Midwesterners—hardworking, unfrivolous (which isn't to say they don't have a sense of humor), dedicated team players. That's a big one at the Big One. And lately it's been a little easier to share a common mission, since there's a common enemy: foreign manufacturers. And the days of layoffs, and careers slowed down by the lack of jobs, are still a fresh memory.

"It's not just a financial commitment that keeps me here," commented one employee. "It's an interest to win. It's as if we're in a battle and you don't want to give up. Because I'd like to see GM in 1990 be building a competitively priced, highest-quality small car with U.S. labor, beating the Japanese. You can see it in the eyes of people, 'Hey, we've been affronted.' "

That's another attitude shared by most GM employees. Pride.

Pride in the size and power of the corporation for which they work.

"If I didn't work for General Motors, I would work for myself," reflected one man who has been with The General since the age of eighteen, when he was a co-op student. "If you're going to work for somebody, you might as well work for the biggest and the best company in the world. Why settle for second or third or 499th?"

Another young manager in public relations agreed. "I haven't met anyone who doesn't have a sense of pride as to what GM is. There are people who walk around with it tatooed on their arms and there are other folks who are quiet about it. I guess I would fall into the tatooed-on-the-arm class."

JOBS

There's only one simple way to describe the jobs at GM: varied. What would you expect at a huge auto company? There are jobs in engineering, manufacturing, computer science, and special-ized, high-technology fields. But The General also has troops in accounting, finance, real estate, sales, personnel, and public re-lations.

The best route to the top is through the financial staff, training ground of chairmen for generations. Cars may be the product, but money is the name of the real game at GM.

"The financial organization within General Motors does tend to move its people along more quickly than other staffs, and it's not afraid to provide an individual with some cross-functional experience," said one alumnus.

The competitive spirit has always been alive and well at GM. Not only has there always been competition from one car division to the next, there also has always been fierce competition for jobs—getting them in the first place and moving up.

"You don't get plopped into the middle of an assignment that you like and other people aspire to. You have to earn that," explained one man.

No automatic promotions here. Staffers say it's more a question of doing your job and doing it well. "There's not such an em-phasis on time and grade any more, or 'How old are you?'," one staffer asserted. "It's more, 'How well are you performing? Are you getting the job done? Do you have the drive and the where-withal to get the job done?'"

From recently hired college grads to MBAs, right on through the ranks, a work-your-way-up attitude is expected. And GM staffers who want to make it go along with the necessity for dues-paying—for a very good reason.

"GM is large enough that, for any job that exists, for my job today, there are five people who could do it as well if not better than I do it," said a manager in his 30s who has no reason to be paranoid. "It's not like I'm indispensable."

But there's a flip side to GM's bigness—job opportunities. All of GM's organization and structure pays off in the formalized rotational system that acquaints most new hirees with many of the job opportunities in the corporation. Overseas assignments are frequent, especially for those identified as high-potential employees. And although there isn't a whole lot of cross-functional transferring—say, from finance into marketing—there is more than there used to be. And there is definitely a lot of job-swapping from division to division, from the offices of heavy industry to the offices of the corporate brass to the glamorous marketing arms. That keeps people fresh.

"Getting on top of the learning curve is one of the most fascinating things you can do," a frequently transferred young man said enthusiastically. Another pointed out the bonus in the job swap: "It may seem as if a person can be stalled for five or six years—for ten years—in this company. But they can catch up overnight just by timing, by being in the right place at the right time, by working for the right individual. All it takes is one or two good breaks. But the key is you can't give up."

There's another key to getting ahead at GM—hard work. Plenty of it. Success story after success story cited not only luck, but sixty- to seventy-hour work weeks. Many staffers said they thrived on it—they wouldn't have it any other way. There's so much to do and learn during the reorganization of GM and the restructuring of the auto industry that there is barely time to sleep. Sure, there's room for the standard work week for those who want it. But not for them personally, not for the achievers.

And those achievers put up with a lot more than long hours. For one thing, there's the bureaucracy.

"You get promoted on how much frustration you can take," a fast-tracker said, recalling the barriers he faced. "I'll tell you how I deal with that. I keep trying to change the organization. I recognize that GM can't make changes as fast as another company just by virtue of the fact that we're so large. There's so much inertia here. I make sure the piece of the organization that I'm responsible for is doing the right things."

To implement change in a company so large "requires twice the effort because you have to prove in advance, before actually doing it, that it could work," noted one staffer. And you have to convince bosses all the way up to listen to it.

"You've got to have a little bit of bulldog in you," explained a staffer. "You have to keep that delicate balance, keep your persistence without being looked at as a rabble-rouser, someone who doesn't fit in as a team player."

But it's worth it to reach that balance nowadays. Many staffers say that getting someone to listen is no longer difficult at the giant. GM now not only listens, but encourages its people to speak.

LIFE

Once inside GM, it easily becomes your life. Whether you're working in corporate or divisional headquarters or at the Tech Center, you're surrounded by enough fellow GM workers to populate your own city. In fact, most GM facilities have their own fire and health-care facilities, their own restaurants, even their own newspapers. It's a lot like being on a military base.

There's also the social side—things like athletic leagues and corporate functions. For the retail sales crew, there are dinners with dealers and trips as payment for jobs well done. True, you'll be working harder than if you were at a desk, but it's hard to get upset about working when you're in Hawaii.

In short, GM can easily become one's whole life. But it doesn't have to be.

DOLLARS AND SENSE

The General pays the troops well. Secretaries here make more than most teachers. College recruits get salaries competitive with those offered across all U.S. industry. Salespeople could make more on commission, but here they get a career and a shot at management. Upper management isn't getting the salaries it should, people say, but adjustments are being made, according to GM spokesmen. And, of course, the million-dollar bonuses for those at the very top have by now become old hat.

"When we go out to the campuses . . . we're equal to or better than the AT&Ts and the Exxons," a GM recruiter said. "We don't really compete with the consulting firms that pay MBAs a lot of money, but we make up for that with a career path. At the consulting firms, you come out either dead or alive."

If the pay is median, the benefits aren't. "You get the best deal in town on purchasing a new automobile, and certainly the GM package of benefits is probably second to none," said a divisional comptroller. "The amount of vacation is extremely liberal." Others mentioned health-care benefits and a stock-option plan that can only be described as generous.

And The General will pay for your advanced degree, give you a leave of absence, and even send you to an Ivy League grad school, if you're good enough to be chosen as one of the year's two hundred GM Fellows. There are in-house training sessions too, hundreds of them. Certain courses are mandatory at certain job changes.

Almost as important for the company's many car enthusiasts are the "product evaluations" of GM and competitors' products—in other words, driving new cars home.

GETTING IN—TRICKS OF THE TRADE

"If I had to do it over again, I'd get an engineering degree and an MBA," said one company recruiter. This sentiment was repeated often by people from engineering to accounting. It's not necessary to have an advanced degree to get into GM, but once you're there, the pressure is on to get one.

It doesn't matter if you're a graduate of an East Coast or California university, since GM is casting its net wider than the Midwest these days. Experience also counts, especially experience at GM, whether gained through a summer internship or co-op program. And take a look at the GM Scholar program at your university: sometimes the scholarship stipend is no more than a token, but later on GM will notice you. One GM scholar met the GM chairman, a graduate of his university, at a university dinner. The Chairman told him that GM would pay for his Harvard degree if he would come to work for the company. He didn't need a second invitation.

"We don't necessarily look for people with straight As," commented a personnel manager. "We do look at grades as one discriminator, but not as an absolutely all-encompassing thing as perhaps consulting firms and investment bankers might look at them. We look at leadership qualities, we look at the work an individual has done on his or her campus or outside that campus experience . . . that indicate leadership qualities and that a candidate can communicate. The ability to work with people is very important." He and his team select 1,500 to 2,000 college graduates each year to join the GM ranks.

For the liberal arts major, the key is knowing what you want within the company. There are many openings in sales, personnel plant management, and public-government relations, for example, that can be filled by generalists. But the competition is intense.

You don't even have to wait for a degree to join GM. The company is still sponsoring most of the graduating class of what used to be General Motors Institute in Flint, Michigan. This cooperative business and engineering college is now independent, and called GMI-EMI, but students can still be sponsored by GM divisions and work their way through college—studying, getting on-the-job training at General Motors, and a paycheck to boot.

THE BOTTOM LINE

The Big One.

BANKS

Banking used to be for liberal arts graduates who could read, add, multiply, and play golf. The business itself was easy. Accept deposits from individuals and corporations, pay out a few percentage points (or none) as interest, and lend the money out to other individuals or corporations at a higher percentage interest. The difference, called "the spread," was profit.

Inflation, recession, high interest rates, and competition have changed all that. You can no longer learn the fundamentals of banking on your lunch hour.

Not that old-line banking isn't still there. There's just more of it. Customers still deposit money, but they may put it in treasury bills (T-bills) or certificates of deposit (CDs). Corporations still borrow, but they may do it themselves by issuing "commercial paper" (IOUs to the public). Banks have had to change with the times—by getting more competitive and more aggressive and bigger.

But not too big. The name of the game is quality growth, improving profitability and return on assets by expanding in the right areas. Interstate banking, investment banking, and garnering quality customers are the focus of the large banks today. Since corporate clients can easily raise money on their own, banking *services* have been emphasized. Calling officers, sometimes called relationship managers, meet corporate financial managers and sell a variety of bank services. Including loans. But more loans go to the smaller customers—the 100-million-dollar corporations that have difficulty raising money on their own.

Today, banks like to think of themselves as financial services companies, offering a wide range of services (for a fee, of course) to individuals, corporations and foreign governments. Cash management systems, consulting, interest-bearing checking accounts, discount brokering. Things can get so complex that calling officers frequently call in specific specialists from the bank to explain the technical aspects of these services.

And it's not only service. Interstate and international banking is also making the big boys bigger. Banks used to be limited to one state, but intense lobbying efforts and relaxed legal restrictions have changed the game a bit. Banks have bought out-of-state savings and loan institutions and industrial banks, and have issued national credit cards. And overseas, the banks are creating financial networks that crisscross the world.

These big banks are called "money center banks," and have headquarters in Boston, Chicago or New York. But there are some others—the "regional banks" and the "California banks." Still, banking by any other name remains banking. Each bank may have a different organizational structure, different job titles and different divisions, but what they all do is the same.

Basically, banking is split into *retail* and *wholesale* divisions, retail dealing with private individuals and small corporations, wholesale dealing with larger corporations. Retail bank officers are either "platform officers" who make (or refuse) personal loans, and branch managers, who run the local branches. Wholesale bankers are lending officers who make (or refuse) loans, analyze the credit-worthiness of their customers and sell bank services to their clients.

International bankers, usually divided by geographic region, handle overseas corporate (and wealthy private) accounts. They may be based in headquarters or at overseas branches.

Correspondent bankers deal with other banks—managing the transfer of billions of dollars that flow between banks every day.

The **capital markets** people try to get the lending officers money to lend. It used to be easy, grabbing some of those free deposits, but today it's very different. People here are more financial-market oriented, less Park Avenue and more Wall Street, trading dollars and foreign exchange, betting on currency trends.

Trust divisions are the quiet area of banking—separated legally from the rest of the bank. Officers invest client money in stocks and bonds, and as such are investment people more than bankers. This was a dead end for bankers just a few years ago, but the Wall Street exposure and recent promotions have made it a much better place to be.

Operations used to be the real dead end. Every loan, every deposit, every banking transaction generates a huge load of data work, and operations people did the processing. It was (and is) more like factory work than anything else, and operations officers used to be more like factory foremen (and were treated that way by lending officers). But it's a very important area of customer service, as anyone with an error in his bank statement knows. And it's had a recent rise in reputation as banks compete in operations.

Still, most people want to go into the **corporate** client side of banking—selling bank services and calling on corporate treasurers and the like. It's the "blue blood" area of banking. Most still begin with credit training, designed to teach the nuts and bolts of the business. Often grueling, with classroom work, tests, and on-the-job training, it transforms eager liberal arts graduates into tougher bankers.

Then the slow route to the top—from credit trainee to assistant treasurer to assistant vice president to vice president. The titles vary with the bank, but the paths don't. Expect up to a year and a half as a trainee, then two to four years as an assistant treasurer, then four to eight years as an assistant VP. Then VP, the first job with real teeth in it.

Salaries are pretty good. Credit trainees begin at $20,000–$25,000. Assistant treasurers make $25,000–$35,000. Assistant VPs make up to $45,000, and VPs can make up to $100,000. Not bad. But that's the real crunch position in banking. It's a bureaucratic business, and like all bureaucracies, banks are structured like a pyramid—they get narrower at the top.

But the field is itself changing very rapidly. National banking is probably only a few years away, and the old line that separated investment banks (which handle underwriting, mergers, etc.) and commercial banks is fading.

And the best thing about it is the exposure. As one young officer stated, "It's such a broad industry and you learn about so many types of companies that you can't go wrong." If you're not sure of what you want to do, banking can show you pretty much everything. And it's an ideal spot for liberal arts majors for just that reason.

Just don't tell that to a recruiter.

BANK OF AMERICA

VITAL STATISTICS

- **locations:** San Francisco (headquarters); offices nationwide and worldwide
- **assets:** $102.2 billion (1984)
- **rank:** 2nd in assets
- **employees:** 89,200

AS SEEN FROM THE OUTSIDE

A lot of little deposits can make a very big bank. That's how Bank of America began—lending to the little guys. It was founded in the early 1900s by A. P. Giannini, the son of Italian immigrants. Then came branches all across California, and lending to the big guys—Aerospace, Agribusiness and Real Estate. Combined, this made Bank of America the largest bank in America—and the most comfortable.

No cutthroat competition on its home turf with the other giants from New York and Chicago. Federal and state laws pretty much kept those banks on the other coast, in other, smaller states. In a booming California economy, Bank of America scooped up almost half the banking deposits in the state and plowed its earnings into a worldwide network that competed with the money-center banks abroad. Big and solid Bank of America had an unassailable position, and because of this a reputation for being a little bit quieter than the other banks.

Not now. Recession in real estate and agriculture, and competition due to loosened banking laws, have brought tougher times at home, and are changing BA's image. Earnings went down, loan write-offs went up, and BA lost its solid No. 1 spot. But a little competition never hurt anyone—and Bank of America is in it for the long haul. Unprofitable branches have been eliminated, and a revved-up sales and marketing orientation has been encouraged. It's not as comfortable as it was, and increasingly, employees are finding their salaries and promotions linked to performance, not tenure. A new bottom-line orientation has emerged.

So BA is changing with the times. It purchased Charles Schwab, the largest discount broker, in 1982. And like the other banks, it is selling its services aggressively. Earnings and the ratios are still down, but some Wall Street analysts are looking to 1986 for an upturn.

And BA is big enough for real staying power. BankAmerica Corp., the holding company, owns the bank, Bank of America National Trust & Savings Association, which has 1,061 domestic and foreign branches and 28 corporate banking and representative offices, including one in New York.

HEARD AT THE WATER COOLER
WHAT IT'S REALLY LIKE TO WORK HERE

We didn't speak with many corporate bankers at Bank of America. So we focused on retail and (middle market) business bankers instead. That's the bedrock of BA. And whether those staffers work in a rural branch or in the San Francisco headquarters, they're all talking about the changes Bank of America is going through.

There seems to be a definite "let's wait and see" mood here. No one seems sure what's happening up on the fortieth floor in the Ivory Tower, as staffers call the BA building in San Francisco.

"There are still people wondering what's going on and where we're going," one employee said. "That needs to be communicated more.

"There have been some management turnovers in the company and that's generated some concern. Lately anyone who leaves makes most officers wonder, 'What's wrong? Why are they leaving? Is it because they're not doing their job? Or is it because they see the ship is sinking?' " That reassurance has to come from senior management, and according to some staffers the company is giving it.

But reassurance isn't the only thing BA staffers need during these times. They also have to be adaptable and pretty resilient. For years, Bank of America has had a reputation for being a warm "people-oriented" company, not quite as competitive as the other banks. And while staffers say the bank is still humanistic, many also say there's more of a bottom-line, sales-driven orientation.

Still, for all the changes and all the concerns, many employees still swear by Bank of America. It might be going through difficult times, but a lot of people are willing to stick by the company.

PEOPLE

As with most banks, BA staffers are becoming more like salespeople and less like traditional bankers.

"We're all very sales-oriented now," said one employee. "That's kind of a new way of thinking for us here, in that we're trying to sell company services to people. Before, people always came in and asked for them."

So BA employees have the traits most bankers have nowadays—"If you don't have a sales mode of thinking, then you won't work out," an assistant VP said. "You have to enjoy being aggressive, going out and calling on people, asking for their business, having to leave your desk. You've got to have it all. It's not just a paper-pushing function any more."

BA staffers have to be flexible in other ways, too; specifically, they have to be prepared to relocate. Bank of America is a large corporation, and many of its employees end up seeing quite a lot of it.

"You're expected to move if necessary," said a young woman with quite a few moves under her belt. "Especially on your first assignment . . . The company will terminate your employment if you don't go where they want you to go."

But some things *are* constant here—like the traditional distinction between headquarters employees and operations types. Corporate employees are seen as, well, more corporate, and branch staffers more casual—even in how they dress. Said one branch officer, "If you're up in San Francisco, it's extremely corporate. That's the culture up there—lots of yellow ties with blue dots. The power tie."

As for people in the boonies? "They're more into whatever style the customers are wearing," he explained. "Out in the desert, they wear casual clothes, slacks and open sports shirts. Back in a city area, it's suits again. Not the routine blue pinstripes, but more of an assortment of colors. We're more 'springy' than San Francisco."

JOBS

The job duties and responsibilities of BA staffers mirror what's happening in banks everywhere. Here you can see clearly the shift the financial world is taking, especially since Bank of America has been so strongly affected.

A young woman summed up the shift everyone there has had to deal with. "We never had to worry before about our market share because no one was in California trying to take a piece of the pie. The pie was so big, we had our portion, which was an understood portion. Now a lot of the Eastern banks have come to the West Coast."

"There are so many bankers here in San Francisco, it's not funny," she continued. "It's very difficult to keep that market share now, so consequently we've got to be more aggressive, we've *got* to be perceived as being more aggressive."

The new focus at Bank of America can be summed up in one word—selling. A twelve-year vet explained how duties have changed. "I was so busy in the late 70s that I never had to go on a business development call because there was so much business coming to the company. But there are so many people out there soliciting your customer, you've got to call on them, you've got to be willing to go to them. There are other people who are willing if you aren't."

Traditionally, BA has had a reputation for quality customer service. And now that's being emphasized even more.

A personal financial service officer explained how she sold customers on Bank of America. "Quality of service—we're large, we're nationwide. And I offer all the vast resources Bank of Amerca has. I can help you put your finger on anything you want with just one phone call. You don't have to search through the directory or call different places if you're interested in a standby letter of credit or you want to do some investing. Call me. That's the niche Bank of America wants to fill." So does the competition . . .

In order to prepare its staffers to service clients, Bank of America offers a variety of training programs in retail, business and corporate banking. According to one staffer, much of the training is decentralized. Within the branch system, there are seven regions, and each region is responsible for administering both operations and credit training programs. Additionally, some branches offer specialized training for those interested in specific areas, such as becoming a personal banker to wealthy individuals. The corporate credit training program is one program that is nationwide, as opposed to regional.

People training in **branch management** typically are assigned a branch in which they rotate through assignments and become familiar with all phases of branch banking. The nine to twelve-month program entails hands-on work, under the guidance of the branch officers. "Our job is to help trainees advance and learn the bank," explained one branch officer. "We don't push them off in a corner and say, 'There you go.' "

Based upon the trainee's performance, he or she is then assigned as an assistant branch administrator. Many times the first assignment requires relocation. Then it's a question of working your way through the ranks, moving from branch to branch.

"If your performance is good, there's no stopping you," commented one fast-tracker. "They'll promote you as fast as they can. Here, you don't have to play politics."

Part of being a successful branch officer is putting up with long hours—according to one branch administration officer, that's typically 7 to 6:30 each day, and two hours on the weekend.

Many branch officers who prove themselves can rise into area management, which oversees a group of branches. Area positions include credit administrator, area administration officer and area manager. And beyond that, they may go into administration and personnel.

As one staffer explained, "The bank has changed its career path. It used to be, get to branch administration officer, and then jump over to become a lending officer, so you can ultimately become a manager. The system's changed now, so you never have to jump over. The direction's more clear now for branch administration officers than five years ago."

A typical **regional operations program** runs from between six to nine months and combines classroom training with hands-on work. Trainees rotate through different departments for varying periods of time, working alongside branch employees, and they are tested on various objectives listed in their "learner control guide" throughout the rotation period. Each trainee is assigned a sponsor in his branch who serves as a sort of guidance counselor, listens to problems and generally helps the trainee get along. Upon completion of the program, graduates usually become assistant operations officers, with responsibility to run the operations portion of a branch system.

But operations staffers don't have to stay with operations. One thing many staffers like about Bank of America is its size—and, thus, the number of opportunities. One woman began in operations, moved up to become an assistant operations officer, then moved over to **business banking**—the retail credit area that handles companies with sales up to about $10 million and credit commitments of about $1 million.

"There's a regional training program," she explained. "You go through the same kind of operations training as an operations officer, but shortened. They don't need to know how to manage the people, they just need a flavor of what banking is all about."

Following the on-the-job operations training, business banking trainees get into the credit portion of the program. Classwork in courses like accounting, financial statement analysis and commercial loans is combined with in-unit training. As with the operations program, business banking trainees work with a sponsor. Commercial business banking trainees work alongside senior officers, writing credit reports, going on business development calls and sitting in on client interviews. "Typically, they'd be working with many different officers in order to understand the different types of credits."

The **consumer credit training program** is similar to the commercial one, with the combination of classwork and hands-on training—and that exposure to different units in the bank. "Many times a candidate will go into lending and not really know what he wants to do. And by visiting each of the units on the job, he can see what he likes best and where he fits best," a former trainee summed up.

Among the different specialties a consumer credit trainee may end up working in are dealer (financing paper for car dealerships); consumer (directing lending for cars, mobile homes, home equity and so on); and personal financial services (being a personal banker to wealthy customers).

Bank of America also offers training in **corporate banking**, designed to train people for work as account officers in either the California corporate banking division (Calcorp), handling middle-market lending, or the North America division, which handles larger corporate accounts. Said a staffer who went through the program, "The best people get into this unit—whether they're hired as MBAs from outside or the best business bankers."

According to one employee, the corporate credit program is much like the programs at other banks—a combination of intense coursework in finance culminating with a credit presentation, and on-the-job training. After the classes are over, trainees are assigned an in-unit sponsor to guide the trainee and make sure the trainee is meeting the prescribed on-the-job objectives. Calcorp trainees rotate through different areas of the bank—operations, real estate, commercial lending and so on, while North American divison trainees serve as backups for their sponsors and may write credit analyses, go on development calls and so forth.

As one former trainee in Calcorp summed up the program, "It's a structured program, but it brings in all phases of the bank. It helps people coming in get a sense of the bank and how large it is. And people who've been in the bank, in one tiny microcosm of the universe, understand that, 'Yeah, the bank's really huge and there are these people over here that I never met.' "

LIFE

The size of Bank of America is one thing that directly affects life here. Because the bank is so large, staffers say it makes a difference who you know. And, in many cases, management tries to make the bank as personal as possible. "The bank really encourages networking," said one staffer.

That seems to be the case. According to staffers, even after training is over, you're assigned a mentor. "You have breakfast and meetings, whatever works best. And if you can't discuss something within your unit, if you're afraid to go to someone, if it's a political question and you're not sure if it would be a faux pas, you can talk to somebody," a young woman explained.

There are also a variety of professional groups organized within each region. While they offer a chance to meet people in a non-work environment, they're mainly designed to sharpen skills. And since many staffers say there's been a communications problem during this time of transition, some of the groups are trying to help solve that.

"Our head of Human Resources has made it a personal goal to get communications training to people," one employee stated.

"So we're having a statewide public speaking contest that the presidents of the speaking clubs are organizing."

But life at BA isn't only work-oriented. There's socializing after hours, too.

"Officers at the banks in the outskirts are real individuals," a branch officer commented. "But they seem to hang around with each other a lot. Maybe after hours or on the weekends playing golf."

Of course they're playing golf. Bank of America might be changing, and bankers might be changing—but they can't be changing *that* much.

DOLLARS AND SENSE

Bank of America is middle of the road where salaries are concerned. "We are not the highest paying financial institution around," said one employee. "There are regional banks that may offer 30 to 50 percent increases to officers—that's how we lose many."

"When I talk to people about why they're leaving the bank, they say it's the money. 'I'm getting a 30 percent increase. What are you going to offer?' Well, it's certainly not going to be 30 percent. These days it's not even going to be 10 percent," she added with a laugh.

But one thing BA is strong on is benefits. And one that wins particular raves is its relocation package, something especially attractive to branch staffers who end up moving a fair amount.

GETTING IN—TRICKS OF THE TRADE

"What they look for is initiative, a self-starter, the same laundry list you always hear," a young woman said.

And that's pretty much the case. Bank of America wants the same candidates everyone wants—aggressive, motivated, bright, etc., etc. Add to that a large dose of so-called people skills, and you've about got the picture.

"If applicants are looking for a branch management program, the most important thing is they have to be mobile," a branch officer stressed. "They've got to be willing to move with the bank."

Anything else? Well, in line with the new climate, would-be BA staffers also have to show that they're go-getters. "Keep pushing through the training department. Make yourself exposed to them—like beating their doors down," a young man suggested. "Just show that you want to get into Bank of America."

THE BOTTOM LINE

Times might be tough for this giant, but it's far from being beaten.

CHASE MANHATTAN

VITAL STATISTICS

- **locations:** New York (headquarters); offices nationwide and worldwide
- **assets:** $85.3 billion (1984)
- **rank:** 3rd in assets
- **employees:** 40,400

AS SEEN FROM THE OUTSIDE

It's a tough world out there. Even for a multinational giant like Chase, the third largest bank holding company in the country. But a reorganized Chase has emerged, playing catch-up in retail banking, and expanding fast into the America hinterlands.

There's a sense of urgency at Chase. It comes partly from the new competitive air in the banking world. Deregulation has let banks expand across the country, and competition means getting there first. Neck and neck, the big banks fight to position themselves for interstate banking—and for the profits. But at Chase there's also an urgent desire to prove it's good and getting better—to put the recent past behind.

The early eighties were bad years for the bank. It suffered bad loan problems with Penn Square Bank, and with the collapse of Drysdale, a New York securities firm, it was left holding its obligations as well. Combined, it meant over $200 million dollars in loan losses. Banking is partly image, and those losses hurt Chase on more than the balance sheet.

But Chase has had a reputation for solid banking skills, and it's banking on them once again. It has the resources to put those skills to work. Chase is divided into three giant operational groups—Global Banking, Consumer Banking, and National Banking. Globally, Chase is everywhere, with 13,000 people in 75 subsidiaries working in 100 countries. In National Banking, Chase has a leading position in electronic corporate cash management and treasury services. And its restructured Consumer Banking group is aggressively pushing its own electronic network. Like its competitors, Chase has emphasized a new attention to service. But coming from establishment Chase, "quality service" maybe means more than just an ad slogan.

Chase's early history was a little antiestablishment. It was founded as the Manhattan Company in 1799, with the mission of supplying "pure and wholesome water" to the citizens of New York. But one of the founders, Aaron Burr, saw it as a way of beating the monopoly in banking held by Alexander Hamilton and his Federalist friends. So he slipped in a little clause that allowed the company to engage its excess capital in other endeavors, including banking. A few months later, the Bank of the Manhattan Company opened on Wall Street. Hamilton was furious, and his quarrel with Burr continued until they dueled in 1804. Burr won. Chase still has the pistols in its collection.

The Chase part of the bank was founded as Chase National in 1877; and in 1955 the two parts merged to form The Chase Manhattan Bank, under the leadership of John J. Mcloy—a former World Bank president and U.S. High Commissioner for Germany. Under him, and in particular under David Rockefeller, Chase acquired a reputation as *the* international bank, with a network few could match and a contact list through David Rockefeller none could match.

Today, under Willard Butcher, Chase is still strong. Now to work on the equity and asset ratios—the key indices of profitability and corporate strength. But Chase is definitely on the move.

HEARD AT THE WATER COOLER— WHAT IT'S REALLY LIKE TO WORK HERE

Chase headquarters at 1 Chase Plaza in New York looks like a modern art museum. High ceilings, open space, walls painted in nonbanker colors of electric green and yellow—and giant paintings by modern artists. The type with bold splashes of black and red.

But somehow it still manages to have the feel of a traditional bank—solid, stolid, slighty stuffy, organized, disciplined and neat. That's what banking was, and that's what Chase is. Just add modern art, computers and aggressive people. Politely aggressive people.

Most Chase people still behave a bit like classy, old-time bankers. Soft-spoken types who think carefully before they say anything. Most sit in row after row of desks on huge floors, the senior bankers occupying offices along the perimeter. But at Chase, the floors are a little bigger, and everything is a little sleeker. And conversations are a little bit quieter. It's a classy, formal place. "Chase has this old-line reputation that gives us an edge in the market," explained one consumer manager.

It's serious and restrained, but not unfriendly. "There's much more of a sense of the personal touch," said a current Chase staffer who used to work at Citibank. "The employees are not treated in the same offhand way they are at Citibank."

At Chase, some traditions are worth keeping.

PEOPLE
"By and large, the people in the credit training program were graduates from the top schools," a former trainee explained. "Not nerdy people though. You have to have a personality to work here. No matter how bright you are, you have to have a personality."

"Generally, the people here were in college athletics. And they played on a team," another staffer said.

Apparently, that helps to fit into Chase.

"You've got to be aggressive, but also a team player," said a three-year vet. "What works in sales and trading doesn't work at Chase. Here, it's collegial."

For all the team playing and similar scholastic histories, "we tend to like generalists," a middle manager said. "People who are creative. People working together from different backgrounds helps the team."

JOBS
A lot of people want to become "**relationship managers**," Chase's way of describing its officers who lend Chase's money, sell Chase's services and make Chase's credit decisions. They're between the client and the bank—and they've been through Chase's rigorous credit training program.

The program has a good and tough reputation, and emphasizes teamwork and a case study approach. Classes of about 30 go through together, and about 200 each year take the program. First comes five to eight months of classroom training, divided into ten to twelve modules covering all the basics a good banker

needs to know—accounting, financial analysis, capital markets—
"a mini MBA." With all the tests and headaches thrown in, at a
very fast pace. "Money and Capital Markets?—we covered the
whole book in a week," said one trainee.

People can't wait for the training program to end. "It's like
final exams that go on for years," said another confident veteran.
Just make 70 percent or over. And that's the mornings. After-
noons are spent out of class learning by doing—with teams of
people from different classes as well.

Trainees catch their breath, then get ready to jump back in.
First it's "Mini Desk" time—described as a "trial run for what
you have to do to keep your job." That means acting as a full-
fledged banker by analyzing and reporting on a specific corporation or client, and then presenting and defending the analysis.
It's called a "desk" because that's where you do the work—all
day and into the night. It's called a "Mini" because it doesn't
count.

But after the trial run it does. Then trainees have five desks,
and they must pass three. So what are they in plain terms? One
former trainee described them: "Each desk is a full-blown analysis. You spend one week on one company. At the end of that
week, it feels like you know more about that company than its
officers. You're fairly taxed. Then you sit in front of some vice
presidents and explain your analysis. They're trying to be like a
credit committee."

It's not for the lazy or the faint-hearted. And it's competitive.
Not everyone passes, but trainees do pull for each other. A little
healthy competitive spirit helps to get you through—as long as
it's against the guys in the other classes. And teamwork is essential.

Once they're out, trainees enter phase two of training, which
is learning by doing and by rotating between assignments or
assisting more senior managers. And although all now have credit
backgrounds, jobs vary considerably. International bankers may
go overseas, corporate bankers based in the U.S. may begin with
analyses at headquarters. One woman started out in risk management—an important area in these debt-ridden days. She uses
her skills to assess Chase's credit risks in the petroleum industry.

But most people who complete the program want customer
contact—making deals, and using their training to advance Chase
and their careers. One relationship manager in corporate bank-

ing enjoys the tight four-person teams and the camaraderie of a common goal. Another enjoys the variety of companies she encounters, and the challeges of leveraged buy-outs, where a lot of debt and a lot of work and a lot of money changes hands. The pace is fast—but they're used to it by now.

Retail Banking, or **Consumer Product and Branch Management**, is very different. Another training program, and another world. All still Chase, but more open, more aggressive, and very energetic. Less Ivy, and more State. Chase is proud of its retail banking—and it's pushing it.

Chase branch managers, the "on the line" people who meet the public and run the branches, count the money and get the deposits, are perhaps the most enthusiastic and entrepreneurial Chase employees. Why? "We're going through a culture change," explained one manager. "We're open to a lot of new ideas."

"Retail banking is one of the great unknown opportunities," explained another branch manager who described the job as "mind expanding—seriously." She meant it. The button-down corporate prestige may not be there, but *everyone* walks through those branch doors. You meet more than corporate VPs of finance.

That exposure to everyone and everything begins in the training program. Trainees meet about "a million branch managers" and spend up to a year rotating among branches and learning the ropes. It includes teller training, new product development and supervisory skills. And then assignment as an assistant branch manager. Then branch manager, and "a lot of responsibility, very quickly," supervising upward of twenty platform officers and tellers, selling and servicing customers on the noncredit side of things, and meeting growth targets set from above. One manager described herself as "burnt-out" after five years on the job.

But the best part of the job is the flexibility. If you feel a bit tired, there's always room for the right people in product marketing—the design and strategy of new financial products to keep the consumer happy. And who better to assist than the branch managers, who meet the consumer every day?

But branch managers have recruiting problems. One branch manager described recruiting at one B-school: "Those kids, they'd rather die than work here." That's not a problem restricted to Chase. Retail banking has an unglamorous reputation in the industry, and the people are seen by corporate bankers as "unclassy polyester-suit types."

Maybe so, but it has its advantages. As one branch manager put it, comparing her route to the "prestigious" credit-training route: "You can get ahead much faster in the branch system, because there are not too many people who are bright and willing to go down into the trenches—like I did."

Operations has the same sort of reputation, and the same sort of promotion possibilities and challenges. People who like operations enjoy the "real work" of banking—overseeing the countless transactions that a big bank processes every day. As one 26-year old stated, "In money transfer, you process a billion dollars a day."

And you'd better be right. There's a training program—the Operations Management Development Program—with in-depth learning of budgeting and systems. Computer work is routine, and as banks get more and more high-tech, "it's a chance to really trailblaze." Supervision skills are important. However computerized it gets, it's still a labor-intensive area, and young managers may supervise sections of forty people or more—many of them ten or twenty years older, and ten or twenty years more experienced.

LIFE

When you're a Chase credit trainee, being a Chase credit trainee is your life. There's simply very little room for anything else.

"On the training floor, it's not unusual to see people working till 9, 9:30," a former trainee commented.

That's probably why trainees become pretty good friends. They're together all the time, working hard and long. And they're all in the same boat.

"The training program is incredible," said a three-year vet. "People become friends for life. It's a lot like being in a big storm. You know, the lights go out, you meet the people next door who haven't got electricity either and talk about sharing flashlights and food."

And after the training program is over? Well, you never leave it behind . . . "I've met guys with the bank for twenty years, and they still talk about their credit class. It's a lot of bonding to begin with," a young man stated.

One young summer intern got hooked on banking in general and Chase in particular after a speech by a Chase senior manager. "He talked about the future of banking as if it were Star Wars—it sounded terrific to me. It sounded like Chase was dreaming about the future."

Apparently, in some cases, the future is already here. But it's not like science fiction at all.

A Chase banker in the Capital Markets division is excited about newer, different kinds of lending projects—like a peat power plant in Maine. No, not oil, not nuclear energy—peat moss; the stuff gardeners use to grow (green) plants.

Chase is changing with the times, all right, and apparently in some cases is ahead of them.

DOLLARS AND SENSE

It may have been Rockefeller's bank, but salaries are pretty normal—$20,000 for BAs, $30,000 and up for MBAs. And the benefits are standard for banks—Major Medical, tuition reimbursement, profit sharing and, of course, free checking.

And to boost those beginning salaries, Chase is big on internal networking. "You've just got to meet the right people," said one young man.

GETTING IN—TRICKS OF THE TRADE

"It's very easy to find people who can do financial analyses, but we need people who are creative," said a young Chase banker on the college interview circuit. "People working together from different backgrounds helps the team—with different approaches to problem-solving."

What kind of backgrounds? Maybe "someone who's spent four years reading fifteenth-century literature and can analyze it well." Chase likes generalists.

It does help to have a little business background. "It never hurts to do the groundwork—accounting and finance," said a young woman just out of training. And do your homework. "I had the names, the key players in the group I wanted," stated a successful applicant who researched the exact area and business she wanted to get into. Chase likes generalists who can be specific.

But the bottom line in today's competitive banking world is sales. "I really don't believe it was the business school courses that got me the job," an MBA said. "I think it was my selling background." A sales background of any type is "an incredible thing to have on your resumé," according to someone who had just that. Extracurricular activities, leadership positions, anything that involves selling or promoting a product or service is helpful. Chase likes generalists who can sell.

The interviews are a bit different in that Chase has one specific credit interview, in addition to others. One staffer commented, "They really want to determine whether you are able to think on your feet and understand basic credit issues." Whereas other banks "fold it in" to other interviews, at Chase, it's a specific and separate interview. It doesn't involve banking jargon. It's just to see if you have that one thing all companies want—common sense.

THE BOTTOM LINE

Chase earns money the old-fashioned way—it sells it.

MANUFACTURERS HANOVER TRUST

VITAL STATISTICS

- **locations:** New York (headquarters); offices nationwide and worldwide
- **assets:** $75.7 billion (1984)
- **rank:** 3rd in assets
- **employees:** 30,300

AS SEEN FROM THE OUTSIDE

> Patient investors may want to consider high yielding Manufacturers Hanover shares for the long pull.
>
> —Value Line

It's not the biggest bank, nor the flashiest. And it still isn't as strong as it wants to be. But Manufacturers Hanover (Manny Hanny or MHC) is quietly changing its goals and its balance sheet. It's slowly shedding its image as the "grandmother" of the money center banks—high quality, solid, strong, a good employer, but a bit uncreative and noninnovative.

It's changing. Take the 1984 purchase of CIT Financial Corporation for $1.5 billion—the largest acquisition in banking history. With the stroke of a pen, Manny Hanny raised its interstate presence from thirty-one states to forty-three. While other money-center banks bid for banks on a state-by-state basis, MHC did it all at once.

Sure, it raised operating expenses and restrained earnings growth. But like the others, MHC has to think long and hard about the future and take those risks, because the future is interstate banking, investment and merchant banking, middle-market lending and consumer banking—and increased competition for these profitable areas.

Now, MHC is well-placed in all of them. In 1985, the corporation reorganized into five sectors: Asset Based Financing, Banking and International, Corporate Banking, Investment Banking and Retail Banking. The reorganization reflected the bank's changing image of itself. Preoccupied with asset growth in the 1970s, it overlent to Latin America and was left in the 1980s with a large bad loan problem. Now it's more content with its position as the nation's fourth largest bank—and like the others, is hungry for a selective, relationship-oriented approach to banking. Sell loans and services—but to the *right* customers.

Profitability is still high and even with the CIT purchase the company raised its ratio of primary capital to assets—a key ratio of bank stability. There's more to do, but the bank is effectively moving forward on all fronts.

Recent high spots? Merchant banking and investment banking now account for one fifth of net income, and INTEPLEX, MH Corporation's computerized financial management system ("the treasurer's work station") is known as one of the best. Manny Hanny is also the world's largest correspondent bank (a bank in which other banks park and transfer their money). And its credit training program has one of the best reputations in the industry.

HEARD AT THE WATER COOLER— WHAT IT'S REALLY LIKE TO WORK HERE

"I think it's maybe a little more cutthroat . . . It used to be pretty chummy around here. It still is; but I think if the bank really wants to make a change, it's going to have to be less that way."

So explained a young officer in the large corporate banking area. Everyone here is talking about change; where the industry is heading in general and where Manny Hanny is heading in particular.

Traditionally, Manny Hanny has been known as a "sleepy bank," as one staffer termed it. And there's still that relaxed feel in the air. But reorganization and "OBM" have changed the bank's philosophy and quickened the pace somewhat. OBM is Overhead Budget Management, and it means zero-based budgeting and a hard appraisal of positions and jobs.

"I was OBMed," explained one manager, describing the corporation's decision to eliminate his position and transfer him to a more profitable area. But, typical of the bank, the planned staff reductions of 1,745 are being done through attrition, not firings. And it's still a very big hirer of entry-level BAs and MBAs. There's just more of an emphasis on performance now—getting people "on the line" and out of the back rooms, selling rather than just analyzing.

Yes, like every other money-center bank, the name of the game is sales. And profits. And bottom line.

And like the others there's an appropriately impressive headquarters building—in uptown New York on Park Avenue—a tall skyscraper with a red lobby dominated by a huge corporate logo. But upstairs the feel is slightly different.

"We're a shirtsleeves kind of place" explained one officer. "There probably isn't much of a distinction from most of the other banks," said another officer. "But . . ."

There is definitely a more candid and casual feel. Professional, yes, but a lot less stuffy than some, and less "go for the guts" than others. Everyone talks about the need to enjoy your work.

PEOPLE

One recruiter described a candidate for an entry-level position who didn't get an offer—someone "too rehearsed and mechanical, you just want to shake that person and say, be yourself!"

That about sums up the opposite of a lot of Manny Hanny people. Sure, they're from the same schools as people at many of the other banks, but there's that unstuffy feel about the place that seems to rub off. Of all the banks we interviewed at, this one wins the award for congeniality and candor. Very few stuffed shirts, and very little of that "I've got to be careful, my boss may be listening" attitude.

Part of that comes from the training program, where people are hired for specific divisions. There's no overhiring with the expectation of weeding out losers. So, early on, there's a strong teamwork emphasis. In most cases it works. One trainee described the camaraderie of training as "Unbelievable. The best part of the program."

JOBS

There's a lot more to the training than the people you meet. It's the starting point for many MHC account and lending jobs, including account officers in the **Corporate Banking Division**. And those are the people we talked to.

Most start out in Manny Hanny's prestigious credit training program, which has the best or second best training reputation, according to many bankers. Let's put it this way: at the other banks, they say their bank has the best program, and Manny's is second best.

But before it begins, many are placed in temporary assignments in the division that hired them, "to get you acclimated to the business, a couple of months to learn how to tie your tie," according to one staffer. Others liked the opportunity to get a feel for banking before jumping into credit training.

Credit training lasts for about seven months, and covers all the usual things. First, there's an overview of the bank and how it operates, then seven weeks of accounting and money and banking classes. Accounting is seen as the toughest class by most, and the first few weeks as the most crucial.

According to one trainee, "the people who didn't do well in accounting were the people who screwed up on the first test. It really builds on that fast."

And those who screw up and make less than a 75 percent average on all tests in the program are out. There's less than a 5 percent attrition rate, but people *are* fired for not making it. In accounting (and corporate finance), there's a second chance. Make between 70 and 75 percent and you're allowed to take a retest a few weeks later. And tutors are available. No one said it was going to be easy.

After money and banking comes spreading assignments for some (taking apart corporate balance sheets and redoing them in a banking format), then more full-time classes in Corporate Finance and Business Law. Most trainees found Corporate Finance the best taught, and the next toughest. The academic courses are taught by outside professors, which can be difficult. "They can always throw a curve ball at you," according to one staffer. Maybe that's why most trainees describe it as being "like going to college again." But, as one trainee put it with a smile, "It's a whole different atmosphere when you're studying for your job. It's a lot easier to get motivated."

The final portion of the program, Credit Analysis, is described by the bank as "the most important module in the program." Many trainees disagree. Essentially, it's designed to give trainees experience writing credit reviews and analyzing a customer's credit-worthiness. But one trainee said it was far too long, another described it as "really just a writing course—telling you how to write a fiscal analysis."

All in all, though, most trainees felt the program lived up to its reputation. Most BAs with business backgrounds found it fairly easy. In the words of one, "80 percent of the time it was a 9-to-5 job, if you were fairly well organized and relatively bright." The other 20 percent? "It could be anything from 8 to 8 and weekends."

So if it's so good, why isn't it a killer program? Two reasons. First, the old teamwork approach—lots of help from fellow classmates. Second, class notes—handouts from professors. According to one trainee, "They really outline the things you need to know. I didn't open a book."

Once out of the program, trainees go to their respective divisions. The best way to get the top assignments is through networking. As one staffer put it, "If you do well, you'll usually have a couple of people asking for you. If you make contacts and see the area you want to go to, it's up to you to go and contact the person in that area, or have one of your supervisors in the training program make that contact for you. They encourage you to go and find a spot for yourself."

One less aggressive officer just listed his top three choices, all in prestigious midtown Manhattan, but found himself commuting two hours to an outlying suburb. His advice now? Network.

Once assigned, trainees usually do backup work for a district, writing credit reviews and doing the grunt work of banking. "You do an awful lot of back office number crunching," one officer said. After five or six months, they become part of a basic unit within the districts—four-man teams that manage and sell bank services to specific corporate clients. As account representatives, they're the generalists in the bank. One young officer described the job as mostly marketing, since he calls on large multinationals that don't need lending services.

Among the services he offers are: credit (revolving credit, letters of credit), foreign exchange, treasury services, currency and interest rate swaps, interest rate caps, Euro-commercial paper, mergers and acquisition financing, and, last but certainly not least, cash management services, which is where a lot of junior employees get their start, selling computerized treasury systems to corporate clients.

It's a lot of learning, updating and competition, and internal bank networking to bring in the right specialists for the specific service a client wants. And there's a social side to it as well. "We have cocktail parties, we get our senior management in to talk to their senior management, go to sporting events with them . . ."

During the first two years, promotion is relatively structured. According to one staffer, "Everybody makes A.S. within the same three- or fourth-month period." A.S. is assistant secretary, the first junior officer position, where client responsibility increases. Assistant vice president "isn't as much of a given," another officer said, "and you really have to prove yourself to make VP." Maybe more now than in the past. There's talk in the hallways of rewarding younger officers more according to performance and less according to a standard scale.

The common streak in some of the more successful younger employees seems to be a willingness to do more than is expected of them. It's hard to get fired in the first few years after training, and it's fairly easy to get comfortable. Successful bankers don't.

The hottest area of the bank is the Merchant Banking division. The most prestige, the blue chip clients and the hot deals. Plus outside hires from places like Goldman Sachs, and thus a chance to work next to some of the best in finance.

Even the corporate division is talking in merchant banking and investment banking terms. And the feeling in the halls is that they will move into offering more of these kinds of services, and become more like merchant bankers or investment bankers themselves. And in so doing, the commercial banking–investment banking distinction will probably become less clear.

LIFE

In the training programs, it's like college life anywhere. Classroom work, homework, cliques, after-hour bar and restaurant hopping. After training, it becomes more like a job—"dealing with politics, senior management, policies . . . You have to be able to distinguish when to jump and when not to jump," said one junior officer. "But you have to like jumping when you're told to jump."

For all the changes, commercial banking at Manny Hanny is still commercial banking—and that means fairly routine hours, a hierarchy to go through, and a sense of order. One officer chose banking because of that routine. "I don't mind working from 8 to 8, if I *know* that's what I'm going to be doing. I can make plans for dinner at 9, and know I'm not going to have to break them."

But there's a bit more informality at MHC than at many other banks. One officer described friends at other banks as more serious, more aggressive. Here, "we yak it up a bit more."

But not in front of the clients. It's still a top-notch bank.

DOLLARS AND SENSE

In terms of salaries and benefits, MHC is competitive. As with other banks, to prevent newly hireds BAs from leaving for MBA school right after training, the bank offers the "weekend warrior" option to some BAs: alternate weekends at Wharton Business school in a 2½ year MBA program, with MHC footing the bill. Then they owe the bank three years of their life, or if they leave in three years, they have to prorate their tuition. MHC also pays the bills on a sliding scale for night school MBAs—100 percent for As and Bs, 75 percent for Bs to Cs, and 50 percent for passing grades below.

The bank wants to keep its BAs. One personnel officer commented that employees thinking about leaving should definitely talk with personnel for placement on a faster track. In several cases, employees have been transferred to the merchant bank or other very visible areas.

GETTING IN—TRICKS OF THE TRADE

It can be tough. In the words of one banker on the line, "We get the cream of the crop BAs." So do other banks, but the numbers favor the recruiters, not the recruits. College recruiting accounts for about one fourth of all new hirees. In a typical period, 967 people were interviewed, 167 were invited to the bank for further interviewing, 54 were offered employment, and 34 accepted the offers.

Recruiters are looking for the bright, energetic employee who knows banking and the bank well. And "time and time again, it's those interpersonal skills that end up being the determining factor," according to one MHC recruiter. Maybe more so at MHC.

One Princeton graduate avoided the college rush and sent a letter directly to the bank. "As at any other good school, when you have twelve other people who are economics majors, 3.0s, and wear a blue suit, you don't have much of a chance."

Everyone advises looking for inside contacts. Interviews are fairly standard. First, recruits meet with the recruiter, then "they hook you up with an Assistant Secretary, then a VP for 15- to 20-minute interviews; very informal, kind of get-to-know-you type interviews." Successful applicants are called back a few weeks later, meet a recruiter again, then spend the rest of the day with officers at the area they're being considered for. Lunch is spent with someone in the training program. BAs take a written test that supposedly determines intellectual capacity. Don't worry if you've done all right on any E.T.S. test.

MBAs skip the test. Many officers feel that currently the bank gets better quality BAs than MBAs, since "commercial banks are just not prestigious places to be." But if you feel that way, don't let it show. The most annoying aspect of MBAs is their "cockiness," according to one staffer. But the bank has emphasized hiring MBAs, since they don't leave the bank for graduate school.

THE BOTTOM LINE

Maybe not the best bank, maybe not the biggest bank, but the opportunities are there.

MORGAN GUARANTY TRUST

VITAL STATISTICS

- locations: New York (headquarters); Los Angeles; Miami; Palm Beach; San Francisco (rep. office); and offices worldwide
- assets: $61.2 billion (1984)
- rank: 5th in assets
- employees: 13,000

AS SEEN FROM THE OUTSIDE

The glittering chandelier that dominates the main banking room at Morgan is suspended by a chain, reinforced by a parallel steel cable—and covered by a velour "stocking." A power winch is geared to lower the chandelier for cleaning at the rate of one foot per minute—no more and no less.

Morgan does *all* of its business in a calm, deliberate, high quality way. They are prudent, classy bankers with the best reputation in banking.

In the somewhat wistful words of a competitor: "They're the best at what they *choose* to do. All the new things, all the good things that people are trying to get into, they're two years ahead of everyone. Except maybe for Citibank."

And for a bank with an old-line, careful reputation, Morgan can be very nimble. The July 1985 issue of *Institutional Investor* reported on Morgan's decision to enter the international bond market. The result has been a meteoric rise from No. 46 in lead managements of new issues to No. 2. In just five years. It's all in how you play the game.

And Morgan does it with concentrated intensity and careful planning. With only a few branches in the U.S., the bank picks its customers very carefully, concentrating on blue chip corporate clients and wealthy private accounts. It's very eager to get into the investment side of banking as well, applying to the Federal Reserve Bank to get into those activities that were prohibited under the Glass-Steagall Act. But, as with the international bond markets, it's already a major presence in the legal areas of investment banking activities, and is currently pushing hard in the mergers and acquisitions realm.

Entering into Wall Street investment finance is perhaps a bit easier for Morgan because of its background as a major trustee—it has one of the largest U.S. trust departments, investing corporate and private pension funds and the like in the stock market.

It hasn't forgotten mainstream commercial banking, though. Yes, Morgan does make mistakes, including loans to debt-ridden Latin America. But it practices what it preaches—that a strong capital base means a stronger bank—and so its primary capital-to-assets ratio is the strongest of all the money-center banks.

All along, Morgan has preserved a blue chip reputation. Founded by gruff, tough J. P. Morgan in 1860, by 1870 it was already a leading banker for the French Government—arranging a ten million pound rescue bond issue after the Franco-Prussian War. Back in the U.S. it was also involved with the blue chip names of the day—GE, US Steel, International Harvester and AT&T.

Under the Glass-Steagal Act of 1933, the firm was split into two. J.P.'s younger son, Harry, went on with others to form Morgan Stanley investment bank, while J. P. Morgan remained a commercial bank and trust company. In 1959, it merged with Guaranty Trust, forming the Morgan Guaranty Trust Company. J. P. Morgan & Company is the parent company, overseeing the operation of five divisions of the bank and several subsidiaries.

HEARD AT THE WATER COOLER—
WHAT IT'S REALLY LIKE TO WORK HERE

Morgan is conservative, quiet, and corporate. It lives up to its reputation. This isn't a place for casual clothes, loud laughter or boorish behavior. In short, it's everyone's idea of what an old-line bank should be.

It even *looks* the way you picture a bank. The headquarters building on Wall Street reeks of old money—an old-fashioned stone building, with the company name etched in the front. A uniformed guard graciously offers to take your coat. It's all pretty impressive.

In the offices where Morgan people work there is plush carpeting covering the floors and large wooden desks arranged in neat rows. Although most people work in an open area, it's rather quiet. Yes, people talk to one another, but their tones tend to be low. Even the telephones seem to ring with a hushed respect here. It all seems in keeping with Morgan's image of a proper, prestigious, conservative bank.

And wherever you go here and whomever you talk to, you can't escape reminders of that image. Ask employees why they wanted to work here and one of the first things they'll mention is Morgan's reputation.

"I perceived it as the top institution in its field, the best people, the most professional," a young man explained. "Classy—if I may use that word."

"Anybody who would not want to go to work for something that's known as the best is probably out of his mind," added another staffer.

J. P. Morgan would be proud.

PEOPLE

"I think the image of Morgan as a stuffy, stiff, Eastern uptight place is just not true," a young woman said. "Certainly it is Eastern. But it also tends to be relaxed and the people tend to have a sense of humor. And they *definitely* have diverse backgrounds."

That certainly seems to be the case, as with many banks. Morgan people with masters in philosophy, or bachelors degrees in comparative literature or environmental studies, work alongside econ majors and MBAs.

But for all the diversity in majors, there is a definite blue-blood feel about Morgan. Sure, there are light-hearted and casual types; but overall there are more people with the "right" background here than at many other places. People are more polished, more East Coast establishment at Morgan.

Some call it stuffy. Morgan people would strongly disagree. Another banker put it this way: "Maybe they're smarter, more professional. But I sure wouldn't go to a hockey game with a guy from Morgan. Maybe the opera."

JOBS

The Morgan Guaranty credit training program—the **Commercial Bank Management Program**, or CBMP as it's referred to—has about as lofty a reputation as the bank itself.

People are hired into the training program proper, not for specific jobs. And since the program is given twice a year, many

people fill interim assignments until the program begins. According to one staffer, "The training programs are filled very quickly, so there's a time lag—usually six months or so."

New hires in interim assignments are able to get first-hand experience in banking prior to the rigorous training. And even those people who don't take interim assignments get prepared before the program begins. According to one employee, new hires are given books to read and assignments to do—"And it's especially key for people with no accounting background to do those. I spent my weekends doing them all."

The CBMP is designed to accommodate both BAs and MBAs. Split into three phases, the program offers three months of coursework in accounting and corporate finance for newly hired BAs in Phase I. In Phase II, MBAs join the BAs for three months of advanced accounting, credit analysis and international economics. Then it's Phase III, the Financial Advisory Division, where trainees do credit analyses. And in all three phases, the training is rigorous.

"What you should expect from the training program as a BA is six months of very intensive work where your entire life will revolve around credits and debits," explained a young woman who recently went through it. "But in the long run, it's a terrific experience."

As for MBAs, one described the program as "a very good refresher. It does cast a new light on some of the things you learned in business school."

Both BAs and MBAs agree upon one aspect of the CBMP; it's a great time to get to know the bank and meet people both in the program and out. And whether trainees find the program "intense" or "redundant," they all agree that there's little competition among people. That's possibly because Morgan trainees aren't given tests or graded on coursework. And there's very little attrition, "the theory being that Morgan hires high quality people, therefore we don't have to lose any," as one young woman put it.

Staffers say there's an emphasis on heavy classroom participation, with trainees expected to answer questions and speak on cases before the class. That's something many former trainees found attractive about the program.

Another aspect of the CBMP that staffers like is the inclusion of foreign office trainees in the program. "That's a very big plus,"

an AVP said. "You start arguing from an American standpoint and then, right away, one of the Foreign Office people will jump in and say, 'Yeah, but we see it a little bit differently. Here's the economics as we see it.' Especially when you're talking about foreign trade and things like that, it adds a great flavor."

Courses in both Phases I and II are taught in a "case study" approach—trainees are given a case; they'll go through textbooks to get the background principles that would apply; and the professor assigns basic questions.

"In Phase I it tended to be more 'let's get the basics down; let's get the numbers on the boards,' " a trainee explained. "In Phase II, that was assumed and it was 'what do you think about this; how does this impact your thinking as a banker?' So it's hard work—you have to grasp the basics quickly, then move on and learn their applications to banking."

Learning those basics in Phase I means rather intensive work and long hours. "The first three months you're in class from 9 to 12, there's a two-hour lunch break that ends up being a two-hour homework break, and then you have another class from 2 to 5. *Then* you spend from 5 until 9 doing your homework—every day, five days a week."

But there's a positive side to all that grueling work. Trainees say they get to know each other well. Plus, as one young woman noted, "the fun side is that people get so hysterical by the weekend that they end up having a wonderful time for two days."

Once Phase I is over, it's on to Phase II. While trainees are still in classroom situations, the assignments are less constant. In between the coursework and assignments, bankers from various areas of Morgan come in and give orientations to the trainees, explaining what their jobs are and what goes on in their departments.

Once Phase II is completed, trainees enter the Financial Advisory Division, or FAD as staffers call it. There they are assigned companies for credit evaluation. About five trainees work under one unit head on the credit analyses. It's up to the trainee to determine how many analyses to do, but one trainee suggests that "you want to write at least two five- to eight-page 'blue reports.' "

FAD is the part of the training program most staffers praise. The pressure is lower, people are more relaxed, and they've got the opportunity to apply their in-class training in accounting and

corporate finance, as well as writing skills, to a real work situation.

It's also a time for trainees to focus on where they want to work within the bank. Morgan employees explain that, during FAD, they meet with different people in the bank, lunch with them, have coffee, and discuss what their areas are like.

Trainees are assigned mentors in personnel with whom they meet informally throughout the training program. Near the end of FAD, trainees and mentors get together, discuss the trainees' interests and the bank's needs, and try to match the two.

One young woman in FAD described it as a "friendly and low-keyed process—no one gets stressed out about it," and that seems to be the case. There appears to be a real effort to place trainees in their primary area of interest. In the case of those people who took interim assignments, many times they'll be placed back in that department if they and the department head agree upon it.

Once employees are out of the training program and have become full-fledged bankers, the learning process still continues. "The first couple of months, you really have to get a feel for the terminology, what's going on around you, how you're fitting in," explained an assistant treasurer. "Plus it takes an awful lot of time to read up on the accounts, read up on Morgan's products and to meet the clients."

But staffers aren't only sitting back and absorbing. In fact, many people say that the main thing they like about working at Morgan is the degree of responsibility that you're given soon after training.

"As much as you can do, they'll let you do," said one young man.

Many newly assigned trainees also find that they're treated as part of the team pretty quickly. "As a junior person, you don't get a feeling of being left out of the mainstream," commented a young woman in Public Finance.

Like most banks nowadays, Morgan is becoming more sales-oriented. People explain that their jobs entail pitching Morgan products, going on calls.

"It's no longer just understanding commercial lending," an AVP said. "Now there's twenty other products that this institution is out there trying to sell. You have to be very analytical and very intelligent to pick up on them quickly and understand how they relate to the client's needs."

Unlike at other banks, however, Morgan staffers have to get used to rotating assignments in different departments.

"They move you around a lot, say every three to four years," said an assistant treasurer. "The idea is to make you a totally well-rounded banker. I think sometimes it's difficult on the client when you move around that much and it's also difficult on the banker. But everyone here is quick enough to pick up the new business, the new client information, whatever. So it takes a while to get used to a new assignment, but I think it prevents stagnation."

And that's something many Morgan staffers like in general. The flexibility of rotating keeps them on their toes and keeps them constantly learning different areas of banking. It also seems to affect their attitude toward working here.

"That feeling that, even if someone's not content with his particular job, he's happy with the institution, comes across," one recent hiree noted. "No matter what gripes he may have, there's a feeling of 'I'm here and I like it.' "

LIFE

During Phases I and II of the training program, life at Morgan means working at Morgan. But staffers say they still manage to have fun.

"People tend to get together in social settings, not only in business settings," one staffer observed.

And since there's little competition in the CBMP, trainees tend to form a cohesive group. "There's a feeling that we're all going to make it, we're all in this together, we're all hired for a reason and we're all going to be here to stay," a young woman said. "And that really eliminates a lot of the tension and nervous anxiety that people in a lot of other training programs may go through."

And staffers say that this team spirit continues after the training is over.

"A lot of your progress depends on your willingness to work with other people," a young man commented. "I enjoy that. Certain people are attracted to it—not taking all the credit but making sure other people get credit for things accomplished. I think that's very true at this institution."

DOLLARS AND SENSE

"I must stress that we do not skip on compensation. Morgan would have no hope of remaining the quality institution it is if we ignored the importance of attracting and rewarding first-rate people."

So said the chairman of the board at a 1985 stockholders meeting. Morgan employees are amply rewarded. BAs start at about $25,000 and get a raise at the beginning of FAD; MBAs start at about $35,000. Add to that a full benefits package including limited tuition reimbursement and reduced commissions on stock transactions.

No, Morgan doesn't skip on compensations.

GETTING IN—TRICKS OF THE TRADE

"It probably is one of the premier banks in the world, but I don't think that should scare anyone off," a former trainee stated.

That's the advice most employees give. Yes, Morgan has a great reputation, but that doesn't mean you can't land a job here.

"Relax. Be yourself. Do not try to be something you think Morgan wants you to be, because you have no idea what Morgan wants you to be, and you're not going to know until you work here," advised one employee. "So relax and tell people what you're all about."

Staffers here say that's the best thing to do in the first interview. Most say that initial meeting isn't intimidating, but then again, they made it. Morgan is after the best—and if you fit, you already know it.

THE BOTTOM LINE

The reputation speaks for itself.

CORPORATE GIANTS

Corporate giants aren't all in the same industry. But then, they don't have to be. They've got enough in common already: they're huge; their offices (and influence) spread nationwide and overseas; and their budgets and revenues are immense. They're also home to bureaucracy, hierarchy, and millions of employees in thousands of different jobs.

The jobs *do* vary from one corporate giant to the next—but only to an extent. They all employ people in finance, in personnel or human resources and other support services. And depending on the industry, there also are many jobs in marketing, sales, engineering, manufacturing, and purchasing.

Marketing and **Sales** attract a large number of recent college graduates and MBAs. Marketing, especially in the consumer products and packaged goods companies, is a high-visibility spot with a track record for producing high-level managers. Depending upon the company, entry-level people typically begin as marketing assistants or assistant product managers with salaries ranging from the mid 20s to the low 30s. Marketing departments essentially work with a company's products or services (depending on the industry), researching what consumers want and figuring out how a product or service should be positioned in the marketplace for maximum effect. Marketing staffers may be heavily involved with the technical staff in product development, the sales staff in product introduction, and the advertising staff in product promotion, as well as with the financial staff in budget planning. It's a great field for people with numbers ability and creativity, since marketing staffers have to understand consumers' needs and wants, predict consumer trends, and develop programs that meet prescribed budgetary goals.

In Sales, entry-level employees usually begin in the field, with a small territory to cover. Pay varies dramatically, since salespeople often earn a commission over their base salaries (which are typically in the low to mid 20s range). It's a job for hustlers, and those who succeed will move up to cover larger regional areas or large national accounts, and eventually enter management and oversee a sales force.

The people in **Engineering** at the corporate giants may have a number of different responsibilities, once again depending on a company's products and/or services. Entry-level engineers generally have an advanced degree, although some companies (especially those with in-depth training programs) may hire engineering students straight from college. Beginning salaries vary, with the norm in the high 20s to mid 30s, and specific jobs also vary.

Regardless of job titles and responsibilities, engineers essentially apply technical knowledge and skill to make a product or service workable, or to enhance implementation or production of that product or service. They may be directly involved with the design of a specific product or a feature of that product; they may work in research and development, coming up with new product or implementation ideas, or they may work in the manufacture of a product. Among the positions on engineering staffs in the corporate giants are those of manufacturing engineer, electrical engineer, petroleum engineer, and many more. Usually companies offer two career tracks for engineers: either a management track, in which an engineer upon reaching a certain technical level can split off into the management side; or a straight technical track, in which an engineer remains doing strictly technical work in his or her specialty.

Purchasing is an area that lately is receiving more and more attention, and attracting more recent graduates. To put it simply, purchasing staffers buy materials or equipment for a company. These may be used in the manufacture of products or services, or, more generally, may be materials needed for the operation of the company. The entry-level position here is usually that of assistant buyer or buyer, and salaries range from the low to upper 20s. Depending upon the specific company and job, a buyer may be responsible for purchasing items as basic as office equipment and paper clips, as sophisticated as plant machinery, or as vital as raw materials for the manufacture of a product. An important responsibility of the purchasing department is to keep costs down. Staffers have to work with a variety of departments within a company as well as with outside suppliers to ensure that needs and budgets are being met and materials delivered at the right time at the lowest possible cost.

Corporate giants also offer entry-level positions in their **Financial** departments, where staff work on budget analyses, accounting, and so on. Salaries here range from the 20s to the 30s depending upon the specific position and company. Typically, an entry-level person enters as a financial analyst. Often there's close interplay between financial and marketing, coordinating the budgets for products and services. Financial staffers may work in a variety of departments—corporate, treasurer's, controller's, accounting, and others. The trend lately has been toward hiring MBAs, although companies with financial management training programs do accept recent college graduates with business, accounting, mathematics, or economics degrees.

The corporate giants offer a wealth of opportunities in other areas as well, such as Personnel, Information Services, Market Research, Customer Service, and other administrative and management positions. And because these companies are so large, you never know whom you may meet: art historian, corporate librarian, archivist, even executive chef . . . you never know.

ATLANTIC RICHFIELD COMPANY (ARCO)

VITAL STATISTICS

- **locations:** Los Angeles, CA (headquarters);
- **revenues:** $24.7 billion (1984)
- **rank:** 12th (*Fortune* 500); 6th largest oil company
- **employees:** 39,900

AS SEEN FROM THE OUTSIDE

ARCO, like the rest of the oil industry, has been plagued by the worst economic conditions in recent years: depressed prices, excess supply, and reduced demand. The company responded in 1985 with a major restructuring program, which included reducing the number of employees from 39,000 to 32,000; authorizing a $4 billion stock repurchase plan; divesting its metals and minerals assets; and shifting its gasoline marketing efforts from the eastern to the western United States.

Drastic actions in uncertain times. But ARCO has a history of risk-taking behind it. Long considered the most liberal of the oil companies, ARCO has a reputation for doing things differently from its competitors. It's considered the oil company with a conscience, with a corporate philosophy devoted to making money on the one hand and contributing to the community on the other, through donations to social service organizations, financial support of the arts, and more.

ARCO's philosophy essentially stems from one man—Robert O. Anderson. He became a major shareholder in Atlantic Refinery when he sold them his oil production company in 1962. Three years later, he and Thornton Bradshaw, a former Harvard Business School professor, began making the less-than-innovative Atlantic Refining a mover—by merging with Richfield Oil in 1966, discovering oil off Alaska in 1968, buying most of the assets of Sinclair Oil in 1970, and acquiring Anaconda (the large copper and aluminum producer) in 1977. All this came together to become ARCO, one of the nation's largest domestic petroleum producers.

But times have changed at the benevolent oil giant. ARCO has traditionally been rated a top corporation to work for in the U.S., and that was reflected in the number of employees who saw Arco as a lifetime employer. But 1985 was the year of the cutback, and when many of the employees left, so did the enthusiasm.

ARCO's headquarters in Los Angeles still stands as an imposing black glass and steel structure, but the employees are getting used to smaller offices, and those who made it through the cutbacks have taken on a sort of "survival of the fittest" attitude. ARCO hopes to emerge as a "lean machine" that's stronger than ever before.

HEARD AT THE WATER COOLER
WHAT IT'S REALLY LIKE TO WORK HERE

"We're going through this transition period, where morale is going to be shattered," commented one staffer. "It's going to take a while to get back where we were."

That's the common feeling around ARCO these days. Big oil has had troubles lately, and ARCO has been no exception. So why are so many people sticking things out? Most say ARCO was a good employer in the past, and they're counting on the company to weather the changes and return to what it was.

One employee whose father was a veteran ARCO man said, "I'm a real diehard. We've gone through a lot of change, but I'm still optimistic. ARCO's very progressive—we're always at the forefront of decisions in the industry. We're bold enough to take the lead."

Some of ARCO's decision making lately has been tough—cutting back on staff, battening down the hatches. But for all the changes, there are some things about ARCO that will remain the same. For one thing, the size—ARCO is a "big oil" company, complete with subsidiaries, red tape, and politics.

But there's another mainstay at ARCO that offsets the "big oil" image. This is a company that's very big on community service. ARCO has established an extensive social responsibility program, encouraging its employees to donate to charities, to volunteer and get involved.

"The more integral a part of the community you are, the better off you're going to be in the long run," said one corporate employee. "It is in our self-interest, but a good healthy community is in everybody's interest."

It's that kind of corporate attitude that keeps a lot of people here. They know these are bad times for the oil industry; they know ARCO is trying to survive. And many of the staffers here want to survive with ARCO.

As one young woman summed up, "There has been a lot of restructuring, a lot of unknowns. When it first happened, I think morale was really low. We were all waiting to see which rumors were true. I'm going to wait and give it six months or so."

"It was a good place to work and I think it will be a good place to work in the future. I'm going to give it a chance."

PEOPLE

ARCO looks for the best and the brightest and it usually finds them—even now, when it's not in a growth period. As one staffer noted, "ARCO does recognize that it has to have good people to survive."

And survival is on a lot of people's minds. Right now, many employees feel it's important to be enthusiastic and have a positive outlook about the company's future. Many of them gave a thumbs up to management's decision to reorganize.

"I like the corporate culture, I like the way they market their product, and I think they're very wise about the way they're running the company," said a three-year engineer at an ARCO subsidiary.

If there's one thing that distinguishes an ARCO employee, it's community service. A business analyst said that was one of the reasons she stayed with the company.

"If someone wants to really be part of the company, it's not just 9 to 5," said one employee who's involved in Junior Achievement, the speaker's bureau, and the Civic Action Program. "Even though they're cutting back, they still find ways to get tickets for kids to go to Disneyland. It's nice, and it's good for the company image."

ARCO rewards its employees who put in that extra effort. "If you put in some time and volunteer, they'll come and pat you on the back—it doesn't go unnoticed."

Most employees give high marks to their co-workers and managers. One engineer who moved from the East Coast to the West said his best friends are those he knows at work. "I think mixing work with pleasure is important—it will get you a long way."

The management at ARCO is known to be conservative, with an "old boy" attitude that goes way back. One woman who was only the second female engineer to be hired at the ARCO subsidiary where she works said, "The people who run ARCO are the people who were out in the oil field years and years ago, and there weren't many women out there at that time. It's hard to change attitudes overnight."

Another employee said, "I haven't been hindered being a woman, but I am not one of the boys. I'm the only professional female in our department. The men don't come down the hall and say, 'Hey, do you want to go to lunch with us.' You feel kind of isolated."

JOBS
Even with cutbacks, there's one key aspect to working here—varied opportunities.

"One thing that attracted me to ARCO was the ability to move around within the company and go to different ARCO divisions," said one engineer.

An industry forecaster who has held three different titles at ARCO in the past five years said, "In a company the size of ARCO, you can pursue a career and have enough transitions in your career so that you're always growing professionally and personally."

There are disadvantages, of course, to working at a large company. "Any big corporation has its bureaucracies, but you treat that almost as a challenge, learning to work with it," he added. "That's one of the professional skills that you wouldn't acquire in a small company."

It's not a bad idea to start "down in the trenches"—at an ARCO subsidiary. One government affairs coordinator said, "I've always had in my mind that I wanted to be at the corporate level. My first position here was just a stepping-stone. But I've learned a lot more and had more exposure and opportunity here. I've moved ahead faster."

"It's not as prestigious as the headquarters—we call the downtown ARCO Tower 'the Ivory Tower'—but there are more opportunities."

Actually, the opportunities depend to a great extent on your field and background. At the **corporate** level, there are very few entry-level jobs since the restructuring. Some staffers say there's a glut of MBAs, but others note that having an MBA in an oil company is a definite asset. A greater emphasis has been put on the financial end of the business.

As an engineer said, "In the world today, the major emphasis is not on new ideas and construction and engineering, it's on finance and financial analysis. In my opinion, it puts the world in a nongrowth mode. Instead of a company being able to advance because of its innovation in technology, etc., it's advancing because its people know how to work the numbers, they know how to read the tax laws correctly."

Jobs on the financial and business side of ARCO are similar to those at any large corporation—staffers may work as financial analysts, business analysts, treasurers, industry analysts, and so forth. And most see quite a bit of the company.

"It's fairly standard for people to move around in the corporate finance area," said a treasury employee. "They like to rotate people every year or so. They want to expose you to a number of different areas. The oil and gas group and the downstream group are very much oriented toward serving the operating companies. The general corporate group gets involved in planning, budgeting, some corporate issues."

Most employees in these nonengineering areas say that ARCO sets no definite tracks for them. "Career paths are not that clear-cut," said an industry analyst. "Most MBAs end up in staff-type functions. They're not involved in the operating decisions on selling gasoline or negotiating contracts. They're basically analyzing, providing internal consulting."

Career paths are clearer on the **engineering** side. Since ARCO is an engineer-driven company, a dual career path exists for engineers—a technical path and a management path. An engineer on the management track may move from junior engineer to senior engineer to supervisor or manager; one on the technical path would move up into a specialized engineering position. "This has been developed more recently," commented a young woman. "Technical specialist—it's a prestigious thing, it's a real honor."

Generally, engineers begin by working in the subsidiaries. For one thing, "you should really get a lot of hands-on experience, get out in the field as much as possible," as a supervisor noted. "You've got to learn to respect the construction hands and what their skills are. If you don't design around those skills, you can't expect those skills to go toward your design. You have to design around the skills of the industry, and without field work, you're never going to learn that."

In the subsidiaries, the engineers have lots of independence, and they prefer it that way. Most engineers at ARCO's Four Corners Pipe Line Co. in Long Beach have responsibility for their projects from conception to completion, including design and specifications, writing financial authorizations, evaluating bids, and watching over the construction.

New hires get their feet wet quickly. While they're assigned to work with senior staffers, it's up to them to pick up all the experience they can, quickly.

"As soon as I got on board here, I was assigned to work with a senior engineer and I grabbed onto his coattails and followed him wherever he went. I know I was a pain in the butt sometimes, but you can't be independent when you first come on board. You have to get all the experience you can off the senior people. You don't want to get burned on mistakes when you're very young in your career."

Engineers work up through different grades, or levels. On reaching a certain level, an engineer can opt to move into management. "The grades apply to salary and position," explained a supervisor. "As far as advancing to the next grade level, the timing is up to you—how aggressive you are—and it also depends on your group. You have a lot of hidden internal competition within each group."

To a great extent, that competition exists because of the nature of the business. One engineer noted that "oil companies are very conservative. To get promoted to senior engineer you generally have to have years of experience, be a little older, or have a Master's degree. But there are a lot of young managers, so there's a lot of competition for management jobs."

There's also a lot of politicking. A young man explained that communication skills are often more important than any type of analytical engineering skill. "If you're doing some great analytical work, but you can't relay that information to people, it isn't worth it."

And communicating is especially important in these rough

times for ARCO. Staffers say it takes "a real optimistic view" to get ahead. "Don't complain," suggested one young woman. That holds for all employees here, regardless of the type of job they have—engineering or nonengineering, management or technical. "You have to spread your name around a lot. It also takes a lot of hard work, a lot of overtime," explained a young man. "And you have to play the politics as well."

LIFE

Lately, life at ARCO has meant worrying about ARCO. ARCO is not the best place for an engineer to work right now because the oil industry has been suffering due to lower oil prices and lower demand.

"We're talking about a very small capitalization program in the next several years," said an engineer at an ARCO subsidiary. "As an engineer, you're looking for a company that has a big capital program. You want a company that's going to spend a lot of money, because that will make things a lot more interesting."

And there's another side to these tough times. One young engineer who was promoted to a supervisory role said, "The politics can get really deep and frustrating at times, especially when a company is in a nongrowth mode as we are now."

But ARCO is still trying to make life here as positive as possible for the people who have made it through the layoffs—and for those who haven't. Despite all the turmoil caused by the restructuring, ARCO offered some attractive deals for people who left the company.

"People are being retired with a nice severance package," one employee noted. "It looks good and it makes people feel that they are valued, instead of just getting laid off. The company feels that it's important to keep people's goodwill."

But what about the good old days when people chose ARCO for their entire career? "I've always thought that was the way to go, but I still think you should have feelers out there," said a government affairs employee. "I've changed my mind since the restructuring."

DOLLARS AND SENSE

ARCO has a reputation of paying very high salaries. And the engineers here have no complaints in that area. According to one employee, "an engineer at ARCO makes more than an MBA."

As for the financial employees, some say they'd be making two to four times more money if they were on Wall Street. "The question is, do you want to work eighty hours a week? Do you want to live in New York?" commented a financial analyst. So many staffers say there's a payoff for their relatively lower paycheck—a more relaxed lifestyle.

Outrageously high salaries may be a thing of the past. "We're in a new trend—oil companies have paid notoriously high, so now there are cuts," said one employee.

GETTING IN—TRICKS OF THE TRADE

Since the restructuring, job opportunities here have narrowed to "very slim" according to one staffer. So people have to be pretty well-qualified to get in nowadays. "It's going to take a top school in your field," a staffer stated. "ARCO does demand high credentials anywhere it hires, whether it be engineering, business, or law. It's not just a matter of getting your degree; they tend to go for the top students."

The best way to break in is to apply to an ARCO subsidiary. The salary is lower (you can expect to make up to 30 percent less than a co-worker at the corporate level), but there are usually more entry-level jobs. Would-be ARCO employees can also get experience through internships or summer job programs at the oil companies. These give you both hands-on experience and contacts.

One engineer said the summer job program was a good way for ARCO to try out someone—and for the employee to try out ARCO. "Four Corners has a summer jobs program and so do the other ARCO subsidiaries," noted an engineer. "Even during these slow times."

Times might be tough, but ARCO is still looking for good people.

THE BOTTOM LINE

Only the strong survive.

AT&T

VITAL STATISTICS

- **locations:** New York (headquarters); offices nationwide and worldwide
- **revenues:** $33.188 billion (1984-post-divestiture)
- **rank:** 1st (among telecommunications companies); 8th (*Fortune* 500)
- **employees:** 365,000

AS SEEN FROM THE OUTSIDE

Aggressive salespeople and competitive-minded product managers take note—there's room for you at AT&T.

Not so in the old days before 1984. That was the year of divestiture, the year AT&T and its seven regional telephone companies (the seven sisters) split off and became independent entities. AT&T was then left with the long-distance telephone service and those sections of old Ma Bell that developed, manufactured, and marketed telecommunications products.

That was also the year the competitive fires really started burning. Before that it hardly mattered. The big, bulky, heavily staffed phone company had little to worry about. It was a government regulated, quasi-public utility and monopoly, and its employees enjoyed the benefits of noncompetition: quiet loyalty, a family atmosphere, and a virtual guarantee of lifetime employment. As long as you didn't rock the boat. With little or no competition that extra edge just wasn't needed. Longtime AT&T employees talk of the days when people with innovative, new, or just plain different marketing ideas were better off keeping quiet.

It's different now. Although vestiges of the past remain, AT&T is now *very* concerned with marketing innovation. It has to be. In the long-distance area, it faces competition from MCI, Sprint, and other companies. In the technologies area, innovation has always been the byword, but now there's a difference: Bell Labs is no longer required by law to keep the doors open and share its technological breakthroughs. Instead, AT&T product managers are interested in selling them—against such heavy-weight competition as IBM. It's a tall order, and the first years have been tough for AT&T.

But reorganization, layoffs, and time are making for a stronger company. AT&T now has two main bases—AT&T Communications and AT&T Technologies.

AT&T Communications is the telecommunications part of the company. It provides long-distance voice, data, and video transmissions. It's also the service side of the company. It still has almost two thirds of the total long-distance market, and 81 percent of the profitable interexchange business. But in the long run, it stands to lose some of that to its competitors. To keep its losses to a minimum, AT&T has invested heavily in advertising (those homey Cliff Robertson ads), marketing (Reach Out America, and other consumer packages) and cost-cutting (interstate rates were reduced by 6.1 percent in 1984). And even with inevitable losses, AT&T expects to keep half the total long-distance market. That means about $1.5 billion or more in operating profits.

AT&T Technologies makes and markets telecommunications products—including digital switches, PBX's (private branch exchanges, or switchboards), and computers. AT&T Information Systems is the principal marketing arm of this highly competitive area of the company. While IBM has remained a force in the computer industry through the information processing side, AT&T hopes to become a major force through the transmission side, developing the UNIX system to allow its computers to communicate directly with one another. Of course, IBM has now announced its own local area network, promising some very tough competition in AT&T's own turf.

But despite the traumas of the divestiture and the problems of competition, AT&T is beginning to find its way. Massive layoffs of up to 24,000 people have shaken old Ma Bell's complacency, and innovations such as fiber optics and light wave voice and data transmission will change things even more. Fewer staff jobs and a more bottom-line orientation are making AT&T a different place. At AT&T, the past is still there, but the future belongs to profit-minded MBAs.

HEARD AT THE WATER COOLER—
WHAT IT'S REALLY LIKE TO WORK HERE

"There are still a few people here who think the orders are just going to drop on our desk," said a tough, no-nonsense Communications manager. "They have to change. That behavior *has* to change."

Yes, sir!

And it *is* changing, all over AT&T. There's a feeling in the air that things may not be so great just yet, but wait a few years . . .

"Once we get a critical mass of highly skilled people, you're going to see a tremendous change," a young product manager promised.

You're already seeing it. AT&T today is a leaner and meaner place, and getting more so. But you can't quite get away from reminders of the Ma Bell days. No matter how many hard-chargers enter the ranks, it's still a bureaucracy. Try running a company of over 300,000 employees without rules and chains of command. It can be a "maddening" impediment to getting things done. On the other hand . . .

"Our strength is inertia," a young Ph.D explained. "We can really push products if things are set into motion. Inertia is on our side."

"But younger employees can get frustrated wading through red tape and going through the right channels. And all those chatty, down-home talks by Cliff Robertson can't hide the definitely political nature of the place. Here, it's far more giant corporate than small town America.

AT&T offices reflect the combination of old and new. From ultramodern labs to older district offices that look straight out of a 1950's movie, there's an interesting blend at AT&T.

And wherever you go there's tight security. When asked about the need for I.D. badges, security guards, and reception rooms, one young staffer smiled and commented: "It didn't used to be like that, before divestiture. We're more like a company now."

PEOPLE

"One of the fundamental qualities of AT&T people—if you can take 300,000 people and find one quality—is that they're really honest people," said one Communications manager.

Okay, so what else is new? But there *is* a dash of old-fashioned

American virtue that seems to permeate the company. It probably stems from the old utility days. There's a conservative, old-fashioned feel.

And there is still that blend of old and new. A Communications employee sees two types of people in her division—the "old technical type" who worked his way up from the ranks, who might have gotten a degree along the way at night school; and the new employee, who comes directly with a college degree, and picks up the technical skills along the way.

That technical orientation permeates the company. Everyone is big on the jargon. They "interface" with people and "communicate" with co-workers. Even the liberal arts majors talk that way.

Maybe it's the continuing technical education most employees receive. Work at AT&T means education as well, in classes at the office and in tutorials on the (AT&T) computers. As one manager explained, "It's an ongoing process. It never stops. If you think you're going to walk in here and learn it in a year, you're kidding yourself. Because the minute you know it, the technology's changed."

You work and learn at AT&T.

JOBS

We talked with people who are on the cutting edge of making AT&T a market-driven corporation: sales and marketing people from AT&T Communications, and product managers from AT&T Information Systems.

Product managers from **Information Systems** used to have it easy. If Ma Bell made it, the public would buy it—the public didn't have much choice. Now they do, and it's the product manager's job to make sure the public chooses AT&T. It was a tall order for people used to taking orders, instead of competitively marketing and advertising, and it meant some changes.

The job was summed up by one product manager as a juggling act, "going through the process of bringing a product to the market, and everything that involves coordinating all the different functions within AT&T to have a successful product introduction."

A nice way of saying "I do everything." Getting market data, setting up a review process with key vendors, talking with the sales force, "interfacing" with the lab staff in order to refine the product, talking with advertising agencies, selling the product to senior management, and then, and only then, letting the public decide.

One manager describes the atmosphere as "slam bam . . . you have to get a lot of things in motion. It pays to socialize, to circulate your ideas, and get a 'buy in' before you start."

Buy in? Don't forget that AT&T is a giant bureaucracy, and many different products compete for AT&T management's attention before any of them ever hits the streets. You need political savvy as well as market savvy.

It's "a hell of a lot of wheeling and dealing," as one manager explained. "What you're doing is negotiating with your interfaces for a certain type of support, then quarterbacking meetings and progress."

It's also a lot of work. A very successful manager who helped introduce MULTIPLEXORS (a group of complex data communications products) had just a year to plan and move the product to market. His advice for success? "Treat product responsibility as a small business of your own."

For all the problems of bureaucracy, clogged channels, and not-up-to-speed old-timers, there's room to move at AT&T now. The key is "grabbing responsibility, stepping into new voids and structuring new jobs." One product manager described two methods of pushing to get a product noticed by AT&T management. The first is bulldozing it through. It can work, but it can also ruffle feathers and eventually hurt the product, and in turn, the manager's reputation.

And then there's his way, which is more in keeping with AT&T's traditional management by consensus. There's a nice jargon word for it too: Matrix management. That means building support methodically, having lower level employees get approvals from their bosses and in turn their bosses getting approval from their bosses—all the way up to the CEO. No surprises, and a lot of lead time; but a successful product with the huge bulk of AT&T behind it. And a promotion for the manager.

AT&T **Communications** people are also talking promotions, and risk-taking, and competition, and sales, and teamwork, and just about every other buzz word ever used in a management textbook. The younger ones particularly are excited by the changes.

"We didn't like bad news in the past," said one young staffer. "You gave your boss bad news and you got chewed out, and that wasn't healthy."

No, it wasn't. And that's why when these people use those tired old buzz-words they mean it. Sometimes they sound like people who've been through intensive psychotherapy—admitting to mistakes, coming clean, being terribly open, and generally getting everything off their chests.

So what do they do besides talk about how good change has been for them? Here's one seven-year vet describing his job:

"I manage the state of Indiana. I have roughly four hundred people in the state, I maintain and manage all the equipment that's necessary to provide long-distance service to residential and business customers—switching machines, the facilities that connect those machines, and dedicated services."

That's on the sales and service side of the company. Just like the old days, but with a dash of risk-taking and competitiveness, trying to keep your customers happy and away from Sprint and MCI. And a lot of team-leading, instilling in employees a spirit that was lacking before.

AT&T Communications has become far more specialized now. In the old days, ideal managers were generalists, and the company encouraged hopping around. Not now. One sales manager exhorted the sales staff to "get out of that service mode. There are other people to do that. Your job is to sell."

Yes, AT&T has changed. Specialization is the key now. In sales and marketing services, people are hired as CSCs, or Communications Systems Consultants, and Account Executives. Depending on the type of customer they'll be servicing or selling to, they take courses in such areas as data transmission, packet, or voice transmission. There's a centralized training center in Cincinnati, and regional sales centers around the country, and many core courses on the computer, so people can work while they train.

In terms of managerial advancement, AT&T used to place new hirees directly into the then-named Management Development Training program. Staffers say the program's still around, but that in line with AT&T's new culture, "they changed the name. Maybe to give it more meaning. It's now called the Management Succession Roster." Only the new AT&T could come up with a snazzy, nonbureaucratic name like that for a training program. . . .

Now new hires are no longer placed directly in the program. First they go to work and prove that they've got the potential to be part of that management succession team. That way both old hands and recent hires get shots at managerial positions, although, according to one manager, "in reality, what we see is that those people with the leadership skills and the academic background are still usually the ones who rise." AT&T has a definite tendency to prefer higher education—Ph.D.'s and MBAs.

Since this is the new AT&T, there's the usual candor in assessing the program. "We've only been doing this for two years," commented a seven-year vet. "We might change our mind. But it seems to be working out better this way . . ."

Then it's to work selling to and servicing customers.

LIFE

"A very political place. Absolutely," commented one Communications staffer.

"There's an old-boy network. You develop a network, learn to work your way around it, develop a relationship with peers who you can rely on when you need to get something done. If you piss everybody off along the way, God help you when you make district level and you don't have any favors to call in."

It's still Ma Bell, it's still a bit clubby, but most employees seem pretty happy with it. Just watch your step.

The fun side of things is the importance of your work. One former academic in Information Systems summed it up: "The satisfaction of the job is that, unlike working in a university, the work you do will probably be used by about a million people."

And it's exciting being on the cutting edge of a new industry. "We're just beginning to see the beginning," one staffer said enthusiastically. "A new way to the top is through technical management."

And working at AT&T, you can't help but be technical.

DOLLARS AND SENSE

Sales staff and sales managers now get commissions, since AT&T is not a utility any more. Benefits include the standard ones, plus tuition reimbursement, plus a benefit all loyal staffers feel obliged to mention at least once: working for No. 1.

Do people quit? "When you're the market leader, why go to the competition?" asked one enthusiastic staffer. A pause. "Unless it's a really good deal."

But most stay with AT&T. One reason is the lingering "we're all in this together" family feeling. Another is the money and opportunity. Particularly for young people. They have an advantage, as one senior manager noted: They don't have to unlearn behavior. AT&T wants young and aggressive people. Now.

GETTING IN—TRICKS OF THE TRADE

Get an advanced degree. You don't *have* to have one, but . . .

"Don't hurry to take a job at the BA level," advised an Information Systems product manager. "You're 22, that means you've got over 40 years to work. Why push it?"

"Build up a repertoire of skills so you can move easily from job to job or assignment to assignment."

AT&T wants educated technologists. But a Communications employee warned against being *too* technologically oriented, with a degree in MIS or another technical degree, unless you like being categorized as a "techie." She strongly advised having an MBA. From a top school.

Interviews at AT&T stress education, top grades, and leadership skills. In sales, liberal arts majors are welcome, particularly those who have gone on to get their MBAs.

From a top school. Or tell the recruiter you're interested in getting one at night. Got it? AT&T likes higher education.

THE BOTTOM LINE

Reach out and get competitive.

COCA-COLA

VITAL STATISTICS

- **locations:** Atlanta, GA (headquarters); offices nationwide and worldwide
- **revenues:** $7.36 billion (1984)
- **rank:** 1st (world's largest soft drink company), 46th (*Fortune* 500)
- **employees:** 40,500

AS SEEN FROM THE OUTSIDE

When Coca-Cola announced that "the Real Thing" *wasn't* the real thing in the summer of '85 and came out with the new Coke, the public was shocked. It was blasphemy, pure and simple.

Coke wised up fast. On national television, it announced that the old Coke was coming back, but with a new name—Coca-Cola Classic—to be sold alongside the New Coke. Many people called the whole turnaround a fiasco and snickered at Coke's loss of face. But The Coca-Cola Company has had the last laugh—increased shelf space and stronger positioning in the highly competitive soft drink marketplace.

The Coke saga began in 1886, when John Styth Pemberton, an Atlanta pharmacist, came up with the original Coca-Cola syrup. In 1891, Asa Candler took over and Coke started to become the company we know today. It was Candler who decided that Coke wouldn't do the actual bottling of the product, and who established what many refer to as the first franchise system: Coke provides the syrup, but it's the bottlers that actually produce the soft drink.

The Coca-Cola Company has come a long way since then, becoming the world's leading soft drink company, a leading citrus marketer, and a producer of motion pictures and television programs. There are three different parts of the business. First, there are the Soft Drink Business Sectors, one for North America and another for the international market. These handle the production and distribution of the syrups and concentrates for such products as Coke, Cherry Coke, Diet Coke, Tab, Sprite, and Fanta. Second, there is the Foods Business Sector, headquartered in Houston, which manufactures and markets Minute Maid juices, Five Alive, Hi-C fruit drinks, and others. And thirdly there's the Entertainment Business Sector, headquartered in New York City, which owns Columbia Pictures, one third of Tri-Star Pictures, Embassy, and Tandem.

For all the diversity, though, soft drinks are still Coke's main moneymakers (representing about 77 percent of its income). And that's no surprise, given that the Coke products are sold in over 155 countries through over 1,400 bottlers and 4,000 wholesalers. As Coke proudly notes, "Brand Coca-Cola is asked for in 80 different languages and enjoyed more than 300 million times each day."

So, no matter how you slice it or say it, Coke *is* it.

HEARD AT THE WATER COOLER— WHAT IT'S REALLY LIKE TO WORK HERE

One young man recalled what it was like when Coke's "Gang of 4" put Diet Coke together: "That was the ultimate cultural change for this place. Up till then, it was 'Thou shalt not change the formula,' 'Thou shalt not mess with the trademark,' 'Thou shalt not even change the shape of it'—Coke's absolutely sacred. Diet Coke was *the* event that fundamentally changed the way we did business. And you can see where it went from there."

It went a long way. Staffers say that in the past Coke had a "southern country club kind of atmosphere. It was 'don't rock the boat; we're making good money, why change?' "

Well, inflation and tough competition from PepsiCo. made Coke think again. And changing suddenly looked good. So the New Coke (the company, not the soft drink) was born. And it's going strong.

There's a youthful, go-get-'em attitude here now—young people are in upper management positions; hard work, risk-taking, and new ideas are the bywords, and everyone seems primed for action. And action they get.

"It's a bunch of wild hustlers who work like hell," summed up one staffer. "It's extremely fast-paced, exciting, and go-for-it."

PEOPLE

If Coke were anything like the ads you see on TV, there'd be hundreds of red-blooded American lads here. You know, the kind who play touch football, shoot the rapids on rafts and are just wonderfully healthy and apple-cheeked. Well, people at Coke *aren't* like the ads. Not that there aren't some red-blooded American kids here. It's just that there's more to them than that.

"It's a fascinating cast of characters here," commented a marketing staffer. "It looks more like the U.N. down here than it does a normal corporation. And certainly not only a southern corporation. There are people from literally all over the world and culturally from all over the United States."

But there do seem to be certain similarities among Coke people. For one thing, most are aggressive, "go-go types," as one young woman put it.

And there's another thing. While Coke employees are hard-driving and success-oriented, they're also big on something you don't usually come across in this type of corporate atmosphere—manners. Basic courtesy. It's quite refreshing, actually.

"They're very personable, very hospitable—it's part of being an indigenous southern company," said a financial staffer of his co-workers.

JOBS

"When most people think about Coca-Cola, they think about the product that we drink; they think about the trucks we see on the street. And that *is* Coca-Cola," said a sales staffer. "But it's not Coca-Cola USA. There needs to be a distinction."

Right. The problem with working at Coke is that very few people outside Coke understand exactly what they do. That's because Coke is split into different groups. The one we focused on is Coca-Cola USA, the largest division of the North America Business Sector. Coca-Cola USA is the division responsible for Coke, Diet Coke, Sprite, Tab, and so on. So far so good. But it's not as simple as that.

To put it simply, Coca-Cola USA's main business is *not* literally making Coke and the other soft drinks. Take the bottle of Coke you buy in a supermarket. Coca-Cola USA sold the syrup to make that Coke to a bottler. It's the bottler who actually winds up producing and selling that particular bottle of Coke.

So Coca-Cola USA actually produces and distributes the syrup or concentrates for soft drinks, as opposed to producing the soft drinks themselves. But that's still not all. As you'd expect in a large company like Coke, there are many jobs and departments—sales, marketing, purchasing, finance, etc. Within those departments, one may have responsibility on the bottler side or the fountain side, (or, in some cases, both). It can get rather complicated.

Not to employees, though. A sales employee on the bottling side explained his group's duties clearly. "It's basically a franchise system. The only product that we sell is the syrup to the bottlers, who in turn sell the cases of the finished product that we drink. In order for us to sell more syrup, we have to have our bottlers sell more cases. And the person responsible for that is the district manager."

Despite its title the position of District Manager is an entry-level one in the **bottler sales** group. A District Manager is responsible for a geographical area and the bottlers within that area. In order to ensure that bottlers are maintaining market share, a District Manager has to keep tabs on each bottler's market, help him analyze his business, and with the bottler, determine the steps necessary to improve his business in order to gain volume, share, and profitability.

Since district managers work so closely with bottlers, they go through an intensive training program that allows them to see every aspect of the business, from the ground up. It's a thirty-three-week program divided into five separate phases. First, there's a two-week orientation in Atlanta that introduces new hires to the business. Then, it's off to the bottlers for fourteen weeks, doing everything involved in the manufacture and distribution of soft drinks—literally.

"They work in production; they work loading the truck; they work riding routes and sorting bottles; stocking shelves," explained one young man. *Plus* they're meeting with sales managers, general managers, and plant presidents. The third phase of the training program is about ten weeks long, two weeks for classroom instruction and eight weeks traveling to various markets around the country for a week at a time. Then trainees go back into the classroom for seven weeks. Finally, there's two to four weeks with field people.

Generally, district managers remain in their position for two to three years. Then they go in one of two directions. Either they move over to the retail side, where they become sales development managers, or they become senior district managers in districts with more responsibility. From there more options open up. Senior district managers may become sales development managers in an important marketplace, or become region managers; sales development managers may become region managers or regional sales development managers.

It's a little different on the **Fountain Sales** side of Coca-Cola USA. As one employee explained, "it's a direct sales organization, really, in that there are salesmen on the street who sell restaurants on why they should have Coke and not Pepsi."

The entry-level spot in Fountain Sales is that of Territory Sales Manager. From there, salespeople can work their way up to larger accounts or a larger geographic responsibility, and later move on to become area managers and district managers. As one staffer summed up, "It's a very traditional selling organization with solid, traditional career paths."

In **marketing**, things are a little different. "For the MBA hustler-type who gets hired in marketing, it's much more random—it all depends on what your interest is, what your specialty is. that will determine how organized or disorganized your career path is."

On the fountain sales side, marketing is split into three groups—marketing services, marketing specifically for Coca-Cola USA, and marketing for national accounts. Servicing national accounts can cover a wide range, depending to a great degree on how sophisticated the client's own marketing department is. Staffers in this area may provide market research, basic data, creative promotional ideas, and so on. As an employee explained, "it can go from 'Thank you, we're just fine without your help.' to 'I've only got four people in the marketing department and we just fired our ad agency. Would you guys help with creative?' So what do we say? 'Hell, sure, glad to.' And we'll shanghai our advertising agency or brand people or do it amongst the marketing people we've got."

One marketing employee explained that moving up in marketing is based almost entirely on individual initiative and planning. "One of the fundamental culture changes around here has been a propensity to pay for performance and promote for performance."

A self-determined career path is evident in jobs other than marketing. A young woman in **purchasing** explained that there used to be a defined career path. Now, "there's a lot of cross-training going on. And the career path doesn't necessarily stay in purchasing. Somebody who's marketing-oriented could make that step from purchasing to marketing, or somebody could move to sales. Purchasing is a great way to learn the background."

The high level of exposure plus the diverse duties a purchasing staffer can get involved with are the key things employees find attractive about their work. One employee noted that purchasing is getting more and more attention at Coke lately, which is the way it should be. "Purchasing can truly affect the bottom line," she stressed. "For every purchasing dollar saved, you affect the bottom line by $16 or $17. That's a dramatic figure, because it takes that many sales dollars to generate a dollar of bottom line profit. It you look at it that way, you can make a real impact on the company."

One thing that helps all Coke staffers, regardless of department, in developing a career path is Coke's performance evaluation system. Both employees and their immediate supervisors outline goals at the beginning of the year; at the end of the year, each employee rates his or her performance, as does the supervisor. At the same time, employees may complete a Career Aspirations and Interests form, in which they may request movement to another area of the company or express interest in a position outside the regular career path. Personnel reviews these forms when there's an opening, and employees throughout the company get the opportunity to try for the job.

But the key to Coke—no matter what department a person is in—is plain old initiative. As one staffer said, "The atmosphere at Coke is right now is lean and mean. That might sound kind of trite, but we're buckling down and there's a hell of a workload for everyone."

There's also a lot of opportunity if you've got the right stuff.

LIFE

So life at Coke can be quite action-packed. And not only on the job. They've just built a health facility, complete with indoor track, racquet ball courts, Nautilus equipment, and professionals on staff to help you develop your own fitness program. And when you come back to work after your workout, you can have a free soft drink (as long as it's a Coca-Cola product).

"One of the other things that's fun around here is that Coke is big on entertaining our customers. And I have yet to meet a poor bottler—they're all millionaires," said one young man. "Some of the entertainment functions and some of the bottler-advertising functions become gala events."

DOLLARS AND SENSE

No one here wanted to talk about salaries. However, word has it that money is quite good. Coke is coming on strong in the market, so it's passed along to the employees.

GETTING IN—TRICKS OF THE TRADE

A lot of people want to work at Coke, so it's tough breaking in. For one thing, Coke can afford to be selective. Since it is a popular company, it's flooded with resumés. What it looks for is people with two or more years of work experiences, or people with MBAs.

As far as getting into sales is concerned, Coke has a very selective recruiting process. There are on-the-road interviews with experienced salespeople. Interviews may last up to five hours, in which the applicant is given a trade math test and a problem-solving case. Those who pass this stage go to an assessment center in Atlanta. There, field managers from the company watch them go through a day and a half filled with a series of role-playing situations.

"They're given a tremendous amount of information, a lot of correspondence that they have to dig through, and three different cases that they have to work with in a very short time," said one employee involved with the training. "Then they make a presentation to a fictitious bottler or fictitious buyer for a retailer that will address the problem they've identified, based on all that information they've been given." While applicants go through the exercises, the field managers assess their performance and look for the nine skills Coke wants to see—organizing and planning, perception and analysis, decision making, decisiveness (i.e. regardless of the quality of your decision, did you stick with it?), oral communications, written communications, adaptability, interpersonal skills, and perseverance.

As you can see, it's pretty selective. And while the recruiting might not be as formal in other departments, it's just as tough. A marketing staffer pointed out that part of the problem is the product. "It's important to understand that we have only a few brands. When you have a limited number of heavily advertised products, you're not talking about a huge number of marketing positions."

So how do you get one of those few positions? Experience and an MBA are virtual necessities. And beyond that, "it's a real trick. You just really have to be good to pull it off."

Interning helps. Coke does have intern programs in its different departments. The marketing program usually looks for MBA students who can handle immediate responsibility, since there's no formal training. There are seminars for interns, roughly once a week, in which staffers from around the company explain their areas and responsibilities, but beyond that, it's up to the intern. "They really gave me a free rein," explained a former intern. "They told me what the problem was and said, 'you put it together yourself.' They didn't say, 'Okay, you will do this and this and this.' So I structured the project the way I could handle it." And she ended up with a job offer.

Getting a job at Coke in any department is really a matter of luck, timing, perseverance, and experience. And a touch of a "go for it" attitude always helps. One young man explained that he got his job "by cornering a guy at a cocktail party."

"I got in by just plain hustling," he concluded. "And I don't think it's any different today."

THE BOTTOM LINE

If you like hard work, an energetic atmosphere, and hustling, Coke might be It for you.

GENERAL ELECTRIC

VITAL STATISTICS

- **locations:** Fairfield, CT (headquarters); offices and plants nationwide and worldwide
- **revenues:** $27.94 billion (1984 sales—pre-RCA purchase)
- **rank:** 9th (*Fortune* 500)
- **employees:** 330,000

AS SEEN FROM THE OUTSIDE

> You are either the very best at what you do, or you don't do it for very long.
>
> —from GE's 1984 annual report

In addition to doing other things, GE made over a billion light bulbs last year. Other things included making refrigerators, motors, turbines, diesel electric locomotives, scanners, radar systems, high-performance plastics, and industrial lasers. Other things also included providing leveraged buyout loans, construction designs, nuclear consulting, and data services. And next year, other things will include airing the "Bill Cosby Show"—GE has bought RCA, owner of No. 1 broadcaster NBC.

But it all began with a light bulb and two companies. One was Thomas Alva Edison's—the Edison Electric Company. The other was a competitor—Thomson-Houston. When they merged in 1892, General Electric was born. It moved quickly to justify its name. If it involved electricity, GE did it. Sometimes a little too much.

It got involved with (electric) power utilities and (once before) the (electric) radio company RCA—and Uncle Sam got a little bit worried. Big was fine. Monopoly was not. So antitrust suit followed antitrust suit. But all along the way GE still grew and grew.

Today it's the eleventh largest corporation in the U.S. And the past of antitrust suits worries GE (and Uncle Sam) far less than the future of foreign competition. GE is moving quickly to make itself more competitive.

That means focusing on what it does best. No more growth for growth's sake. The company has organized itself around six "core" businesses: major appliances, motor, turbine, transportation, construction equipment, and of course, lighting. Plus two other areas, high technology (that's where RCA comes in) and services. In services, GE already owns one of the largest diversified financial companies in the U.S., the General Electric Financial Services, Inc., which has $18.5 billion in assets.

Focusing also means training and education. Particularly for engineers and financial types. GE is far better than most colleges for a postgraduate degree. There's a huge estate in Crotonville, New York, that offers management development courses, plus programs around the country conducted jointly with universities for postgraduate engineering degrees. And there's training program after training program, all over the U.S.

HEARD AT THE WATER COOLER— WHAT IT'S REALLY LIKE TO WORK HERE

Ask GE employees what it's really like to work at GE and they'll tell you they can't—it's too big, each area has a different atmosphere, it depends on what type of work you do.

But whether a person is a financial analyst at the sleek Fairfield headquarters (complete with art gallery, outdoor running track, and health center) or an engineer at the less-than-sleek steam turbine plant in Schenectady, there are some constants.

First, GE is all over the place and so are its employees. Most people *aren't* working at posh headquarters. But most don't seem to mind. As one young woman said, "GE's actual environment isn't as nice as Burroughs or IBM. Both of them have shag carpets and nice couches. And GE doesn't concentrate so much on work environment. It concentrates more on the employees."

One of the main ways it concentrates on employees, especially young ones, is thorough training. GE offers comprehensive training programs—including the Manufacturing Management Program (MMP), the Edison Engineering Program (EEP), the Information Systems Management Program (ISMP), and the Financial Management Program (FMP). Since they're all integral parts of working at GE, we spoke with people from all of them.

The second aspect of GE that affects everyone is its size. It's big. And since GE's training programs are designed to give participants experience in different GE jobs, that means trainees cover a lot of areas—and a lot of ground. That's a plus for young people who aren't quite sure what they want to do, who want to see what jobs are out there while they're working.

As an applications engineer summed it up: "If you don't know if you want to make light bulbs or engines or boats, then GE is great." And it's just as great if you don't know if you want to be a financial analyst or a corporate auditor, a programmer or a systems analyst, a plant manager or a field engineer.

PEOPLE

Just as it's difficult to describe the real GE, it's difficult to sum up the typical GE person.

"I don't think you really have your stereotypical GE engineer," said a recent EEP grad. "It's a varied company. They're into appliances, jets, engenees, nuclear, batteries . . ."

And they're not only engineers here, either. There are financial staffers, information systems employees, and more.

But while GE is definitely varied, participants in the training programs have something in common—they're fresh from school and they're young. "It's all young people, people just like yourself, out of colleges from all over the U.S.," a former ISMP maintained. "They've all got the same concerns you have." So making friends is easy.

Trainees don't only have age in common. Most have technical backgrounds—Bachelor's degrees in engineering, computer science, math, or business. And since many chose GE because of the chance to rotate through a variety of jobs and locations, most are flexible. They have to be.

"If you don't like travel, if you don't like change, you won't like GE," a two-year vet warned.

And atmosphere and people change from place to place. Employees at headquarters or in the service offices of GE are more formal. At the plants, managers and trainees might wear suits and ties, but "we take our jackets off. It's not at all stuffy."

Stuffiness isn't the GE style. "Remember," a five-year employee stressed, "this is a manufacturing company. And the way you succeed is to get your hands dirty."

Which is something GE people aren't afraid to do.

JOBS

GE prides itself on thorough training, and that's just what it offers new hires in its programs. Most of the programs offer a combination of classroom study with rotating work assignments, designed to give trainees experience in different areas of the same general field.

The **Manufacturing Management Program (MMP)** is a combination engineering/management training. And like the other GE programs, it offers its participants experience in a variety of jobs. It's that combination of management opportunities, job diversity, and hands-on work that attracts many of the MMPs, especially those with Bachelor's degrees.

"I wasn't sure what I wanted to do," said a young woman. "And the GE program had a lot of direction and a lot of corporate support."

Support, yes. But MMPs have to be prepared to perform. "We're considered management material," one MMP said. "And they expect a lot from you. No one treats you like a trainee. No one sits there and holds your hand."

Essentially, MMPs follow a two-year program—classroom work combined with four six-month work assignments. The classroom coursework kicks off with a two-day orientation period. Then, during the first year of the program, all first-year MMPs take a one-week Manufacturing Concepts Course at a conference center. The second year, a Manufacturing Technology Overview workshop is held, again away from work. But that's not it as far as classwork goes. MMPs also attend a mandatory nine-month series of courses on Manufacturing Leadership at their assignment location, designed to go along with their day-to-day work in manufacturing. And it's pretty in-depth stuff.

For the MMPs who aren't swamped and don't think that's enough, they have the option to enter the Advanced Course in Manufacturing. "Through the advanced course, I have six hours toward my Master's in engineering," one go-getter said. "It takes twenty-five to thirty hours outside of class to get through. And it's pretty technical."

Indeed it is—with coursework covering subjects like electrical engineering, robotics, and more.

And while all this in-class and after-hours work is going on, there's a regular job to be thinking about. During the course of the two years, MMPs hold jobs in three of the four GE manufacturing engineering areas—Quality Control, which often involves work on the factory floor; Manufacturing Engineering, which entails design, development, and production of tools, equipment, products, and automation systems; Materials Management, which deals with the ordering and purchasing of materials, as well as work with production schedules and cost control; and Shop Operations, in which the MMP is involved in the actual manufacturing process as a supervisor to plant personnel.

MMPs rotate through job assignments designed specifically for MMPs only—which means that their job trainer is always another MMP. Normally, an entering MMP gets two weeks of training from the MMP currently holding that job. Then he or she sits down with the manager to review progress and identify goals.

The job areas vary—from high-volume/low-tech fields like major appliances, to low-volume/high-tech fields like factory automation. And MMPs often give input as to their preferred areas.

"I wanted old line, big manufacturing," one young man said. "So they put me in Schenectady, which is as old as you can get, and in Steam Turbines, which is as big *and* as old as you can get. I was supposed to be there for six months but I stayed eight. There's a local MMP representative at each location, and we hit it off real well."

Another thing many MMPs like about the program is that while it's rather structured, there can be flexibility for those who push for it. So assignments may last longer than six months, if the MMP convinces management that it's feasible.

Being sent all over the company does have its advantages. MMPs point to the opportunities in the manufacturing field. Some call it "the up and coming field at GE." And there seems to be room to advance fairly quickly.

According to a former MMP, "There is an age gap in manufacturing that's very prevalent here. So the MMPs about my age are just drooling when they look at the jobs ahead. The people in those jobs are in their late forties and fifties. So it's a great chance for people my age and younger."

"Most of us want to see if we can run our own plants," an applications engineer stated. "That's about 1,000 people, a $500- to $600-million business. And here you can run that at a fairly early age. If at age twenty-five you went out on the street, knocked on a door and said, "I want to run a five to six hundred million dollar company,' they'd slam the door in your face. But here you can."

Another current MMP mentioned that her manager is a former MMP, and in turn his manager is a former MMP, "so this program is a jumping-off place to bigger and better things."

A successful former MMP summed up the program simply. "If you're an engineer and you don't want to do research and development, the manufacturing program is great."

GE also has a program for engineers who *do* want to do R&D— **The Edison Engineering Program**. Like the MMP, the Edison Program is a combination of rotating work assignments and education (in this case all graduate-level work) over a two-year period.

And again, the assignments are varied. A recent graduate from the program reeled off some of the possibilities. "I did some Computer Aided analysis over in our design group; it could be out on the production floor, it could be in manufacturing engineering, it could be in automation . . ."

That diversity is one of the key reasons participants feel the program is valuable. As one automation engineer pointed out, although a degree in mechanical or electrical engineering might seem limiting, "there are many different ways you can go. You could be a strict design and development person, you could be a product engineer, you could be a manufacturing engineer. The Edison Program allows you to get a feel for what each type of engineering involves."

Along with their work assignments, Edison Program engineers with both Bachelor's and Master's degrees take a mandatory course—the "A" Course—their first year. The course runs a full academic year and covers a range of engineering disciplines.

"It's pretty intensive," a young man stated. "It exposes a mechanical engineer to things in electrical engineering you might not have had in school, and vice versa. There's some Thermo, some Fluid, that kind of thing that a lot of people might not have been exposed to."

Edison Program participants discover that the combination of work and intensive classwork makes their first year fairly grueling. "I think the thing that surprised me most was the amount of work," said one staffer. "I'd heard about the "A" course, but it ended up being a lot more work than I expected."

When the second year comes, the amount of classwork is largely up to the individual. Employees decide which classes they want to take, either GE courses and seminars or graduate study at a school. And GE pays tuition for Edison engineers who take "approved graduate courses at outside institutions." That's an opportunity many employees take.

But staffers say it's not enough to perform well on the job and in the courses. "You've also got to market yourself a little too. If your section manager has five hundred people working for him, you're not necessarily going to stand out unless you try a little harder and make yourself stand out."

Being in the Edison Program helps, though. One young man referred to it as "one of the little tools that helps you stand out amongst the rest of the company."

Once an engineer has gone through the two-year cycle, he or she interviews throughout the company for a job. "Typically, you end up going back to one of the jobs you had as an assignment," a former EEP stated. "They've seen you, you've seen them, and it ends up being a very short interview."

Staffers say there's little turnover among EEPs either during or after the program. And one of the reasons for that may be that GE comprehensiveness. Beyond strong experience, there's the prestige within GE associated with the program. "You've sort of been identified as a high potential candidate," a staffer said. "They'd like to keep you. They give you a good offer coming off the program, a good salary. There are more opportunities for an Edison engineer, I think, than for someone who was hired directly out of school."

The **Information Systems Management Program** is yet another of GE's programs designed for "managerial material." Covering two years of combined education and hands-on rotating assignments, the ISMP is aimed at people who want to integrate computer-systems work with management. The blend of the technical and managerial is what many ISMPs find attractive.

"The first year coursework is really technical. And as you go into the second year, it gets more and more managerial. You're learning decision-making techniques, communications skills, how to manage your manager," a successful former ISMP explained.

ISMPs take graduate-level courses over the two years, generally lasting one to three weeks each. The highly technical first-year courses include three weeks on Advanced COBOL Programming

Techniques, two weeks on Data Base Technologies, and two weeks on Software Design Engineering. ISMPs work on their assignment for a period of time, then go away to a central location for the coursework with all the other ISMPs. The same arrangement applies to the second-year courses, which are primarily devoted to management skills, but include a two-week course in On-Line Systems Design Characteristics.

"Your first six-month rotation is generally selected for you depending on your major," a former ISMP stated. "There are rotations in information systems, manufacturing, engineering, finance, payroll. They try and ease you into the environment by giving you something where you're aware of the information and the surrounding application. It's just the system itself you have to learn."

After the first six months, ISMPs are encouraged to go to the ISMP administrator at their assignment and discuss where they want to go next. The administrator is also there to offer advice during assignments.

As with the other training programs, ISMPs are reviewed annually and rated in categories. Based upon those ratings, some are termed high potential—"hi-pot for short"—and they tend to become the most mobile in careers and geographically.

Most ISMP assignments begin with programming, something many ISMPs aren't thrilled with, but accept. "I hate programming like anyone else," a successful staffer said with a laugh, "but you have to do your time. It's a pain in the neck, but thank God I did it."

After the two years, when the lower-level programming assignments are over, ISMPs usually graduate initially to a project leader position. "You generally have offers from the managers you worked with," a three-year vet said. "Then you decide where you want to stay."

Given the flexibility of the ISMP program, more than one career path exists. A business analyst explained that, after graduation, ISMPs can follow a horizontal path, which concentrates more on programming; a vertical path, which moves from programmer to program analyst or designer to project leader and then management; and a third, more technical path, which leads to a systems engineer position.

Finally, there's the **Financial Management** Program, yet another GE training program, which consists of rotating work assignments and courses over about a two-year period. FMPs cite the six-month rotation schedule and the diversity of assignments as the factors that interested them.

"It's a well-developed program," a current FMP said. "The coursework is basically from a college textbook, the functional courses take us out and show us the manufacturing process, and the rotating assignments are giving us the hard experience. Just a year and a half in the program has made me more competitive and helped me progress."

FMP classes are held once a week for two hours. The first-year curriculum focuses on accounting and financial reporting; the second year includes business planning, auditing, and management and presentation skills. "It's not like getting an MBA," a young woman stressed. "The courses are very GE oriented, 'this is the way we do it at GE.' They're a supplement to your job."

While the courses may not be MBA equivalents, strong performance is expected. FMPs need an 85 percent average in their coursework overall, 80 percent to pass a specific course. People who fail a course are allowed to repeat it; if they fail two, they're out.

The first assignment is based on an FMP's major and any work experience. The FMP may be assigned in account operations, cost accounting and analysis, operations analysis and planning, auditing, or information systems. Responsibilities grow through each rotation. And FMPs explain that you have to be as flexible as the program itself.

Like many of the other program participants, FMPs are evaluated every three months in an informal FMP-manager meeting, then formally after the six-month period, when they are told how they have performed and where GE sees them moving.

Following graduation from the program, most FMPs apply for jobs within the location they're currently working. But some apply for positions on the prestigious Corporate Audit Staff—a fast-track program for select FMP graduates that entails three to five years of almost constant travel auditing GE components all over the country and the world.

"That's the real fast track, because you're going all over GE, meeting people. And it's a real commitment," a young woman explained.

Some people join the Audit staff on a trial basis, work for a month, then decide whether to stay. And those who do stay on for a year but then decide they'd prefer a new assignment can be reassigned a job elsewhere in GE. Most people who get on the Audit staff stay, however, for "the successful people get placed at a higher level after it."

And that's what most FMPs say about their program, too. While there have been reported complaints (one staffer mentioned that many people believe the program is too accounting-oriented; so there is talk of change, specifically in the curriculum), the FMP program comes in for quite a bit of praise.

"I really see myself progressing at GE. There's a lot of interaction with upper-level managers. They look at us and try to determine who will be in their position," a young man summarized. "The FMP is developing young managers in a unique situation."

So those are a few of the GE entry-level training programs. That's right—a few. GE also has a Technical Marketing Program, Field Engineering Program, Software Technology Program, Research Technology Program, and Chemical-Metallurgical Management Program. Add to all these training programs the many GE locations and you've got quite a diverse company.

"Until I started working here, I had no idea how big they were or how they were put together," an engineer remarked. "There's a lot of these very small companies under this umbrella called General Electric."

And there are also a lot of entry-level opportunities.

LIFE

For trainees, life at GE means a lot of work. But it also means a lot of team spirit.

Trainees in the programs go to orientation together, they go to classes together, and they usually stay in touch after the training is over.

"You build a network that is unbelievable," a former ISMP noted. "I could go to at least three other components; one in San Francisco, one in Florida, and one in Canada, and get a job there—just because of the contacts I've made through the ISMP program."

But there are drawbacks to life at GE: trainees usually have to relocate at least once. And sometimes people are assigned to areas that are far from home and far from where they wanted to be. That's probably why many GE employees stress the need to find the right job within GE.

As one satisfied former MMP said, "This job stood out even though it was still making light bulbs. Everything they said has happened and a little more. It's great, because I'm stuck in the middle of Ohio and the job's got to make up for a lot."

DOLLARS AND SENSE

"The money isn't that great. My friends are making more, but I've been in eight different departments so I've gotten more experience."

That statement by a recent graduate of the MMP program sums up the feeling of many GE employees—the money's OK, but that's not their main reason for being here. The training and the jobs are.

According to an ISMP, the salary starts lower than those for direct hires at other companies, but every six months ISMPs receive about a 12 percent raise. There's a similar system in the FMP program—with the six-month raises based on grades and performance.

Still, money isn't the key to working at GE. As one young woman stated, "I have experience. I know I can make more money at other companies. But as long as there are opportunities at GE, I'll stay."

Another woman agreed. "Headhunters go crazy as soon as you graduate from the training program, but personally I've been satisfied. GE has done a lot for me. And I wouldn't look at another company now."

GETTING IN—TRICKS OF THE TRADE

First of all, you don't need a Master's degree to land an entry-level job at GE. Most of the programs accept people with Bachelor's degrees in—depending on the program—business, finance, computer science, engineering, math, and so on. Secondly, while GE wants people with a "technical twist," they're also looking for people with managerial and "people skills."

"The first thing we look for is GPA. It's just because we get so many resumés," an ISMP representative involved in recruitment explained. After looking at GPA (a 3.2 was one cut off point mentioned), recruiters look at major, work experience, and interest in the field. And because the programs are geared toward management, GE reportedly has found that purely technical skills aren't enough.

There's a similar emphasis in the other programs as well. Said one former MMP, "If you can't deal with people, you won't make it in manufacturing. The technical skills are a given. So you have to stress things some people don't think are important—especially interpersonal skills."

Getting into the Edison Program involves much the same blend of technical experience, good scholastic record, and people skills. One Edison engineer recommends making a follow-up phone call after the first interview and asking more questions—"anything to initiate a conversation. And maybe you'll get your resumé back on top of a pile." Co-op programs while in school are also a plus, as they demonstrate hands-on work experience and initiative.

As for becoming an FMP, again it's good grades, work experience and extra curricular activities. Generally, the recruitment process involves an on-campus interview, followed by a plant visit or on-site interview with managers of the training program you're applying for. Often there's lunch or a meeting with people currently in the program—something that current trainees said was extremely helpful in getting a feel for GE.

In brief, whatever area you're interested in, at GE you need something more than strong technical skills. "Everyone has the preconceived notion of an engineer who sits at a drafting board, doesn't look up all day long," an automation engineer said. "But there's very little of that these days. It's much more of a go-get-'em type of thing."

So whether it's for an engineering, an auditing, or a systems analyst position, the people GE wants have to be as diverse as the company itself.

THE BOTTOM LINE

GE likes its employees bright.

MATTEL

VITAL STATISTICS

- location: Hawthorne, CA (headquarters)
- revenues: $1.05 billion (1985 sales)
- rank: 1st (largest single toy manufacturer and marketer); 334 (*Fortune* 500)
- employees: 17,000 worldwide

AS SEEN FROM THE OUTSIDE

The bumper stickers on the cars in the parking lot say "Mattel: We're Having *Fun!*" They mean it. After all, fun is what they sell.

Mattel has come a long way since it was started in 1945 in a garage. Then it was a manufacturer of dollhouse furniture with a staff of eight. Now it's a toy-making giant, a large multinational corporation based in Southern California that sells toys around the world.

How did it get so big? Just ask "Barbie." Mattel introduced the world's most famous fashion doll in 1959. It was the doll that had everything—a boyfriend (Ken), a large glamorous wardrobe, cars, houses, and more—and it proved to be a huge success. She might be 27 now, but she's not over the hill yet. According to the company, 85 percent of all fashion dolls owned by girls in the U.S. are Barbie dolls.

Mattel hasn't stopped with Barbie and her well-heeled lifestyle. In the early 60s came Chatty Cathy, a talking doll. Then Hot Wheels toy cars hit the road in 1967, another roaring success.

While the old standbys are still pulling in purchasers, Mattel has been busy coming up with new items. Among the newer products that are delighting both children and management are Rainbow Brite, a soft doll, and the Masters of the Universe line featuring good guys He-Man and She-Ra. In all, the company markets nearly 450 products.

Coming up with all those new toys takes a lot of people. And that's what Mattel has. But most of them aren't the ones with the great new ideas—more than 10,000 are in manufacturing plants in the Far East. At company headquarters, 2,000 people work in design and development, marketing, product planning, and operations to design, tool, market, and sell toys.

Company headquarters look more like those of a big business than Santa's workshop—on the outside, at least. Located next to the 405 freeway just south of Los Angeles International Airport, Mattel's headquarters consist of a one-story administrative wing attached to a six-story structure that houses design and development, product planning, and marketing.

The sales and marketing functions are a lot like those in any other company involved in consumer products, and design and development of toys is as involved as designing cars or airplanes (which Mattel does—on a small scale). Mattel employs mechanical engineers, industrial designers, illustrators, and graphic artists. And, in fact, many employees worked in aerospace and automotive companies before coming to Mattel.

Now, instead of working on cars, they're working on Hot Wheels. But those small products still mean big business.

HEARD AT THE WATER COOLER— WHAT IT'S REALLY LIKE TO WORK HERE

Here's a place where the business is toys. So, in some places at Mattel, the work looks a lot like playing. Sure, employees are here to make money. But they do it through fun and games.

Especially in design and development. Mattel apparently believes that people need a free and creative environment to come up with great toys. And that's just what the design and engineering people get. Here it's jeans and T-shirts, wandering around, chatting in the halls—and, of course, toys.

Each floor in design and development is equipped with a small shop stocked with materials to build models, and there is a larger, more complete shop on the main floor. Employees are also encouraged to use the shops in their off-hours for personal projects. Sometimes those personal projects become a company-wide game.

"We had a competition where everyone was given a bucket of parts to build something that would play king of hill," said an engineer. "Everyone would build a contraption, put it on top of this dirt mound, and then flip a switch and apply power to it. These things would battle and try to knock each other off. It was something one of the workers came up with—it wasn't a Mattel function, but Mattel gives us the freedom to do that."

It's less fun and games and more bottom line and profits, however, in the other parts of Mattel. Staffers in marketing and other noncreative departments wear suits instead of jeans. When impromptu meetings spring up in the halls and elevators, everyone's talking business. But the business is toys. And that makes a difference.

PEOPLE

As you might expect, people here are generally fun-loving, outgoing, all those cheerful adjectives. But, beyond that, all similarities end.

"You meet so many diverse people here at Mattel," said a young man in design. "If you want to find a weird hobby, you can find experts on any sport or hobby that you would care to meet. It does tend to attract a very diverse crop of people."

It's not only sports and hobbies that make everyone so different. There's also quite an age range here. "It's an excellent blend of young and old workers," said another designer. "In our department, we have a lot of people with twenty- and twenty-five-year anniversaries."

What keeps them here so long? Actually, there are a few reasons. On the practical side, Mattel allows people to do what they want for a career. According to one recruiter, Mattel now has a "dual ladder" career path: different levels of jobs that are strictly technical and other levels of jobs for people who want to go into management. Before this, with one level of jobs, those who didn't want management could reach a certain level. Now, under the dual ladder, a worker can remain a designer for his entire career if that's what he wants.

According to an artist, "A senior staff designer has the equivalent pay to a manager. If you want to stay on the board and design, you can do that. We have a guy here that's done Hot Wheels for ten to fifteen years. He doesn't want to become a manager. He likes to draw cars—that's all he does is draw cars. He's really good at it, too. He can whip cars out fast. But when it comes to drawing people, he can't. So he can't design Masters products and he stays on Hot Wheels."

It's not only doing their own thing that keeps people at Mattel. There's another reason, too. Working on toys for children seems to be infectious. As one woman noted, "You find a lot of people who are long-time employees. When you stay here a long time, you tend to stay young."

You also tend to stay fairly noncompetitive. As an assistant product manager in the marketing department said, "There really isn't a sense of trying to be better than someone else. It's nice from that standpoint."

A designer concurred. "It's pretty lighthearted competition. You're not dealing with bombs here."

JOBS

The fact that the product is fun and games doesn't mean that work here is easy. Sure, there's a free-spirited environment and people are relaxed—but a lot of work goes into the toy business. The vast number of new products introduced each year, coupled with short product cycles, means that a lot of work is processed—and processed quickly.

A typical toy goes through a three-year cycle. The first year, designers come up with an idea for a toy and make the initial models. In the second year, development staffers step in and the toy undergoes product development in which safety, reliability, and manufacturing feasibility are studied. In the third year, the toy goes into production.

In addition to the design and development staffs, sculptors, modelmakers, fashion designers, and artists all contribute their part to the toy. And then there's the product planning and marketing staff, who work throughout the whole cycle, not to mention the sales department. So actually, making toys isn't child's play. It's a sophisticated art and it's big business. And as in any modern industry, the jobs tend to be highly specialized.

Entry-level people in **design and development** quickly learn that Mattel means business. There's little time for training. New hires are expected to hit the ground running and learn what they need to know on the job.

There are a variety of positions in design and development. Artists and illustrators are assigned either to product design or packaging, and they do a number of different tasks.

"If you come in as a package designer, that's all you do," said one artist. "If you come in as a product designer, all you do is product or what they call 'visual design.' I really enjoy product—it's important to do a nice package, but it's easier to change a package. In product, it's harder to change, so you have to keep on top of the project so it doesn't get away."

The people who come up with the toy ideas are the designers, the people responsible for your He-Mans and She-Ras. But having a warrior with half-inch biceps spring from your head isn't the whole picture.

"I really enjoy my job because it takes full advantage of my skills," said a designer with a background in mechnical engineering. "My favorite things are brainstorming, coming up with new ideas, and making the first model or 'bread boards,' as we call them. A lot of times that's where the fun is."

Being a designer and having a hot new toy on your mind isn't all fun, however. Once a designer has an idea, "there is a fair amount of red tape involved" getting it into production. An engineer added that, while coming up with an idea is the fun part, seeing it changed by marketing, or simply getting shot down, can be tough.

When designers come up with new ideas, they have to make a presentation to management. These presentations are both a boon and a bane to engineers. One designer pointed out that it's a good opportunity to talk to the top management on a one-to-one level.

"The most exciting thing about working at Mattel as a designer is that you get to present your invention personally to the top management of the company—the president, the vice president of marketing, and the vice president of design and development. You're on a first name basis with the president. Here I was, just out of college, and the president is shaking my hand and calling me by my first name. It's exhilarating."

Once a toy has gotten the go-ahead, it moves on to development. "That's where you have engineering done on CAD/CAM systems," said a designer. "They deal with the people who are going to make the molds. My job in design is to come up with the first bread boards and to get approvals from all the big groups—safety, marketing, and things like that. As soon as I get those, the toy is officially taken over by somebody else."

Moving up in design is generally a matter of coming up with good toys. What happens as designers climb the ladder? Well, not much, apparently. One young man who got hired after interning at Mattel said, "I started as a designer. I got promoted through a few levels—engineering designer, preliminary designer. It's all the same job. They just give you different titles and a little more money."

While design and development people are treated like stars, marketing, product planning, and other jobs within the company are just like similar positions within other industries. "The real world," as one employee termed it. "Politics, people, the grind . . ." This is where three-piece suits and hard-driving attitudes are the norm. Design and development may come up with the ideas, but the final go ahead is given by **marketing**, and as a result, people tend to move up faster in this area. "This is a marketing-driven company," observed one woman.

But the turnover is much higher in marketing, and so is the pressure. "Marketing tends to burn people out; there are so many long hours. It's a little hard to tell in marketing when you've done your job well. Design is satisfying because they pay you to be creative and that's fun. People recognize you. It's frustrating, though, because designers don't have any power over what ideas get chosen, that's all in marketing. In marketing, I have power. If I don't like something, it won't go."

But you don't have that power at the beginning. In marketing, most people start out as assistant product managers doing a lot of paperwork—like listing all the products in their area, working with documents issued to authorize new products, and more general drudge work.

"You also write memos, attend meetings. You do a lot of schlepping around getting product," explained an assistant product manager. "When I started, I was like a glorified clerk. I was the world's highest paid secretary."

A lot depends on how much a manager is willing to delegate to his or her assistant. Those assistants who are lucky end up doing much more than clerical work, and doing more of what a marketing director does. That entails making product decisions, coordinating the activities of design and development, making decisions on packages, and marketing strategy.

There's a lot of clerical work at the lower levels in **product planning**, too. Assistant product planners have the primary task of scheduling deadlines for product due dates and production scheduling. And it's sort of like working at a library at the same time, since product planning acts as an information clearing house.

"Each product planner is assigned to a group of products,"

said one manager. "Product planning was formed to centralize responsibilities for one toy. If anyone needs to find out anything about a toy, he can go to one person." As a young woman explained, "Product planning works on a three year scope—toys in production, the next year's products going into production, and the following year's toys in planning. Its responsibility is to make sure schedules are being met."

But it's not as cut and dried as it sounds. She added that the job isn't "for the type of person who feels they can get their work done in one day. Every day, no matter what level you're at, new situations come up."

"You can't miss a deadline," stressed an artist. "That's the bottom line here. I've never seen too many deadlines slip here." He added that the competitive nature of the toy industry has resulted in some basic changes that have accelerated the pace.

LIFE

"There is something special about Mattel because of the environment—it's constantly changing and constantly challenging," said a product planner. "And there is that balance between three-piece suits and blue jeans."

On the three-piece suit side, in both product planning and marketing, it pays to be diplomatic. "You have to put in your time," said a staffer. "You can't stand up and say, 'I'm good. I have ten years experience.' You have to start from scratch."

In marketing, people get to know just about everybody in the company, yet it's so busy there isn't much interaction with the rest of the marketing staff.

But Mattel tries to keep the atmosphere light. In order to keep the creative juices flowing, the company sponsors a lot of activities for the employees. Each Halloween, for instance, employees are encouraged to dress up, and awards are given to the most creative costume.

Still, the company isn't everyone's life. "It's kind of like a family, but it's not real close-knit," one staffer noted. "Every Halloween during "Halloween Happenings," you get a lot of people dressing up and going out there. It's fun. But you get a lot of people out there just watching them. They stay for ten minutes and then they disappear."

DOLLARS AND SENSE

A lot of engineers don't consider designing toys when they get out of school. But little do they realize that it pays as well as jobs in aerospace.

Engineers start in the high 20s, while a marketing person will start in the high 20s or low 30s. "The salary depends on some other things—where they went to school, what kind of GPA they had, what kind of experience they've had," a recruiter said.

Add to the competitive salaries a strong benefits package and, yes, Mattel is similar to an aerospace company. But there is one difference—at Mattel, you can buy the company's products at the company store.

GETTING IN—TRICKS OF THE TRADE

One way *not* to get into Mattel is to try anything cute with personnel. An engineer who was bound and determined to work at Mattel said, "I got the name of a woman in personnel, called her every day, sent her red roses. Nothing happened. The most you can expect from personnel is that they will forward your resumé to an appropriate manager. If you can get that person's name, they would be the person to do wacky things with."

The resourceful engineer was able to get a job by writing the president and saying that he had a great invention he wanted to show the company. "Of course at the time I had no great invention," he said, but added that he quickly put together an electromechanical gizmo that showcased his talents. He got an interview and a job.

In design and development, a good number of the employees have come from Arizona State University, where Mattel sponsors an annual toy design contest. Winners are usually considered for a paying internship program, in which the students work at Mattel during the summer of their junior year. Many are hired after graduation. Mattel is in the process of expanding its contest to campuses in the east, including MIT.

In marketing, it helps to have an MBA. A marketing staffer who came over from design said that while an MBA isn't absolutely necessary to do the job, "if you want to come to marketing from the outside, it really helps to have it. Practically everyone they've hired from the outside as an assistant product manager has an MBA." He added that Mattel looks for people "with energy, because it's a very time-consuming job. You work long hours, much more than in design."

Prior work experience is also critical for those looking to get into marketing or product planning. A personnel staffer said that of about seven hundred people who were hired last year by the company, only a small percentage were at entry level.

THE BOTTOM LINE

If you're creative, work hard at play, and are young at heart, Mattel has room in its toy box for you.

XEROX

VITAL STATISTICS

- locations: Stamford, CT. (headquarters), nationwide offices
- revenues: $8.97 billion (1984)
- rank: 38th (*Fortune* 500)
- employees: 103,500

AS SEEN FROM THE OUTSIDE

Xerox's first general-use office copier weighed 648 pounds, was as large as an office desk, and made seven copies a minute. Not much by today's standards, but that was in 1959. It started a business revolution, and transformed a small struggling company named Haloid-Xerox into a giant corporation named Xerox—with $9 billion in revenues in 1985. And that's not enough for 1986.

Xerox is now ready for its own revolution—selling its way into the broader market of office systems and automation. Sure, it developed photocopying, but now it sees its growth in systems.

Not that photocopying isn't profitable. It is, but other companies have eaten into Xerox's once overwhelming share of the market. Today, Xerox has about 50 percent.

Not bad, but Xerox wants growth. And the future is more than proper. Xerox's office systems concentrate on what it does best, using photocopying, printing, and document storage as a base for an office system—and to sell it well.

The sales force is key. Xerox's salespeople used to compete against each other, which was good for the division, but not good for "Team Xerox." So Xerox has merged them into one giant group of 4,200 salespeople who will sell all Xerox office products. Twenty million dollars was spent training 3,500 of them, all former photocopier salespeople, in computers. It's a big commitment—but Xerox is ready.

HEARD AT THE WATER COOLER—
WHAT IT'S REALLY LIKE TO WORK HERE

Xerox is known as a sales-oriented company. And that's the truth. Sure, you've got your engineers, financial people, and support staff working here. But it's the salespeople who have made Xerox a household word. And they're the people we talked with.

Xerox seems tailor-made for people who love money, competition, money, hard work, money, selling, and money. Do you copy? To work at Xerox, you'd better believe that money makes the world go round.

That almost single-minded concentration is obvious when you walk into any of the Xerox sales offices. It's actually a bit like walking into a bank vault. Step off the elevators and there's no visible reception area—just doors with Xerox signs beside them. To get behind those doors, you've got to punch in the correct number code into an electronic lock. Only then do you get the pleasure of seeing a reception area and offices.

At some of the sales offices there are great views outside the windows, but the offices or cubicles themselves tend to be a bit drab. Decorations are virtually nil—save for award plaques occasionally hung behind someone's desk, or sales charts lining hallways or posted on doors and bulletin boards. Those Xerox employees who fancy themselves interior decorators might pin up a snapshot of their boat, but that's about as far as it goes aesthetically. Xerox cares more about good business than good looks.

That's not to say it's a dry, stuffy, super-corporate environment. Sure, it's a *little* corporate. But there's a looseness about Xerox offices. People wander around, poke their heads into co-worker's cubicles and chat. Everybody seems to know everybody else, where they are, how their accounts are doing. And it seems as though there's always a conversation going on somewhere—usually about business, of course, but in a relaxed way.

One staffer summed it all up: "It's more loose, more easygoing than a lot of companies. Sure, it's high pressure, it's highly competitive, but all the players have a lot of fun."

And that's the best way to make money . . .

PEOPLE

"I wear my white shirt and my wingtip tassels, but still I'm not a stuffed shirt," said one young man. "I can have a good time. And that's the kind of person we get here. We don't get real straight-arrow business people like IBM."

What you do get here are superachievers who seem to know what they want.

"Most of the people here are outgoing; they're aggressive and they're motivated by money," an outgoing, aggressive staffer said. "I think that's a real biggie. Everyone's income-motivated."

"Once you get here, your training will be intense, but you'll get through that. Then you just have to be successful and never accept no for an answer," a fast-moving young woman said.

"You have to be somebody with a high level of enthusiasm and energy and somebody who understands that this is not an easy business," a manager added. "It's a tough business—long hours and long days. And it can be extremely frustrating *and* extremely rewarding."

Still, Xerox people aren't only workaholics. Sure, a lot of them are. But there's another side to them, too. "I've developed a lot of friends here," one staffer commented. "It's a young, progressive environment. And anyway, we have to be good talkers. We have to be social to survive in this business."

But Xerox employees don't just survive—they succeed, or die trying.

JOBS

Sales reps at Xerox learn selling the old-fashioned way—door-to-door. That's what entry-level "New Business Representatives" do.

"You get a territory, a couple of towns, and you just start knocking," an account rep said. "It gets depressing at times, you're knocking on all these doors and getting a lot of rejections."

But new business reps persist. And many realize that it's a great way to learn sales. Hirees are trained in basic selling skills, where they learn an approach called "SPIN"—Situation questions, Problem questions, Implication questions, and Needs payoff. Essentially, the rep begins the sales calls with a situation question, such as "What kind of work are you doing most often?" Then it's on to problem questions, "Are you having difficulty copying red ink with your present copier?" Ideally, the customer will agree that there is a problem. So the sales rep moves to an implication question.

"What you want to do through implications questions, like 'Doesn't that affect employee morale?' is build the need up as large as possible," explained a fast-tracker. "So that it comes to the point that they're saying, 'Give me an answer to my problem.' That's when you go to the needs payoff, when you're basically saying, 'Wouldn't it be of value to you if Xerox would solve that problem?' "

It sounds easier on paper than it is in practice. New business reps are trying to sell non-Xerox customers on Xerox—and that takes a lot of confidence, perseverance, and just plain optimism.

"You've got to be able to put up with the rejections and just keep going," a former new business rep stated. "You can't take any of it personally."

A thick skin isn't the only thing new business representatives need. They've also got to be self-motivated. It's up to the individual to get out there every day, keep knocking at those doors, and meet the quota. Those who do meet their quotas and survive the rigors of door-to-door selling for a year to a year and a half move on to become Account Representatives. Most account reps handle about fifty midsize companies that are already Xerox users. It's still a lot of work, a lot of hours, and a lot of selling, but it's not quite as tough.

After roughly six months in the field, account representatives are sent to Xerox's international trading headquarters for sales, service, and administrative employees in Leesburg, Virginia, for a three-week course in selling skills. As one staffer explained it, "You go down to Leesburg and it's like a big brainwash. Everything's Xerox, Xerox, Xerox. You walk out and you're ready to conquer the world. You're flying high. It's good medicine. You're really psyched up on the company."

Xerox employees say that the training facilities are like a large university, the courses "very, very intense," covering subjects like time management, customer care, managing priorities, and in-depth sales training involving role-playing. And the training doesn't stop after that first three-week course. Each year, employees are sent back for at least a week to brush up their skills, learn new specialties (like high volume training), and make their selling even more profitable.

Account reps who've been through training and proved themselves in their field eventually move on to other assignments. They may become High Volume Marketing Executives, and support about ten other account reps on high-volume business; they may move up into a "major customer selling environment" as account managers and have responsibility for large regional accounts; or they may be National Account Managers and handle major national accounts.

Those people who don't stay as generalized sales reps (handling an entire product line) may also narrow down their focus and become Specialists in any of the Xerox categories, handling only personal computers, typewriters, or large copiers, for instance. But whatever position a Xerox salesperson is in, one thing is constant—there's always a lot to learn.

First, there's product knowledge—knowing everything and anything about the complete line of copiers (fifteen to twenty models), the different personal computers, laser printing equipment, electric typewriters, facsimile equipment, and printers, to name just a few categories.

And that's not all. "You not only have to know what each product does, you've got to know what the competition's does," a successful rep stated. "And what kinds of applications the customers have that are applicable to the product."

No wonder one young woman maintained that "you're inundated with data and learning and it's constantly changing."

And somehow, in between digesting new numbers and learning about new products, Xerox staffers sell. And sell and sell and sell . . . A rep will have three to four sales calls a day. And those calls are the part of the job that most people like.

"It becomes a game, and I enjoy it," an enthusiastic go-getter said. "It's two people, the customer and yourself, talking business, and it's 'who's going to win . . . ?' The biggest thing I've found is having them trust you. Look them in the eye and have them see that trust. Most of the time you get good business out of it."

Some people never want to leave their sales positions (and their sales commissions), and at Xerox, they can stay as sales reps for life. But people who continually get that good business and who want to manage people instead of accounts may be chosen as management candidates. Would-be managers go through a panel interview process, an hour and a half session in which they're presented with six situational questions. The applicant is expected to take four members of the panel through the problem-solving steps, and is graded on his or her performance. If you come out with a top grade, you become a "ready-now" candidate for sales management, meaning that, should a manager's position open up, you're "ready now" to step into it.

Good sales technique and high performance aren't the only things managerial candidates are expected to have, though. Staffers here stress that it's important to let everyone know that you're interested in moving up. And it's good to apply the selling skills you learned in the field right in your own backyard.

"I know who makes the decisions for my next career move," said one young woman. "And that's the person I play to." At Xerox, the selling just never stops . . .

LIFE

"Without numbers, you won't go anywhere," a two-year staffer said. "Every month, this district will put out a list of where all the sales reps stand against plan. And it's a little incentive. You don't want to be at the bottom of the list. So you compete with everyone in the office."

Yes, as one would expect, since this is a high-pressured selling environment, the competition can get a bit intense. But most employees don't seem to mind that.

"Sure, there's competition inside," said one young man cheerfully. "It's good, it's healthy. You want competition because it's going to make everyone do even better."

And that's how a lot of Xerox people feel. It's not cutthroat, but just plain old competitive. Staffers talk about their accounts together, they compare their sales over drinks after work. And they seem to get along. But no wonder. They're all doing the same thing—working very hard to make those sales and beat that competition.

"I never saw myself as a workaholic," a recently promoted employee said. "But coming here, now I work like a nutcase. I leave here at 7, 7:30, go home, eat, then work again."

"I haven't taken even two weeks off for vacation in years. And there are nights when all of your friends are going out for drinks and you've got to stay home to write proposals," echoed a young woman.

So is this life in the fast-lane worth it? You bet.

"At the age of 25, I never expected to make this kind of money," a fast-talking young man said. "When you get a bonus check for close to $30,000, you'll keep working."

Who wouldn't?

DOLLARS AND SENSE

Here's where all the hard work pays off. Xerox sales reps get paid 60 percent salary and 40 percent commission, which means that those who hustle can make out like bandits.

Generally, new people start out at around $20,000, but the income potential in the first couple of years is about $35,000. After that, the sky's the limit, with salaries of $70,000 not uncommon. Most people are pretty satisfied with the money picture here.

"My first year out of college, I didn't plan on making the kind of money I made here," said one happy employee. "I was thoroughly thrilled by it. It made me work even harder. The motivator was money—and Xerox knows it. That's why everything here is compensation driven."

Most employees are after the high sales that will win them one of the many incentive awards. When Xerox says it's incentive driven, it's not kidding. Among other things it offers "spiffs" on products it wants to move.

"They want all the sales reps marching to the same tune," a staffer explained. "If they raise the compensation on one product, the know all the reps will be pushing that one product. The reps will be making money on it and the company will meet its objectives."

And that makes Xerox profitable and Xerox employees very happy.

GETTING IN—TRICKS OF THE TRADE

Sales technique will get you everywhere. The one thing every Xerox employee stressed was "closing" the interview, asking right out for that job when you're done talking.

"*Ask for that job!,*" a manager emphasized. "So many people walk out and don't ask for it. And what I'm trying to learn during that interview is whether this person can sell me on himself. If he can, he can sell a product."

It's not all that tough getting the interview with Xerox. It's big on hiring people straight from college with BAs. The key is most definitely the interview itself. It's not a time to be polite and genteel. You just have to take off the kid gloves and show them you can sell yourself as well as you could sell a copier.

There's also a test people take before the interviews—basic skills like language, math, and so on. "They also ask what it is that motivates you and what you want your income to be," a sales rep explained. "They have a list like $10,000, $20,000, $50,000. And obviously, if you're going to be in sales, you want to put $50,000 to let them know you're income-motivated."

Beyond that, staffers recommend leaving an interview knowing when the interviewer will call you. "And if you haven't heard from them in three to four days, give them a phone call," a successful woman said. "Because it's that kind of persistence that they're looking for."

As for the final word? One staffer summed it up succinctly. "To work here, you can't take no for an answer. No is unacceptable.

THE BOTTOM LINE

Selling makes the world go round.

ENTERTAINMENT

If the glamour of sitting around a movie set or a recording studio, schmoozing with the stars, is what draws you to the entertainment world, forget it. The only people who regularly do that are the secretaries and the folks who are already rich and famous themselves. Everyone else is too busy trying to claw his or her way to the top to have time to hang out with the talent. Entertainment is a hard-driving, jockeying-for-position business.

There are no figures available for the number of people who work in records or film. A major studio may have under a thousand employees, although that number can jump dramatically when production is in full swing. During the boom period of the seventies, the record industry hired new people by the bus-load; but when the crash came in 1980, many were laid off. Things have settled down a bit now, but an average record company now employs only three hundred staffers. And the competition is fierce in both fields—there are probably as many people trying to break in as there are already working.

So, once you break in, how do you rise to the top? The answer is, any way you can. But if there is no standard path for career advancement—and there isn't—the one sure thing in both records and film is that nearly everyone starts at the bottom. Schooling is not a requirement, although a student film award or time spent at a college radio station may help. People without experience frequently begin in reception or the mailroom; those with a little industry background might jump in as someone's assistant. But from there, moving up takes luck, timing, contacts, ambition, and the ability to find a way.

Now for the good news. Money in the entertainment industry can be pretty good. Entry level positions in film usually start around $20,000 at the majors—not enough to buy a house in Malibu, perhaps, but not bad. People who figure out a way to move can do a *lot* better. A mid-level studio executive may earn $150,000, and for a top producer, director, or highly placed executive, the numbers can boggle the mind. Records are not quite as lucrative, with starting salaries usually in the high teens. Only a very few in the music business make incredible amounts of money; most will settle in the $60,000 to $80,000 range. Still, an income in the high five figures is nothing to sneeze at, and just think of all those free records and concert tickets . . .

The most "glamorous" career in the record industry is **Artists & Repertoire** (A&R), which involves finding and signing new acts for the label. A&R people sift through hundreds of tapes, visit young bands in scuzzy bars, and listen to as many records as possible in their search for hits and trends. The route to A&R can be from a secretarial position, from the legal department, or from virtually anywhere in the company. The only thing that people who move into A&R should have in common is an ability to spot "diamond in the rough" talent.

Runner-up for most glamorous job, but even more difficult to get, is that of **Producer**. This position involves working with artists in the studio, deciding on songs to be recorded, supervising the "mix," and watching the budget. Producers sometimes come from A&R, sometimes move up from being recording engineers. More and more often these days, the producer is the musician himself. This is one of those jobs that can pay off big . . . if you produce the hits.

The people who are probably under the most pressure in the record industry are those who work in **Promotion**. A field promotion job involves getting a label's new records on the air in a given area. These may number from five to twenty a week, and they are competing against all the other labels' new cuts. Promotion people try to get their records on the air by playing them for radio station programmers. They also have to stay on top of the numbers of requests, sales, and the "rotation" (the number of times a record is played each day) at other stations, all of which can influence a programmer's decision. Promotion people have to demonstrate an inventive and almost fanatical ability to get people to listen to music. The route upward for field staffers who don't burn out is to regional and then national promotion manager, and then to VP of the department.

Top management at a record company usually comes from these three areas, A&R, promotion, or producing. But not always. Sometimes legal types get the top spot—as Clive Davis did at Columbia. And sometimes the big jobs go to "outsiders," such as Irving Azoff, former manager of The Eagles, who recently moved into the presidency at MCA Records.

One thing that records and film have in common is that people with the ability to anticipate the public's taste may make a bundle, but they always have to remember that they're only as good as their latest hit. If the lucky streak runs out, they, and everyone connected with them, can be back on the street. That makes for a lot of insecurity, up and down the ladder.

Aside from the insecurity and the potential for big money, working in film production is completely different from working in the record business.

The job that nearly everyone in film, tape, or television production wants is that of **Producer**. There are a lot of variations on the theme, but, in general, producing means finding a "property" like a book or script, putting together the "package" of writer, director, and stars, overseeing the shooting of the show, and finally, ushering the project through editing and release.

There is no set way to become a producer. Very occasionally, someone will be promoted into the position, but producers are usually self-made. If you've got the glimmerings of a story idea and some money behind you or a friendly director who's willing to string along, you can call yourself a producer, and a lot of people do.

Some routes toward this goal are better than others, and **Development** is one of them. Developers look for story ideas in magazine and newspaper stories, talk to writers and their agents about scripts or books, and develop these ideas into finished and, ideally, shootable scripts.

One entry-level development job is that of **Story Analyst** or **Reader**. This position involves reading scripts or books that are submitted to the studio, summarizing the plot, describing the characters, and recommending the property—or not—for production. On many lots, readers are unionized and make roughly $600 a week. Others use only freelance readers, who may be paid anywhere for $50 to $100 per assignment—with no fringe benefits. Ouch!

Another possible route to producing is through Production itself, the nuts and bolts of the business; scheduling and budgeting the show, bringing in the equipment, hiring the crews, and shooting the picture.

The most basic entry-level job is that of **Production Assistant** (PA), which involves making copies of the call sheet (which tells cast and crew who, what, when, and where), collecting time cards, running for coffee and general "gofer" duties. PAs who work on the set are approved and controlled by the Directors Guild, and this means that after working two hundred low-paying days they can move up.

What they move up to is the position of **Second Assistant Director** (AD). Seconds draw up the call sheets, get cast members in and out of makeup and wardrobe, put out the production report (which tells the studio who did what, for how long, and why), make sure the crew knows what's going on and is ready, and act as a liaison between the shooting company and the office. It's at this point in their careers that most people start wondering if it's all worth it. Second ADs are the first in and last out on the set, which frequently means sixteen-hour days. And the fact that they're the lowest men on the totem pole with any responsibility means that they get the brunt of everyone else's politicking and frustrations.

If they last, they go on to become **First Assistant Directors**. First ADs are the ones who shout "Quiet!" and "We're rolling!" on the set ("action" is reserved for the director) and they are responsible for scheduling a show—deciding, for example, whether to shoot the airplane stunt on Wednesday, or postpone it until the weather looks better. They also decide what time everyone should start work and when it's time to quit. And sometimes the First AD will get a shot at directing a "second unit" (scenes that take place away from the main, or first, unit without sound or principal actors involved). Because they are responsible for everything that happens on a set, First ADs take the heat when shooting is behind schedule or over budget.

Then they move up to director, right? Sorry, try again. If a First AD decides to move up (and a lot of them don't) one possible next step for those who can wangle it is to the position of producer. Those who want to leave the set, but don't want to try their hand at producing yet, may become a **Unit Production Manager** (UPM). This position is equivalent to that of top sergeant in the Army, and is usually the first to be filled on a production. The job involves the initial "boarding" (scheduling) of the show, budgeting, hiring the crew, renting the equipment, securing the film stock, and making sure that the cast and the exposed film negative are insured. As shooting goes on, the UPM works with the First AD to revise the schedule, and reports to the producer and the studio as to the status of the project. Producers sometimes don't want the studio to know *everything* that's going on in a production, so UPMs have to be good diplomats.

Because UPMs have a thorough grounding in the nitty-gritty of the production of a show, they often become producers—if they also have a hot property under their arm, a lot of ambition, and the ability to navigate through the studio hierarchy. Many decide to stay where they are.

One last job description. The **Studio Executive** decides what projects a company wants to get involved with and is responsible for the successful production, marketing, and release of a picture. These people move into their positions from development, producing, legal, and frequently from one of the major talent agencies. The life span of an executive at a given company may be as short as three years. If the hits aren't rolling in by then, it's time for everyone to move to a different studio. Imagine the Mad Hatter's tea party with millions of dollars at stake and you're close to the idea.

And that's entertainment. A lot of hard work and long hours, a lot of insecurity and muscling for status, and some big rewards if everything goes right. Did we mention that it can also be a lot of fun?

A&M RECORDS

- locations: Los Angeles (headquarters); New York
- revenues: N/A
- rank: 6th (pop records)
- employees: 280

AS SEEN FROM THE OUTSIDE

A garage in Hollywood was the birthplace of A&M Records. In 1962, Herb Alpert, a former Army trumpeter, and Jerry Moss were playing around with a song written by a friend, adding an Americanized mariachi rhythm, and overdubbing the roar of a bullring crowd. Scraping together a couple of hundred dollars, the two friends produced the record they called "The Lonely Bull" by The Tijuana Brass. When the record started to take off, Alpert and Moss immediately formed A&M Records and released a "Lonely Bull" album. Sales were good, but when the song became the theme of "Clark's Teaberry Shuffle" ads on radio and TV, the numbers went over the top. A&M's Brass had turned to gold.

Chairman Moss, Vice Chairman Alpert, and President Gil Friesen, who joined the company in the mid-sixties, have a long-standing commitment to offbeat pop music. In the old days artists like Sergio Mendes, Procol Harum, Paul Williams, Cat Stevens, and Quincy Jones found a home at A&M. The tradition continues today with Bryan Adams, Joan Armatrading, The Police, Simple Minds, UB40, and Sting. It's a commitment that has meant a hearing for many artists who otherwise might not have found an audience. And it's a commitment that has made A&M the largest independent label in the country. Not bad for a couple of guys experimenting with a tape recorder in a garage.

HEARD AT THE WATER COOLER—
WHAT IT'S REALLY LIKE TO WORK HERE

No one has ever described working in the record industry as laid back. It's a high-pressure, fast-paced business, where yesterday's hits don't mean a thing if tomorrow's hits aren't in the pipeline.

But A&M is one company that tries to foster a low-key attitude in the midst of lunacy. As one staffer put it, "There isn't a lot of yelling and screaming here—this place runs on positive reinforcement. And it all comes down from the top."

One employee described it as a "homey company," and the relaxed atmosphere is part of the physical setup. Quaint, cozy bungalows house some of the comfortable offices, and none of the buildings is more than two stories high. The offices are part of a two-block complex on the site of the old Charlie Chaplin Studios in Hollywood. In fact, the footsteps in the cement on the lot are reported to be Chaplin's.

Still, there's no doubt that you're walking into a record company here. If the receptionist with the Grace Jones hairdo doesn't tip you off, the music blaring out of the offices will. And despite the effort to keep it relaxed, things *are* hectic—phones are ringing, people are running around worrying about this or that deadline, and there's a general feeling of excitement.

A&M staffers pride themselves on the differences here, though. As one put it, "It acts like a major label, but it's close-knit. Everyone knows each other and when push comes to shove and you really have to work on something, people know each other well enough and they all have the same goals. It works well."

PEOPLE
Committed young workaholics who live and breathe music would fit right in at A&M. How else would you survive the long hours and the pressures inherent in this industry? Enthusiasm is the most important requisite. As one earnest young man said, "It's a sin to become jaded in this business."

That enthusiasm usually shows up long before you start here. Nearly everyone had jobs in music-related fields prior to landing at A&M—working in college radio, retail record stores, "fanzines," playing in bands. One staffer started his own record import company, and when he lost his backing, took a job as a receptionist at A&M. "I really paid my dues, went the whole route, and had to start all over again. But I love records, and I love music."

Loving it makes the long hours easier to take, too. And there can be other rewards. As one fast-riser stated, "Days can be 9 A.M. to midnight, because you have to go to shows all the time. But I love going to shows and I love being able to meet the artists. I had to pick up Sting at the airport and I was thrilled to death. I'm still star-struck. If it starts getting to be work to go to a show then you're in the wrong industry."

JOBS

There are a lot of hot seats in this business, but Artists & Repertoire (A&R) and Promotion are generally conceded to be the hottest.

A&R is where it all happens first. This is the department that decides which artists will be signed and then ushers the bands through the studio, all the way to choosing album art and liner notes. Every other department of the record company depends on A&R—if they haven't signed the artists, there aren't going to be any hits.

This is one company that accepts unsolicited tapes for consideration, and the number of tapes that the A&R people have to weed through in search of a potential hit can be mind boggling. "I get a hundred tapes a week, on average," said one weary staffer. "I'm always two months behind. And you only pursue one out of five hundred tapes."

Deciding what to pursue is the heart of the matter. It's not just a case of personally liking what you hear. The artist also has to be commercial and fit into the A&M roster. As one veteran explained, "A lot of stuff that you hear is signable—but not for a major. We're playing hardball. We have trouble getting Joe Jackson on the radio, so we're not going to sign someone who needs a lot of development."

Even a tape that seems commercial won't always be signed. "At times I'll hear things that I know are hits, but they're not A&M. We're not going to spend big bucks to get recognition for a generic band when we could use that money to do a Sting video. One thing you hear around here is 'they're very good, but they're very pop.'"

A&R people are always looking for the next trend—their jobs, and the company's bottom line, depend on it. The burn-out rate can be high. As one veteran put it, "You can get fired at one place and then hired at the next—where they just fired all their people. And if a company doesn't have any hits for a while, they may fire the entire A&R department."

But there are compensations. As one A&R staffer said, "People see me come in at noon and leave at three and say, you've got a great job. What they don't realize is I've got a lot of work outside the office—going to clubs, going to showcases, in the studio. Then you hear your record on the radio and you tell them, *that's* where I've been. It makes it all worth it."

The task of getting the record on the all-important radio falls to the **Promotion** department. And it's not easy. A&M may be trying to "break" anywhere from three to seven records a week, while Warner Bros. and CBS, the giants of the industry, may be working fifteen each, and the other labels may contribute ten or twenty to the pot. Radio stations generally "add" only three or four new records to their playlist every week, so the competition for airplay is enormous.

Promotion people attempt to get a record added by playing it for the station's program director. That can be tough. As one staffer said, "Everyone will listen to Sting's new record, but a new artist . . ." Being part of a label with a reputation for quality, like A&M, helps.

A lot of promotion people try to increase their chances of getting adds by spending time with program directors, doing favors for them—and spending money. But knowing what records fit a station's playlist is important here. "Of course you take people to dinner and to clubs—but it's not about $100 dinners. It's about the music and whether it works for them or not. And you're taken more seriously if you have a street sense of the music."

But the radio add is only the first step. Getting the record played (or "rotated") frequently is the key to moving it up the charts. As people like to say here, "the job's not done until the record's No. 1."

Wednesday is the cutoff point for radio stations to put together their playlist for the following week, so Monday and Tuesday are incredibly hectic. On Wednesday, promotion people catch up on paperwork and have a national conference call to talk about what's been accomplished, what the goals are, what the new "breakers" are. Thursdays are spent going over R&R (*Radio*

& Records, a trade publication), *Billboard*, and advertising and sales figures with the marketing people. Then on Friday they start calling stations again setting up for Monday and Tuesday. It never ends. As one young man put it, 'It's fun and it's an adrenaline high, but it's such a rat race. You can't survive more than three or four years—you're always under the gun."

Another added, "It's tons of work—that's why there's so much pressure. You get a record add at a station and the sales department doesn't care. They want to know what the rotation is and how it's moving up the charts."

That's why people who don't love the business and who don't love the music don't last long in this industry. One enthusiast summed it up, "Work is the same thing I do for fun. I mean, I get *paid* to ask guys to play Bryan Adams or Sting."

LIFE
A&M prides itself on being a small, artist-oriented company. That's important to a lot of people here. "Take Joan Armatrading," said one staffer. "She really hasn't had what you could say was a major hit, but they've stuck with her because they value her music and her talent. That says something to me."

Of course, A&M wants to—and does—make money, but other considerations do enter in here. One music lover said, "The bottom line *is* a buck, and it's no picnic. But it's one of the few businesses where decisions are not completely based on the buck. If you're considering dropping a brand of soap, that's one thing. When you're talking about dropping a band it can get very emotional."

The fact that this is a small label also means that top executives know everyone in the company, and that's good for morale. One young employee said, "I can call the president and he'll take my call. It makes you feel special, and that's what A&M is about."

There's a feeling here that no one starts at the top, everyone works his way up. As one go-getter put it, "Once you're in, you're part of the family. Even if sometimes you feel as if you're getting the shaft when you have to run around looking for fresh-squeezed orange juice for Sting, still you're in, and if someone decides to leave you might move up." Added another, "They want people who will be some place else a year later. They promote from within, and we're small enough so that enthusiasm and talent still make a difference."

And enthusiasm for the music is still the bottom line here. As one staffer said, "People are here because they love music—and that attitude toward music and toward the artist is why this is the largest independent label in the country." Asked why *he* was at A&M, he said with a laugh, "I'm in it because I can play music in my office and no one tells me to get to work."

DOLLARS AND SENSE

This is a glamour industry and people in glamour industries make a lot of money, right? Not necessarily. Since the boom of the seventies and the bust in 1980, budgets have been tight in the record business. And a lot of people want to get in, so salaries reflect the oversupply of eager beavers.

Entry-level jobs can pay in the teens and the next step up may bring in $20,000 to $30,000. Sure, there are some thirty-year-old millionaires around, and that does inspire people. But money isn't what keeps people here.

Said one young man, "I'm making $20,000 a year and I know guys who park cars that make more money. But this is a great place. I know people who are willing to take a cut in salary to work at A&M."

Because these people are music lovers, the "perks" that come with being at a record label help. "If I were working at another job I'd be spending a lot of money on concert tickets and albums anyway, so it balances itself out in a way," said one staffer.

The general perception here is that if you love music, love what you're doing, and work hard, the money and the success will come. And loving it is the bottom line. As one young woman put it, "I really don't think I could be happy doing anything else."

GETTING IN—TRICKS OF THE TRADE

In order to get in, you already have to *be* in. One publicity assistant explained it this way; "It's a very incestuous field. They like to hire from within the industry. Once you're in, no matter how you got in, you're better off than someone who's out."

Internships, college radio, and working in retail record outlets are recommended ways of breaking through the barrier and making contacts at the label. "We get stacks and stacks of resumés and everyone has degrees, but it's the experience that's important, and who you know," said one staffer.

Once you do get in, be prepared to start at the bottom. The reception area and the mail room are the favorite beginner spots. As one cum laude graduate said, "Sometimes people take it for granted that you're a moron when you're working as a receptionist. They assume that is your destiny in life, to sit there and answer phones. It was hard for me."

But it pays off. As one veteran said, "It's tough rolling posters when you have a college education. But if you want to be the president, if you want to be the next Gil Friesen, roll those posters!"

THE BOTTOM LINE

For the confirmed music lover who thinks small is beautiful.

LORIMAR-TELEPICTURES

VITAL STATISTICS

- locations: Culver City, CA (headquarters); New York
- revenues: Lorimar: $364,674,000 (yr end 7/85)
              Telepictures: $112,210,000 (yr end 12/84)
- rank: N/A
- employees: Lorimar: 640
              Telepictures: 335

AS SEEN FROM THE OUTSIDE

When Telepictures Corp. and Lorimar announced their merger at the end of 1985, the theme song for the union might well have been "This Could Be the Start of Something Big." The merger brings together two relatively young but well-established entertainment companies, whose interests complement, rather than compete with one another.

Telepictures Corp., a New York-based company, was founded in 1978. Its prime revenue generator has been television distribution, along with the co-production and distribution of game shows and animated series. The company also brought to the merger five TV stations, *US* magazine, as well as magazines aimed primarily at the youth market.

When Lorimar was founded in 1969, it was a small company operating out of a smaller office in Beverly Hills. A hit TV series called "The Waltons" changed all that, and the company has never looked back. President Lee Rich and Chairman Merv Adelson have led Lorimar from success to success in television production, from "Eight is Enough" to a string of nighttime soap operas, headed by "Dallas" and followed quickly by "Knots Landing" and "Falcon Crest." Feature film production has not done as well as television at Lorimar. Such notable hits as "Being There," "The Postman Always Rings Twice," and "S.O.B." have been offset by a spate of forgettable, sometimes expensive, films. But, hey, this is Hollywood, where big risks and bigger money are the name of the game.

In order to spread some of that risk and, to quote Adelson, "build a diversified communications company," Lorimar acquired advertising agency Kenyon & Eckhardt (K&E) and video producer Karl Video Corp. (producer of "Jane Fonda's Workout") in 1983. In the summer of 1985, Lorimar picked up another advertising firm, Bozell & Jacobs, which was merged with K&E to create an advertising giant with billings of over $1 billion.

It is too early to tell how well the two companies will work as a team. But with a renewed commitment to feature films, a hefty slate of network, syndicated, and first-run programming in the works, the combined film libraries available for distribution, and the outside interests, this should be a powerful combination.

HEARD AT THE WATER COOLER—
WHAT IT'S REALLY LIKE TO WORK HERE

Want to get in on the ground floor of a company that's aiming for the big time? This is one Hollywood "mini-major" that's trying hard to go for the gold and doing a pretty good job of it. But there are growing pains. As one staffer put it, "In the old days everybody knew everyone else. Now you walk down the hall and no one knows you. It's losing its personal touch, but I think that's a phase it's going through. It's just growing too fast right now, but it should settle down."

Even with the rapid growth and diversification into other entertainment-related fields, a commitment to television and feature film production remains the cornerstone at Lorimar-Telepictures. And that means a commitment to successful programming. Nicknamed "the mouth that roared" for his outspoken statements, President Lee Rich was described by the *Los Angeles Times* as "a super salesman, schmoozing with and cajoling network executives till he gets what he wants." What he and Merv Adelson want are shows that are at the top of the ratings every week, like "Dallas."

Nor does anyone here forget that "Dallas" alone brought in over $60 million in revenues in 1985 in its first year of syndication. And that's the bottom line: shows that people like, shows that last (or that have "legs," as they say in Hollywood), and shows that keep on earning dollars in as many ways and in as many markets as you can find.

But with all the pressures of trying constantly to come up with hits, and with all the problems that go along with a fast-growing corporation, this is one company that still keeps a sense of humor. The tough-talking Rich jumped out of a birthday cake at a recent party given in the sleek offices on the MGM lot. As one employee observed, "How corporate can it get if the president of the company jumps out of a cake?"

PEOPLE

Sure people here are hard-driving and ambitious. Sure they're after the big money and the fame that are part and parcel of the Hollywood dream. But stepping on others on your way to the top is not the style at Lorimar-Telepictures.

As one fast-riser put it, "People aren't petty or backstabbing, and that flows down from the top. That's what I've always liked about this company. People are honorable and direct and good at what they do."

And this is one company that tries to foster a comfortable atmosphere even in the high-pressure world of show business. A young production staffer recalled, "Someone was making popcorn in the microwave and all of a sudden our chairman, Merv Adelson, is running down the hall wearing jeans and a polo shirt, yelling, 'where's the popcorn, I gotta have some popcorn!' Basically it's pretty relaxed around here."

Still, the pressure can get tough and that can make things pretty tense occasionally. But as one employee explained, "This really isn't a screaming kind of company. It's family oriented and families will scream at each other sometimes, but people are treated with respect here."

Even so, the bottom line is never very far away. As one staffer put it, "You're talking about a lot of money here—we're family but we're not folksy."

JOBS

Putting together a television show or a feature film and then getting it on the air or into the theaters has to be one of the most difficult, gut-wrenching, and "iffy" ways anyone has come up with to make it big. There's no room for pessimism in this business.

As one optimist explained it, "You have to remember that you're going to have to walk through fifty different doors before a project comes together. It can be very frustrating—so much can go wrong and it takes a long time to get anything done. But when you see something come together, that's where it all gets to be worth it."

Scripts, books, treatments (story outlines), or story ideas come in to producers from agents. These are read and evaluated by readers in the story department or by the individual producer. If the producer likes an idea, he or she first decides whether it would be right for a MOW (movie of the week), mini-series, pilot, series, feature film, or other genre, and then takes it upstairs to discuss it with the executive concerned. If the executive likes it, and the idea is aimed at network television, the story is pitched to one of the big three. If the network likes it—and doesn't have anything else on the air or in development that's similar—there may be a script order.

At that point, a writer is brought in (who may or may not have been the writer of the script or treatment submitted) and approved by the network. Outlines, a first draft, revisions, the polish, and then the final draft are all written and approved. If all these steps make it through the network, you may get a film order. Then the director must be selected—and approved—and the major casting has to be done—and approved.

In the meantime, business affairs has been checking the copyrights and negotiating with the writer, director, and cast, and the production office has "boarded" the script (breaking it down into logical shooting days) and budgeted it. If the network approves the budget and agrees on a license fee, production goes into full swing. Actors and crews are hired, equipment is brought in, locations are found, sets are built, wardrobe and props are designed, bought or rented, and the show is finally shot. Then post-production takes over—editing, adding sound and music, and finally, the all-important credits.

Then, if the network still likes it, you may have a show that gets on the air. Once. If the Nielsen ratings are bad, it's back to the drawing board—and months of work, thousands of dollars, and the time of hundreds of people are down the tube. As one employee put it, "It's a long, hard process, which is hard to believe sometimes when you see what gets on the air."

Features are a little simpler, because you don't have to deal with the networks. But the budgets are bigger and the risks are higher. And we've all seen a picture come into a theater and leave again at the end of the week. It happens all the time in this business.

Is it any wonder then that these are high-pressure jobs—even at a friendly company like Lorimar-Telepictures?

One director of production described it this way, "It's certainly not calm here, although everyone tries to remain calm. But there is a lot of pressure. There's an immediacy—decisions have to be made on the spot—and what we do has a financial impact."

That pressure can make itself felt in long hours, too. One young man who has moved up the ranks said, "We work under deadlines all the time, so I'll work sometimes on the weekends and until 10 or 11 at night."

But because he *did* have the chance to advance he doesn't begrudge the time. "The opportunity I've had here is incredible. I've never once resented any of it. If you start resenting having to give up a Saturday for your job, then you're in trouble," he continued.

It is too early to tell how the merger of Telepictures and Lorimar will affect employees of the company, but the general feeling is that it will only open up new opportunities. A staffer said that although a few people had been laid off as a result of the merger, "both companies are growing so rapidly that most of the excess should be taken care of by growth."

And opportunity is something most employees think there's plenty of at Lorimar-Telepictures. As one young employee put it, "Here, they do give people a chance. A lot of times they'll say, 'You don't have the experience but we like the way you handle things and we'll give you a try.' Of course, if you're bad at it, you're out of there."

Still, opportunity does not mean starting at the top. Usually you start at the bottom—and the bottom can get pretty low. One young go-getter, with a BA in communications, got a job making big urns of coffee at 7 A.M. Because the job involved a lot of lifting, she had to challenge the head of the department to an arm wrestling match before he was convinced she could handle the job. How does she feel about the experience? "At first I was really depressed about it, but I figured what the hell, if that's all that's available, I'll take it,' she explained. And it turned out to be a great way to meet people—nearly everyone in the company visits the coffee machines at one point. Now she has moved into a coveted production spot and has plans to be a producer—eventually.

And production jobs *are* coveted. "You may go nuts, you may have problems, but I have to kick myself because I know I'm lucky. A lot of people would kill for this job. It's fun working on the MGM lot, it's fun being able to talk to Larry Hagman. And there's always someone knocking on your door who wants the job," she continued.

Working your way up is the name of the game here. People starting in the mailroom or Xerox room and have become secretaries or assistants, then production coordinators or program executives, then associate producers or producers, managers or directors of departments. Some have gone on to become VPs.

It's a company that prides itself on hiring and promoting from within. And that's good for morale. As one staffer summed it up, "They do move people up. I'd have to feel it was possible or I'd leave. Sometimes I feel like a Barbie Doll, I'm so happy here."

LIFE

Lorimar-Telepictures is struggling to remain a "mom and pop" atmosphere, despite its rapid growth. It doesn't always work. One staffer said, "Sometimes things don't go right. At times people will just disappear, they'll be gone and you wonder what happened. But it's the nature of the business."

Still, they do try hard.

One production newcomer explained it this way, "They really do make an effort to keep people informed about what's going on and they try to keep it like a family, even though it's growing so big." Asked how they keep employees informed, she said with a laugh, "We get internal memos all the time. I swear nothing happens around here that doesn't get a memo. One comes through the interoffice mail almost every day."

Corporate meetings are also held roughly every six months to keep people informed about what's in production, what shows are being developed, and anything else that might be going on around Lorimar-Telepictures.

Making an effort sometimes means doing things a little out of the ordinary. "Wrap" parties are normally given for shooting crews at the finish, or wrap, of a production—and staff employees aren't invited. So management decided to throw a monthly "wrap" party for the entire company, so that no one would feel left out.

But growth is a fact of life at this company, and that has an impact. A newly promoted manager explained it this way: "This is still an evolving company. It is a family, but it's not a small family anymore. Having all the new faces changes things—it can't stay the same." Still, that growth offers opportunities to those with an eye for the main chance. As one go-getter puts it, "This is a great place to be because it's going to be big and it's nice to get in on the ground floor."

DOLLARS AND SENSE

This is Hollywood, and the money is *never* very bad in Hollywood. But it's not great here, unless you're at the top.

Entry-level personnel can expect to make between $300 and $400 a week—enough to live on, but nothing to write home about.

Overtime is something of a sore point at Lorimar-Telepictures. One employee explained it this way: "We don't put in for overtime here. You can, but you won't make yourself very popular doing that. I want to get ahead here and I do get a lot back, but you have to pay your dues."

And getting ahead is what it's all about in this industry. People in middle management or production positions can make anywhere from $30,000 to $60,000 a year and up. Once you get past that level—if you *do* get past that level—the sky, or your agent's negotiating ability, is the limit.

As one ambitious staffer put it, "Money is absolutely a big draw for me. I see people making a lot of money and I know I'm brighter than they are. I can do it and I will."

GETTING IN—TRICKS OF THE TRADE

Oddly enough, not that difficult—if you're determined and willing to start at the bottom.

Production is the toughest nut to crack because so many people are trying to get in. In fact, one frustrated corporate employee called it "almost hopeless." Still, lack of experience and naivete are the biggest obstacles. As a high level production staffer said, "We will see people, but if someone just gets out of film school and wants to be a director . . ." She recommends starting at a smaller film company to gain sophistication and knowledge of the industry before knocking on Lorimar-Telepictures' door.

Temping at the company is a frequently cited way to get a foothold. And it's a good place to get an overview of what's available. One young fast-riser who got her start as a temp explained, "I worked in music, in syndication, in publicity. People forget that there are more facets to the business than just shooting." Another added, "I was temping here when a job opened up. You get an inside shot at things, and they know you."

Internships are also available in some departments, and that can lead to full-time work.

But sometimes, the easiest avenues are also the most obvious. One young man was told by a friend to just go and apply for a job. "Most of the people I talked to about it were discouraging, they said it was impossible, too nepotistic. Anyway, I did fill out an application and a few days later I got a call for a job." In the two years since then, he's been promoted to a manager of a department, and has his eyes open for further moves up the corporate ladder.

As always, persistence and concentration are the keys to breaking in. Counseled a veteran, "If you're hell bent on getting in, find something you're qualified to do and don't give up. If you're talented, you'll make it."

THE BOTTOM LINE

Not as big as the "majors," but on the way.

MCA / UNIVERSAL

VITAL STATISTICS

- **location:** Universal City, CA; New York
- **revenues:** $1.65 billion
- **rank:** N/A
- **employees:** 17,700

AS SEEN FROM THE OUTSIDE

The initials "MCA" don't stand for *M*oney *C*orporation of *A*merica, but no one would be surprised if they did. Make no mistake about it, this is a huge entertainment conglomerate, the most successful producer of prime-time network television in the country. And a few other things you might have heard of, such as "E.T.," "Jaws," and "Back to the Future."

Founded fifty years ago by Jules Stein as the Music Corp. of America, a band booking agency, MCA has meant big business for a long time. When Lew Wasserman was named chief executive in 1946, he continued, with Stein, to build the company into one of the most powerful talent agencies in the U.S. In fact, the company was so powerful that it was allowed to function as both an agency and a producer for television, a practice not usually tolerated under antitrust restrictions. When MCA acquired Decca Records in 1962, however, and with that takeover, Universal Pictures, the government yelled monopoly, and MCA got out of the agency business and became basically the company it is today.

The company comprises MCA/Universal, producer of television shows and features; MCA Music, a powerful force in the music publishing business; and MCA Records, producer of the "Miami Vice" and "Beverly Hills Cop" soundtracks and distributors of the Motown and I.R.S. (Go Go's, R.E.M.) labels. Here we'll primarily be concerned with the film production side of MCA.

Money, power, and clout are all important words in the glitzy world of Hollywood, and even more so at MCA/Universal. The company's world headquarters on Lankersham Boulevard in Universal City, north of Los Angeles, has its own zip code.

But Lew Wasserman has added "businesslike," "conservative," and "stable" to his list of important Hollywood words. Called by one MCA executive "the most powerful man in the state of California," Wasserman has strived to overcome the Hollywood image with tastefully decorated offices, and conservative business practices and dress codes. And it's worked.

Being the biggest producer of network television shows, having the only stable management team in Hollywood, and being traded on the stock exchange in the range of $45 to $50 a share doesn't guarantee visibility outside California, however. One group of MCA executives, sitting down with a major New York bank to talk about financing a project, met with polite indifference until one banker finally put it together. "Oh, you're the E.T. people!" Right. And the "Miami Vice," "Kojak," "The Breakfast Club," "Magnum, P.I.," "Amazing Stories," "Rockford Files," "Murder, She Wrote," and "Hitchcock Presents" people. The list goes on.

HEARD AT THE WATER COOLER—
WHAT IT'S REALLY LIKE TO WORK HERE

Want a little security in the most insecure business in the world? Hope your "dress for success" suit can come out of the closet in the land of sequins and leather? You may have come to the right place. MCA is the biggest, most conservative, and most stable company in Hollywood.

Lew Wasserman, MCA president Sidney Sheinberg, and their management team in the Black Tower on the Universal lot have shaped a corporation that's come to be known in the industry as "The Factory." Sure they make movies, TV shows, hit records, and plenty of them, but the bottom line is important here. We're talking product—did it "open" at the box office, what were the "overnights" (ratings), did we get a network pickup? This is not a studio that allows runaway production or huge overages. Cost control, businesslike, and the "MCA way" are familiar words on this lot.

"It's like working for Chrysler," commented one veteran.

Looking at the executive suites in the Tower, you can understand his point. No movie memorabilia or show biz glitz here—

these offices are plush, elegantly decorated, filled with fine French antiques. And the people who work in the Tower dress the part. While the "penguin" suits that MCA was famous for may not be required uniform any longer, this still isn't the place to wear your latest Italian haute couture silk threads. Quietly conservative is much preferred to flash. It's an image designed to foster a "power presence"—and that image is tended carefully.

Even outside the Tower, in the more free-wheeling TV and movie production offices at the studio, the image is stressed. Production coordinators on a new show are issued a manual that tells them exactly how their offices should be set up (credenzas *behind* the desk, with scripts for distribution on the right, shooting schedules on the left).

This is a big, powerful company, and it's not about to let anyone forget it. But that has its advantages. As one producer put it, "It's so huge and so stable, the odds are better for you and for it being around for a while."

And that's important—and unusual—in the volatile, insecure business known as the Hollywood entertainment industry.

PEOPLE

"Everybody in Hollywood wants to be something else, every one's an aspiring . . . fill in the dots," said one young production staffer. "You have to be a little bit of a dreamer."

People at MCA are no different. Budding directors, producers, screenwriters, and actors are working in the mailroom, as lot runners, assistants to producers, script readers, production assistants, and Universal Studio tour guides. All are looking for their chance, hustling the deal that will make *their* dream come true. As one VP said, "It's one of the few industries where you have a good shot at making a huge score in the early years."

But these dreamers have a few things in common. Like being willing to put up with long hours, intense pressure, heavy competition, and the risk that they may be out of a job if the show or project they're working on is cancelled or goes into turnaround (a polite industry term for being put on the back burner).

One young associate producer, who averages twelve-hour days, said, "It's a real commitment that you have to make. I have no social life, and can't foresee having one—unless the network doesn't pick us up for more episodes. We're waiting to hear, but I could be out of a job very soon. One good thing about working here, though, is that if this show flops, I have a very good chance of getting on another one."

That small bit of security is what keeps a lot of people at MCA—and what attracts them in the first place. "It used to be perceived as boring if you worked for MCA. But the climate of the times has changed and now the conservative attitude and stability are much more alluring than they used to be," explained one executive.

Still, you can't be the type who hates risk and longs for security, even at MCA. Said one staffer, "The first thing I'd tell someone who was interested in working in the business is forget stability, forget your retirement pension. But the glamour and money usually overcome all common sense."

JOBS

MCA/Universal isn't known as "The Factory" for nothing. "It's like a playground, there's so much product," a fast-rising employee commented.

And the amount of "product" means opportunity—for those who are willing to take the initiative.

One go-getter, who became an associate producer on a new television series after only six months at MCA, had tried for six years at another, smaller production house. "There's a real opportunity here because of the amount of work. At a smaller place, you might get one chance in three seasons to get a job like this."

How does it feel to have finally landed an "above-the-line" position? "I've never worked harder in my life. Weekends, into the night. Never any eight-hour days and no overtime—but I do get a single card credit! It's great to see my work on the screen. The greatest motivator, scary but wonderful."

Because of the number of television shows and features MCA has consistently produced over the years, it has always been a real training ground for new people in the industry. One production manager, who got his start as a production assistant (PA) at Universal, said, "Just because of the sheer volume of work you would get the experience and they would have to move you up. You'd be young and new and dumb and you'd get thrown a problem you had no idea how to handle. But there's nothing like disaster to teach you what to do."

And, people like to remind you, this is the place where Steven Spielberg got his chance. Signed to a seven-year contract by Sid

Sheinberg while still in college, the young director went on to hit the jackpot for himself and the studio in 1975 with "Jaws."

One of the biggest problems at MCA, and at any other studio for that matter, is that once you're in, you're really on your own. Lines of progression up the ladder from PA or assistant to producer/director/writer are unclear—there are no obvious stepping stones from one position to the next. As one employee who *has* risen through the ranks said, "You have to be your own starter, you have to initiate everything. No one is going to promote you or set you off on a direction."

Glenn Kaplan, talking about the industry in *The Big Time*, put it another way. "People don't move upward in a rational career system. They seize opportunities, exploit chaos, and promote themselves shamelessly."

Many of the jobs are union (on a film set, all of them are union). You may get a set job as a Director's Guild (DGA) trainee or PA and then move up to second and then first assistant director (AD), but the logical progression ends there. Newcomers are often surprised to find that ADs don't necessarily go on to become directors. In fact it rarely happens. ADs usually go on to become production managers and from there, sometimes, associate producers or staff production executives.

Technical set people, such as the assistant cameraman, script supervisor, sound boom man, makeup and hair stylist, gaffer, grip, or set dresser, usually move up through the union ranks to more elite specializations within each craft. While good technicians are highly regarded in the industry and equally highly paid, these "below-the-line" people (collectively known as "the crew") only rarely move into the "above-the-line" positions of producing, directing, and writing.

One young production coordinator, who's been with MCA for about a year, feels that the studio is very supportive and willing to let you learn the skills that will help you move up. "They're good that way, they do encourage you to go for it."

But even with that encouragement, it's not easy. "There are just so many people here, it's easy to get lost in the shuffle. And outstanding work is not necessarily rewarded with a promotion. You have to schmooze people you think might help you, take the initiative yourself."

Still, with all the problems posed by the sheer size of MCA/Universal and the lack of a defined structure for moving up, that size offers many benefits and opportunities. One ambitious young woman said, "If you're smart and not shy, you can get a lot of experience, get exposed to a lot of things. It's a great training ground."

LIFE

Even if MCA is bigger, more stable, and more conservative than other studios, it's still The Business—and that means insecurity. Shows can get cancelled, projects put into turnaround, and the executive that you're assisting can find him or herself back on the streets (and featured in the "trades" as the latest in a long line of independent producers).

But MCA has a continuity of management, and management that consists of industry people rather than bankers or insurance brokers, so you get the feeling that you have a chance of being around for a while.

For people coming to MCA from other production companies, the size and departmentalization are a big adjustment. Elsewhere a show, whether television or feature, is housed in one production office with everyone from the coordinator to the writers and producer sharing the same roof. Here, things are broken up by department, with production staff in one building, associate producers in another, and producers in yet another.

"You may never meet the producer of your show except at the Christmas party," said one staffer. "You don't work for the show here, you work for the corporation."

That can have its advantages, though. "It does introduce you to people on other shows, which can be a plus if your show gets cancelled or you've finished shooting. It can give you a place to go," she continued.

"The main thing you have to deal with here is the corporate structure," said one young producer. "But once inside the structure you can get a fair shake if you've got the talent, energy, and the willingness to work."

DOLLARS AND SENSE

In the old days, this studio was famous for paying as low as they could go. "Once someone was established, had the experience —and could command a bigger salary—they would leave Universal."

Not anymore.

Pay now is generally on a par with the rest of Hollywood. And that tends to be high, compared with other industries.

As one production man put it, "They've realized you're absolutely nuts to hire cheap labor on a $20 million film. It's worth a little more to get good people to protect the investment."

Nonunion, entry-level positions can start in the range of $400 a week, and quickly zoom up from there. And if you get sent to shoot on a distant location, higher rates are paid.

As with most other studios, rates tend to be lower for television personnel than for features—but not always. "If you want more money it's not impossible, but you have to be very sure of your position," one employee explained.

In general, the perception is that the salaries and the benefits are very good. And benefits can include free screenings of new films, tickets to concerts at the Universal Amphitheater, and records on the MCA label, along with the standard insurance, health, and vacation packages.

"Let's face it," said one executive. "It's one of the highest paying industries in the world—but it's feast or famine. You get hazard pay while you're working for the times you won't be working."

GETTING IN—TRICKS OF THE TRADE

"The key in this business is to get a job. If you can somehow get your foot in the door, maybe you can move from there."

That advice comes from Frank Price, chairman of the MCA Motion Picture Group, in a recent *Cosmopolitan* interview.

One executive said, "It's not what you know but how big is your Rolodex and who will return your calls. If you're just out of school you may not have a telephone, let alone a good Rolodex."

"The production department has pretty much decided not to hire people right out of school anymore—there are exceptions— but it's basically policy at this point," explained one production coordinator.

So how do you get a start at MCA?

College internships, working for smaller production companies as a secretary or a PA, working at your local or state film office, are all ways to get some valuable experience. MCA itself does have an internship program run through its personnel office. But it is small and the pay is smaller—in fact, it's nonexistent.

Good office skills can be a start—typing, a facility with numbers, and a smooth phone manner can get you in the door as an assistant or a secretary. As one young man, who's first industry job was as a clerk, said, "No one wants to start out like that, but sometimes it's the only way in."

Or you could consider working as a Universal Studios tour guide. Pay starts at close to minimum wage, but you do get to know the lot and many guides move up to production office runner, and from there to assistant coordinator.

A word of caution, though, came from one production staffer. "When you're just starting out, don't talk about what college you went to. So many people in Hollywood don't have degrees—I worked for one producer who hadn't even finished high school—and they're threatened by it. That's not true once you get past a certain point in your career, but in the beginning. . ."

The biggest key to getting in is to do your homework—as in any other industry.

One veteran advised, "See movies, read film magazines, read the trades. And talk to people—if they don't have anything, but you're smart and nice and interesting, they may send you to a friend who does. But most of all persevere, persevere, persevere."

THE BOTTOM LINE

If you want the brass ring badly enough and you don't mind the risk, the opportunities are there.

WARNER RECORDS

VITAL STATISTICS

- **locations:** Burbank, CA; New York; Nashville
- **revenues:** N/A
- **rank:** 2nd (pop records)
- **employees:** 300

AS SEEN FROM THE OUTSIDE

When Jack Warner decided that his family movie studio needed an outlet for sound tracks in 1958 he wasn't envisioning a record industry giant. But that's how it turned out.

The company started small. Along with motion picture sound tracks, Warners liked comedy albums (Bob Newhart, for example) and novelty songs, such as "Kookie, Kookie, Lend Me Your Comb." It didn't stay small long, though. Warners merged with Reprise Records in 1961 and started getting into the burgeoning rock scene. It did very well in that market, and by the time WEA (Warner-Elektra-Atlantic) was formed in 1970, Warners and WEA were playing cat and mouse with CBS/Columbia for the top spot in record sales.

Warner Records and WEA are both wholly-owned subsidiaries of Warner Communications, Inc. and operate independently of each other. Well, sort of. The three labels, Atlantic, Elektra, and Warner, each produce their own records, which are then manufactured and distributed by WEA. Overseas the individual labels disappear and become WEA International. Confused? Don't worry. The distinctions can get a little blurry to an outsider. At any rate, working for Warners is not the same thing as working for WEA or Atlantic or Elektra.

Although Warners, along with everyone else, was hit by the industry crash at the end of the seventies, the company has bounced back. Its best year to date was 1984, powered by sales of eleven million copies of Prince's "Purple Rain" album. Individual figures aren't available, but the combined revenue for Warner Records,

Warner Music, and sister corporations Atlantic Recording and WEA was $817 million. And while all the numbers aren't in yet, 1985 looks even stronger, with Prince's success being joined by that of Madonna and Dire Straits.

Still, not everything's rosy here. While the record company and the WEA conglomerate are doing well, the parent corporation Warner Communications, Inc. (WCI), was the target of an expensive takeover attempt by Rupert Murdoch in 1984. And WCI suffered other heavy losses before selling its Atari, Panavision, and Franklin Mint units.

Because of WCI's problems, *Forbes* considers it especially vulnerable to corporate raiders in 1986. That could mean changes at the record company. But whatever the difficulties at the parent corporation, no one doubts that, so long as it is allowed to follow its policy of developing, signing, and supporting hot new acts, Warners will continue to be one of the leaders in the record world.

HEARD AT THE WATER COOLER— WHAT IT'S REALLY LIKE TO WORK HERE

Warners is everything you'd expect an industry "major" to be. The artist roster is filled with glamorous names, the office walls are lined with gold records, and sometimes the streets seem to be lined with gold, too. As one employee said, "They don't skimp on money here. Everything's done with exquisite taste." And the pressures are everything you'd expect in a record company of this size. Warners may not skimp on money, but that's because it expects to make a lot of it.

What you don't expect is the relaxed, noncorporate atmosphere that you find here. Being relaxed means dressing the part. As one staffer commented, "The only dress code here is—no shorts!"

Warners occupies a redwood and glass "condo," as many employees like to call it, on the edge of the Burbank Studios. No hi-tech chrome and plastic here—this is the domain of green plants, brown paneling, and old jukeboxes. And that helps. As one departmental director put it, "I have a sliding glass door out to a patio that's filled with ivy and trees. It's like being in a ski lodge. You don't even notice that you're spending eleven hours a day at your desk."

Putting in an eleven-hour day is not unusual here. Office hours in the record business are long anyway, and then there's a new act to see at a club, or a "working dinner," or a Warner artist's concert to go to. And the industry downturn in the late seventies and early eighties, when hundreds of people were fired, has resulted in tighter budgets and smaller staffs.

That means pressure, even at Warners. As one industry veteran explained, "Trying to figure out how to break a new act is a strain. You can make a good record and still not know how to sell it. You have a tremendous workload and you have to become accustomed to working in a high-pressure situation without being able to hire the help that you'd like to."

But the pressure comes with the territory in the record industry, and if you can't take the heat in this kitchen, you'd better get out, and fast. A lot of people do, but Warners has a history of hiring people who *can* take it and who stay here for a long time. Very unusual in such a fast-paced industry. As one old hand said, "I wouldn't leave here to go to a better record company because I don't know if there *are* any better companies than Warners. I wouldn't go from the frying pan into the frying pan."

PEOPLE

This is a glamour industry, and it attracts people who want the bright lights and the stardust. But if they can't do the job, they won't last long at Warners.

"This is definitely not a 'hey baby, let's have lunch' kind of place," one staffer said. "Everyone's a real music fan. It's a treat to work with people who are in it for the music, not sex, drugs, and rock 'n' roll."

This is one business where you have to be a salesman, whether you're in the sales department or not. If you're not selling the record itself, you're selling a new artist to management, or promoting the record to radio stations, or trying to come up with new merchandising gimmicks or album covers that will sell. One executive put it this way, "You have to know how to walk into a room and work that room from corner to corner to the middle. We can't use any wallflowers in this business."

But being a world class hypester doesn't get you far unless you love what you're selling. And these people love music. As one VP said, "I really still am a groupie at heart. Every time I start thinking I'm getting stale a new artist comes along, or an established artist comes up with something new, and I get excited all over again. I can't wait for 1986 to get going so we can break some of the new records we have."

JOBS

There are a lot of people here trying to figure out what combination of sound waves could be the next million seller. And a lot more trying to figure out how to get those sound waves on the air and on people's turntables, and increasingly, disc players and VCRs. It's a mixture of crystal ball-gazing, business acumen, and hard work. And it's not easy.

It starts with the people at **Artists & Repertoire**, of course. They listen to the hundreds of tapes that come in, which can sometimes be hazardous to the ears; go to grimy bars at two in the morning to hear new bands; and watch what all the other labels are doing to try to predict the trends before they *are* trends. It's a job for optimists. As one A&R director said, "You're really sitting around hoping everything you see is going to be a smash."

And it's a job for people who are sure of themselves. One staffer tells the story of an A&R man here who heard a group that he liked, but because no one else seemed interested, got cold feet and dropped the act—which went on to have major hits at another label. "You have to be secure about yourself and your judgments," she said. "If you really like it, you have to risk being wrong. You should not hedge your bets—*always* follow your instinct."

But having the right instincts is only the beginning. Once an artist is signed, all the contractual fine print has been agreed to, and the record is produced, it has to get on the air. Which is when the promotion people start their pitch.

Warners **promotion** staffers keep track of hundreds of radio stations, about half of which report programming information to *Billboard*, *R&R*, and *Cashbox*. Promotion people convey this and sales information to radio programmers in their efforts to persuade the programmers to "add" a record to their play lists. And they have to develop a rapport with those programmers. As one promotion man explained, "I try to come to them as a friend. It's more than 'hey man, play my record'."

And there are a lot of records to play. Warners releases anywhere from five to forty in a week, which can make things busy for promotion people. If a record doesn't hit, fingers may get pointed. Said one promotion veteran: "I wish every record we have would go to No. 1, but we all know that's not possible. We get the brunt when a record doesn't do well, but you get used to it. You can 't take it personally."

Once the promotion people get a record added, employees in sales and marketing come into the picture. WEA has "single specialists" who make sure that singles are in the stores, particularly if a station is "on" a record. Warner salespeople work with the singles specialists and the rack jobbers and keep track of national airplay to be sure records are in the stores for listeners to buy. Doesn't sound that interesting?

Listen to one sales manager who rose through the ranks. "The regional managers are the eyes and ears for Warners on the streets. You work with the promotion people, you cater to the acts when they come in on tour in your market, you get involved in merchandising. It was a great job and I learned an incredible amount."

How he moved up through the ranks is instructive, too. After putting in time at a record store he took a pay cut of $175 a week to work for WEA in its Chicago warehouse as an order picker. After being the low man on the totem pole, he became a single specialist for WEA, and later a Warner Bros. regional sales manager. He's still moving up.

Getting a record on the air and in the stores is only half the battle, however. The acts have to be recognizable and in the public eye if their music is going to sell and keep on selling. This task falls to the publicity staff, who deal with the press; people in video, who come up with product for MTV and related markets; and the people in artist development, who handle touring.

Since the advent of MTV, touring has slacked off, although it's making a comeback. Two men work in artist development at Warner's, one in L.A. and one in N.Y., and they hope to add a third in the Mid-west this year. At a large company like this there may be as many as twenty tours on the road at a time, which spreads these guys pretty thin.

Most people get into artist development through sales or promotion, but one young man started as a road manager for a Warner group. "While I was doing that, working my ass off and going crazy, I met the Warner's guy assigned to us. He was taking people out to lunch, buying people dinner, flying in for the show. And I thought, that's what I want to do." After he finished the tour, he started hanging around the studio, running errands and picking people up at the airport—for free. It paid off, and he landed a development job.

Was it worth it? "I work seven days a week, twenty-four hours a day, all the time. I love live shows—it's the most exciting thing in the world. This is the world's best job, but who else would want it? You have to be stupid to work this hard for so little money. I love it!"

Guess that means "Yes."

So that's what it's like working at Warners. A lot of long days and long nights, a lot of hard work, a lot of pressure and not necessarily a lot of money—but there's always the music.

LIFE

While Warner Records itself has only three hundred employees, WEA and WCI between them have several thousand. This can mean occasional problems, no matter how hard they try to act like a small label. "It's so big that sometimes communications are bound to get screwed up," said one staffer.

The bigness can be a real advantage, though. Because it's a successful industry major, Warners has the ability to attract and keep top artists on its roster. And it has the money and the willingness to go after and stand behind unknowns. "They give full investment and support to bands that take a long time to break. They give chances to artists. That means a lot to music and it means a lot to the people who hear them."

But the pressure is still intense. Said one high-level staffer, "You have to be good. There's no room for screw-ups. You're talking about a lot of money being spent on any given campaign."

Even so, most people thrive on the atmosphere here. As one young VP said, "There are crazy days when I'm having a nervous breakdown, but that's what gets me off. I love the excitement and the pressure."

DOLLARS AND SENSE

Salaries here are all over the map, with middle-management people making anywhere from $30,000 into the high five figures. Of course, it can go quite a way up from there—and quite a way down. When the bottom fell out of the record industry in the late seventies, money got tighter at all levels.

One employee who survived the crash agreed to handle his

department by himself, so Warners doubled his salary—bringing it into the *mid* five figures. Still, salaries are generally comparable to the rest of the industry. And the potential for big money is there, but not in the beginning. As one veteran put it, "Anybody who really wants to get in has to have the stamina to put up with some financially unrewarding years."

GETTING IN—TRICKS OF THE TRADE

It isn't what you know here, it's what and *who* you know. Warners just doesn't like to hire people unless they've worked for a record company before. The old catch-22.

Many staffers suggest retail record stores as a good place to start and a good place to meet label representaives and learn about the fundamentals of the business. College radio is another preferred jumping off point, giving you contacts with record promoters and sales and marketing people.

If you're interested in A&R, you might learn about the new bands in your area and write about them in rock papers or book them into local clubs. Said one A&R director, "You shouldn't be sitting at home in your living room listening to records saying you can tell what's good and what's not. You should be going to clubs because you really like doing that, you really like hearing new bands." And the clubs are where you'll meet not only the A&R staffers, but other industry types as well.

Secretarial and mail room jobs represent one avenue, but most of these people have industry experience and are trying to work their way up, too. Still, it can be done. An executive here who started as a secretary offered this advice: "When I first started I'd do anything, I wouldn't care if they asked me to walk a tight-rope. You have to get coffee, or work in the mail room or answer phones. Everybody does it."

But being willing to start at the bottom is only part of it. Counseled one old hand, "I look for somebody who understands deadlines, who doesn't start looking at the clock when it's six, who is fanatic about the job and fanatic about the music."

THE BOTTOM LINE

The big time, with a bullet.

WALT DISNEY COMPANY

VITAL STATISTICS

- **locations:** Burbank, CA (headquarters); Anaheim, CA, Tokyo, and Orlando, FL (theme parks)
- **revenues:** $1.65 billion (1984)
- **rank:** N/A
- **employees:** 28,000 (including theme parks)

AS SEEN FROM THE OUTSIDE

It seemed laughable to industry pundits back in the early twenties. Who wanted to watch the adventures of a squeaky-voiced animated mouse and his girlfriend? But Walt Disney and his brother, Roy, proved the experts wrong, and soon millions of people around the world were laughing at the antics of Mickey and Minnie. A legend, and a gold mine, had been born.

The gold mine lasted a long time. The brothers set a standard of excellence and originality for animation that is still held up as the ideal, and America loved it. Even when Walt's vision went too far ahead of the public taste, as in *Fantasia*, a box office bomb when it was first released, the legend continued to grow. By the time the sixties rolled around the Disney name had become synonymous with wholesome, quality family entertainment.

The "Wonderful World of Disney," the weekly Mickey Mouse Club, Disneyland, and the beautifully crafted cartoons, all had the Midas touch and all seemed an enduring part of the American way of life. And then the world changed, and Disney couldn't seem to change with it.

It tried, cautiously, but not much worked. Some expensive attempts were made, such as *Tron* and *The Black Cauldron*, to win back the family audiences from *Star Wars* and *Close Encounters*, but the public didn't go for it. *Splash* was one Disney hit, but it was an isolated success. Whether the creative well had run dry here or the country's tastes had changed too much, no one wanted to see Disney's "G" rated films anymore.

Even the theme parks weren't doing as well as they once had.

The rides and exhibits were becoming old hat, and there was stiff competition from outfits like Six Flags. The company was moribund. As the *New York Times* put it, "Between 1966, when Walt Disney died, and 1984, his company was essentially in suspended animation."

The crisis point came in 1984, when the company successfully —and expensively—defended itself against two corporate raiders. When the dust finally settled, two new members had been elected as Disney's top corporate officers: Michael Eisner, chairman and CEO, and Frank Wells, president and chief operating officer.

Eisner, former president of Paramount, and Wells, Vice Chairman at Warner Bros., immediately started a revitalization effort at their new company, and so far things have been going their way. Eisner's first prime-time television series, "The Golden Girls," has been a success in its first season, two Saturday morning animated cartoons have been sold, and the "Disney Sunday Movie" will debut on ABC in February.

The theme parks are also undergoing some updating, and Wells's idea to advertise the parks on television has paid off— attendance has gone up almost 10 percent since the campaign started. In addition, the company has announced a new Disney park in Paris and has plans to break ground in 1986 on a multi-million dollar film studio in Florida. Hopes are high for the new regime's first important film, *Down and Out in Beverly Hills*, starring Nick Nolte and Bette Midler, and initial box office receipts are very good. The film's "R" rating represents a milestone for Disney, and the film has been released under the company's adult distribution label, Touchstone.

It's too early to tell whether Eisner and Wells can put the romance back into the American public's love affair with Disney. The estrangment goes back twenty years, and the company's "just for babies" image is a tough one to change. If they fail, however, it won't be for lack of trying. A year from now, this new team hopes to be singing "Baby, Just Look at Me Now."

HEARD AT THE WATER COOLER— WHAT IT'S REALLY LIKE TO WORK HERE

"Who's the leader of the club that's made for you and me?" You guessed it, the mouse is *still* the king around here and there's no way anyone is ever going to forget it.

If the Mickey mailbox outside the studio post office doesn't give you the idea, the Mickey clocks in the halls, the Mickey coffee mugs on the desks and the Mickey T-shirts, sweatshirts and jackets on nearly everyone's backs will.

Mickey's pals aren't forgotten either. The entrance to the Burbank lot is on Snow White Boulevard, and you can stroll down Dopey Drive or Donald Avenue. As one awed newcomer put it, "It's really overkill. They go to the limit with this stuff."

The fantasyland that Walt created goes beyond the famous mouse and his friends. With the meticulous green lawns and well-groomed flower beds thriving in the warm California sun, the place looks more like a college campus than a movie studio. And you get the feeling that everyone here belongs to the Mousketeer Fraternity.

One Hollywood veteran who went to work on the Disney lot commented, "When I first started I thought it was amazing. I just wasn't used to people liking to go to work that much. I've always enjoyed my job, but this was silly."

Not everyone is as skeptical. Said one enthusiast, "It's one of the nicest places I've ever worked. People are always smiling and saying hello. You're always happy here."

Still, things are changing. No one expects—or wants—the Disneyland atmosphere to disappear completely (after all, Michael Eisner wears Mickey T-shirts, too). But with all the projects in development and production there is a lot of new blood and new energy, and that means the studio isn't as comfy or as sociable as it used to be. It also means many of the old-timers have been laid off or retired.

One staffer said, "It used to be if you wanted to make the big money, go elsewhere, but if you wanted the security, come to Disney. That's changed."

Turning a sleepy studio into an industry major is no easy task. Whether Eisner and Wells can do that without losing the unique Disney flavor remains to be seen. As one newcomer put it, "Everyone's waiting to see what we do. We're in the limelight now and there are a lot of expectations."

PEOPLE

"This is going to sound syrupy," one staffer said, "but people here are *nice*, that's the only way to describe it."

Walt's company was known for being a small, friendly studio

that made people happy, in the theaters *and* at work. To a great extent it still operates that way. "We're a first name company," said a personnel recruiter. "Walt Disney didn't want anyone to feel subordinate."

Nor did he want anyone to feel insecure. A lot of people have been at the studio for more than twenty years. As one put it, "When Walt hired you, you were hired for life. It was almost like a Japanese company in that way."

The advent of a new management is changing things somewhat. "There is an old Disney personality and it's middle of the road, very family oriented and, well, nice," one employee explained. "The new people coming in are more aggressive, more the standard Hollywood types. But it doesn't seem to cause a conflict, it's more of a mix."

However many industry hotshots may be moving into the studio, there's a tradition here that just won't go away. Commented one newcomer, "When you say Disney, you conjure up Mickey and the parks. It's part of American culture and it flows through the lot. It's a real family here and everybody is very into the whole Disney phenomenon. That's not going to change."

JOBS

People here make films and television shows, and as in other studios, entry-level jobs range from that of script development story analyst, to runner (staff assistant here), to production secretary. And with the new regime taking charge, there are a lot of film and TV shows being made at Disney these days.

That can make things pretty busy. Commented one production staffer, "I came here because I was bored at another studio, but this is going to extremes! I've never worked harder in my life."

The **theme parks** employ thousands of people (or "cast members" as they call themselves) who do everything from running the rides, sweeping the streets and dishing out food, to making Mickey Mouse hats. Cast members have to have strong legs to be able to stand around on the asphalt all day in 90-degree heat, and cheerful, outgoing personalities. How else could they cope with the forty thousand people who visit Disneyland alone every day?

But what Disney is famous for is Mickey and the gang, and it's **animation** that makes the big difference between this studio and any other. Working in animation is different from any other film job. Said one veteran, "There's a lot behind those cutesy characters." He's not just whistling Dixie. It starts with the story, of course, but once that's perfected the animator goes to work designing and developing the characters. Each one has to have a look and personality uniquely its own and each one has to come alive on the screen. As one staffer explained, "The characters practically have to think and breathe or the audience won't be able to relate."

While the animator is working on the character, the production team selects and records an appropriate voice. A staff person then sits down with the tape and figures out, phonetically, exactly where each word begins and ends and what the voice modulation is. That hard-won information he puts line by line on an "exposure sheet," each line representing one frame of film.

And then the work really begins. The animator starts drawing the character's actions, in pencil, synching picture to sound using the exposure sheet and a cassette of the recorded voice. While the characters may be fantasy, animators often draw from life, acting out the story themselves in front of a mirror. Said one man, "If you get to know an animator you'll recognize his characters, because they'll all have some of his mannerisms."

The animator puts the character's actions, including lip sync, on paper as briefly as possible. The assistant animator then goes to work, refining, adding a few more drawings, and trueing up proportions. He, in turn, is backed up by a breakdown artist, who adds more drawings. And then the "in-betweener" steps in, penciling in the last drawings—the ones that go in between the others.

All that takes a lot of patience and a very long time. As one department staffer said, "You're sitting in a room drawing the same character on a sheet of paper for a year or a year and a half. It's a *very* demanding occupation."

Once the drawings are completed, the camera crew photographs them onto 35mm black and white film. After the print is approved by the director, the people in the animation Xerox department copy the film onto transparent cels (a single transparency). And then people in the paint department start their work. And it *is* work. Painters color each cel by hand—and in an average animated feature there are 460,800 cels. Finally, the animation cameramen photograph all the moving colored transparencies, cel by cel, over stationary painted backgrounds.

The people in the editorial department add a few sound effects and some music and, voila!, you have the magic of Disney.

If you think it sounds like a long, painstaking process, you're right. As one animation executive commented, "It comes down to dedication. It looks like fun, but it's not easy and it's a lot of work. The reward is in hearing the audience laugh and knowing you had a part in it."

Added a staffer, "I love it. Everybody wants to be able to draw pictures and play with cartoons all day. I'm one of the lucky people who gets to do it."

There are other rewards, too. People who work in animation at Disney are all members of the Screen Cartoonists union and they make good money—salaries of over $800 a week are not unusual. And moving up is not as difficult as it once was. In the old days it could take as long as fifteen to twenty years to go from trainee "in-betweener" to full animator. Now, with the increased amount of product coming out and the generally higher turnover in the business, that time can be cut to as little as three years, if you're good.

Nearly everyone in the department has a fine arts background, but being a competent artist isn't enough. "Most animators can make something move, but the gifted ones are those who bring a character to life," explained one VP. "In order to do well you almost have to be born to it. But there are a lot of career assistants and they are very respected and very much in demand."

Staffers who work in animation tend to be a close-knit group, partly because no one else really understands what they do. And unlike crews on "live" productions who move from short-term project to short-term project, these people work together for years on one show. And it's generally not a high-pressure environment. Hours are 8 to 5 with an hour for lunch. Toward the end of a show, as the deadline looms, everyone goes into overtime and starts working weekends, but even then people stay relaxed. "It seems impossible but we always make the deadline," said one staffer. "But you don't feel the tension. We're generally a laid-back breed—maybe it's a slow heart-rate or something."

Some people have worried that, with the advent of computer animation, human animators would be out of a job. But this is not true at Disney. Of course computers can be used to do a lot of the technical, repetitive work, and they're unbeatable for figuring out changing perspectives and movement trajectories for inanimate objects. But as one human put it, "As long as you want characters with life and personality, animation has to come from people."

LIFE

It all starts at Disney University. Almost every new employee who comes through the gates goes through a six-hour training session, learning the Disney tradition, finding his way around the lot, having his picture taken for the weekly newsletter, and getting his Mickey name badge.

Those who haven't gone through orientation yet are being encouraged to do so by the new management. Said one old hand, "They're not making it a requirement, but they *really* want everyone to do it."

And every month the University team puts on a three-day corporate update program, called Disney Way I, for all salaried employees. Being a part of the Disney "family" is important here. Besides the normal company picnics and softball games, there are golf team tournaments, bus trips, cruises, and Halloween costume parties, most of which are coordinated by the Mickey Activity Center. Last Christmas the center organized a street fair on Dopey Drive, and employees were encouraged to bring their families to enjoy the games, exhibits, and food tables.

Nevertheless, the real fact of life here now is the new regime and all the changes and hopes they bring. And the path is not always smooth. One auditor (accountant and costs estimator) who recently finished a show here said, "A lot of people I worked with had no understanding of production. When you need a check for a prop on a show, you need it *now*, not in two weeks. I was told all the time to stop putting pressure on people, to stop rushing. It stems from everything being geared to the slower pace of animation."

If the pace has been slow, it is quickly picking up. "We hit the ground running," said one new production hand. "It's been busy from the day we walked in. New management is not taking this one step at a time." With one animated feature nearly in the can, five "live" features being prepped or shooting, the Sunday night television hourly anthology, the "Golden Girl" series, and a new pilot that just got a go-ahead, this group is out to show their stuff.

"They're workaholics," said a production executive. "I've been here the last three weekends, but management's been here, too. I had a meeting with the chairman Sunday afternoon and he'd been here since eight."

"There is a lot of money being spent right now," he added. "This is their first shot and they want everything to be perfect. It's all *got* to be a big success, otherwise . . ."

Otherwise, everything could change overnight again. But hopes are high. True, feathers have been ruffled and some old-timers are apprehensive that the sterling Disney image may get tarnished. "You'll hear 'Walt wouldn't have done it that way' sometimes," said one veteran, "but people are starting to be enthusiastic. Something is happening here and everyone's getting excited."

Added an enthusiastic newcomer, "You have to remember that there's nothing we're doing here that isn't for the family. But it isn't going to be Davy Crockett or Spin & Marty anymore."

DOLLARS AND SENSE

People in establishment Hollywood expect to make decent money, and they do here. Most staff and all set and animation jobs are unionized on this lot. Disney usually pays scale, which means that a secretary may make over $500 a week and a camera operator may top $1,500. Even a beginner in the mailroom (or "traffic," as it's called here) can expect to gross $350.

Benefits are reasonably good, too, and there's always the company store, which offers hefty discounts to staffers. The commissary is subsidized, too. So no one is starving, even though entry-level people aren't getting rich. But the Hollywood dream is very much there. Said one young go-getter, "Compared to jobs in other industries, pay rates here are pretty good. But if you get to the top in this business, you can make a killing."

One last thing, just to remind you of where you are: the paychecks all have Mickey's smiling face printed on them.

GETTING IN—TRICKS OF THE TRADE

If you like the idea of wishing upon this particular star and think you want to be a part of the wonderful world of Disney, then join the club, and this time we don't mean "M I C." There are a lot of people out there who want to work for this company. "I tried for a year to get in," said one young man who finally made it. "If you don't know anybody, it's really difficult."

As with other studios, knowing someone and having a background in the industry helps, but then it's still tough. Even entry-level clerical jobs frequently go to applicants with previous experience in the business. These positions open up more frequently than production or creative slots, but landing one of them doesn't guarantee much, unless you're a hustler. As one mover and shaker put it, "Starting out as a secretary is hard because you won't get the exposure. Being a traffic messenger is better, because you deal with everybody. I think that's what helped me."

There are no formal internship programs here, but many of the departments have interns who work for college credit, and interns frequently land permanent jobs. Putting in time at one of the theme parks is a route that staffers often recommend. The hours are long, the work is hard, and the pay can be very low, but it can be fun and it's a foot in the door.

So, the bad news is, there aren't a lot of job openings here. The good news is, that's because Disney promotes from within. If you can get through the front door, your chances of moving up are pretty good.

THE BOTTOM LINE

Disney's not just for kids any more.

FEDERAL GOVERNMENT

The biggest myth about federal government employment is that it pays poorly. The *average* white-collar government employee today earns over $30,000—and when you factor in civil service benefits, including job security, you've got a pretty good deal.

But there are drawbacks. You won't get rich, and you must contend with an enormous bureaucracy that can be stifling. And no matter what happens, that bureacracy cannot and will not disappear. The federal government is too large to make do without one. It employs over 1.5 million white-collar workers, working in every state of the Union and most foreign countries. Job opportunities are similarly large, ranging from file clerks to public relations experts, from computer programmers to ambassadors.

Rather than describe 1.5 million jobs, it's better to start with the process of obtaining federal employment. The best way to start is to decide what *type* of employment you want, and then check out career paths at the various departments, agencies, and quasi-governmental agencies. Get hold of the U.S. Government Manual (which can be found at most libraries, or ordered from the Government Publishing Office). This is a very detailed book that describes every government division, and lists current high-level officials. Boring reading, maybe, but it lists everything.

Then write the appropriate agencies to obtain a civil service rating. There are no longer any general tests; instead, applicants receive blank SF171s. Remember those letters and numbers! That's Standard Form 171, which is essentially a blank government resumé form. Since this may be the only contact an applicant has with the government, it's best to be thorough and comprehensive. Fill it out completely, mail it in, and wait.

Sometimes the wait can be too much. One applicant we talked to mailed a form in, forgot about it, and two years later received a reply inviting him to send more particulars. It's better to write a cover letter to various departments, and to request meetings in person (to which you should take another copy of that SF171).

Federal Job Information Centers, located in state capitals, also post openings and addresses to write to for positions; they also have a never-ending supply of blank SF171s.

Federal positions have detailed job descriptions and civil service ratings attached to them. They're designed to be fair—equal pay for equal work—and to reduce favoritism. The ideal of federal employment is that people are hired on their merits only. Except for political appointees, of course.

As in other fields, knowing someone is the best way to a job. So, go out and meet people, use friends and local Congressmen, it possible, to open doors, and with luck you'll get in.

Once you are in, you'll get a civil service rank. The Federal Pay Schedule is divided into eighteen levels, and subdivided at each level into ten steps. The lowest in the civil service is GS 1 Step 1, for which the salary is $9,339 a year. The highest is GS 18, for which the salary is theoretically $84,157. But the government puts a cap on high level salaries, currently at $68,700.

No, you won't get rich, but you won't starve. Not by a long shot. And promotions tend to be steady. Stick it out and it's hard to be fired and relatively easy to rise through seniority.

The following profiles cover two departments. The Smithsonian, which has a quasi-governmental status, and the Department of State.

THE SMITHSONIAN INSTITUTION

VITAL STATISTICS

- locations: Washington, D.C.
- revenues: N/A (non-profit institution)
- rank: world's largest museum complex
- employees: 6,000

AS SEEN FROM THE OUTSIDE

Ride up the subway escalator and step out onto the Mall in Washington D.C. You are now in the center of the District of Columbia. Look around you. Due west is the Washington Monument. To your east is the Capitol. Everything else you see (with the exception of one Department of Agriculture building) is part of the Smithsonian Institution.

It's hard to avoid the Smithsonian in D.C. or anywhere else. It's the premier research and museum complex in the United States, with a specific, and very large mission: "the increase and diffusion of knowledge among men." Well, maybe not too specific. (The mission has gotten even broader since those words were written—women are included now.)

What kinds of knowledge? Virtually all kinds. Get ready for a long, but only partial list.

The Smithsonian maintains twelve museums in Washington and New York City devoted to science, history, technology, and art. Among others, they include the National Air and Space Museum (NASM), the National Museum of Natural History, the Freer Gallery of Art, the Hirshorn Museum and Sculpture Gallery, and the National Museum of American History. (The National Gallery and the Kennedy Center come under the same board of regents, but under different boards of trustees.) As the "custodian of the national collections," these museums (along with several storage facilities, including a climate and humidity-controlled technological wonder in Maryland) contain more than 100 million artifacts.

As if that's not enough, the Smithsonian also maintains a zoo in Washington, a marine station in Florida, a tropical research center in Panama, Astrophysical stations in Massachusetts and Arizona, and a natural preserve on the Chesapeake Bay. It also publishes a magazine—aptly named *Smithsonian* magazine.

Quite a list of activities. It all began with 105 bags of gold, willed to the U.S. in the early 1800s by James Smithson, a gentleman English scientist who never visited the U.S. After congressional wrangling over what to do with the money, whether to fund a library or start a school, Congress decided instead to invest most of the funds in State of Arkansas bonds.

Not particularly in keeping with the mission of extending knowledge to all mankind . . . And worse was to come. Arkansas defaulted and it looked as if James Smithson's dream was about to fall apart in a tangle of partisan politics. Some things never change, particularly in politics. Then John Quincy Adams, congressman and former president, rode to the rescue, reclaiming the money, prodding and pushing, until in 1846 Congress finally authorized the creation of the Smithsonian, and the job of following up on that large mission.

The job began with the setting up of the Smithsonian's curious administrative structure—headed by a Board of Regents consisting of the vice president of the United States, the chief justice of the Supreme Court, three senators, three representatives, and six private citizens. As well as the real head of the Smithsonian, The Secretary.

The secretary and his administration oversee the conglomeration of museums and research institutes, manage the budget (some of the money comes from the government, and some from private donations) and maintain the unusual position of the Smithsonian as an independent federal agency. They have more freedom than most government agencies, but they're not completely independent. The secretary also supervises the Smithsonian employees, most of whom are government civil servants. But not the secretary himself, who's not a civil servant. Don't ask why! Just understand that the Smithsonian is a little complicated.

And from its unusual beginnings to the present day, it has been less interested in form and more in getting the job done, sometimes in spite of the federal government. It's been blessed with strong secretaries who have cajoled, begged, and borrowed their way into millions of dollars for Smithsonian activities. And unlike many federal agencies (or private corporations, for that matter) the Smithsonian is famous for a budgetary first—building and completing the National Air and Space Museum in 1976, on time and under budget.

Sounds as if these guys could give a few pointers to the people up the street on Capitol Hill . . .

HEARD AT THE WATER COOLER— WHAT IT'S REALLY LIKE TO WORK HERE

It's big. And, for all its good points, it's still a giant bureaucracy. People are proud of the first, and complain a lot about the second.

"This place is so huge, there are just so many facets one could fit into," marveled an employee who loves the diversity of people and interests. "The phone book is a hundred pages long."

That means many people, and that means bureaucracy. And that's the principal complaint of virtually everyone here. In that sense they're no different from other D.C. government employees. It's *in* to complain about bureaucracy. Which isn't to say there's not justice in those complaints.

Even if the Smithsonian is only a *quasi*-governmental agency, it has plenty of that grand old government standby—red tape. Uncle Sam foots half of the $300 million dollar budget, so you can expect it. One woman said that her job was fine when she could do her job, but "these days, unfortunately, you spend most of your time making sure people fill out forms right."

A mid-level employee was more graphic. "There are some days you want to go home and pound your head against the wall because you've been dealing with someone who's just a total and complete jerk about something."

But he quickly added, "Then there are other times when I have to sit there and say to myself, I'm getting paid to do two of the things that are most important in my life—astronomy and photography."

And that's the key to the Smithsonian. People in jobs that involve things they *love*, not just tolerate. It's the bureaucracy that they tolerate.

PEOPLE
"There's a lot of really high-powered people who pass through the Smithsonian. You get that only at perhaps two or three

top universities in the country," one employee said proudly.

In the scientific and art worlds the Smithsonian has a very high reputation, and according to many staffers, funding comes through more quickly.

In D.C. the Smithsonian also has a reputation for being a refuge for eccentrics—a bird watchers' and bug collectors' haven. Some Smithsonian people disagree about that label, however. One said that Smithsonian employees were "not at all eccentric, they're fine people."

Another scientist said that the best thing about the Smithsonian *was* the eccentrics. "They're there and it's one of the things I like about the job." It depends on your definition of an eccentric.

But there is a difference between Smithsonian people in general and the rest of Washington. And it's a refreshing one. As one employee explained, "To other people, Smithsonian people appear a little standoffish or aloof or something, but I don't consider that eccentric. They are just very devoted to what they are studying. *That* I find in some ways very refreshing. They are people who can get that involved with something."

And their enthusiasm is contagious. Just visit the Smithsonian and see.

JOBS

As a NASM curator described it: "This kind of work attracts people from many different backgrounds. You need to have technical people who know electronics and computing and exhibition. You need cabinetmakers, and mural painters, and researchers. People who know how to take care of rust on an object . . ."

If you're into rust, this may be the place. The Air and Space Museum has a collection of 23,000 items, including airplanes, missiles, engines, propellers, and rocket motors.

That's the best part of Smithsonian jobs—caring for and studying collections of sometimes unusual things (sometimes rusty things) that have a scientific value, and are often very interesting. The jobs reflect both the range of the collections and the breadth of the original mission.

There's no one "typical job" at the Smithsonian, and no one typical set of responsibilities. Researchers may be studying things that range from spiderwebs to moon rocks.

The jobs most people dream about are the curatorships, positions filled by scientists and art historians and technological specialists who study, manage, and research the museum collections.

It's not all ivory tower research at the Smithsonian, however. Curators often describe the jobs as involving a lot of administrative work, preparing exhibits, arranging for shipping and insurance of borrowed items, writing catalogs, supervising the preparation of collections. An art curator described her job in terms of peaks and valleys, the peaks coming when she arranges exhibitions, the valleys when she handles the administrative work.

Researchers may not have to worry about shipping and insurance, but they do have to think about funding for research projects, and writing. At the lower levels, as one scientist explained, "you're expected to produce two or three substantial scientific papers a year. This job is measured in terms of writing, copy, output."

"It's like being a research biologist in a university, except instead of teaching I have to run a huge collection," explained a researcher who studies arachnids (for the uninitiated, spiders and their relatives).

Running those collections involves technicians, museum specialists, and collections managers. And then there are the registrars, the "librarians" of the museums, who figure out and catalog the exhibits. Finally, display and production people put on the visual "shows" that make a museum interesting to the general public.

As one production coordinator said who produces the still and motion picture images that are projected on the Planetarium walls, "it's like playing in Santa's workshop—and you get paid."

LIFE

Like a lot of D.C. people, many Smithsonian employees drive in car pools from the suburbs to their jobs. Specialists from one area get to know people from other areas, and share gossip and hobbies.

It's not all typical D.C. talk. One person described his "long time star-gazing buddy, the former director of the Natural History Museum. His specialty is fossil sea urchins."

Morale may be high, but it varies from museum to museum. When asked about problems, one person replied, "I found that being honest gets you in trouble." That sounds more chilling than it is. Essentially, when people spoke off the record, or when we talked to former employees, their complaints were similar to those made at all museums, about money, and about who *really* does the work. Some women in the arts felt that the field was still dominated by men, and that opportunities were still a bit limited. And of course everyone complains about paperwork. In many senses, problems sound like those of academics, such as not having enough time to devote to study.

But most people at the Smithsonian are not only happy but very enthusiastic. There's too much work, maybe, so that people writing books or trying to get grants must come in on weekends, but at the same time, it's fun work. And people enjoy it.

DOLLARS AND SENSE

Government employees get government salaries, which vary tremendously depending on the grade of the position (see government profile). In general, salaries are good. Some areas pay less than others. Art curators face competition from hundreds of other aspiring art curators, so art museums can pay a salary that one former employee described as a "pittance."

But others disagree. A former freelancer said, "I am a civil servant now. I find it preferable to have a secure existence, a regular paycheck, regular hours."

Security is the name of the game when working for Uncle Sam. It has its advantages.

GETTING IN—TRICKS OF THE TRADE

"For people who want to do what I want to do, there are only three slots, and they open up only once in a generation."

That's from a specialist researcher. At higher levels, jobs may be very hard to find, to say the least. They require Ph.D.'s, and are usually advertised in specialist magazines and university journals and talked about on campus.

Other jobs come a bit easier. One curator stated that "very few people come directly into a curatorial position. You have to start doing other things first."

A lot start by working somewhere else, developing an expertise, then getting hired by the Smithsonian. One person we talked to started out by training at the Metropolitan Museum of Art in New York, then heard about a Smithsonian job though the grapevine, grabbed an interview, and got the job. Another person with a background in Russian studies (and an English major) got a job writing a history of the Apollo Soyuz space project, "got my foot in the NASA history door that way, got to see a couple of missions take place, got to know the astronauts . . ." and then got hired by the Smithsonian as a full-time curator. She mentioned that the field is a bit more open today, with fledgling air and space museums opening up around the country.

Another person at the Air and Space Museum managed to "gate-crash the opening gala. I had a friend working there, and I decided it was a really neat looking place to work." He met some people, kept his ears open, and eventually landed a job as a part-time aide, showing people around the building. Once in, he quickly moved to a full-time job.

Where there's a will, there's a way.

THE BOTTOM LINE

There's only one Smithsonian.

STATE DEPARTMENT

VITAL STATISTICS

- **locations:** Washington, DC; 230 embassies, consulates, and offices worldwide
- **revenues:** none
- **rank:** 1st (out of a field of 1)
- **employees:** 3,700 Foreign Service officers; 3,700 support staff

AS SEEN FROM THE OUTSIDE

The State Department is like a small multinational corporation that forgot about profits. It does everything—but with a difference. The official United States government department responsible for planning, implementing, and conducting foreign policy and diplomacy.

Most of the people we call diplomats the State Department calls Foreign Service officers. The Foreign Service is the official career diplomatic service that staffs the embassies and missions and runs the department, under the politically appointed secretary of state and (some of) his deputies. The Foreign Service is split into four "cones" or areas of responsibility: political (which analyzes and reports on foreign political trends); economic (which analyzes and reports on foreign economic trends); administrative (which manages the embassies); and consular (which issues visas and assists individual Americans abroad).

The State Department itself is split into "bureaus," by region and by function. These bureaus are all staffed by FSOs from the four cones. And then there are the embassies, or missions abroad, which are also staffed by FSOs.

Yes, they're everywhere.

HEARD AT THE WATER COOLER—
WHAT IT'S REALLY LIKE TO WORK HERE

"State"—that's what everyone calls it. It sounds like a college, and in many ways that's just what it is. There's a clubby atmosphere at the State Department, a feeling of camaraderie and belonging. Even the main building in Washington has a shabby, comfortable feel to it—pastel walls, old wooden desks, overcrowded hallways, people running around in tweeds and polyester. And *everyone* is always studying something—an exotic foreign language, maybe, or political reporting techniques.

Then again, how many colleges do you know that offer courses in weapons training, defensive driving, and how to keep your mouth shut if you're taken hostage? There might be a college atmosphere here, but nobody forgets that it's serious business, too. There's a plaque at one entrance to State filled with the names of people killed abroad while on duty for the State Department. And many of those names were added recently.

Since this is the federal government, it's big business, too—with a healthy dose of bureaucracy.

"There are hundreds of forms," complained one staffer. "It seems as if you have to fill out a form to go to the bathroom."

Along with the red tape comes a government lingo, complete with acronyms. People talk about OERs (officer efficiency reports), CDOs (officially, career development officers, but the standard joke has it that they're really career destruction officers). FSOs don't ask for specific assignments, they "bid for posts." And they learn then and there that "needs of the service" (another popular State Department term) come before the needs of the individual. In other words, where you want to go doesn't matter as much as where *they* want you to go.

Still, for all the headaches, many FSOs wouldn't give up their jobs for anything. "Where else would I get paid to learn languages, travel overseas, and feel that I have a real impact?" asked one rhetorically. "It's tough sometimes, but it's worth it."

PEOPLE

"The Foreign Service is like your family. You join a community of people who will keep turning up for the rest of your life," commented one woman.

That's how most FSOs seem to feel about their co-workers.

Working in the Foreign Service isn't like working for any old corporation. You're part of the government; your job affects foreign policy; and often you're overseas a great deal. So it's no wonder FSOs wind up feeling a strong camaraderie. It's a unique job.

And there's more. According to one young man, "A lot of us are eccentrics. We didn't fit in back home. Getting away is an escape, and the Foreign Service is a pretty good way to do it."

Well, that might be an overstatement. But there is an undeniable wanderlust that most FSOs seem to share. Even while many of them prefer the high-visibility, cushier Washington jobs, they're still people who love traveling, and foreign languages and cultures.

Since the Foreign Service is a highly selective employer, with stringent tests that must be passed, FSOs on the whole are an academic bunch.

"The group of people in my A-100 course (the introductory Foreign Service course) were the sharpest group of people I ever met," said a young man.

They're also highly competitive. It was a struggle getting in and it's a struggle getting the good posts. Not that there's open backstabbing. No one ever insults anyone in the Foreign Service. There's always a nice way of putting someone down, and these people are experts. There's a little item referred to as a "corridor reputation," which is what your co-workers think about you and your skills, your maturity and technical expertise, your diplomatic acumen.

"In plain English, it means talking about someone behind his back," said one consul.

JOBS

Diplomacy has changed a lot since the days of striped pants and top hats. Sure, diplomats still discuss foreign policy at cocktail parties, but they also run offices, fix embassy plumbing, guide congressmen on junkets, and write press releases. Officially, they're not even called diplomats but Foreign Service officer (FSOs). And, as with officers in the Army, rank means a great deal.

An FSO isn't just an FSO, but an FSO with a number. Most beginning FSOs are 6's on a department scale that begins at 9 (starting salary $13,000) and ends at 1 (starting salary $57,500). After 1 comes a scale for ambassador and other top-level people.

Confused? There's worse to come. There are numbered steps from 1 to 15 assigned in addition to each numbered rank. And there are protocol (diplomatic) ranks ranging from third secretary to ambassador. So a beginning FSO is usually an FS6, Step 1, Third Secretary who dreams of becoming an SFS1, Step 15, Ambassador. But rank isn't everything. There are also the four "cones"—political, economic, administrative, and consular. So our beginning FS6, Step 1, Third Secretary is also a Pol officer, Econ officer, Admin officer, or consul. In layman's terms, he's a diplomat. Ah, bureaucracy . . .

But most FSOs start out as students. They're not immediately sent out to a foreign embassy post. New hires begin with training at the Foreign Service Training Institute in Rosslyn, Virginia (just a metro stop away from the department).

First there's a few weeks of basic orientation, then more specific job and language training, for those who require it, usually lasting up to seven months. During this initial period, FSOs are told what their "cone" assignment will be, so course work usually focuses on that specific area.

But not always, as one old hand pointed out. "Almost everyone will take the consular course," he noted, "since almost all first tour officers have to spend part of their tours doing consular work, generally working a visa line." (In other words, stamping visas, which a first tour officer described as "like being a bank teller.")

Once FSOs have completed training, they're sent overseas for their first tour of duty, which lasts for eighteen months to two years. And as a rule that's when they start working in their specific area of responsibility. A senior Foreign Office secretary summed up the four cones rather succinctly, and cynically.

"My current impression is that the consular and commercial types stay more than busy carrying out essential functions; the admin people run around frantically trying to take care of themselves, as well as about double the amount of personnel in any given embassy that is necessary for normal operations. And the political types attend constant parties, try to look wise, frequently turn out political reports that *might* even be useful, but nevertheless are usually caught by surprise when the big ones happen."

Okay, that's one view of it all. But it's a bit more complex than that, and to be fair, a lot more difficult.

The **political officers** are the ones who usually consider themselves the *real* diplomats. Their work involves analyzing foreign government trends, writing cables to policy makers back home and meeting with foreign dignitaries, foreign ministry people, and foreign business people. But the bulk of the job consists of listening, reading, and analyzing.

"You go to a lot of parties and you listen. Then you run home and write it all down," explained a five-year vet.

Many political officers wonder if anyone actually reads or uses what they write. The State Department receives a deluge of cables written by political officers based all over the world. So it's easy for the cable you consider to be the definitive analysis of the French election to get lost.

There's a more personal downside, too. As one young man stated, "the political cone does seem to be the lightning rod for a lot of frustrations at State." He went on to say that "other officers envy the political officer his 'substantive work,' the production of reports that go back to Washington to be read, and that might get his name known to the movers and shakers in Washington."

Most FSOs want to wind up as political officers. In the words of an FSO who began in administration, but finally made it to the political cone, "Politiccal officers have more prestige. Admin officers and consuls, they're like blue-collar workers. They're part of us, but . . ."

But they have to get their hands dirty. And they disagree *very* strongly with that "blue collar" image. The typical administrative or consul response is that they do the *real* work, while the political officers are out writing obtuse cables. **Administrative officers**, in particular, do a great deal of scut work. They manage the embassy, handle the budget and keep the limos running.

"It's like being president of a small company," boasted a rookie. "You're in charge of everything and everyone depends on you."

Sometimes everyone depends on you for too many things—things that don't quite fit the popular image of a diplomat. "There was this huge party and none of my workers were around," recalled a former administrative officer. "I was in charge—literally—of delivering the chairs. Everyone is standing around in white tie and tails and I'm in jeans carrying chairs in. I felt like a bum." On the other hand, because administrative officers work with many foreigners, they often have a better feel for the country and its local politics than some political officers.

Consular officers tend to feel more like assembly line workers. "You know what we called the consulate in London? A visa mill. I spent two years, eight hours a day, stamping visas," explained a consular officer.

A lot of the consul's job is rote work, but many find fulfillment in helping Americans in distress. As one former consul proudly said, "For every political officer who perceptively analyzes the course of the Islamic revolution in Iran, there are ten consular officers who've reunited a family of refugees, helped an elderly tourist whose husband died overseas, or issued a replacement passport to someone who has lost the one he arrived with."

LIFE

Two years is the usual duration of an overseas tour of duty. Sixty percent of a typical FSO's career should be spent at embassies and missions abroad. But many FSOs fight bitterly to stay in D.C. Why?

"Frankly, it can be dangerous," explained one who recently returned from the Middle East. "I'm not wild about being shot. Or even thinking about being shot."

And part of the reason is plain old homesickness. "It's funny," mused a staffer. "You go away for two years and you expect everything to have stopped from the minute you left. Then you come back and everything has changed."

Politically, D.C. is where the action is. Particularly in the political area, FSOs might find themselves actually *making* policy. Working on the country desks (offices assigned responsibility for a specific nation or region), they will interact with Congress and other government agencies, and get a chance to be listened to. Once that happens, they don't want to leave. And they fight to stay.

But for many people posted abroad life can be colorful and occasionally glamorous. You get to meet all kinds of people, and to visit exotic places. Not a bad life . . .

DOLLARS AND SENSE

The money isn't all that bad, either. FSO base salaries are in the mid-20s, and there are some very nice perks. You get to travel to places that few other Americans see, you have free language training, and the benefits in government are better than in private industry.

"Some of the housing you get overseas is amazing," raved one young man. "A single guy, I graduate from a one-bedroom apartment in D.C. to a five-bedroom house with two gardeners and a maid." (Note to the taxpayer—these last are paid for by the individual, not the government, except for higher level types with entertainment responsibilities.)

Besides free housing, or a housing allowance, you may get commissary privileges, reduced rates on cars, liquor, maybe even a car and driver (officially for official purposes). You also get a diplomatic passport, which means that you can rush through customs, never opening a suitcase.

As one FSO stated, "It's like being rich without being rich."

But then there is the downside. The best perks wind up coming in the worst places—the hardship posts—where even with cheaply hired maids and official housing you have to contend with danger, boredom, and heat (or cold). So you do earn those perks.

GETTING IN—TRICKS OF THE TRADE

Throw away your resumé. There are no formal requirements to get in. But there is a hitch. Remember the SATs? The people who wrote them also wrote the Foreign Service Written Examination, a dream test for Trivial Pursuit fanatics, with hundreds of multiple choice questions about history, English, economics, and political science.

If you pass that, then it's on to an oral examination. Pass that and you're in—almost. Then there's a security check, a health check, and a long wait—up to eighteen months. And of 10 to 25,000 people who take the written exam each December, only 250 finally get accepted. But it sounds worse than it is. For the written test, many FSOs recommend reading a basic high school history textbook as well as a major metropolitan newspaper. As for the orals, "it's not what you know; it's how you say what you know. During the interviewing, it's often a case of style over substance," a new hire pointed out.

Not style in the trivial sense. The orals include a group interview where people are asked as a team to agree on a specific policy item. There's a lot of polite arguing, and negotiating and interpersonal skills come to the fore.

Once in, it's still not over. New hires come in as "Career Candidates" on probationary status for a period of several years.

So relax and be yourself. There's a real mix of people in the State Department. An Ivy Leaguer elaborated: "I expected an Ivy League bias here. A lot of the old guys are Ivy—Harvard and so on. But the younger people aren't. There are more southerners and midwesterners than I thought."

THE BOTTOM LINE

Put away your pinstripes and top hats and put on your traveling shoes.

FINANCIAL SERVICES

What is financial services? What isn't financial services? It's a catchall phrase that describes companies that make money in many ways, all financial, all profitable. And if some areas aren't profitable, maybe other areas are. Call it diversified financial services, a supermarket approach to finance. And it's the name of the game on Wall Street and in the world of finance. For now. Services may include brokerage services, investment banking, insurance, credit cards, personal and commercial banking, commodities trading, real estate financing. You name it and some firm does it.

The only problem is to figure out which companies fit the bill. Some are included in industry surveys and some aren't. Almost everyone calls Merrill Lynch and American Express financial services firms. But then there's Sears, which owns the large brokerage house Dean Witter Reynolds, and there are the investment banks, which offer more specialized services for bigger clients. They're usually classified as investment banks. But then there's Bear Stearns, which is also a trading and brokerage house, and is public and growing fast. And there's Citibank, which is known primarily as a commercial bank, but which also has an investment bank and is trying to do everything. Definitions can get confusing. But it all boils down to one thing—making money with money in many different ways. And that starts with "the Street."

Wall Street's best-known business is probably that of **brokerage services**, which serve as intermediaries between buyers and sellers of stocks and bonds. The largest employer of brokers on the Street is Merrill Lynch, which has thousands of Retail Brokers, who sell stocks and bonds to the public, and hundreds of Institutional Brokers, who deal with the large blocks of securities bought and sold by the large pension funds and other bulk buyers. Brokers also work on the floors of the stock exchanges, conducting transactions for investment firms on a salaried or freelance basis.

All the broker jobs require a lot of hustle. People usually start out with a small salary and a lot of ambition. It's primarily a commission business. The more a broker encourages clients to buy or sell, the more the brokerage house pays in commission. So you can't always trust your broker . . .

Salaries vary widely, with a base salary usually in the 20s, and commissions ranging all the way up to the millions.

Before stocks or bonds can be bought or sold, they have to be *issued*. That's where **Investment Banking** comes in.

Essentially, investment banks advise corporations in need of money how to get it, and then help them get it. The options can get very complex, but often it starts with a simple choice. A corporation may decide to issue stocks (or equity, in financialese), which give their buyer partial ownership of the company and a right to future earnings (dividends). Or the corporation may decide to issue bonds, in which case the buyer in effect lends money to the company and gets back the principal with interest later. And, in both cases, the investment bank earns a commission.

The job of getting corporate clients and earning money falls in the first place on the **Corporate Finance Department** of an investment bank. Here employees work in teams to develop financing ideas, write prospectuses, bring in clients, and work out the financial and legal details of financing deals with corporate lawyers.

Entry-level people are usually hired as Analysts. In this position they work for more senior members of the team, crunching numbers, checking legal documents, and doing grunt work like arranging luncheons and meetings. It can be a great way to learn the ropes, but it can also be like a prison sentence, working all hours of the day and night. The pay is excellent for BAs, usually starting in the 30s (unless you calculate it on an hourly basis, in which case it can hit minimum wage levels). But in a good year bonuses can come too, amounting to a few thousand or more extra.

Analysts are usually expected to leave after two years and go to business school, but occasionally very smart, very lucky, or very well-connected analysts move up to the MBA hire position, that of Associate. The work is the same, but there's more responsibility and more supervision. And more money—from the 50s on up. And as associates move up the ladder to senior vice president, the bonuses get larger. At the level of Managing Director, or Managing Partner, take-home pay gets into the $200 thousand range, or more.

Public Finance positions are similar, although the action here involves public organizations: utilities, state and local government, and other public organizations. Here you are dealing more with bonds than with stocks.

Once a stock has been issued, someone has to buy it, and that's where the **Syndications and Underwriting** people at an investment bank come in. The investment bank buys the entire issue, and then sells it to other investors. It takes a lot of money, so often new issues are presold to other investment houses as well. This is called syndication. Announcements of syndications are usually made in the long "tombstone" advertisements you see in the financial press, listing the firms that have bought into an issue. (What you don't see are the squabbles and bickering over who gets what position in those announcements.)

Then comes a hot area of any investment bank—**Sales and Trading**. Institutional Salespeople take issues and sell them to block buyers of securities. It's a lot of phone work, a lot of socializing, and a lot of money. The salary range here is very wide, from $30,000 on up to several hundred thousand.

Traders also earn good money. Traders use the bank's or a company's money to make profits by buying stocks or bonds low and selling them high. Traders specialize in either stocks or bonds, and usually get to know certain categories within those broad specialties. It sounds simple until you get into stock options, market trends, and complicated matching strategies, and . . . well, don't ask. Base salaries are in the $30,000 range, but bonuses are the reason people are out there trading. Bonuses vary tremendously, based on what a trader makes for the firm, length of service with the firm, what sort of deal he or she has cut with the firm, or all three. Take-home pay usually begins in the 50s, and after a few years goes into the $100 to $200 thousand range and beyond. But, of course, that depends on the market.

And that's not the end of it. Investment banks and brokerage houses also employ researchers (also called analysts, but different from the previously mentioned type of analyst) who study and recommend stocks and bonds based on research in specific industries or financial areas. Firms also hire people in merger and acquisitions, who advise on and conduct the current rash of corporate takeovers. And then there are the computer people who keep the action going.

And there's more in the more diversified financial services companies like Merrill Lynch and American Express. The list goes on—sales and marketing people in credit cards or travel-related services, real estate specialists, insurance staffers, money managers . . .

Where there's money, there's a job—or, rather, many jobs.

AMERICAN EXPRESS

VITAL STATISTICS

- **locations:** New York (headquarters), Minneapolis (IDS), San Francisco (Fireman's Fund), and offices worldwide
- **revenues:** $12.89 billion (1984)
- **rank:** 1st (diversified financial services companies)
- **employees:** 76,447

AS SEEN FROM THE OUTSIDE

It all started with the merger of three companies in 1850, and a simple job—moving money and freight safely, profitably, and quickly. American Express agents rode along—on horses, trains, and carriages. That's where the "Express" part of the name came from. And they were fast—for the 1850s.

Today, the same Express is moving financial data at the speed of light (well, *almost* the speed of light) along electronic cables and telephone wires, as the company strengthens its formidable position as a leading diversified financial services corporation.

That's a long way of saying "financial supermarket." It's the big thing on Wall Street nowadays. As the regulatory walls crack, and the old distinctions between commercial banking, brokerage houses, and investment banks blur, many firms want a bigger, more comprehensive piece of the entire financial pie. Why offer only personal banking services to a client, they have asked themselves, when we can also collect a fee on that client's stock purchases? Why let some other firm get the money?

That's the mentality. And American Express has a nice built-in advantage in this respect: the twenty million credit card users who charged upward of fifty billion dollars in 1985. Add Travelers Cheques (fifteen billion dollars worth purchased in 1984) and travelers services, and there's quite a potential market for other services as well. And a lot of profits. Along with a few other services and items, this part of the company generated over half of its net income of $140 million in the third quarter of 1985.

That's the backbone of the company—Travel Related Services, Inc. It's a marketing dynamo, tying card use and travel services to such diverse activities as direct mail selling and discount vacations. It even publishes magazines, including *Travel and Leisure*. Appropriate for the company that invented the counter-signed travelers check.

This unity among things that at first may seem a bit diverse is the new company hallmark, and it's smart marketing. American Express is as much a marketing and operations company as a financial company.

Five major businesses are grouped under the American Express umbrella: Travel Related Services, American Express International Banking Corporation, Shearson Lehman Brothers, Inc. (investment banking), IDS Financial Services Inc. (financial planners who also sell life insurance, mutual funds, etc.) and Fireman's Fund Insurance Companies (property and casualty insurance). All are autonomously run but increasingly linked. And as much of the company settles into its new corporate headquarters in the World Financial Center in New York City, those links are getting stronger.

HEARD AT THE WATER COOLER—
WHAT IT'S REALLY LIKE TO WORK HERE

"There aren't many people here who don't get the job done, as unlikely as that may seem," commented one staffer.

The big job of 1985 was moving into the new headquarters, a beautiful building almost at the tip of Manhattan Island, on the river side of the World Trade Center. American Express Tower is "new" modern—marble floors of gray, green, and maroon, pink granite exterior walls—and has a sophisticated state of the art telephone system that should link all the far-flung offices. But there have been problems, with overtight security and telephone hassles.

And there were problems for us as well. American Express didn't officially let us come in and interview. We had to rely on interviews with a few friends who were willing to talk. So this is a brief look at a huge company through the eyes of a few people, concentrating on the Travel Related Services section.

PEOPLE

"There're a lot of typical blue suit banker types here," commented one employee with experience in operations and travelers checks. But don't confuse blue suits with dull. Everyone we talked with stressed image, the right look, as being essential.

What kind of image? A fast mover, an entrepreneurial type from a top school with good interpersonal skills and a bit of hustle. That's what American Express likes, and increasingly that's what you see. According to some insiders, it's come a long way since Robert Townsend described it in his book *Up the Organization* as a "company rich enough to do . . . almost everything wrong."

American Express likes to think of itself as an entrepreneurial company, built around small groups of movers and shakers, people with an entrepreneurial attitude who can also fit into a large corporate environment. But they do mention some things that tell you this is still a large corporation. What does a good employee need, for instance? "Poise," summed up one young man. "A little knowledge and a good presentation and you're fine."

Presentation? As at many large market-driven companies, at American Express the marketing begins at headquarters. People who want to stay here have to be good at it.

"That can make or break somebody," one staffer maintained. "I've sat at worldwide meetings—we had one last year in Hawaii— with 250 people and listened to somebody who's really not getting across. Maybe he's missing the point, maybe he's jittery, a little nervous. But you know that guy isn't going anywhere."

"A good personality—that's the big thing," another staffer added. And at American Express, good personality is not just a buzz word. They mean it.

JOBS

Travel Related Services hires primarily MBAs into a graduate management training program, where employees are routed throughout the company to gain exposure to all its aspects. The old unity theme again. After nine months they go on to their specific area: finance, marketing, systems, or operations. And then they start moving some more. "There's a high turnover here," said one staffer, "people get bored after two years."

Turnover at American Express doesn't necessarily mean leaving the company. Many transfer within it, moving from line to staff jobs and back again. People stressed the company's policy of promoting from inside. And the jobs are diverse, from new product development (analyzing market trends and coming up with new card services) to the more mundane jobs of financial and market reporting.

People like the opportunity for movement, and the implicit risk involved. "There are so many things going on, and we're going in so many directions at once," one staffer said with a smile, "that *hopefully* everything will come together. But that's not necessarily the case."

One mid-level employee described the management style as "management by challenges—they throw you impossible tasks." That's on the entrepreneurial side. On the corporate side, with growth targets dictated from above, hustling is necessary in order to meet them.

"Management is looser," said one veteran. "But the goals are there. And they change depending on the priorities of the guy above."

Working at Amex, you don't forget that it's a hierarchical place. It's too big not to be.

LIFE

So, when they're not hustling or networking or maintaining the right image, what do people do here? Well, they travel, for one thing. American Express employee travel offers nice deals to employees, spouses, and friends. And, of course, there are officially sponsored company meetings, often in resort centers around the world. After all, it's a worldwide company.

DOLLARS AND SENSE

The company would not officially discuss salaries, but apparently starting salaries are in the mid-30s, for MBAs. Beyond the travel perks are expense accounts for travel and entertainment that are quite generous. Then there are other occasional bennies like a "Be My Guest" American Express pass to a restaurant. "You walk right in, spend anything you want," a senior staffer said. He contrasted the older employees with the new frugal types: "The guy who works for me went to a diner—*I* spent 190 bucks."

Other benefits include medical and disability insurance and

tuition reimbursement, and reduced rates on stock and money-market transactions.

And on the career side, there are "a lot of in-house seminars to upgrade people's skills."

GETTING IN—TRICKS OF THE TRADE

In order to get in you'll need an MBA from a top school. And show poise and entrepreneurial spirit, of course. At American Express, you can't leave home without them.

THE BOTTOM LINE

With a little smart marketing, your future can be gold . . . or platinum.

BEAR STEARNS

VITAL STATISTICS

- locations: New York (headquarters); 6 U.S. offices; 5 international offices
- capital: $1.8 billion (1985)
- rank: 11th (among Wall Street firms in capital)
- employees: 1,000

AS SEEN FROM THE OUTSIDE

> We have this expression about we love people with PSD degrees, not necessarily MBAs, and PSD stands for poor, smart, and a deep desire to become rich . . .
> —Alan "Ace" Greenburg, CEO,
> in a television interview
> on CNN's "Strictly Business,"
> March 24, 1985

Bear Stearns is known as the tough guy on Wall Street. A company of blunt-talking, hard-charging traders and investment bankers without the fancy Ivy League degrees and the prestigious blue chip client lists of the other investment houses. But with a deep desire to become rich.

And that's the way "Ace" wants it. The blunt-talking, hard-charging CEO of the firm doesn't mince words. What he does is make money and make his company grow. The total capital of the firm has rocketed from $56 million to $500 million in the past six years. Profits have reached $168 million. And in 1985 the firm went public, selling $200 million worth of itself to the public.

With more capital, Bear Stearns is getting broader based—moving more money and people into retail brokering, stock clearing, international investment and services, real estate, public finance, and corporate finance. All the services a mainstream investment house offers. And it's getting more blue chip clients. But some things probably won't change. The firm still prefers to concentrate its people and money in selected locations and areas—it doesn't want to become Merrill Lynch. And top people are still called partners, and those partners are still charging. Sure they are—they own a lot of stock.

Bear Stearns moved particularly quickly in public finance, entering the business in 1978 and making itself one of the leading underwriters of tax-exempt municipal securities by 1985. Meanwhile, Bear Stearns' investment bankers raised $5.5 billion in public offerings for corporate clients in 1984, and moved strongly internationally as well, serving as lead manager on several European bond issues.

But the heart of the firm is the trading floor—a huge crowded room with rows of blinking video screens, where traders buy and sell stocks, bonds, and government securities for Bear Stearns' accounts and client accounts. It's where split-second trading decisions can mean millions in losses or profits.

And it's where Ace Greenburg sits.

HEARD AT THE WATER COOLER— WHAT IT'S REALLY LIKE TO WORK HERE

"I worked in a commercial bank before," explained a bond trader, "and it was boring, stodgy. Here, it's as close to a casino as you can get."

In more ways than one. People play for high stakes here and you never forget it. How you play the game doesn't matter, it's winning that counts (as long as it's legal). And that's what makes Bear Stearns tick. Money. Bottom line. Profits. Wall Street without the pinstripes. It's performance that counts first—and last. "If you don't perform, they don't care if you're from Harvard or Tulsa, Oklahoma," explained one salesperson.

Bear Stearns is different from its competitors Morgan Stanley and Goldman Sachs. Forget bureaucracy, job titles, and formal channels of communication. The firm is a series of separate "fiefdoms," as one partner explained, with different bosses, opinions, and styles. Put six Bear Stearns partners in a room and ask where the stock market is going and you may get six different opinions; but one will be right. And that one will make up for any losses. But they all share the basics of a Bear Stearns philosophy: Cut your losses! Cut the bull! Make money!

"They sort of delight in being street urchins," one bond trader said of Bear Stearns' partners on the trading floor. "You really live by your wits down there."

And you win. Or you leave.

PEOPLE

Bear Stearns people are those who respond to a challenge. It's a mixed bag of BAs, MBAs, English literature majors, history majors, Civil War buffs, and sports fanatics. Like some other firms, Bear Stearns is big on hiring sports people—people who can *compete*.

That attitude permeates the firm. When asked to describe themselves, Bear Stearns people use words like "driven," "compulsive," and "aggressive." But that's the way people are up and down Wall Street. At Bear Stearns, however, there's a difference. "There's a typical investment banker look," explained one investment banker, "but not here."

People talk of the differences between Bear Stearns and the other investment houses, where analysts sit in large rooms at the mercy of a partner's whims. Not here. There's less need to be ingratiating to your boss, dress in the right suit, and have the right look. Just do your job. And the people reflect those differences. They're a bit less diplomatic than the people at the other houses, and a *lot* more outspoken.

JOBS

There's no one list of responsibilities for entry-level positions, no formal training program, and very few "typical" days or experiences. "Everyone we hire is on a 'by exception' basis," explained one partner, and that means very few formal spots, or defined duties.

As for training programs: "We have what we call a 'formal informal' training program," said a partner in bonds. "If you have a formal program, and you say the trainee has to be two weeks in the utility debt trading area, well, when he gets over there he may want *four* weeks!" So Bear Stearns makes do with a "down and dirty" training approach, learning by doing in the area you want to make money in, for as long as it takes (within reason) to learn the ropes well. It will also pay for classroom work on the outside—in anything related to the business.

Corporate Finance and Public Finance, the deal-making areas of an investment bank, are where a lot of people want to end up. Entry-level employees usually start out as analysts. Essentially, the job revolves around proposals and financings—trying to get clients, and then arranging various methods for the clients to raise money, including issuing bonds and stock. Analysts are usually placed in teams headed by a partner, and work with that partner in structuring these deals, doing everything from getting cups of coffee for clients to preparing spreadsheets and analyses on specific ideals.

At the beginning it's more coffee than spreadsheets. Or things like staying with a financial printer until a proposal document is fully and correctly printed. One young analyst spent forty hours straight waiting, reading, correcting, and talking with corporate lawyers at a printhouse—with a few hours out for catnaps.

Long hours of work ("the average is at least sixty hours a week") make this a far from cushy job. Essentially it's an "everything" job, doing everything necessary to bring a deal to the table. That means calling clients, talking with the firm's operations people to make certain the details are taken care of, telling the people at the trading desk (who sell the bonds) the ins and outs of the deal, crunching numbers, and working weekends when a big deal is being completed. It's fast-paced, detail-oriented work for people who are hungry to succeed. "I'm self-motivated and I live in absolute terror of making a mistake," joked one young analyst. But it's not really a joke.

Everyone stressed that corporate finance is far from being glamorous. "I don't think it's any great feat to be chosen for a job where they're going to work you to death," said one young analyst who loves his work.

You'd better love it, and *want* it. "I don't understand how a company makes decisions," explained an analyst. "I know the transactions, but the whys and the hows—that's what I'm seeking and acquiring, little by little . . ." And it's that desire to understand and know finance that keeps them going. Not the money; that comes later.

On the trading and sales side, it comes a bit quicker—if you're good, or lucky, or know the right people (the kind who buy stocks or bonds). **Institutional Equity Salespeople** sell stocks to institutions, the large pension funds, and money managers who buy and sell huge chunks of stock. Each sale generates a commission for Bear Stearns and its salespeople. And that means big money.

But you earn it. "It's phone work, all day long on the phone," explained one salesman. It's selling to clients at breakfast meetings, lunch meetings, and you guessed it, dinner meetings. "Sometimes it's nuts," explained one salesman, "three or four dinners, and a hockey game on Saturday night—and all in between phone calls. At the end of a good day, my throat's sore."

Needless to say, "You can't be shy in this business at all," as one person advised. Successful salespeople start out as assistants to partners, and then, preferably on their own initiative, start cold-calling potential clients. In time they build relationships, and *then* they start earning the megabucks.

Institutional Traders sell or buy blocks of stocks, bonds, and other financial instruments for Bear Stearns and client accounts. It's not a job for faint hearts. "On a busy day," one trader said, "it's all yelling and screaming. It appears very chaotic. But once you get there, it's all very orderly." Well, somewhat orderly.

An entry-level person is called a trainee or a clerk, and rotates among different sections to get a feel for the many different types of financial instruments traded. "We deal in relative values," explained a partner, and if a salesman calls with a client hot to spend millions and save on taxes, the trader had better know what specific bond or stock issue gives the client "the most bang for his buck." That comes from seeing everything.

People start out with grunt work—filing, learning, and listening to their bosses yell on the phones. The trading terminals have 150 buttons on the phone board, and as one successful young trader put it: "It's implied that your eagerness to do business depends on how quickly you answer the phone" and make those trades. Eager people are given a few small accounts, and build a reputation and a feel for the market from there.

"It's instant glory or instant failure," explained one trader. "In this business you know on a daily or even hourly basis how you're doing." Another said, "You can go wrong with good intentions and lose three million bucks." And then you have a problem. So it's not for faint hearts.

LIFE
There's a hardworking casualness about Bear Stearns. Just don't be late for meetings. The minute a meeting begins, the doors close, and latecomers are not tolerated.

Otherwise, there's a more casual feel about the place. Everyone stresses making your own way on the job, "grabbing responsibility" and "running with the ball."

"If you can prove you can make money for the firm, they'll turn you loose!" stressed someone who did. And that's the motivating factor here. One person described it as "sink or swim." No one's going to tell you what to do. Just do it!

Social life at the firm is secondary. "We'll go out for drinks across the street at Harry's; you can call that socializing if you want," said one analyst.

DOLLARS AND SENSE

"One of the things that bothers me about people coming to interview is that they seem to think that everyone starts at $50,000 a year," complained one trader. "And they read bizarre stories in the *Wall Street Journal* about Harvard MBAs averaging $125,000 a year."

Don't even dream about it. Everyone stresses that money shouldn't be that important at the beginning. "If you're given a job with a reputable company on the Street, don't worry about starting salary, take it!" advised a bond trader.

Experience counts for more, and with it comes the money. One trader said that Bear Stearns trading seats are reportedly worth a million dollars each. But you have to *earn* the right to use them.

GETTING IN—TRICKS OF THE TRADE

One person who interviews on college campuses says that peer pressure, and not a real desire for the job, motivates a lot of people to interview at investment banks. So it's the interviewer's job to cut those people from consideration.

Whatever the motive, it seems that a lot of people want to work for an investment bank. One person in the corporate finance department spent one day at Yale and came back with resumés from 172 people, of which he planned to interview 14 (of which one or two will get hired). He estimated that nearly all of them had the required intellectual capacity, and probably half had the right type of personality. "How do you decide?" he asked rhetorically.

"It's absurd . . ." said an investment banking partner, who went on to explain the importance of having the right contacts to even be considered. If it's that tough, how do people make it without the connections?

In corporate finance, an MBA is becoming almost a necessity, just as at the other firms. An MBA from a good school, and a decent work background, will get you an interview through the front door, from a recruiter on campus. The same goes for the undergraduate campus interviews—you need good grades and luck.

People in corporate finance also stress that there are large numbers of high-paying, interesting jobs outside the paneled walls of the corporate finance department, too, in syndications, trading, and research. They recommend trying for those jobs as well. "Very few people starve on Wall Street," one banker said with a smile. Some of these less popular, less hyped jobs pay as well or better, and the competition is far less intense.

Internships are available to undergraduates, and many start out that way, getting to know the firm before the job interview. But those are also hard to get. Persistence is essential. One person who "came for a summer job and never left" advised calling fairly frequently. Use the "I'm in the neighborhood and thought I'd drop in . . ." approach. Just be careful. There's a fine line between persistence and being a pest.

The sales and trading side of things is an excellent place for liberal arts BAs. A Bear Stearns partner pointed out that the firm wants people with different backgrounds; you can't talk business all the time, particularly at hockey games.

Bear Stearns interviews tend to be informal. On the trading and sales side, a partner explained, people meet with an interviewer, and go over everything—job, schooling, business desires. "Their whole life. Then we have the person go around, see other people, other contemporaries, then some old goat like me . . ." And maybe over to Harry's for a drink with some more people.

A salesman recalled asking someone during an interview if he knew whether he wanted to work in stocks or bonds, in selling or trading. The interviewee didn't know, and the salesman didn't recommend hiring him. His advice? On the resumé and during interviews: be specific!

"It's never all rosy. It's easy to say 'screw it'. So you should know that you *want* to do it." He paused. "Or at least *think* you want to do it." With so many people trying to get in, it's your job to convince them. Be tough, persistent, and *know* what you want.

THE BOTTOM LINE

A lot of people are bullish on the Bear.

MERRILL LYNCH

VITAL STATISTICS

- Locations: New York (headquarters); offices nationwide and worldwide
- revenues: $5.9 billion (1984)
- rank: 1st (among stock brokerages); 1st (among Wall Street firms in capital)
- employees: 42,200

AS SEEN FROM THE OUTSIDE

The ads say Merrill Lynch is "a breed apart," but in fact Merrill Lynch is many breeds—all financial, but *very* diverse. Anyone can find his or her niche here, since Merrill offers a multitude of financial services to a multitude of different types of people. Size is Merrill's biggest asset—it does almost everything everywhere. And who hasn't heard of Merrill Lynch? It's the nation's largest securities firms and more. It's a global investment and financial services company that has more offices, more registered representatives, and more capital than any other firm. It's a big player in most markets, and known to all.

In many ways, Merrill Lynch invented the modern securities business. When a Wall Street salesman, Charles Merrill, formed a partnership with Edmund Lynch in 1914 and created a medium-size brokerage house, Merrill Lynch was just one of the pack. But Charles Merrill was shrewder than most, and by the time the Great Depression began Merrill was already out of the stock market. Good timing! He got back into active management in 1949 and noticed that the general public didn't trust and didn't use most brokerage houses. So Merrill changed his house. He opened up the stuffy offices that looked like old-time banks, renamed his brokers "account executives," and started advertising heavily. With the motto "investigate, *then* invest," he convinced Middle Americans to buy securities by showing them Merrill Lynch research reports. No stuffiness, no secrecy. It was open, democratic, *American*-style investing—and it worked in a very big way, catapulting Merrill Lynch to the very top of the stock market heap.

Merrill Lynch has had some bumpy years since then, particularly in the early 1980s, when those average Americans once again got out of the stock market. Profits went down, unproductive or less productive people were laid off, and management reoriented itself to the old tried-and-true Merrill Lynch formula: marketing securities and financial services just like any other product. Find out what the public wants. If you don't have it, invent it, tell 'em about it, and sell, sell, sell.

Critics of the company call it a "jack of all trades, master of none," but no one denies that it has the market power to sell almost everything. As a "wire house," it has the electronic connections, and thousands of (human) brokers to market a new issue quickly and efficiently. And it's pushing to enter the ranks of the best in name as well as size in all its diverse financial activities. So far, it's succeeding well, winning back its number one spot in the eyes of many on the street.

To do this job, Merrill Lynch is organized into three large groups—Consumer Markets (the brokerage), Capital Markets (the investment banking part), and Real Estate and Insurance.

Merrill Lynch & Co. is the name of the holding company. Merrill Lynch Pierce, Fenner & Smith, Inc. is the subsidiary dealing in securities, options contracts, commodity and financial futures contracts, government and municipal securities, and investment banking. Merrill Lynch Realty, Inc. handles real estate services. And Merrill Lynch Life Agency, Inc. sells life insurance and annuities.

Together, they make up one of the largest and most comprehensive financial services companies in the world. And the world's largest brokerage—with five million customers.

And that's no bull . . .

HEARD AT THE WATER COOLER—
WHAT IT'S REALLY LIKE TO WORK HERE

Merrill Lynch is business. Big Business. And no one here forgets it.

Headquarters is a big black box of a building across the street from the *Wall Street Journal* and the World Trade Center. This is the financial district of New York City, the capital city of all the financial wheelers and dealers in the world, and Merrill Lynch is right where the action is. Everyone rushes around, dressed up and buttoned down. Merrill Lynch even has a Brooks Brothers clothing store right in the building. No need to wander around looking for blue pinstripes and wingtip shoes—Merrill Lynch staffers can buy them on their lunch hour.

The rush stops at the notoriously slow elevators—Merrill may be high tech, but its elevators aren't. People still talk of a trader who lost a $40,000 deal when stuck between floors, without a phone. But soon they'll be moving, and the elevators should be faster. Part of the company is going to New Jersey, and another part down the street to the new World Financial Center.

Inside the black box that is still its headquarters, the colors are red, gray, and blue. A red lobby, tasteful gray in the offices, and blue suits—with an occasional khaki or brown thrown in for self-expression. And the bustle and hard work continues: analysts studying financial data, traders shouting numbers at each other, and management quietly trying to figure out how to make these guys earn more. At Merrill, the bottom line counts, particularly now. Costs were skyrocketing, and management was well aware of the smaller and leaner firms that were closing Merrill's lead. Money is the name of the game, here, and everybody knows it.

As one young man said, "You *have* to be money-oriented. That's the only reason we're working so hard."

PEOPLE
Merrill Lynch people are as diverse as the financial services they offer. First there are the traders. "You've got to be a crazy person who drinks and smokes cigarettes. You've made a lot of money, but you'll die at forty," one trader said with a laugh. At Merrill, just like anywhere else, you don't forget the "clubby environment," where everyone knows everyone else, and everyone occasionally yells at everyone else. "You just have to get hardened," said someone who did.

Research analysts are quieter, more solitary—they interact more with computers than people. And then there are the account executives. "A breed unto themselves—individualists, entrepreneurial types," explained a former account executive. "Your destiny is in your own hands."

But maybe because Merrill is bigger and deals with so many clients, there always seems to be a streak of everyday Main Street

America. Even Merrill Lynch investment bankers don't seem as stuffy and formal as elsewhere. Merrill is organized into small units where everybody knows everybody else, and it's hard to be stuffy.

And that's about it at Merrill Lynch—smart, mainstream people in big time Wall Street.

JOBS

At the lower levels, Merrill is *the* place to be. "I don't think there's anywhere else in the business world where you can get this kind of exposure," said a very young financial analyst with very big dreams. Merrill Lynch has some of the best training programs on Wall Street.

The hottest is the **Corporate Intern Program**—eighteen months of hopping all around Merrill Lynch. It starts with a week of orientation; then trainees go to the Account Executive Training program—nine weeks at a retail sales office, then they study and take the General Securities Exam (the GSE), then they take four weeks of Sales Training, then they go into Securities Research, then Marketing Services, then elective assignments almost anywhere they want at Merrill Lynch.

Yes, it's very comprehensive. "We're kind of 'corporate nomads,'" said one intern. And if you're interested, Merrill will foot the bill for NYU Business School at night.

"It's the best program on the Street," a former intern said, highlighting the advantages of being exposed to all of Merrill Lynch (including lunch with the chairman and other bigwigs). It's also very good training. "I consider it a specialized business school in finance," said an intern who just passed the GSE. "I would rather be doing nothing else."

Problems? No one, inside or out, could talk of any—except maybe a dose of green-eyed envy from non-interns. "I've been called the 'Golden Boy,'" an intern said, laughing, and quickly added that his hard work and can-do attitude dispelled any resentment from hardworking non-interns. Well . . .

But later on things can get tougher. Interns may get to pick the area they want to end up in, but from then on in they're one of the pack. Merrill expects them to stay, and eventually form the nucleus of middle and even upper management, but meanwhile it expects them to produce.

And that can be a problem for someone who lets the program

go to his or her head. One former intern found himself laid off during a crunch in his section of the market—from golden boy to unemployed.

Others, less golden maybe, but just as smart, start out as research analysts and financial analysts. Both positions are part of investment banking programs, where analysts are trained to back up the bankers and crunch numbers for two years, and then leave for an MBA.

Research analysts in the Public Finance Group are expected to get up to speed quickly, working on all stages of a financing, from research to working on the actual issuing of securities. One analyst summed it up more simply: "We take a practical financing problem, translate it into investment banking jargon, produce an investment banking solution, then translate that into a practical solution for our client."

What that means is a lot of computer work on Merrill's IBM PC ATs, analyzing the cash flows and ratios of a deal; and a lot of grunt work, checking the numbers and phrasing of proposal documents that may be hundreds of pages long. "Weeks can go into the 90- or 100-hour range," one staffer said, describing his most recent project. "We put together a 100-page book in an evening, it was printed that night, and delivered the following morning." It sounds a bit worse than it was. A lot of the information is "canned"—standard "boiler plate" banking jargon, and a lot of a proposal is taken up with numbers, already studied, crunched, and re-crunched by the same hardworking analysts.

"There's a lot of grunt work, gofer work," added a research analyst. "And the words 'I can't' are not to be heard."

Financial analysts are also working the long hours. Merrill Lynch Capital Markets hires analysts out of school, trains them for four weeks in accounting, securities, and the ways of the firm, and then puts them to work backing Merrill investment bankers. People go into the general investment banking department, or into one of the specialized groups like Mergers and Acquisitions. But in any area, it's a lot of number crunching again, learning how to analyze and present the complicated financial transactions of Wall Street.

"Everyone thinks they've gotten in over their head at first," commented one analyst, who described the very steep learning curve of the first year.

"You are forced to learn the practical aspects of business school," said another hardworking analyst, who described the sexier parts of the job—meeting corporate lawyers, chairmen of the board, all the movers and shakers of the Street. It's an excellent exposure, and an excellent job to have on your resumé for business school.

In some ways, even the atmosphere is collegiate. Analysts work in teams, in small offices called "bullpens," and fellow analysts "become kind of your second family," as one person described it. "We cover for each other." Supervisors are associates with MBAs who work under a managing director of an area.

One difference, according to another analyst, "I never pulled an all-nighter at school—but I've pulled around eight here."

Investment banking may be glamorous, but there's that price to pay—a lot of hard work.

Sure, there's a mentor system, the senior guys help out, but all the same, the work must be done—and many stay until all hours of the night doing it. (Of course, Merrill foots the bill for food.)

After two years, most analysts are expected to pack up and go to B school. Most do—and most find it far easier to get in with that Merrill experience.

For nonfinancial types, Merrill has computers to offer—lots of them and lots of people running them, programming them, and fixing them. Merrill is known on Wall Street for its commitment to computerized financial services (it has one of the largest computer systems in the U.S.) and it hires top-notch computer people to uphold its reputation as one of the best-wired houses on the Street.

There's a **Computer Systems Intern Program** for those people; a **Systems Programming Class** for computer scientists, and a **Business Applications Class** for those without programming experience.

For both types, there are some definite benefits. As one former IBM programmer put it, "At IBM, there's so many of your type. You're one pea in a pod." Not so at Merrill. Here, "you're made to feel that you're the best and the brightest."

Traders might disagree. As with any computer system, there are "down times," and during these the floors may resound with uncomplimentary remarks about computers and Merrill's devotion to them. What kind of remarks? Don't ask.

People who don't make it in the internship programs can also start out as part-time or full-time **sales assistants** at regional brokerages—retail and institutional. One broker who tried this route explained that it's not for proud types: "You have to start at the bottom—and I mean the bottom."

The job is assisting the account executives by handling phone calls, typing, "sweeping the floors." But if you're good, you may get a piece of what the account executive makes and then a shot at being an account exec yourself.

Some interns eventually choose to become account executives as well, skipping some of the early grunt work and jumping into the real work of selling securities.

It can be rewarding, but also intimidating. "It's all up to you," said one staffer. "You sit at your little desk with your Quotron and telephone book, and it's all up to you." You've got to start calling and getting clients interested in buying stocks or bonds or other investment instruments. And that's where the name Merrill Lynch has its advantages. "The only thing they remember is Merrill Lynch. They certainly don't remember my name," commented one account executive.

So, all the low level jobs at Merrill lead to the same thing— selling or helping to sell financial services to the public or to corporate clients.

And at Merrill the account executive is king or queen. "Ninety percent of the departments here at Merrill exist for the account executive," a former corporate intern explained. Management may sometimes have its problems, but the real work is selling those stocks and bonds to the public. That's where the real money is, too.

LIFE
According to some interns, there's not much time for life after Merrill Lynch—maybe because leaving at 10 P.M. and waking up at 6 A.M. doesn't exactly motivate you to spend those few free hours dancing and drinking. Sleeping, maybe.

So interns make Merrill Lynch their life. There's a team spirit— "We're all pulling for one another," commented one staffer.

But later on some of that glow fades. Older Merrill staffers complain about morale problems from layoffs in the 1980s, the politicking and the management changes that have confused or annoyed more than a few. Size is another problem. When you're big, it's easy to get lost in the shuffle, and more than a few people cite complaints with operations people and administration.

Account executives and sales people sound the most content. They don't have the time to complain. They're cold-calling potential clients all day long—"You just keep going," said one energetic staffer, "some days till 8 or 9 at night" handling rejections, client problems, and new accounts.

Then come the commissions—a lot of green money for all the hard work. "As long as you're producing, you don't have a morale problem," said an institutional salesperson who produces.

And producing is what jobs and life at Merrill Lynch are all about.

DOLLARS AND SENSE

One person said it all—for all Merrill Lynch interns. "You are paid well and you *will* earn it." That makes Merrill Lynch no different from most Wall Street firms.

Interns receive salaries in the mid-20s to low 30s, and standard benefits including health and life insurance.

The only complaint most people have concerning money here is the lack of time in which to spend it. After internships or sales assistantships are over, account executives average about $30,000 a year. But there are stories of people who top $100,000 the first year as well. You get what you put in. That's the fun part about being a stockbroker.

Merrill may add perks like several-thousand-dollar bonuses and free lunches, juice and coffee for interns, but the real benefits are intangible—a learning experience that's probably the best on Wall Street and a chance to see every aspect of the securities business to decide where you fit in.

GETTING IN—TRICKS OF THE TRADE

"Fortunately, I was granted an interview at Merrill. That can be the hardest step," said one young woman who made it in.

Maybe it's the ads on TV—everyone applies to Merrill. The corporate intern program receives thousands of resumés for fewer than twenty openings, and it's not much better for the research analyst and investment analyst positions.

Good grades, "outstanding qualities of leadership, initiative, and accomplishment in both academic and extracurricular activities" are essential. Better yet—get to know someone who already works there. A good way to get a foot in the door is working as a summer intern or part-time sales assistant (in New York or any local office). Then, next year, apply for a plum entry-level position.

On interviews, mention outside interests. "God knows there are enough people who get 800 on their GMATs," said an investment banker on the interview circuit. "I'd rather someone who's a real go-getter who had a 3.3 instead of a 4.0."

In short, Merrill is looking for that well-rounded person—who can sell.

THE BOTTOM LINE

The big one: the most jobs, the most capital, the most diverse, and the most applications.

HIGH TECH

The fad is over. For the first time in years, the number of people majoring in computer science dropped in 1985. And it's about time. Jobs in the computer industry require talent, brains, and hustle—it's not an easy fast track to money.

Generally, high tech companies hire entry-level people in the technical areas of product design and development, research and development, and production and manufacturing, as well as in the nontechnical finance, marketing, and sales departments. But even those so-called nontechnical areas usually require some degree of technical expertise and knowledge. After all, technology is the business, so staffers have to understand that business.

Product Design and Development and **Research and Development** staffers are the hands-on people at a high tech company, and they generally start out with engineering and computer science degrees. They're the ones who come up with ideas, and test and modify them until they become salable products. Obviously, the actual job duties depend upon the product. Staffers in hardware design work with an aspect of the computer they're developing, while those in software enter as programmers, developing applications or systems programs. Whatever the specific position, typically they work in teams that are long on brainstorming and short on rigid structure. Hours are flexible, as are chains of command. Pay varies, the average starting salary for college grads being in the mid-20s, the mid-30s for advanced degree holders.

Production and Manufacturing staffers are involved with actually getting a product made. They'll work overseeing a plant, supervising the line people and developing ways to enhance manufacture of the computer or computer product; so responsibilities range from the purely technical to personnel management. Usually beginning as production supervisors, staffers in this area can move up to become production managers and plant managers. Salaries are about the same as those for design people.

Marketing is becoming a fast-track area in most high tech companies, especially as competition rises and sales slump. The marketing department in a high tech firm, as in other industries, works with the development, introduction, and positioning of a product. Most people enter marketing as an assistant product manager or product manager, responsible for one aspect of a product or the entire product itself. They work with the technical staff in developing the product, troubleshooting, and giving input as to the market's needs. They work with the sales department in the product introduction and with finance in keeping the product within budget.

As marketing staffers climb the ladder, they move into areas of greater responsibility. Product managers past the entry-level stages may be responsible for an entire line of products, and may move up to become product marketing managers and oversee an entire division. While it's theoretically a nontechnical area, most companies prefer staffers with technical degrees—especially given marketing's interaction with the design and development staffs. Starting salaries vary, with the average beginning salary in the upper 20s to low 30s.

Sales staffers are the ones who get out there and sell the high tech products. Again, a technical background is preferred, as salespeople have to fully understand the product they're selling and present it comprehensively to the potential buyers. They're briefed by the marketing staffers when a new product is introduced, and then go on the road to convince customers to buy it. As with any sales job, it requires hustle. Depending upon the company and the products offered, sales reps may be responsible for one product line or a complete category of products. Typically, sales reps begin with a small territory or account, then graduate to larger geographic responsibilities, higher volume territories, or large national accounts. Base salaries begin in the mid-20s, but money improves with improving sales technique, since most sales jobs include commissions.

Financial staffers, as with their counterparts in other industries, work to support the other staffs. Analyzing budgets, doing cost projections and planning, employees in the financial departments usually enter as assistant financial analysts, then move up to positions with more responsibility. It's often a high-visibility department with a fast track toward management. Beginning salaries are in the upper 20s to low 30s.

APPLE COMPUTER

VITAL STATISTICS

- locations: Cupertino, CA (headquarters); factories in Fremont, CA; Garden Grove, CA; Carrollton, TX; Singapore; Malaysia; Cork, Ireland; and sales offices nationwide
- revenues: $1.9 billion (1985 sales)
- rank: 234th (*Fortune* 500)
- employees: 5,400

AS SEEN FROM THE OUTSIDE

Apple Computer is an American success story in the rags-to-riches tradition. It's one of a handful of companies that can boast of starting in a California garage and growing into a multimillion-dollar player in the international personal computer industry.

Actually, founders Steven Jobs and Stephen Wozniak were more interested in making devices that could tap into the telephone system for free calls when they first got together. They never made any such equipment, but somewhere in their tinkering, they came up with an idea and a system for a simple computer. And they chose a simple name for it: Apple.

The first models were expensive toys compared to the highly sophisticated and powerful machines of today, but they captured the imagination of kids and businessmen who were ready to move into the twenty-first century. More importantly, Apple caught powerhouse corporations such as IBM and Xerox napping, and grabbed a lion's share of the personal computer market.

Apple Computer Co. was formed in 1977, and in 1980 Apple went public with the largest initial stock offering in corporate history, selling five million shares at $22 each. One after another, Apple turned out popular top-selling computers: the Apple I, Apple II, and Apple II-Plus machines, and made them fixtures in schoolhouses and homes throughout the nation. The stock soared to $62 a share in 1983.

Unfortunately, Apple fell victim to its adolescence and its own success. Jobs, Wozniak, and the other executives began believing that they had the Midas touch, and decided to go head-to-head with IBM. In 1983, Apple introduced the Lisa computer for business users. It also ignored its popular "open architecture" design and shifted to closed systems that didn't allow for easy expandability.

Lisa was a flop, and it soon became obvious to Wall Street that the Apple style just wouldn't cut it in the business market. As a result, Apple brought in as president John Scully, a straitlaced executive from PepsiCo Inc., a master of selling consumer products, and handed him the reins and the mandate to provide the company with tougher, less laid-back supervision.

The Macintosh computer was launched in January 1984. It attracted a large following of personal users, but couldn't crack the office/business market. Suddenly, Apple, a company used to doubling in size every year, was on a rollercoaster ride. Profits fell 6.1 percent in one quarter of 1984, then soared 500 percent the next.

It was obvious by 1985 that the entire personal computer business was in a deep slump. Four Apple factories were closed for a week due to oversupply, and the Lisa was scrapped. Stephen Wozniak left Apple and, by May, Jobs had also left.

A new era began at Apple.

HEARD AT THE WATER COOLER— WHAT IT'S REALLY LIKE TO WORK HERE

Well, Apple hasn't let go of its hold on the public imagination, that's for sure. As one staffer noted, Apple has a reputation for being a "laid-back, California-type place that is also hugely successful."

"That's an important combination in this part of the country," he continued. "Everybody out here believes the mellow lifestyle will conquer the earth. And here's this little off-the-wall computer company with people in flowered shirts who are pushing around those stuffed shirts at IBM."

Apple may have been through some lean times, but the image persists—and employees like it that way. "If you ever wanted to be a techno-celebrity, this is the place," commented one.

Of course, the celebrity status ends once an employee drives onto the sprawling Apple Computer corporate campus in Cupertino, California, south of San Francisco. Behind the wooden walls of the one-story buildings, the mood is serious, although not grim. It is pretty obvious that IBM has gotten up, brushed itself off, and gotten back to work. And it's pretty obvious that there's a new hand at the helm, someone who's determined to fight.

There's a new mood at Apple. Fun and freedom are no longer part of fringe benefits. And the unofficial T-shirt worn by computer development division staffers says, "working 90 hours a week and loving it."

As a software developer said, "Look, this is still the second largest maker of personal computers, so it is successful. There's a new attitude here. Nobody gets down, they just get down to business and they make computers. There's a new emphasis on marketing and sales, because you have to go out and prove yourself and your computers to the rest of the world."

"It isn't as much fun, but it's not bad."

PEOPLE

It's a young, brash company, and as you'd expect, there are a lot of young people here—the average age reportedly is twenty-nine. So there's definitely a youthful spirit here, that goes hand-in-hand with the laid-back image.

But youthful and laid back doesn't mean nonconformist any more. Apple is a big company with a business image to uphold. So not everyone here is running around in Hawaiian shirts and jeans. Sure, product development and design staffers are as casual as they were. But corporate executives wear suits, junior staffers and salespeople wear jackets and ties, and suits when they're on the road.

For all of Apple's size, it's still an entrepreneurial company. Its roots lie in personal initiative and an impossible dream. And that seems to have affected a lot of people here. Many staffers are dreamers, people who are bent on making it.

"If there is one dominant characteristic about the people here, it's that they're optimistic and always looking forward," said a hardware designer. "People who come here have personal goals of being successful and they want Apple to be successful and not just survive. They want to get ahead and be somebody, so they don't get depressed or sit and worry when things go wrong."

Part of wanting to get ahead here is believing that the worst of times is over. "Even through the bad times with the market slumping and all, you didn't hear any complaining or bitching in the corridors. We keep working and we know that when the market recovers Apple will be ready."

JOBS

Apple employees have to believe in computers, and that means more than just tinkering with them. Key to being an Apple staffer is being a self-starter who can be relied on to work hard, work smart, and work long hours, if necessary, without supervision. That requires a special kind of maturity.

"The nicest thing about working at Apple is that, from the start, you are given your own piece of a project and expected to perform," said an engineer. "You don't waste your time for years waiting for a chance to prove yourself. They want you to start working right away."

Jumping right into work doesn't have to be difficult here. There's Apple University, a "university without walls" that offers seminars and, occasionally, weekend retreats for people at all levels and in all departments. And Apple has a team approach to work, so new employees can keep their eyes and ears open and pick up quite a bit.

As a young woman only a few years out of college said, "You get a good education here, not just about computers, but about business. You learn from watching and working with the other people. Sooner or later, you fall in and start to feel very creative and start blue-skying new ideas with the rest of them. And maybe one of them will be a breakthrough."

That's the attitude people need to succeed around here. But it's not enough to believe in yourself and have technical know-how. There's another serious consideration about working here—Apple's future is tied to mass sales. That means that, regardless of their position, staffers must always think in terms of sales and marketing, or this is the wrong place for them. So today's Apple employee is part computer maker, part marketing whiz, and part salesperson.

"In a way, it makes no sense to make a computer that doesn't sell, or to try and sell a computer that you don't understand or don't like," said one staffer. "If there's something you don't understand, you learn it the hard way—spending long hours until you have it right."

Apple staffers find out every six months how they're doing, when performance reviews are made. It's a big picture place, where employees get involved every step of the way—from development to packaging to sales. And staffers who know only their own area of expertise quickly pick up the others.

"When I came here, I didn't know anything about sales, and I didn't think I cared to do sales," an employee said, "I was in marketing, and after a while you get committed. I knew how to develop the product and I had ideas on selling it. In a way, it's an opportunity to show what you've got."

This doesn't mean that there aren't specific jobs. For instance, Apple is always looking for electrical engineers, mechanical engineers, and computer science majors, most of whom are recruited right out of college, to do **product and development** work. The difference here is that there are no set guidelines and there's no single track for moving up. It all gets back to being self-motivated and having personal initiative.

When Apple hires people for **marketing, finance, and operations** management, it looks for students with an MBA or a graduate school degree with a specialty in these areas. As for Apple's extensive national **sales** force, it doesn't hire any inexperienced salespeople. They are drawn either from the ranks of employees who show a desire to sell, or from other computer companies. The sales force is *very* new, even for Apple. Most of it sprang up during the boom year of 1984, when Apple introduced both the Lisa and the Macintosh. In a then-typical and somewhat manic Apple fashion, they advertised, interviewed, and hired the sales team in 100 days. New recruits went through a three-week crash course called Sell With Apple Training (SWAT).

But for all the innovation that Apple still represents to many, you can't get away from one fact. It's not the young upstart any more. It has become big business—and that affects staffers, especially in the nontechnical areas.

"There is a strong corporate feel here and a 9-to-5 mentality, although the hours are usually longer than that," said one young woman. "And hard work and performance count for a lot, both for getting ahead and for learning the trade."

LIFE

"The first thing people want to know when they find out you work here, is about the Ping-Pong table," said one young junior executive in marketing sales. "I wanted to see it, too, on my first day. But it was gone. Anyway, the story has it that Steve Jobs had a Ping-Pong table set up in the reception area and any time you wanted to play, you could."

Yes, life at Apple used to be just a bit free-wheeling . . . And, wait, there's more. "You could watch movies any time you wanted, too," he went on. "There was a sort of recreation room set up somewhere with a video cassette recorder, projection TV, and a library of movies. And you could sit there and watch all day."

Okay, Apple was *very* relaxed. But that was back then, when Steve Jobs made it look as if young people, hard work, and easy living could conquer the earth. But what about now? It's not quite as relaxed and it's a bit more serious.

"Life here comes down to one of two things—either you know your stuff or you don't," said a staffer. "Most people here find this type of environment invigorating. It's like you're completely exposed. You do your work and there's no place to hide and no one to blame."

That doesn't mean it's super-competitive. This *is* Apple, re-member, home of the original "work should be fun" ethic. So staffers avoid backstabbing and stepping on one another to get ahead. "There's competition here, but it's directed against the challenge, not against each other," noted a young woman.

Life at Apple seems to revolve around personal challenges. Just look how it started. Well, the entrepreneurial spirit that was born in a garage and pervaded Apple's halls isn't dead. It's just that, as Apple is becoming more like a typical corporation, it's the individual employees who are keeping those entrepreneurial flames burning.

"A lot of people here see Apple Computer as a stepping-stone in their careers," said a secretary. "And the [Silicon] Valley is filled with people who left Apple and started their own computer companies doing specialized work, or project work for Apple. Everyone is always thinking of greater things."

DOLLARS AND SENSE
We weren't able to learn about salaries here, but the company reportedly pays rather well—even during the slump. According to company literature, "since we realize that even A-teams have superstars, our guidelines have no maximums."

In addition, Apple offers stock options, profit sharing, and stock-purchasing plans. And there's one more thing—a "Loan to our Own" program. Apple lends employees a computer to take home and, after a year, it belongs to the employees. No strings attached. But maybe a mouse . . .

GETTING IN—TRICKS OF THE TRADE

If you're the right person for Apple, you usually know it. Working here means belonging to a different world, with new heroes and values.

"The computer and engineering types have already done work that distinguished them from the rest," said one designer. "Many are the ones who built a computer for a school project and actually made it work. A lot have already accomplished some feat in the computer world. They know what they're doing, they know computers, they know the same computer people, and they bring a lot of ideas to the company."

As you'd expect, the keys to landing a job here are technical skills and knowledge. Apple recruits heavily on college campuses for engineers and computer science majors. It concentrates on colleges with the top reputations and, obviously, doesn't hit all campuses. But it's always looking for quality people from anywhere.

"If you're interested in working at Apple, send us a letter about you and tell us something about yourself, plus a resumé," urged a woman in the personnel service department. "We screen all resumés and give everyone a response. In general, we ask people who look good on paper to come in for a visit."

If you're one of those people who looks good on paper, you'd also better look good in person. "It is a lean, aggressive company," said one recruiter. "There aren't many places to hide deadwood. Apple can't afford to make a mistake hiring people, so it's very discriminating and selective."

Perhaps the best way to get into Apple is to join its summer jobs program. Each year, Apple hires a good number of college students, engineers and computer science majors, for the summer. A majority of them return after graduation for full-time positions. A growing percentage of Apple employees started this way.

So if you want to get your hands on all aspects of the computer business, from development to packaging and sales, Apple could present you with a big challenge. It wants smart, driven self-starters.

THE BOTTOM LINE

It hasn't gone to seed.

ASHTON-TATE

VITAL STATISTICS

- **location:** Culver City, CA (headquarters); distributors and dealers nationwide and worldwide; 4 subsidiaries overseas
- **revenues:** $82.3 million (1985)
- **rank:** 3rd among independent software producers
- **employees:** 459

AS SEEN FROM THE OUTSIDE

When you think of corporate acquisitions, you don't usually think of a software company. And when you think of royalty payments, a publishing company comes to mind. But they're both big parts of Ashton-Tate's business philosophy.

The company doesn't hesitate to buy software products, arrange royalty agreements with their authors, and then market them. It also doesn't shrink from buying other software companies, or, at a minimum, interests in companies that appeal to it. Most recently, it signed agreements to buy MultiMate International Corporation, the company that produced the word processing package MultiMate Professional Word Processor.

Apparently this aggressive marketing and acquisition stance works. Ashton-Tate has come a long way since it was founded in 1980 as Software Plus, Inc. The company changed its name to Ashton-Tate in 1983. Tate is for George Tate, the late cofounder, and Ashton is for . . . well, there's no one by that name, but it sounded snappy. It started by marketing its dBase II system, and the money Ashton-Tate made was pretty snappy, too—$465,000 in revenues its first full year of business.

Today, the company's products are concentrated in two areas: data base management and multifunction. The dBase family includes dBase II (designed to operate 8 bit microprocessors) and III (for the newer 16 bit machines), dBase/Answer and dBase Run Time, among others. Its other big products are Framework, a software package that combines spreadsheet and word processing programs, and Framework II, which combines a larger, faster, and more powerful spreadsheet with an advanced word processor. The company also has a publishing group that it maintains is the largest among the microsoftware vendors.

According to company reports, as of March 1985, the company had worldwide shipments of over 546,000 dBase units and 63,000 of Framework. That's a lot of products. So the major problem is getting them to the marketplace. To do that, Ashton-Tate has developed a distributor-dealer network in the U.S. There are six major distributors and fifty major dealers, and then another layer of two thousand dealers. The distributors sell to retail stores and provide product support, merchandising, and other support efforts. These domestic distributors, according to the company's annual report, accounted for 50 percent of the company's revenues in 1985. The dealers are retail operations and account for 16 percent of the company's sales.

Ashton-Tate makes no secret of the fact that it is out to attract more business from the original equipment manufacturers (OEMs), and has stepped up its efforts in this area.

Internationally, the company has four foreign subsidiaries—in the United Kingdom, the Netherlands, West Germany, and Spain—as well as dealers and distributors in the key European and Latin American countries and in Asia, Australia, and the Middle East.

So Ashton-Tate is on the move . . . And, if there were an Ashton, he'd be proud.

HEARD AT THE WATER COOLER—
WHAT IT'S REALLY LIKE TO WORK HERE

Ashton-Tate is young and growing, and it's in a fairly new industry. So it doesn't have to operate by the old rules. And it doesn't.

Unless the old rules included having a parrot on the premises. For a while the company was receiving phone calls and visitors for the nonexistent Mr. Ashton, so they decided they might as well wing it. They came up with Ashton, the parrot and company mascot.

Parrots aside, there are other clues that this isn't your average company, like an open office setup that looks as if it were designed by the people who did "Miami Vice," with plenty of lavenders and yellows.

"There's not a lot of mahogany around," said a marketing manager. But he wasn't referring to the office decoration as much as the management style. Ashton-Tate is big on the new-fangled "management by walking around" and letting employees get their job done their own way.

But as a company becomes successful, usually bureaucracy follows. One manager did say that policy books are coming to Ashton-Tate. Still, staffers say it's unlikely that the strict corporate policies that characterize many older businesses will be imposed. As one employee said, there's a big difference between establishment-type businesses and companies like Ashton-Tate—growth.

In the established fields, "everyone has it figured out, but here, we're blazing a trail," a young man said. "We're establishing some of the rules and precedents the industry will operate under."

And they're given the room to do it.

PEOPLE

"There's a lot of identity between us and the company," said a manager.

Like the company itself, people here seem generally easygoing. But as a marketing employee noted, the concept is "working hard, building, developing, growing."

"The people here tend to talk about business," a financial analyst added, "but we laugh a lot."

It's all part of being in a fledgling industry. Several people here have worked for major corporations in established industries such as oil and packaged goods. And they say that the other companies were much more formal.

Here, people are allowed to be themselves, so you see the range from the corporate to the casual. But they try not to let anyone feel *too* left out. So there's a custom of "Friday Dress Down Day"—for everyone.

JOBS

"Ashton-Tate is marketing driven," summed up a marketing staffer.

Ashton-Tate is a little unusual for a software company. Nearly half of its employees are in marketing: a two-hundred-strong department. Now it's beefing up its research side, housing it in separate quarters. Up till now, its major.product lines have been acquired either from other developers or other companies. (Actually, Ashton has even acquired other companies when it thought the product was right.) Maybe that's why there's such an emphasis on marketing and finance.

On the **marketing** side, the career path is clear—from technical marketing specialist, the bottom rung on a project, to project manager or assistant product manager. At the product manager level, staffers are responsible for a specific product. A product manager explained how the department gets into the technical end. "We develop the marketing requirements and take these to the development organization," he said. "They tell us whether they can build and design the product. Consequently, the better technical understanding you have, the better off you are."

There's a downside to marketing, which is long hours. "Nobody tells them to work long hours, and we don't hold weird meetings on Saturdays," a manager said. "People work long hours because they have a lot of responsibility and like what they're doing."

A senior manager in the department said, "We don't hire people with the intention of having attrition, because the biggest cost of software is in human resources, not the cost of material."

With this in mind, the company takes great care in hiring. Most employees come to the marketing department here with experience either in computers or in marketing in another industry.

What's it like in **finance**? Well, there are several elements to this department, including the basic accounting department. But that's not the finance we're talking about. Financial Planning is the name of part of the game, and part and parcel of that group is acquisitions.

A young senior financial analyst explained that there is no set track in his department. But you'd better have an MBA or CPA. The entry-level job is that of assistant to a senior financial analyst. Then it's a move up the ladder to financial analyst, then senior financial analyst, supervisor, and finally manager.

The first couple of months are tough, an analyst noted, since Ashton-Tate doesn't have a formal training program. As with the marketing side, you're thrown right into the work at hand. Because of this, prior experience helps—and so does a lot of confidence.

The normal workday starts at around 8 A.M., according to one analyst, and usually ends between 5:30 and 6 P.M. But when time comes around for budgets or acquisitions, things are different. During budgets, "you can work to midnight," and acquisitions, while not all that frequent in the course of a year, do add to the overtime. So the downside in this group, as with the others, is the long hours. And there is a lot of pressure.

But at Ashton-Tate people don't mind the pressure all that much. As one employee put it, "you have the impression you make a difference and there is a lot of interface with management."

LIFE
Sounds like a pressured, rushed, high-tension ulcer haven, doesn't it? Guess again. There is party time, though not on the same schedule as in the past.

"When the company was small, there was a party every other week." Now things have changed slightly. The parties are held only once every quarter because of the number of people. Pretty tough.

But Ashton-Tate doesn't settle for the ordinary. For example, the opening day of the baseball season was sufficient reason to set up a tent in the parking lot and celebrate.

The company is generous with freebies as well, and every employee has a satin Ashton-Tate jacket with his or her name on it.

And when there's not a party, people gather at a local sushi bar. It's not just one group, as a staffer stressed. People come from every group within the company.

DOLLARS AND SENSE
Since you can enter a software company in so many different ways, it's hard to peg the salaries. One senior executive said some may start at $20,000, and others at $30,000 to $35,000 and up.

But all agree that the pay is "pretty good." And there's more than just pay. There's the stock ownership plan under which employees can buy into the company every six months at a price below market value. It's a complicated formula that changes every six months, but usually runs 85 percent of the lowest price during the period on the offering date.

The company also has a 401K plan (sort of an IRA) to which

employees contribute, and the company kicks in 25 cents for every dollar. Then there are the "Ashton Awards." Three employees are selected each quarter, based on their contributions on the job, and receive $2,500 each.

And there's more. There are bonus plans not only for senior management, but also for everyone else each quarter. If the income plan is met, everyone receives an extra 2 percent of salary during the quarter. If it's exceeded, it's 3 percent, and if it's 90 percent of the plan, it's 1 percent.

"There are a lot of incentives," one employee said. And since there aren't many layers of management, "you can really shine here."

You can also make a nice living . . .

GETTING IN—TRICKS OF THE TRADE

So you want to work at Ashton-Tate? Well, it's a long process. First of all, the company works primarily through headhunters. There is no campus recruitment at this time, although one senior management official said this would be starting up shortly. The details of the program still remain cloudy.

Everyone here emphasizes that selection is a long process. Basically, there's a screening interview, then a second round when the candidate talks with several people who would be colleagues, and a final interview, when the candidate is interviewed by a high ranking executive. Since the company believes in carefully screening its prospects, the time they take before hiring may be several months.

What do they look for? A senior executive described his criteria. First, potential. "The individual has to show the background and the personality to run a division within eight years." His second criterion is "a proven record of accomplishment." He explained more fully, "nobody works a 40-hour week here and the individual should show drive and a mature understanding of what the demands are going to be."

During that interview process, he added, candidates should know the right questions to ask and, if they don't, "we don't hire them."

So what are those right questions? It all depends on the department you're applying for. As with any computer software company, there are many ways to enter—technical, marketing, finance, or various other departments. But whatever the department, employees need a working knowledge of computers.

It's all very logical. Obviously, technical staffers have to know computers inside and out. In the nontechnical positions, as an employee pointed out, "you don't have to have formal training in computer science, but you'd better be able to use them."

And you'd better love computers. As one employee stated—"Software or sex . . . that's a hard decision." If you're Ashton-Tate material, you'd better have a tough time deciding.

THE BOTTOM LINE

A little corporate, a little loose, and a lot of software.

HEWLETT PACKARD

VITAL STATISTICS

- **locations:** Palo Alto,CA (headquarters); offices and plants nationwide and worldwide
- **revenues:** $6.04 billion (1984 sales)
- **rank:** 60th (*Fortune* 500)
- **employees:** 82,000

AS SEEN FROM THE OUTSIDE

The first Hewlett Packard product was the model 200A oscillator. Why model 200? "Because the number sounded big." It was produced in Dave Packard's garage, and the paint on the instrument panel was baked on in Dave Packard's kitchen oven. A light bulb was used as the amplitude control device. It was a small beginning for a five billion dollar, *Fortune* 500 company, and a classic American entrepreneurial success story. But unlike at many other companies with small beginnings, that entrepreneurial spirit of innovation and individualism stayed on.

Now there's a new challenge at HP. Loosely organized individualism and innovation don't work as well in today's super-competitive and super-integrated office computer market. So HP has to change.

So HP has innovated itself into a more centralized bureaucracy, and it is staking much of its future on a new computer line. People at HP are talking in code these days. Tight security and code words like "Firefox" surround the new "Spectrum" computer line, which they hope will serve as the basis for HP's three separate families of computers, the 1000 (for factory use), the 3000 (for commercial use), and the 9000 series (an engineering work station).

As a unified line, Spectrum represents a different approach for HP. Like the computers it wants to sell, the company is moving to integrate and unify its engineering and marketing functions. The hope is that along the way HP doesn't lose its unique character as an exciting and innovative place to work.

This is a company that emphasizes enjoying your work, beginning with the tight small teams that surround a product or a project. All HP offices, all over the world, have only two floors, to keep the bosses and workers physically together. HP calls its managerial style "Management by walking around," and this positive approach has made the company famous outside the engineering field as one of the best places to work. And innovation is a byword here. Among other things, the company put the slide rule into the museum, introducing the first hand-held scientific calculator.

Today, HP manufactures computers, peripherals, electronic test and measuring instruments, medical electronic products, and analytical instruments in over thirty cities in the U.S. and abroad. It also has support offices and distributorships in over seventy countries.

It's a long way from Dave Packard's garage, and there's more innovation to come.

HEARD AT THE WATER COOLER—
WHAT IT'S REALLY LIKE TO WORK HERE

"At IBM, I wore a navy blue wool suit and I was not out of place. When I interviewed here I was in a navy blue wool suit and I stood out like a sore thumb," said one young employee who has put away her "power outfits."

Hewlett Packard is not a 9-to-5 company. Jeans are okay, open neck shirts are okay; there are volleyball courts at the offices in Palo Alto and even higher level employees play—if they want to.

It wants you to get the job done, but it's not big on telling you how. "We look for people who can work very well in an unstructured environment with very little direction," said an enthusiastic product manager.

"When I first started working here my boss said, 'I don't care if you work forty hours a week, thirty hours a week, or sixty hours a week. I care about whether you have done what I expect you to do,'" a manufacturing engineer explained.

Yes, there's flexi-time and a "flexible outlook," and a real concern for the employees. It's almost an American version of the best of a Japanese company. No, they don't sing the company song every morning, but at least at one plant, calisthenics are part of the morning routine. Teamwork and consensus are highly valued.

With the computer industry in the doldrums, HP has been retrenching, but in a typical HP way. Everyone (except the sales staff) is taking every other Friday off without pay. Everyone stays in his job, but everyone makes a little less. Teamwork again, sharing the best and the worst. Even the chairman took a 10 percent cut.

Employees describe HP as "a big company with a lot of small decentralized businesses." But things are now getting more centralized, and a bit more corporate.

"We have so many geniuses at this corporation—it's really true," said one engineer. "And things happen because those geniuses make them happen. They know how to do it, so they just do it. But what happens when they leave, or they move? We have to end up reinventing the wheel." So HP is now becoming more systematic, "more process oriented." And maybe a bit more like a mainstream company. Some employees praise HP's speed in implementing these changes, others say it's taking too long. It depends on where they are. No one seems to doubt that HP management is doing its best.

One employee said it best: "The company's not perfect. But it's very intelligent."

PEOPLE

"It's really a little scary sometimes. We do have somewhat of a clone environment, where a lot of us tend to have similar styles," said one employee who loves HP.

There is an "HP Way," a corporate style that employees are expected to have. The open offices and work places symbolize the unsecretive, unpolitical, and un-backstabbing attitude that employees share. They also share a lot of enthusiasm. Other companies talk about it, but at HP it seems more than just hype. Employees come across as honest, a bit earnest, and always emphasizing the positive. It can be grating to those who aren't willing to make what one person described as "a culture change."

"It's kind of frustrating," another employee explained. "They value so much being positive, helping people, patting people on the back. But there are times when the situation is just bad, and you've just got to state it that way." Nevertheless, she wants to make a fit—so she's learning to use her "hard-nosed East Coast attitudes" positively.

That's the way it is at HP. Be an individual, but make sure you get along the HP way. Oddly enough, for some it can be intimidating. One employee described his first day at the office just that way—having everyone overhear his telephone conversations, and overhearing everyone else's. That fear faded. "All of a sudden I found I was becoming more productive—because there were no barriers."

HP people are open and young. The company has grown very fast—almost half the employees have been there for five years or less. Even the newer employees share the fundamental HP attitudes.

"I think there's a lot of hype around HP," one two-year vet commented. "But a lot of it's justified. People who have worked at other companies can't believe how apolitical it is here. I've seen some politics, but nothing malicious."

The best HP people are open, flexible, and nonpolitical.

JOBS

Just like HP people, HP jobs are open, flexible, and nonpolitical.

"When I look around HP, look at the people in the top jobs, they're there because they worked hard," a young man commented. "You don't see people in top jobs because they're politically savvy. Some near the top aren't savvy at all. If they were, they'd be in higher positions."

So what about the lower positions? HP has targeted fifteen basic entry-level areas—ranging from development engineers, production engineers, and manufacturing engineers to marketing engineers, financial analysts, and sales representatives.

They all have something in common—a team organization that is as small as possible. Organized into divisions and divided into teams, HP engineers see a lot of each other all the time. We talked to people in the Product Marketing divisions and the Manufacturing divisions—two of the most important areas of the company.

Product Marketing is currently seen as *the* nontechnical route to upper management, according to a staffer who transferred into that area from faster-moving finance. It's still pretty technical, though. "Most marketing staff are engineers," said one nonengineer. "They're always throwing techie terms around."

And, appropriately, people in the low level positions are called marketing engineers. They have responsibility for a specific product and report to the product manager, who has responsibility for a line of products. The product manager in turn reports to the product marketing manager, who is responsible for the marketing of all the products of a division. It sounds cut-and-dried, just like anywhere else, and to a certain degree it is. But only to a certain degree.

"When we get in a crunch in marketing, when we can't get some things done, well, heck, we'll send for some people from manufacturing, and some people from the lab. We divvy up the work and get it done," said one manager, extolling the virtues of HP's casual flexibility. "We can restructure a whole division in a month."

That flexibility is essential, because the work is so varied. What does an HP product manager do on a typical day?

"There is no typical day, because it's such a random set of events," insisted a manager. "My job ranges from conceptualizing a product, working in the lab defining it, developing it, introducing it, pricing it, positioning it, training a sales force to sell it, and then talking to customers." The fun part, according to another manager, lies in managing the "trade-off" between design and marketability—helping lab engineers design a product that will sell.

That's where teamwork comes in. Product people work in small teams, but they interact frequently with other teams in the labs and in various support functions. And, of course, with the sales force and customers. "I'm the eyes and ears of our organization" explained a manager. And the mouth. "You almost give a pep rally to the field," said another manager. The field? "That's what we call our sales force."

For all the teamwork and flexibility, people are evaluated in a very structured and individualistic way. There's a formal evaluation once a year, which is linked directly to raises. Essentially, all the employees in a division are ranked in terms of their contribution, not just by their boss but by a group of managers. Then the ranking goes up to the division manager and his staff. Then come raises and promotions. "There are pluses and minuses to it," explained one higher level manager, "but what I try to focus on with my people is that their contributions to the company are highly visible not just to me and my boss but to other managers in the division as well."

Just don't be last on the list, and make those "contributions." That's the HP way of saying "do a good job." "Developing a product, coming up with a clever way to train the field—it's all in what we call contributions," explained a fast-tracker. HP may love teams, but "an individual can make a hell of a difference."

It's the same in **manufacturing**. One manufacturing engineer chose HP for its small, decentralized approach. "I was looking at other jobs where I was going to be working in a department of several hundred people. Here I work in a department of maybe thirty or forty." At HP, it's not unusual for the bigger bosses to know your name.

That's been changing a bit. One engineer described how her division manager would come and walk around the production floor fairly frequently, doing the old "HP management by walking around." But he doesn't come as frequently anymore. As the company becomes larger and more centralized, there's more to manage, and less time for an individual approach.

But there's still a special HP feel. One division has informal Friday morning coffee breaks, where you talk to "your boss and your boss's boss, continually reinforcing that support group." And all engineers emphasize the fact that HP is a technical elite with some of the best people in the field.

Then there's the flexibility. "I knew if I came here and decided that manufacturing wasn't what I really wanted to do, I could change," said one engineer. "They encourage change because it only enriches your knowledge base."

So even with the current cutbacks and changes, there's a lot of satisfaction with the "HP way." As one person put it: "It's understood there's a lot of change going on—but people here are used to that."

LIFE

"Even though the company is large, they try to promote what they call a family atmosphere," said one staffer.

That means team sports, beer busts, company auctions (including a raffle for lunch with CEO John Young, which got bid up to $1,000). Plants and offices are situated in pleasant areas, with easy access to good universities, which is in keeping with

HP's encouragement of training and external education. One staffer talked about all the wonderful cultural and social opportunities at HP, but then added, "we don't intend to become a country club." And not all participate. It's there if you want it.

There is more attention paid to employees here than at most firms. One manufacturing engineer described the monthly get-togethers over dinner with the boss. "No spouses. Just the seven of us. We talk and socialize and develop that support between each other without the pressures of work." At HP, that's not uncommon. "Sure, some people feel they're getting screwed some of the time," asserted another manager. But on the whole, HP really is a pleasant, upbeat place to work. And there's life after work.

DOLLARS AND SENSE

One recent hiree said it all: "As for money, the offer was one of the lowest. But it wasn't that important compared with everything else."

Starting salaries in the mid- to upper 20s are complemented by the usual benefits—health, dental, and life insurance, and a retirement plan. Plus bonuses and a stock purchase option. And a closed-circuit television system that allows employees to continue their education at work, taught by professors from Stanford University.

Other benefits are more intangible. Relative job security, and one of the lowest turnover rates in the industry. People aren't fired, and people don't quit.

GETTING IN—TRICKS OF THE TRADE

"Get an engineering degree and get high grades. It's not easy, but it's the best way to get in," a young employee advised. And for product marketing, "the ideal combination would be a technical undergraduate degree and an MBA."

As one senior manager said, HP is looking for the "cream of the crop," and interviews are tough and very specific. So be prepared.

"When I came here I had the toughest technical interview I'd had in all my interviewing experience," explained one recently hired engineer.

That was an on-site interview, with a potential first-line boss.

Most employees begin with personnel interviews that are similarly tough. HP wants people with "outstanding leadership potential, a history of achievement, and an ability to take risks," asserted one headquarters employee. And these are not just buzz words. Be prepared to explain and defend your resumé. And while some higher level managers say that great grades aren't emphasized, new hirees say that in fact they were.

HP recruits at over one hundred schools, so going to the "right school" isn't as important as having the skills and attitudes HP wants, and an ability to fit in with the "HP way." While people are recruited at a local level, HP plugs resumés into an electronic data base available to all managers at different locations.

And for all the toughness of the interviews, this is one of the few firms where someone would say: "We also look for people who want to have fun. People who consider work from a social standpoint as well."

THE BOTTOM LINE

Technical excellence, hard work, and fun.

INTERNATIONAL BUSINESS MACHINES CORPORATION (IBM)

VITAL STATISTICS

- **locations:** Armonk, NY (headquarters); offices and plants nationwide and worldwide
- **revenues:** $45.93 billion (1984 sales)
- **rank:** 1st (world's largest supplier of information processing equipment)
- **employees:** 395,000 +

AS SEEN FROM THE OUTSIDE

There's no avoiding IBM. And that's something the other computer companies get a little tired of.

No wonder. Even its competitors concede that IBM is the undisputed leader in the field. Where "Big Blue" goes, the others follow. Well, of course IBM followed the others into the personal computer market. But now the IBM PC has a one-third share of the total personal computer market, and the other computer companies are forced to come up with IBM clones. It's all in the name.

But IBM didn't start out as IBM. It began with three other initials—C-T-R—and Thomas Watson, a former employee of a three-letter competitor, NCR (National Cash Register). The Computing-Tabulating-Recording Co. was formed in 1911 when the Computing Scale Co., the Tabulating Machine Co., and the International Time Recording Co. merged.

Three years later, Thomas Watson joined CTR, and in 1924 the company was renamed International Business Machines, or IBM.

Under Mr. Watson (always *Mr.* Watson at IBM) the company acquired its distinctive conservative character, and a reputation for good service. It also acquired a motto—"Think!"—which Watson used to exhort his sales force.

And it worked wonders. Today, IBM is ranked No. 6 on the Fortune 500. It's the world's largest producer of computers and electric typewriters, doing business in 130 countries. Big Blue is still rolling on, most recently into the telecommunications field. In 1984, it bought the remaining shares in the ROLM Corporation (a major manufacturer of computerized business communications [PBX] systems), and acquired a 16 percent interest in MCI Communications (the nation's second largest long-distance telephone service).

In competition with another three letter competitor, AT&T, IBM is getting into telecommunications. Meanwhile, AT&T is getting into computers. The battle is just beginning . . .

HEARD AT THE WATER COOLER— WHAT IT'S REALLY LIKE TO WORK HERE

It's tough to hear *anything* at the water cooler—unless you're one of the IBM army. This is a company that firmly believes in Uncle Sam's old saying that "loose lips sink ships."

"Once you're accepted and you do your work, you won't be let go," said one employee, "Unless, of course, you start stealing secrets and selling them to the Japanese companies!"

Or if you talk to outsiders about the company. IBM has a very strict interview policy, we were told—so we weren't able to get interviews with employees through an open route.

But we didn't give up there, and we managed to scout out a few personal contacts working at Big Blue. And, through them, we learned that IBM apparently isn't keeping employees from talking because they're unhappy. On the contrary, IBM isn't hiding anything but trade secrets (something we didn't ask about), and real employee enthusiasm. You just have to get behind the tight security to uncover it.

And security there is. Some IBM offices and plants have a double security check, for employees and nonemployees alike. Staffers wear picture ID badges. It's like walking into a fortress. But those inside the fortress walls find the atmosphere less military than parental. It's all part of absorbing and accepting the IBM way.

One staffer explained IBM's principles. "There are golden rules here—like respect for the individual. Everybody has to have respect for the next person, whether they're doing the job or not. Respect for the individual is our No. 1 priority."

It's even set down in print. IBM puts out a booklet for employees, stating the company's philosophy. Listed as IBM's "enduring principles, the cornerstones of its success" are number one, respect for the individual, two, customer service, and three, excellence.

One employee summed up IBM succinctly, "They'll take care of you if you take care of them."

And that's what IBM staffers do—very quietly.

PEOPLE

There's the traditional picture of the IBM employee—white shirt, blue suit, serious, loyal, and dedicated. A sort of corporate Boy Scout, if you will.

So what's the truth behind the myth? First of all, scrap the uniform—sort of. "It doesn't necessarily have to be a white shirt, blue tie kind of thing," said one staffer. "I don't think they won't hire you if you wear a *blue* shirt. As a matter of fact, I did wear a blue shirt when I was interviewing."

Basically, IBM is big on "professional appearance," like most major corporations, but maybe a little more so. Although an employee pointed out that employees on the production lines are allowed to dress casually, "as long as it's neat." So much for the myth of suited employees from the bottom on up.

But, obviously, clothes don't make the employee. What truly seems to distinguish an IBM employee is dedication—both to work and to the company itself. It's actually a two-way street. IBM has a policy called "full employment," meaning no layoffs. "You have their promise," said a staffer. "And it has never been broken. So you do have a lifetime career with IBM."

That's why employees repay IBM's loyalty to them with loyalty to the company. As one employee explained, "It's a career here. It's not a question of 'I want a job; I'll work at IBM.'" So IBM staffers, on the whole, do their best not to rock the boat. And who can blame them? All in all, it seems as if they've got a pretty good deal.

As long as they believe in what IBM believes in.

JOBS

Corporate benevolence doesn't mean that employees don't have to work hard here. One staffer termed the work "demanding," adding "but they do take care of you." Of course.

Still, as far as moving ahead goes, it's up to the individual to a great extent. Like many other technical companies, IBM offers different jobs in a variety of departments—from sales and marketing to technical positions in design and development, production, manufacturing, applications programming, and much more.

Given the number of different positions, training also varies. In some areas, it's on-the-job training; in others, employees go through formal training programs. But for all the differences, there are similarities from job to job and department to department in IBM.

First, there's IBM's "Open Door Policy." Employees who feel they have a problem with their manager can go over his or her head. "It's called 'skip level,' " explained a staffer. "And, actually you can go all the way to the top if you're getting a raw deal. You can go *all* the way—up to the chairman of the board."

There's also something called the "Speak Up Program," under which employees with a question, complaint, or comment that they don't want to discuss with their manager may mail in a Speak Up Form. According to a company brochure, "you'll get an answer by the person deemed most qualified to give it. And your anonymity is assured." The answer will be mailed to the employee's house, and only the SpeakUp administrator will know his or her identity.

In addition, IBM believes strongly in promoting from within—something most employees find very attractive. Especially those who intend to work their way up into management. Said one such staffer, "Management is all from the ranks. It's nothing like 'here's a guy from GE who just snuck in there.' "

As with other high tech firms, there's a dual career ladder for technical staffers. Upon reaching a certain level, staffers who qualify may elect to branch off into the management side or stick with a purely technical career track.

"You come in as an engineer and, theoretically, you can get into the management chain, get into higher level management and become president of a division," explained an employee.

Promotion and pay are based largely on a merit system. Employees sit down with their managers, discuss job responsibilities, and make out a performance plan based upon them. After that, managers periodically go over the performance plan with the employees. There's no formal time frame established for those meetings. As one staffer described it, "A lot of managers will say, 'Hey, why don't you come into my office one day. Stop in any time and we'll bull.' " When the formal performance evaluation period is up, an employee and his manager discuss how well the employee met the plan and fill out a Performance Planning, Counseling and Evaluation Form, which is then reviewed by the manager's manager.

One employee summed up the process: "Basically, if you do well for the company, they'll reward you. If you don't, they won't. It's really as simple as that."

Very simple. But it does require initiative on the employee's part. To get ahead, staffers need the usual combination of hard work, motivation, and dedication. That's no secret—even at IBM.

LIFE

"Years ago—say ten, twenty years ago—there was a little rally song, the whole works," said one employee. "That's what I've heard. They used to have meetings where they'd say a pledge of allegiance, sing the little IBM song, that kind of stuff. Today they don't do that."

No, but IBM is still quite big on company activities. Said one staffer, "It's a family-oriented company. They take care not only of you, but your family as well." Events like "Family Day"— outdoor festivities complete with amusement park rides, food, children's shows, and more—are offered to employees and their families. The IBM Club sponsors children's movies and Christmas shows. There are IBM athletic teams and recreation centers. As one employee commented, "There are probably pages of the stuff that they do for all of us."

IBM is involved in community work as well, such as donating land to towns and counties for athletic use. "In fact, if you're involved in a community activity and went to IBM and said, 'We need money to start this—like a day-care center or a fire station— they might even donate money to that particular fund," said one staffer. "And they give time off to employees who belong to community activities. So it is community conscious."

But they don't have a company song. At least, if they do, they're not telling.

DOLLARS AND SENSE

We were unable to get exact figures. According to IBM literature, "IBM intends to maintain an average level of pay that is higher than the average level of pay for similar skills in other companies with which IBM competes for employees or with which it competes in the marketplace." Put more simply, employees say pay is "above average."

As for raises, "you have two ways of getting more money— either through time or through the performance system."

IBM also offers a strong benefits package—the usual medical, disability, and dental, plus hospitalization and surgical insurance. And there's more. IBM also allows employees to take educational leaves of absence (without pay) after two years with the company, or social service leaves of absence (with pay). It offers a scholarship program for children of IBM employees. And it sends staffers to teach at colleges and universities as temporary faculty members (with pay).

And that's *still* not all. There are also special IBM prizes and awards. And there's the IBM Suggestion Plan, under which employees submit suggestions for company improvement. They don't just win the company's praise, either. "I know of one person who got $25,000 for suggesting something," said one staffer.

Not bad.

GETTING IN—TRICKS OF THE TRADE

Times are tough in the high tech industry, even at Big Blue. "The computer industry is in a lull and IBM is holding its own. But in this situation, it will stop hiring." Especially given IBM's practice of "full employment."

But people do get jobs at IBM, even in the slump times. How do they do it? Well, IBM doesn't make it difficult. To begin with, it is probably one of the few companies that usually hires people through personnel, *not* contacts. Staffers say you *should* send your resumé to personnel—both to the main office and to the offices in the areas where you want to work. Grades are important, employees say, but other items on your resumé are equally so. "I didn't have the highest grades, I didn't have a 4.0 average, yet I got in," commented one. Extracurricular activities definitely help, employees stress. And, obviously, computer skills are a real plus. One staffer who had built a computer in college believes that was "20 percent of why I got hired here."

Once you get past that first, hardest step and are called in for an interview, the focus is on interpersonal skills. Employees say that typically you'll go through a day of interviewing, meeting a number of managers. "You just have to show that you're willing to do a little more than the next guy," suggested one go-getter.

So IBM is looking for the usual list of qualities—interpersonal skills, technical knowledge, professional appearance, and a good academic record. Beyond that—well, one staffer summed it all up: "It's terrible to say, but a lot of it is luck. I just wrote them a letter, got accepted, and it's worked out real nicely."

So landing a job at IBM isn't really a great mystery.

THE BOTTOM LINE

Great—if you're IBM compatible.

MICROSOFT

VITAL STATISTICS

- **locations:** Bellevue, WA (headquarters)
- **revenues:** $140 million (1985 sales)
- **rank:** 2nd software company in the U.S.
- **employees:** 900

AS SEEN FROM THE OUTSIDE

In the high tech microcomputer wars, where new casualties are announced every week, Microsoft proves day in and day out that it's anything but soft. The hard-charging company, led by its thirty-year-old founder and chairman of the board, William Gates, continues to score business coups, including strong alliances with such companies as IBM, Apple, and others. Its operating systems set the industry standard, and it continues to do battle in the retail market with applications that are front-runners.

That kind of success is pretty heady—especially since it is only ten years since Gates and co-founder Paul Allen decided to throw their hats into the ring of the infant microcomputer business. They wrote a BASIC programming language for the first commercially available microcomputer. In 1975 —and by 1977, they had five employees and annual sales of $500,000.

Microsoft BASIC caught on and the company was off and running. But here Microsoft parted ways with some of its competitors. Instead of specializing on either systems or applications software, Microsoft concentrated on both. A rather logical move, actually, and one that many analysts believe was the key to Microsoft's success. After all, the systems software controls the internal operations of the computer while the applications software guides the computer through its tasks. Reaching customers of two kinds—the OEM (original equipment or hardware manufacturers) and applications (the retail customer)—gives the company a two-edged sword with which to attack the market.

And that's just what Microsoft has been doing. Things took off with BASIC and other languages, and in 1978 the company licensed Microsoft BASIC to Radio Shack and Apple Computer. In 1980, it licensed the UNIX operating system from Bell Laboratories and developed its own enhanced version for 16 bit processors called XENIX. By 1980, annual sales were $8 million and the company now had forty employees.

But the big coup came in 1981, when IBM introduced its personal computer and used the Microsoft MS-DOS operating system, plus the company's BASIC, COBOL, and other products. This really put Microsoft on the PC map, and by 1982 fifty microcomputer manufacturers had licensed this operating system. Year-end sales were $34 million and the company had grown to two hundred people.

While it was working on systems, the company was also developing applications software. It began rolling out these products in 1982 with Multiplan, Word, Chart, Project, and Access. In 1984, it introduced a full line of applications software for the Apple Macintosh computer. Its latest triumph concerning the Macintosh was in beating Lotus (the number one software manufacturer) by introducing Excel, a spreadsheet program, before Lotus was able to market its competing Jazz program.

Microsoft has been pursuing international markets with equal energy. In 1985, international sales accounted for 30 percent of total sales, according to a company report, and Microsoft now has subsidiaries in England, Australia, Germany, France, Japan, Korea, and Canada. The company announced last year that it would be opening its first overseas production facility in Ireland. It also strengthened its position in this market with several joint development agreements with companies including Intel, Tandy, and Lotus. And its crowning recent achievement is a long-term joint development agreement with IBM for operating systems and other products.

So Microsoft might be No. 2, but its dual approach to the business has put it in a strong position for the future. Industry observers expect to see this privately held company continue to grow. After all, if it's come this far in ten years, who knows what it will do in the next ten?

HEARD AT THE WATER COOLER—
WHAT IT'S REALLY LIKE TO WORK HERE

In the good old days, chaotic was a good word to describe Microsoft. Things have changed though, especially with the hiring of president Jon A. Shirley, a veteran computer management type. Structure has come to the company now. But as one employee explained, "They bring structure but don't stifle the atmosphere."

So the atmosphere is as freewheeling as ever. That's how staffers keep coming up with innovative products. No strict corporate policies, no time clocks to punch, or heavy politicking here. Instead it's creative, relaxed, and individualistic.

And is it ever individualistic! Just take a look at the offices. Staffers get to decorate them however they want. Anything goes—especially where the program developers work. We're not just talking about interesting prints on the walls, or clever coffee mugs on desks. Here it's stereo systems and electric bass guitars set up and raring to go . . . literally.

One young man describing the loose atmosphere here elaborated a bit. "I walked down to my roommate's office and he has an electric bass—so I picked it up and played a little.

So that's what Microsoft staffers mean when they say the company is relaxed. And there are other, more formalized signs of it too—like Friday beer busts and flexible work hours. It's come in when you want, leave when you're finished. At least for the technical staffers. Marketing folks still work standard hours, since they're dealing with outside companies.

So it's not all party time here. In fact, while the atmosphere is free, the pressure to perform is intense. But this pressure "comes from within, not from management," stressed one staffer. And while hours are flexible, they may be long. Seventy- to 80-hour weeks aren't uncommon. After all, there is a job to be done. But Microsoft gives employees the freedom to do it their way.

"It's a place where vision is rewarded," said one staffer. "Employees buy into the dream."

And a lot of people here seem to think it really is a dream company for them. As one young man summed up, "we're running around like a bunch of spoiled children."

But that's how they come up with so many successful products.

PEOPLE

After rolling out all the usual comments—"bright," "creative," and "the people are wizards"—one staffer came up with the most succinct description of his co-workers. "A lot of people here were the geeks in college."

Most Microsoft staffers didn't fit into a rigid structure, and here "they rise above it." And outgrow their nerdy past . . . But there are other types, too.

One employee described his punk haircut when he first came to Microsoft to join the technical side. It's gone now, but management didn't have anything to do with that decision. "There are very cool people here," he concluded.

As one might imagine, since punk haircuts are no problem, neither are pinstripes and power ties. There's no pressure to conform. This is a company where people are encouraged to be themselves.

JOBS

Yes, it's free and easy here. But there is a job to be done. As at most high tech companies, the main job areas are in marketing and technical development.

A look into the applications systems department gives a good picture of what's happening at Microsoft. The two basic sides to marketing within the department are product and programs. Typically, a new employee will start out here as a **product manager** or **program manager**. Don't let the title "manager" fool you, though. The only thing a new employee may manage is part of a product.

Essentially, program managers work to produce a product. These are the inside types who do a lot of research and work with developers on products—in this case software that will be sold to the general public. Product managers work with the market itself. They're on the outside, talking with salespeople. They may be assigned to handle several products or a single, important one. The next step is to senior product manager and then group product manager. All these jobs are filled by marketing people with strong technical backgrounds.

On the technical side, people come in as **programmers** and then move up to become **technical leads**, (a mid-level technicial position). Later they may move into a manager's position, supervising people working on the development of new software.

This career path might seem rather cut and dried; but the work itself certainly isn't. For one thing, there are those flexible hours. One technical lead described his typical day in terms of "getting up at about 10 or 11 A.M., then going for a jog or a swim, then rolling into work in the early afternoon." After meetings with others in his section, he may go home for dinner, and then return to the office and work until 10 or 11 at night.

Sounds simple? Well, it's not. This technical lead was actively involved in the Excel project for the Macintosh computers. The hands-on part of developing software usually takes six to eight months or more before it reaches the market.

There are no formal training programs here; systems training is purely on the job. "You're thrown in," one employee said. "If you don't know how, you learn fast on the job. A lot of people bitch about it." But the fact of the matter is that you're on your own.

"You can fall into a 90-hour work week and stagnate, so you have to regulate yourself," commented one young man. He terms this "the worst downside" at the company.

Microsoft has a system for rewarding its technical people who want to remain purely technical and "become craftsmen at systems design," as an employee put it, rather than move eventually into management. This is where the position of technical lead comes in. There have been cases of "fantastic programmers who go into management and fall flat." If that does happen, however, a bruised ego might be the worst result. In many other corporations you can't go back to your old job. Not so at Microsoft.

One manager explained that there's no time frame established for people to move up. "They may be put in charge of a project very rapidly."

LIFE
"It's almost like a college dorm," was how one employee described life here.

So while business is an integral part of life at Microsoft, most people feel as if they're working with friends. That sort of attitude is something management encourages. And they add to it in their own way, by showing concern for their employees. One person described how a co-worker needed a special chair under orders from a chiropractor to alleviate a back problem. "He casually mentioned this to his group supervisor and the next day, the chair was there."

DOLLARS AND SENSE
The average in the industry is about $25,000 for a college graduate just entering the business. And according to one staffer, Microsoft pays above average. How much more? No one would say, including management. It's a private company, so it can afford to be secretive.

GETTING IN—TRICKS OF THE TRADE

Microsoft may sound too good to be true. But before you go charging in, remember—it is highly selective. An executive in personnel said that there is "always an opening for software design engineers" but that they have to be good students with math, physics, or computer science majors, and have solid references.

The company recruits at some of the top engineering schools in the country, and for those who miss the recruiters, "we review every resumé that comes in, and if it's for a technical position, it is reviewed with the technical people. They indicate whether they want to talk with the person."

In marketing, they look for MBAs with strong technical backgrounds. After all, you have to understand what you're marketing.

And watch out for the interviews! One technical person described how, at the college campus interview, the first screening, "They lull you into a sense of security. Then, Bang! You're into the technical stuff."

If the college recruiters like you, you're invited for a series of interviews at the home office. These interviews may last two days, during which time candidates will talk with several people in the relevant department. According to one employee, they make you write a program, and if it's good, they hire you. "There's no standard b.s."

From the other side of that interviewing desk, it's not so cut and dried. One senior management executive said the company is "careful" about hiring. The screening interview is the time when a prospect is "really grilled." Microsoft wants to find out "how creative the person is—and we need to know how they will react when they get into a stressful situation." This executive emphasizes several key points. First and most obvious, qualifications, and second, "willingness to do what it takes to get the job done."

"I'm impressed with a candidate who has made a mark," she said, adding that this is tied in with experience and specific development. "We test their technical ability," but also, "we look for people who have had success, because people do tend to repeat that successful pattern."

The next area she studies is "flexibility in thinking." She explained that since there is a lot of discussion at Microsoft, "a person has to have an open mind to deal with people who have different opinions." Ambition also comes into play, though she noted that "we want someone who is aggressive but not someone who wants to be president in eighteen months."

But perhaps the most important thing, especially at individualistic Microsoft, is to "Be yourself." As long as yourself is technically competent.

THE BOTTOM LINE

Free-thinking, individualistic and fast-moving.

LAW

There are a lot of lawyers out there—more than 700,000, to be a bit more exact. And the majority of those 700,000 people aren't in the government or in corporations, but in private practice. Private firms run the gamut from small-town to prestigious big-city to nationwide "storefront" practices, such as Jacoby & Meyers. So a lot of lawyers simply aren't in the big time.

And no wonder. Getting into a top firm isn't easy at all. As a matter of fact, it all begins in the first year of law school. Tradition has it that the only way people land jobs at the big name firms is by knocking themselves out the minute they start their first year. Everyone says you have to forget your family and friends and devote yourself to studying, to making Law Review and making the top 10 percent of your class, or you won't have the opportunities you want. And everyone is usually right . . .

Those students who manage to land at the top of the class are ahead of the game, because that's what most firms look at when they're hiring summer associates and regular associates. Most firms offer a summer associate program, which is aimed at second-year law students. Designed to let the student learn about the firm and what it's actually like to be a lawyer, it's also the way firms can assess potential full-time associates. And since the selection process is rather rigorous, firms wind up competing for the same top 10 percent of the class. So those who become summer associates at a top firm should be prepared for the summer of their lives—not necessarily in terms of the workload, but in terms of entertainment. The top firms want the top students to choose their firm, so often it's a no-holds-barred summer filled with such nonwork events as baseball games, dinners on the town, boat rides, and so on. In short, it's a real courtship.

It's not all fun and games, though. The law firms do expect summer associates to work and prove both their interest in and grasp of the law. Those who do well usually wind up with an invitation to join the firm after graduation. Actually, they'll probably have a lot of job offers. Once one firm offers a summer associate a job, the other firms come flocking around, trying to convince this particular legal eagle that *their* firm is even better. Then there's another round of pampering. Quite a change from the rigors of law school . . . But people who have been through all this advise making the most of that time, for once you have made your decision, the courtship ends—and the work begins.

Then it's back to law school for your third year, and typically, to a bar review course, before the bar exam itself. During that last year of law school, firms come on campus to interview students. And this is where going to a top law school can be a definite plus. One of the big differences between the top schools and the rest of the pack is that the big firms *have* to give an on-campus interview at the top schools to everyone who wants one. Elsewhere, you're knocked out of the box a lot faster.

It's not only a matter of accessibility, either. Traditions die hard, and one tradition is that the top firms prefer to hire from the top schools. It's not always the case, naturally, and firms *do* hire students from the lower tier schools. But having a degree from one of the hallowed law schools certainly doesn't hurt your chances of making it into the big leagues.

For the most part, associates join their firms right after graduation. Some associates, however, do enter laterally from other firms, judicial clerkships, the D.A.'s office, and so forth. Sometimes those associates who enter laterally begin at a level above that of the fresh-from-law-school staffers. But the typical entry-level job is that of first-year associate.

First-year associates handle the lower level work at a law firm, researching and writing briefs. By the second year, associates take on more responsibility. They become more involved with cases and strategy, and may take on duties such as taking depositions (the pretrial questioning of witnesses for the opposition) and more. From the third to the eighth years, there's increasing responsibility and expertise. Depending on one's field, an associate will be doing anything from making courtroom appearances to handling takeover battles. This is the time when associates really need to shine, for it's usually in the eighth year that associates learn whether they're to become partners, and to have a chance for the very big bucks.

Not that associates are paid badly. That's something everyone likes about landing a position at a large firm. The jobs are tough, long on hours and pressure, but the money is most definitely there. Starting salaries at the large firms begin in the upper 30s and range up to the mid-50s. These large firms can afford to pay top dollar. They're bringing in a decent amount themselves. Essentially, firms charge clients by billing hours of time and work. And at the big firms, there are many areas in which they can serve a client. Most of the larger firms are "full service" firms, offering expertise in a variety of areas in the law. The three most prominent areas of a firm's practice typically are corporate, litigation, and tax.

Corporate law is the area in which a firm represents a corporate client. A corporate practice covers numerous specific duties such as public and private financing, compensations and benefits, securities law, investment agreements, leveraged buyouts, and more. One aspect of corporate law that has lately been getting a lot of attention is Mergers and Acquisitions (M&A). M&A lawyers either help one company take over another or help prevent its takeover by another company. It's a high visibility, high pressure spot that attracts many people with combination law and MBA degrees.

Litigation is the area for lawyers with a dramatic flair. While the forum of litigation is the courtroom, there's a lot more to being a litigation lawyer than making like Perry Mason. Litigators stress that while the work can be exciting and may appear to be flamboyant, they're not only standing before a judge being convincing. There's a lot to be done before that even comes to pass— such as hearing all the facts and trying to construct them into a favorable case, deciding where the case should be tried, and more. In fact, litigators try not to bring a case to court. More favorable to their client, and thus to them, is to settle out of court. So it's a combination of attention to detail and persuasive skills that makes for a strong litigator.

Tax lawyers are the numbers people at a law firm. They work mainly with business transactions and financing. Among their duties are such things as structuring tax shelters and limited partnerships, dealing with leveraged buyouts and liquidations, stock offerings, and general tax counseling.

Full service law firms also usually offer practices in other areas, including Antitrust, Labor, Banking and Financial Services, Real Estate, Products and Liabilities, Environmental, Bankruptcy, Trust, and Estates. And more. One thing about the law is that where there's a problem and some money, you know there's got to be a specialty.

DEWEY, BALLANTINE, BUSHBY, PALMER AND WOOD

VITAL STATISTICS

- **locations:** New York (headquarters); Washington, DC; Los Angeles
- **revenues:** $44.5 million (1984)
- **rank:** 55th largest law firm; 47th (revenues)
- **employees:** 71 partners, 189 associates, 32 paralegals

AS SEEN FROM THE OUTSIDE

Everyone remembers the victorious Harry Truman holding up a newspaper with the headline "Dewey Defeats Truman." Well, that Dewey, the Republican politican Thomas Dewey, is the Dewey in Dewey, Ballantine.

That's the simplest way for non–legal eagles to identify the firm. But its history precedes him by forty-three years and several name changes. And Dewey wasn't the only notable to practice at Dewey, Ballantine—the firm was also the home of U.S. Supreme Court Justice John Harlan before he entered the judiciary.

Historically, the firm has been considered one of the traditional bastions of Harvard-groomed Republicanism. It has made a transition since those Dewey days, though. Along the way it's handled some rather diverse cases. In 1948, it represented Anheuser-Busch, which was sued when a man found a fly in a bottle of Bud (settled out of court since the fly was unavailable for examination). More conventionally, the firm worked on several of the major railroad reorganizations from the early 1930s to the mid-1950s. It counseled the co-defendants in a civil antitrust suit in which the federal government sought to divest duPont and members of the duPont family of their stock in General Motors and U.S. Motors. And it continues to take on large cases.

Now its major emphasis is on corporate and tax law, with a growing real estate practice. Its client list includes such major corporations as Mobil and American Can. Underscoring the firm's growth is its recent opening of a Los Angeles office in addition to its already established New York and Washington locations.

Thomas Dewey might have been defeated, but the firm that bears his name is still moving on . . .

HEARD AT THE WATER COOLER—
WHAT IT'S REALLY LIKE TO WORK HERE

The old "white shoe" image lingers at Dewey, Ballantine—and the firm's appearance certainly reinforces that. Its downtown New York office occupies space from the fortieth floor up in a building located in the heart of the Wall Street area. The requisite portraits of the firm's founders stand in the reception area; floors are interconnected by spiral staircases; office windows overlook the Hudson River and Manhattan. It's all rather impressive.

But walk inside an associate's office and it's a little different. It's usually deluged with papers—in the tax department, the latest congressional proposals; in corporate, mountains of documents to be reviewed. The mood is unpretentious—right down to the fact that the walls are often devoid of the diplomas and bar certifications its occupant possesses.

And that lack of pretension is what many people like about being at Dewey, Ballantine. Sure, it's professional and somewhat conservative. But that's not to say that everyone is straitlaced and buttoned up.

As one associate said, noting the old "white shoe" organization image, "change has been dramatic in the last few years."

PEOPLE
"It's a hard-working, intellectually oriented group," summed up one young man. "But not to the exclusion of fun, jokes, and appreciation of the ironies in the things we do."

Fun? How about when, after closing a transaction with Kenner-Parker Toys, the company sent boxes of Care Bears, classic edition Monopoly sets, and Izod shirts—"literally crateloads of stuff"—to the three associates who worked on the case. "So we went around one day like Santa Claus giving out these things," one of them recalled. "We were real popular in the firm for a day or two."

But for all the fun, people at Dewey, Ballantine are dedicated to their work. They made it into a big law firm and they're going to do their best to stay here.

"All the people here are overachievers who had staggeringly good grades," said one lawyer.

Generally, he added, "everything you try to do, you try to do perfectly. But when you freak out because you left out a semicolon, that's when you really start to worry about whether you're in contact with the rest of the world."

JOBS

Much of Dewey's reputation comes from its large corporate practice. According to one associate in the corporate department, "The work has nothing to do with law school. In fact, I've probably been in the library five times since I've been here." It's different for litigators, he explained, whose work involves more issue spotting (finding aspects of the case favorable to the client), problem solution, and memorandum writing. His work includes such things as having someone drop something on his desk and saying, "draft an intercompany loan agreement."

Once an associate has demonstrated competency to the firm's lawyers, he or she begins to work directly with clients. As an associate becomes more senior, he or she has more interaction with the clients and then must look to the younger lawyers for assistance.

"Everyone rises within the system by getting work, developing relationships in the firm, and selling the product, which is legal services," said a senior associate.

But, naturally, the type of work people get differs. The junior associates do more internal work, such as drafting and production of documents. The more senior associates spend more time communicating with clients and preparing the overall transaction.

In the **corporate** department, an associate may be working on five or six major transactions at once, including some securities work, institutional work, and merger and acquisitions (M&A) negotiations. The general consensus is that the M&A transactions can be a lot of fun. "It's one of the few chances that corporate has to be adversarial," said one lawyer.

The generally nonadversarial nature of the corporate practice can be "a refreshing bargaining of equals," said an associate. Unlike specialties such as labor law, which are "very partisan, and you have to buy the philosophy of one side or another," corporate law challenges the wits of two well-represented parties, "neither of which has a real bargaining advantage."

No matter how refreshing the work is, sometimes people do question their career. As an associate commented with a smile, "Sometimes I wonder about the social utility of protecting the incredibly rich. Then I shake it off and say, someone's got to do it. It's a dirty business but it's got to be done."

And for those whose sense of social consciousness is aroused, the firm encourages pro bono work and is very supportive. "That work runs the gamut from criminal appeals to employment discrimination to immigration work," an associate explained.

Comparing an associate's role in the corporate department with that in the **litigation** department, one corporate associate commented, "The guys who litigate in a high stakes game like this are senior partners, and junior guys are lucky to sit at the counsel table. To get real advocacy experience, you're better off going to the D.A.'s office of the Corporate Counsel (which represents the city in litigation)."

According to some employees, most junior litigators end up with the less glamorous side of litigation—deposition work, motions, and a lot of memos. "The comparative degree of responsibility between a third-year litigator and a third-year corporate person is staggering. The third-year litigator might be researching law and brief writing, with no real courtroom skill and not much client contact. But a third-year corporate lawyer may well have sole responsibility for several different transactions."

Other lawyers (especially those who are in litigation) disagree. And there is another side to it. For those who enjoy writing and want to learn trial skills, litigation does offer that opportunity. In addition, the firm sends its young litigators for training by the National Institute for Trial Advocacy.

And it's not only the training that many associates like. There's also an electricity in the litigation department when it comes alive for a fast-paced transaction. "It can be exciting to watch it all happen so quickly," commented an associate. "It's exhilarating."

Another strong emphasis at Dewey, Ballantine is on its **tax** practice. One tax associate chose Dewey because it's a "large, good tax firm—and the atmosphere is more congenial than at other firms." He added that one of the big pluses at Dewey is "the greater degree of contact between partners and associates." It's not unusual for a partner to spontaneously ask an associate out to lunch, or for partners to take associates out to dinner when a project is completed. And the hours in tax are better.

Whatever department associates are in, they've got one thing in common—they're all wondering about their chances for a partnership. As with all big firms, that tense issue builds up as the associates' time with the firm increases.

One associate discussed the issue candidly. "Sure, the partnership money is great, but I can't say all the partners are my buddies and that I'd like to hang out with them for the rest of my life. Let's face it, there are two partnership chances—slim and none. You can be the best they've had in three years, but if you're operating in an area where they have enough partners and not enough new business, it doesn't matter. You won't make it. It's the luck of the draw. So much depends on timing. It's impossible to predict."

To be so concerned with making partner is to have the wrong focus, he added. "You should be more concerned with the training and what you think you can learn."

"It's a long career path," said another associate. "Sometimes it feels interminable."

LIFE

"Dewey doesn't have the reputation of being a 'sweat shop,' like Skadden, Arps or Fried, Frank, where they work you to death and then spit you out," summed up a young man. "But you spend a hell of a lot of time here. People are surprised when they get into the system and have two all-nighters in a row."

So to a large degree, people are "married to the place," as an associate put it. "Sometimes it seems you spend 90 percent of your waking hours here. Time is a luxury."

Said another, "The job is all-consuming. There's not that much time for a personal life. Just keeping in touch with old friends takes up all your available time."

Add to the long hours an unpredictable schedule, and life here looks quite busy.

"We work really hard, but we play really hard, too," remarked an associate (who was working the day after Thanksgiving). "In between, there is very little time to rest, so you become a basket case very quickly. You've got to be prepared to give up personal time."

So, to the extent possible, the firm tries to ease the lifestyle frustrations with numerous firm-sponsored activities. If associates don't have the time to see their friends, at least they can see each other in a nonwork situation. In addition to impromptu lunches and dinners, the firm has the Christmas Party, the black tie Spring Dance (with spouses), firm and department dinners, summer activities that include the summer associates, and the Annual Dinner, when firm members have an opportunity to lampoon partners.

The almost monthly firm dinners include the traditional "Wranglers Speech," which updates the attorneys on the recent activities of the firm. Held at the Harvard or Yale Club the first or second Tuesday of most months, the dinner allows the people from the downtown, midtown, and D.C. offices to mingle. And talk about work . . .

DOLLARS AND SENSE

The fact that the money is excellent adds to the job satisfaction here. According to the National Law Journal's annual survey of top law firms, Dewey's starting salary for first year associates was $49,000 in 1985. Problem is, like most big law firms, there's really no such thing as a merit raise. "You have to feed yourself with a pat on the back," an attorney stated. "And sometimes you'd like to see it in a paycheck."

Still, it's a sure bet that no one here is suffering . . .

GETTING IN—TRICKS OF THE TRADE

Although you don't have to have the classic Ivy background, being at the top of the class is an important prerequisite. "Where you go to law school is important, but not as much as it was thirty years ago," said one associate. But let's be frank—an Ivy pedigree still opens doors. "If you don't go to Harvard, you'd better have great grades."

There is a heavy focus on the interview process throughout the firm. "It's important to get new, talented people, because what we are really selling is the services of our lawyers, so we develop our product by developing our lawyers," commented an attorney.

Second year associates on up do the interviewing. Much attention is given to recruiting summer associates, who are often asked back as associates after their year in law school. Once candidates have made the initial cut at the on-campus interview, they are invited to the firm. During a half day of interviews (usually five) and a luncheon, attorneys evaluate the applicants and send on their recommendations to the ultimate decision makers.

And, aside from the obvious intellectual skills, what are the interviewers looking for? How people carry themselves is very important. "Time and time again, people look good on paper, but when they get here, it's not good enough. You have to have people who deal well with clients. It's critical that they be competent enough to think on their feet, joke with a client, and be assertive."

Said one experienced interviewer, "Within ten minutes you can usually tell if you like them—and there is usually a general consensus."

Some other thoughts on what makes a Dewey, Ballantine person: "To determine good judgment, I ask them about life decisions they have made. I look for a willingness and desire to work hard, and whether that was exhibited in their past behavior."

"I look for self-reliant, aggressive and independent people."

"If you don't have enough initiative to get things started on your own and are waiting for someone else to push you along, you're dead."

"If you're a bit too polite, from what I've seen, you get eaten up, because the other guys, it seems, always have someone ready and willing to devour you—and can't wait for the opportunity."

THE BOTTOM LINE

Old line, but not old-fashioned.

FRIED, FRANK, HARRIS, SHRIVER & JACOBSON

VITAL STATISTICS

- **locations:** New York (headquarters); Washington, DC; London
- **revenues:** $65 million (1984)
- **rank:** 29th largest U.S. law firm (based upon National Law Journal's annual survey of the top 250 firms, September 30, 1985)
- **employees:** 81 partners, 222 associates, 55 paralegals

AS SEEN FROM THE OUTSIDE

Fried, Frank, Harris, Shriver & Jacobson is one of the Wall Street law firms that people refer to in reverent tones. It's considered by many to be a "lawyer's law firm"—that is, a firm that general legal counsel turn to for the answers for complicated legal issues. But it's not an old line, "white shoe" firm like many of the others; it has a reputation for liberalism and aggressiveness.

Yes, there are aggressive liberals in the world. And Fried, Frank competes in the big leagues of corporate takeovers, where only the strong survive. They've worked on some of the biggest headline cases, including Limited's bid for Carter-Hawley-Hale stores, and "white knight" Phillips Petroleum's acquisition of General American Oil Company of Texas. White knights are the good guys in corporate takeovers, coming in with friendly bids to "protect" companies from, you guessed it, unfriendly bids. Nice guys, huh?

Well, wait a minute. Fried, Frank also represented Burlington Northern Inc. in a successful bid, despite "poison pill" preferred stock issued by the "target" company to fight off the attack. That was a company that didn't want to get taken over, but did anyway. And that was due in part to Fried, Frank.

Let's call them tough guys with a good pro bono record, and a top reputation in takeover work, which some say is second among New York firms only to Skadden, Arps. And a high-powered practice revolving around sophisticated domestic and international financial transactions, working with investment banks and large corporations. Not that it doesn't do other work, including personal and corporate civil criminal law.

It all started with the creation of the New York office before the turn of the century. And like virtually every other law firm, the history of Fried, Frank, involves long lists of names and dates.

First there was the law practice of Charles A. Reigelman, a partner in the firm of Reigelman and Back, which operated before World War I. Reigelman moved to Leventritt, Riegelman, Carnes & Goetz, which became Leventritt, Reigelman, Carnes & Schwarz, which in turn became Limburg, Reigelman, Hirsch & Hedd—a firm that Walter J. Fried joined as associate in 1932.

Twenty-one years and five name changes later, Hans J. Frank became an associate, and in 1946 he and Leslie A. Jacobson became partners. Sam Harris joined the firm in 1947 and became a partner in 1949, the same year the Washington office was established. In 1955, the firm operated under the name Strasser, Spiegelberg, Fried & Frank (we're getting closer . . .).

In 1971, Sargent Shriver joined the firm—and that's when the firm adopted its current name. And that's when the Washington firm got a new name, too—Fried, Frank, Harris & Kampelman (Kampelman was the former legislative counsel to Senator Hubert H. Humphrey, who joined the firm in 1955 and became head of the Washington office in 1957).

The New York office has grown fast, doubling in size in ten years. And in 1970 the firm opened an office in London. The offices still carry those names, and the firm's tradition for a non-stuffy, non-WASPy, aggressive practice with a touch of liberalism.

HEARD AT THE WATER COOLER— WHAT IT'S REALLY LIKE TO WORK HERE

Located at the southern tip of Manhattan, right across from Battery Park and the Staten Island Ferry, Fried, Frank offers its attorneys some tranquil views of the harbor from their office windows. Those vistas are quite a contrast to the often intense atmosphere inside.

Actually, even the interior of the Fried, Frank offices is misleading—halls are spacious, carpeted, and for the most part, quiet. But pretty hectic work goes on in this seemingly calm environment. This is the big leagues. So associates here are dealing with big cases, long hours, heavy pressure, and general craziness.

How do they stand it? Well, there's something accessible about Fried, Frank. It might be a big firm, but it's certainly not stuffy. Employees say the mood here is "looser" and "more liberal" than at the other legal megafirms—especially the "white shoe" establishments. And that's what keeps them sane when the heat is on.

As one young lawyer put it, "The environment is unstructured, spontaneous, *and* demanding. I feel comfortable being myself here . . . I felt less that way at other firms. But here people have a sense of personal freedom."

"It's a sociable place," concluded a young man. "You can walk in on anyone and ask them questions. You can get addicted to the support systems."

Support systems? Legalese for people.

PEOPLE

As you might expect of staffers in a Wall Street law firm, many people at first seem reserved. They're lawyers, after all, and that means they think before they speak.

But being reserved isn't the same as being stiff and formal, and those are two things Fried, Frank associates *don't* seem to be. As one associate remarked, "At some firms, my jokes would get stares, but here people appreciate them."

At other firms, he added, "I didn't feel I could gesture with my hands, or I felt that I had to wear a suit all the time. Those restrictions can be stressful."

And stress is the last thing these people need. They get enough of it on the job. That's why Fried, Frank people are pretty tough. Actually, a lot of associates here feel that the more stress there is, the better. Some associates say they're at their happiest when the adrenalin is pumping in the heat of battle—even though that adrenalin has to keep pumping for a long, long time.

"The hours are unbelievably long and unpredictable, sixteen-hour days, seven days a week," commented a litigator. "On the other hand the work is, by and large, fascinating, and that's the single most important factor."

But you can't ignore those hours. As one young woman said,

"I'd like it to be as interesting all the time as it is when I'm working real hard—but without actually working so hard."

JOBS
First of all, while the work is tough, it also places attorneys here on the cutting edge of many transactions in the financial world. And that keeps a lot of people happy with their jobs. Who wouldn't enjoy the glamour attached to the high visibility of their cases?

"It's great to read about the case you're working on in the newspapers," said one associate.

The **litigation** department has one of the highest profiles, although the firm also has strong departments specializing in areas such as tax, corporate, bankruptcy, and real estate law. And that sixty-attorney-strong department is what we focused on.

The firm's function as special counsel, rather than as general counsel, is very apparent in the activities of the litigators. "We deal with the problems that general counsel is not comfortable with," noted an attorney.

Firms that act mainly as general counsel to a few big clients have to spend much of their time—and their associates' time—nurturing the client. "But here we're concerned only with, for example, the merger, and those cases don't drag on forever—they're usually over in thirty days," said one litigator.

"It makes it easier to be a lawyer if you're special counsel," he added, "because it makes it easier to reject an unwanted assignment and to tell the client to take their business elsewhere."

Some Fried, Frank lawyers in litigation chose this field over corporate because of the client control. As one young woman commented, "In corporate, the clients always want it done yesterday. I felt more in control in litigation. Because clients aren't in litigation, they don't tell you what to do."

Several associates who said that they had "short attention spans" prefer the fast-paced, quick-solution nature of being special counsel. In addition, the special counsel atmosphere encourages flexibility. Litigators aren't just involved in big deals, but also in areas such as arbitration, bankruptcy, commercial contracts, and white collar crime.

New associates quickly get their feet wet. "Fried, Frank gives its associates a lot of responsibility early on," said a lawyer. And unlike the "big case" firms, where litigation associates are relegated to "more tedious tasks," Fried, Frank's litigators get a lot of early exposure in taking depositions and arguing motions in court.

A young man who had worked at another firm before coming to Fried, Frank commented, "The pace is much quicker here; there are fewer people doing more work."

And that does have its downside. An associate pointed out that the lack of structure makes things a bit disorganized. "But I like bureaucratic chaos," he quickly added.

Senior associates have to trust the juniors to get a job done—and done correctly. "You don't have the luxury of double-checking the junior associates," commented one lawyer. That means that a junior associate has to be able to pick things up quickly, has to be someone who "trusts himself, asks questions, and doesn't flounder."

Those junior people who fit the bill find the setup a beneficial one. "Working here teaches you to make your own decisions," said one associate. "People at all levels will let you do as much as you demonstrate the ability to do."

But that doesn't mean associates are left to figure out everything by themselves. They attend numerous seminars outside the firm (for example, a two-week trial advocacy seminar during the summer) and there's an in-house training program. Different partners give nuts-and-bolts courses on a variety of legal specialties on a bimonthly basis.

Associates may become involved in even more diverse activities here by participating in Fried, Frank's active pro bono program. Traditionally the firm has always had a strong commitment to pro bono work—volunteering legal counsel on special issues—and it's in the pro bono area that Fried, Frank's image as a liberal law firm thrives. It's big on cases that involve "significant" social issues. For example, it has represented Haitian refugees, and worked with school desegregation. One attorney explained that the firm is more likely to take on an incredibly expensive pro bono case if it affects the rights of many people, rather than if the win affects only one person. The pro bono work is a great way for associates to expand their experience, working with social and constitutional issues that they would otherwise never deal with, given the nature of their regular workload.

Training and pro bono work aside, associates also learn about all aspects of the firm's practice at work. Like many top firms, Fried, Frank has a rotation program that allows associates to test their skills in various departments during their first two years. Within that time, the associate declares his or her chosen department.

"That's when you get moved from an inside office to one with a window," one associate explained with a smile.

And that's when the pressure mounts. At that point in their careers, associates are handling quite a bit of responsibility—and they're trying to make sure the right people notice. While associates are dealing with the peaks and valleys of their cases, they're also dealing with the typical worries and tensions of their careers with the firm—are they catching the eyes of the right heavy hitters, are they showing their worth, and so on. In short, it's the age-old question, "Will I make partner?"

One young man noted that associates are most marketable between their second and fifth years. "That's when associates decide whether to move on or stay. And it's a tough judgment to make."

It's also a tough workload. As an associate pointed out, it's in the firm's interest to keep piling the work on. In effect, the firm gets the most for its investment in associates in their "third, fourth and fifth years, in the minds of the partners. They don't have to limit your use with clients. They get their money's worth."

While partners are getting their money's worth, associates are debating the "somewhat indeterminate future. You never know until it happens," said an associate. "Things can happen, like the firm's practice could dry up in your area, you could make some disastrous mistake after six years, or—unknown to you—you could have alienated some key person."

But associates here seem quite optimistic about their destiny. "Whether or not you make partner, you're good enough to be your own lawyer after working here," said one associate.

If you *don't* make it, though, there is a quandary—where to go from here. After all, at that point attorneys are making the kind of money they may not be able to match elsewhere. And chances are that in another position, the attorney will not be working with the same type of high intensity cases.

But, unfortunately, that's life . . .

LIFE
Life here inevitably has a lot to do with work. The nature of the practice calls for heavy interaction among its attorneys—sometimes at 3 o'clock in the morning.

Associates explained that during the high pressure nights, they order dinner in. (The firm pays, of course.) There's a snack at 2 A.M., then it's breakfast at 8. Hours aren't always that late, naturally, but you do get a hint that they're not uncommon: the firm's cafeteria serves dinner till 8 P.M.

"Sometimes I feel as if all we do is push papers," an associate grumbled. "I'd like to do more physical things. When you don't get outdoors for a while, you start to feel like a wreck."

To avoid having flabby, unfit lawyers from too many all-nighters, too many take-out dinners, and too little exercise, Fried, Frank offers its employees a special discount at a health club nearby.

And the hours aren't always that grim. As one associate explained, those super-intense periods (which may extend over four months) may be followed by a lull in action. And when work doesn't involve a compressed time frame, "there's no expectation that you stay late."

That's a contrast to some other firms, where, according to a young lawyer, "there is a pressure to bill (typically at least 2,000 hours a year), which makes for an unpleasant work environment."

Fried, Frank does other things to make staffers' lives more pleasant—and to reinforce the team feeling. Unlike some firms which have "tea and crumpet" get-togethers, Fried, Frank encourages interaction among its staff members through holding weekly Friday afternoon open-bar cocktail parties.

Recognizing the different lifestyle needs of its associates, Fried, Frank has also accommodated its attorneys by offering employment on less than full-time bases. "Fried, Frank is more flexible in terms of women and women with children," said one young woman who has worked a three-day week here. Not only that, but Fried, Frank has more female partners than the vast majority of other big firms.

DOLLARS AND SENSE
Certainly, the fact that the firm pays top dollar was—and is—a powerful incentive for the attorneys. As one attorney said, "I was bitten by the bug of the big Wall Street firm . . . and decided, if I'm going to play, I'm going to play in the big leagues."

According to the NLJ survey, the firm's starting salary for first year associates is $52,000—including a $3,000 bonus. That kind of money is awfully attractive, especially to young people who were recently starving law students. One such mercenary soul came clean. "I decided I wanted to work only at a large New York firm because they pay the best. And much to my surprise, I enjoyed the people and the work."

But he does enjoy the money, too.

GETTING IN—TRICKS OF THE TRADE

It's no secret that being at the top of the law school class is a prerequisite for being considered by any of the top firms. And although in recent years the firms have been choosing their young associates from more than just the Ivy League institutions, odds remain in favor of candidates at the top schools. Among the best bets are Harvard, Yale, Columbia, and NYU, to name a few.

It's not that top candidates from lesser known schools don't get placed, but as one Ivy-educated associate admitted, "there's a sharp distinction between those candidates who are actively recruited and those who have to stand on their heads to get in."

For those law students who are actively sought after, it's somewhat like being "a pro-football recruit with all the firms going through elaborate moves" to woo the candidates.

Becoming a second-year summer associate is a way toward getting a permanent offer from the firm in the third year. Fried, Frank reportedly has asked back 80 percent of its second-year summer associates. Because the firm's reputation stands on the quality of its lawyers, the recruitment process focuses on the day-to-day running of Fried, Frank. Associates actively participate in the process.

Those who are on the Recruitment Committee—which is made up of 50 percent partners and 50 percent associates—do the initial interviewing at law schools. Applicants who make the first cut are called in for a "full dress" interview with three partners and are taken out for lunch or cocktails by two associates. The luncheon "aims at making them comfortable and gives the candidates a chance to ask questions they wouldn't ask a partner," explained a young woman.

All the interviewers fill out a questionnaire about the candidates, which is then evaluated by the Recruitment Committee. It's hard to pinpoint what it takes to do an interview "right," since it's so often intertwined with the power of personal chemistry and establishing a rapport with strangers in a matter of minutes. "People should relax," advised one woman. "Make an effort to interact."

But candidates should always guard against being too relaxed and ending up revealing more than they should. One associate explained, "It's easier to spot poor judgment in a candidate than to be assured of good judgment." For example, "one candidate told the associate in detail how he made money scalping concert tickets (which happens to be illegal) over the summer. That was poor judgment."

Obviously. Recruits like that stand out—for all the wrong reasons. So what are the right reasons for standing out? Generally, everyone said they looked for articulate people with high energy and self-confidence. More specifically. . . .

"Chutzpah."

"Diversity."

"Flexibility."

"An outgoing person."

"Nerve."

For all those descriptive words, one litigator said, "It's easy to pick out the stars and those who won't fit in. It's the in-between that's hard." So it all boils down to one thing—"It's a gut feeling."

THE BOTTOM LINE

Liberal—and pretty tough to boot.

SKADDEN, ARPS, SLATE, MEAGHER & FLOM

VITAL STATISTICS

- **locations:** New York (headquarters); Washington, DC; Chicago; Los Angeles; Wilmington; Boston
- **revenues:** $129 million (fiscal year ending March 1985)
- **rank:** 1st in gross revenues, 3th in size
- **employees:** 121 partners, 428 associates, 150 paralegals

AS SEEN FROM THE OUTSIDE

The aristocrats of law, those firms that have been around for decade upon decade, have been taught a lesson by a relative upstart—you don't need a blue-blooded pedigree to be successful.

The thirty-eight-year-old Skadden, Arps is proving that being young and aggressive has definite assets. Other more established firms were afraid to sully their hands in the ungentlemanly world of corporate takeovers. Not Skadden. Now it's one of the undisputed leaders in the field. And it's making a lot of money at it.

It all started just yesterday, according to the legal profession. More precisely, it was in 1948 that Marshall Skadden and Leslie Arps (from Dewey, Ballantine), and John Slate (legal counsel to Pan Am), formed the firm. Initially, the practice revolved around case-by-case referrals from other law firms and from clients. Eventually, referrals led to Skadden's success. And the firm's first associate, now chairman, Joseph Flom, played a key role.

In the late 1960s, hostile takeovers became more and more common in the corporate world. Many full-service firms didn't handle that type of work. Flom was an expert in the field, Flom worked at Skadden, so Skadden got the business. And it started carving a niche for itself in the tumultuous merges and acquisitions (M&A) field.

It's a full-service firm now, with practice areas including corporate, litigation, antitrust, tax, labor, energy, real estate, trusts and estates, bankruptcy, and more, and offices in New York, Washington, Boston, Wilmington, Los Angeles, and Chicago. But for all the growth and all the diversity, it's the M&A area that gets the lion's share of attention—and excitement.

Skadden's M&A work is the stuff newspaper headlines are made of: the Allied Corporation–Signal Companies takeover battle, the Capital Cities–ABC merger, General Motors' acquisition of Electronic Data Systems, TWA's defense against a proposed hostile takeover by Carl Icahn, the sales of Hughes Aircraft to GM . . . the list goes on and on. And so does the firm.

HEARD AT THE WATER COOLER— WHAT IT'S REALLY LIKE TO WORK HERE

If you want a "white shoe" firm complete with dark wood paneling, oil paintings of the founders, dark carpeting, leather couches, gray-haired parnters in conservative blue suits, and a reverent hush, don't come to Skadden, Arps.

Here the surroundings are modern—white walls, light carpets, modular furniture. It's successful and professional, yes, but it's informal, open, and most important, it's young. That makes a big difference.

There's a bustling atmosphere at Skadden, Arps. Young people walk briskly through the halls. As a senior associate pegged it, "It's jackets off, sleeves rolled up, and let's get to work."

And work they do. "Skadden has a reputation for working hard—that's putting it in the best sense," commented a young man. "And the negative side is that it's accused of being a sweatshop."

Most of the people here don't seem to view it that way. Sure, they're putting in long hours, pulling overnighters and dealing with mega-pressure. But that's what they've chosen to do. And who can blame them? For all the headaches, it's easy to get addicted to the hard-driving spirit here.

One associate recalled her first impression of Skadden, Arps. "It was extraordinarily different from any other law firm that I set foot in. It was exciting, it was electric, you felt energy when you walked down the halls."

And you still do.

PEOPLE

What kind of people end up at Skadden? Well, as one would assume, they're a lot like the firm—hard-driving, unafraid of work, and able to deal with pressure.

"In certain respects, you have to have a type A personality," commented a young man. "You have to be just raring to go. That doesn't mean you have to be keyed up all the time on a tightrope. But the clients have come to expect a supercharged, go-getter atmosphere."

And to a great extent, that's just what the clients get. This isn't the place for people who want a humdrum 9-to-5 existence. A lot of that is due to Skadden's focus on merger and acquisition. There's no question that M&A requires a "unique type of person," as one employee termed it.

How unique? Well, an associate explained, "A merger and acquisition lawyer needs to be able to work twenty-four hours. And in the morning, when the sun rises, you ought to be able to take a shower, put on a clean suit, and go right back in."

That doesn't happen all the time. But still, that kind of "can-do" attitude permeates the place.

"I think that's another reason why the atmosphere here is so informal," noted a young man. "It's because the pressure is non-stop and it's very intense. So it's a 'M*A*S*H' mentality."

"This is the loosest bunch of people," an associate commented. "I had to work this weekend and there were partners here laboring right alongside associates. There's none of this 'I'm the partner; you're the associate; get your ass in the library.' It's just not that kind of place."

JOBS

Here's where all the excitement stems from. Skadden might be best known for M&A work, traditionally a dynamic area, but the electricity is felt throughout the firm.

The M&A practice is where Skadden really shines. It's a tough field, so the lawyers in that area have to be pretty tough, too. And it starts from the very beginning.

"As a first year M&A lawyer, because of the way transactions are structured, you're going to get a lot of responsibility whether you like it or not," an associate said.

"The pressure level is there. I think that's what's difficult getting used to as a first year associate. Law school's all kind of play-acting, and all of a sudden you have a real client, there's real pressure for merger and acquisition lawyers, there's a lot of money at stake, and it's a high-risk game for your client. That translates into a lot of pressure for the client's lawyer."

It also translates into a lot of hands-on work and a large dose of excitement. Since Skadden clients are heavy hitters, a first-year associate can conceivably be working on a case that's being followed in the *Wall Street Journal* or the *New York Times*. So it's a far cry from law school, but many people find it a great deal more fun—and a lot more educational.

One lawyer described working in the M&A area and watching the more senior people at work. "To work with them daily, to be negotiating till 3 A.M., or to pull an all-nighter and come back and start negotiations again—and to watch their level of intelligence, if anything, just get better and better as the transaction goes on—it's amazing to watch."

It's not only first-year associates who learn the game quickly. Summer associates also get a real view of life in the fast lane at Skadden. As one former summer associate explained, Skadden believes in giving its summer associates a true learning experience. Yes, there are the requisite baseball games and nights on the town. But there's also a taste of the real legal world.

"You're not treated with kid gloves, as with some of the other firms; you're not sheltered," said one staffer. "They don't want to give you the impression that being a lawyer is 2½-hour lunches, talking to a client a couple of times on the phone, and then going home."

Summer associates aren't assigned to a specific area. As in most large law firms, they're able to go from department to department and case to case in order to better understand the work and the firm. They may get involved in drafting and negotiating sessions, depositions, and court proceedings—virtually everything a junior associate could expect to do.

"You can poke your nose into anything you want here—practice tax law, get yourself on a trial or litigation, or write a brief."

And as one former summer associate explained, being able to experience all the phases of the firm's practice gives you a very different picture than you get from law school. "I worked with one woman who said, 'If I ever get a tax assignment, I'll die.' She was sure she hated tax. Well, she left at the end of the summer a tax lawyer."

After the summer is over and job offers doled out, quite a few summer associates return to join the ranks as new associates. Skadden usually assigns junior associates to whatever area they choose, and they're given a "liaison partner" during their first six months here. That partner essentially checks over the associate's work and often supervises the assignments. And after the six months are over, new associates should be set to go. There's training for them, too—a litigation program, corporate program, legal writing program, trial advocacy workshop, and more—designed to better prepare associates for the work at hand.

There's no time frame set here for responsibility. It depends on initiative. "Everything seems to turn on individual ability," commented a products and liability staffer. "At least that's been my experience. If you can do it, it doesn't matter what class you're in. There's no rule here that says, 'You don't do depositions until you're at least second or third year.' If you just walk through the door, and they think you can handle it, you do it."

And a lot of people do. That kind of self-motivation seems to be the rule across the board here—whether a person's in corporate, litigation, tax, or whatever. One attorney noted that it's best early on to find a niche here, so you don't get lost in the shuffle, or inundated.

"For instance, in the corporate department, there will be eighty partners. And you can get phone calls from a lot of these guys. They'll be looking for someone to help them on this or that. So it's important for you to have a couple of people looking out for you, making sure that you don't get sucked into everything that comes down. It took me about six months to realize that."

Once associates start settling in, they take on more and more responsibility. And as you'd expect, that's when a lot of people here really begin to enjoy their job. But it does take some getting used to.

The people who succeed at Skadden don't seem frightened about failing—at the beginning at least. One corporate lawyer said, "You just learn by having someone say, 'Here, do this deal.' Sure, you make mistakes, but you learn from them."

Another noted, "Especially in a large New York firm, you're going to take some lumps, no question about it. You have to be able to pick yourself up afterward and just continue on."

Continuing on here means moving on to bigger and better things. "As much as you can handle," as one associate said, no matter the department. A corporate lawyer explained that, after two and a half years, she was handed a joint venture deal to work on. "It was a tricky deal, it was brutal, and I felt it was a turning point for me. Once we got that deal done, I felt I knew how to run a deal from soup to nuts."

And a litigator noted that "in the cases I work on, to a large part, on the other side I'm dealing with a partner. So I have to assume that it's easier here for a go-getter to get ahead, that the reason I'm dealing with a partner on the other side is that they don't want to give associates there the same responsibility I'm given here."

So Skadden might mean hard work, but if associates put in the time, they'll keep moving. Said a senior associate, "The cream really rises to the top here."

It may sound like just another line, but at Skadden, Arps, you believe it. Just look at Joe Flom . . .

LIFE
Okay, life here *does* revolve around work to a great extent. It's the nature of the beast.

"You could get a phone call from a partner saying 'such and such a corporation just called us up and they're the target of a hostile takeover and they want us to represent them. We're flying out to Chicago in two hours; meet me at the airport,'" explained a young woman. "It's unpredictable and, to an extent, there are long hours."

So what? As she concluded, "On balance, on a scale of 1 to 100, the inconveniences that I've had maybe amount to a 10, but the excitement would go well over 90. Not everyone would feel that way; it's not for everyone's temperament."

That's the key to life here. While associates put in their time and deal with the pressures, they're doing it because they want to. And that forges a common bond.

Still, it's not all work. Skadden, Arps offers its associates memberships in a health club, and there are firm-sponsored running, softball, basketball, squash, and bridge teams, to name a few.

DOLLARS AND SENSE
Here's where the hard work pays off. Skadden pays top dollar to its first-year associates—$52,000, including a $3,000 start-up allowance.

Summer associates make out well, too. "You're paid as a first-year associate, so instead of scraping by as a second-year law student, you're all of a sudden being paid $900 a week. That's a lot of money for anybody, let alone somebody who's used to nothing."

GETTING IN—TRICKS OF THE TRADE

If you didn't go to Harvard, you have nothing to worry about. Skadden is bullish on hiring from non-Ivy schools as well as Ivy—you just have to be a go-getter.

"The partnership at the firm comes from a wide variety of schools, many of which would not be perceived to the outside as the top tier," said an associate. "In many interviews, they want to know what your pedigree is. But not at Skadden, Arps."

Another associate on the interview circuit stated it a bit more strongly. "In 99 percent of the cases, I don't know where anybody came from, and I don't care." Okay—so what does Skadden, Arps care about? In brief, the ability to work hard, dedication, intelligence, and the "right" personality. If you're a schlemeil, I don't think you'll fit in here, said one associated bluntly.

Skadden, Arps follows the interview process of most large law firms, and most associates here stress that, while it's the resumé and the grades that get you in the front door, it's personal dynamics that get you the job offer.

Beyond showing that you've got the brains, Skadden also wants people who have the drive. "You have to enjoy playing hardball and you have to enjoy taking responsibilities," said one young man. "I think we do the most sophisticated kind of work in the country. And you have to enjoy it. But, frankly, I don't see how anyone wouldn't."

And that's the real key to fitting the Skadden, Arps profile—plain old enthusiasm.

THE BOTTOM LINE

The tough guys.

MAGAZINES

Very few people work for magazines; they work for "books." That's what most staffers call magazines. And there are books and there are books.

There are the "trades"—the publications geared to a specific industry—and there are the "consumer books"—magazines, for, yes, consumers. There are a lot of both of them—about 11,000 magazines are published in the United States. And there are quite a few people working in the magazine industry—about 89,000.

But despite what the numbers suggest it's not easy breaking into magazines. First off, most of those 11,000 publications are small "mom and pop" operations. This means that most of those 89,000 magazine employees are working for the biggies. According to the Audit Bureau of Circulation, there are only about 450 publications that count as heavyweights, comprising 75 percent of circulation and over 90 percent of advertising revenues.

Circulation and advertising are the two revenue sources. And the two are closely linked. While a magazine generally earns less than half of its income from circulation (readers buying the magazine), its guaranteed circ rate (the number of people who buy each issue) is what determines advertising rates for space in the magazine. That's where the real money comes in; typically, over 50 percent of a magazine's income is from advertising revenues. And advertisers are lured to magazines not only by a strong base circulation in terms of numbers, but also by the customer profile. Certain magazines appeal to certain people; so do certain products.

So there are two main sides to magazines—the editorial or

"edit" side, and the business or "publishing" side. Editorial staffers have to put together a product that will draw readers, thus advertisers; business staffers have to sell the product effectively to both readers and advertisers.

As with newspapers, the two sides are distinct. That's called "the separation of church and state." And there's not that much interaction between the two staffs, which is rather logical. Probably because the two sides have different interests and different responsibilities, they tend to exist in different worlds.

Editorial employees are typical journalists to a great degree, involved in their subject, accustomed to long hours and tight deadlines, and used to fairly small paychecks. Business employees are more typically corporate—salespeople and marketers, dealing with the bottom line, and usually making a bit more money. Magazine salaries for both groups depend largely on the type of magazine—trades tend to pay less, large consumer magazines more. As with any company, it all depends on how much money the magazine makes.

The entry-level editorial position on most magazines is that of **editorial assistant**, which is more secretarial than anything else. The starting salary range is $10,000–$19,000. Editorial assistants are there to serve as apprentices, learn the ins-and-outs of the publishing business, and help editors in whatever way they can. More often than not, that means typing, answering phones, taking care of correspondence and other scut work. Depending on the publication and the editor, editorial assistants may also write brief pieces, help with story ideas and actually do a bit of editing.

On many news magazines, a typical entry-level position is that of **researcher**. Like editorial assistants, researchers don't make a lot of money and do a lot of gofer work. Researchers generally check facts on stories and pull information for writers and editors.

The next step up is **writer** (salary range $15,000–$40,000). Writers on a magazine write. It's that simple. What they write varies from magazine to magazine, and from writer to writer. Most are assigned stories by editors; usually writers have a specialty area—a subject, a division of the editorial department (such as fashion, health, etc.) or a specific section of the publication (a column, news briefs, etc.) Some magazines have a hierarchy among writers, moving up to senior writer or copy chief.

Assistant and associate editors (salary range $18,000–$45,000) usually are editorial assistants and writers who've moved up through the ranks. Typically, assistant and associate editors work as editors for a small department or a section of a larger department. They usually assign stories and photographic shootings for their area and may write copy.

The next step up is an **editor** (salary range $40,000–$65,000). At many publications, editors aren't called merely editors, but fashion editors, science editors, sports editors or simply senior editors. Editors have responsibility for an entire editorial department, and supervise the editorial assistants, freelance and staff writers, and junior editors within that department. They're usually the ones who come up with major story ideas, make sure editorial content from the department is consistent, and arrange major photographic shootings.

Those publications that have bureaus in other locations also have **bureau staffs**—headed by a bureau chief, who is responsible for managing the bureau, assigning stories and possibly writing stories (depending on the size of the bureau). Larger bureaus also have writers and reporters on staff.

Editorial departments of magazines also have **copyeditors** (salary range $17,000–$40,000) on staff, who check magazine copy for grammar, style and usage; **assistant art directors** ($20,000–$40,000) and **art directors** ($50,000–$70,000), who work with the design and layout of the magazine.

The highest editorial slots are those of **managing editor** and **editor-in-chief**. They work with both editorial and art production sides, and are responsible for the entire content of the magazine. Managing editors and editors-in-chief work together, leading editorial meetings, coming up with new thrusts or looks for a publication and making sure that the magazine is in on schedule and on budget.

Then there's the business side, which includes advertising sales, circulation, and production.

Generally, the lower-level jobs in ad sales may also be the highest paying. **Advertising sales representatives** (sometimes called category managers) often make commissions on their sales. And that can add up to quite a bit. Basically, sales reps try to get advertisers to buy, maintain or increase space in the magazine. They fill out "call reports," explaining who they've called and the outcome of the meetings. Those reports go to the advertising director, who has managerial responsibility for the sales staff. Often there's an intermediate person—sometimes called regional manager—who is responsible for sales in a certain region.

Working in **circulation** isn't making phone calls to get people to subscribe. It's actually marketing the publication to the public. Titles vary at the different companies, but essentially circulation staffers begin by being responsible for a certain "source" of subscribers and buyers—direct mail, television, inserts and so forth—tracking the response from that source, coming up with new ways to reach people through those means, and analyzing the results. Circulation staffers move up to being responsible for a larger source area, and then into supervisory positions.

Production staffers work in putting the magazine together. These are the people who work with printers, typesetters and engravers. Depending on the position, a production person may coordinate advertising and editorial production, check the quality of the product, ensure that completed mechanicals are delivered to the printer, and so on. Salary ranges for production staffs run from $21,000 for an assistant to $50,000 for a production manager at a large magazine.

There's one other important person at a magazine—the **publisher**. Publishers are the top dogs on the business side of a publication, in charge of advertising, circulation and production—usually not editorial.

CONDÉ NAST

VITAL STATISTICS

- location: New York
- revenues: N/A (privately held)
- rank: 1st among fashion magazines
- employees: 1,200

AS SEEN FROM THE OUTSIDE

Condé Nast publishes *Vogue*, *Glamour*, *Mademoiselle*, *Bride's*, *Self*, *House & Garden*, *Gourmet*, *Gentlemen's Quarterly* and *Vanity Fair*, as well as some sports magazines. These magazines give the company its clout and its reputation for covering fashion and style with almost no competition. In fact, the individual magazines sometimes compete with each other. It's a nice problem to have and not a major one.

Each magazine is designed to appeal to a specific audience—*Vogue* to the classy and well-heeled, *Mademoiselle* to the young and college-educated, and *Glamour* to the working woman from 18 to 40 years old. That last category is a large one, and the magazine has well over two million purchasers—the largest selling fashion/service magazine in the world.

The inspiration came from Condé Nast, a dapper innovative publisher who believed in "class publications." He began by publishing *Vogue Patterns*, then in 1909 purchased *Vogue*, the then-weekly magazine of society and fashion news. His philosophy was that *Vogue* "should appeal not merely to women of great wealth, but more fundamentally to women of taste." He stuck to his beliefs and, with success, added other magazines to his stable, including *Vanity Fair*—a witty, irreverent and, of course, classy, commentary on life.

Their tradition has continued under another man, S.I. Newhouse. Newhouse bought the company in 1959, added those sports journals, revived *Vanity Fair*, introduced *Self*, and purchased *GQ*. And he kept the quality high. *House & Garden* was repositioned as a decorator magazine, and *Mademoiselle* had a dash and vim added to it that maybe Condé Nast himself wouldn't have liked. But times change, and so do tastes.

HEARD AT THE WATER COOLER—
WHAT IT'S REALLY LIKE TO WORK HERE

Look at the Condé Nast magazines—glossy and polished, filled with pictures of perfect people, ideal houses, fit bodies and gourmet food, not to mention clever articles, noteworthy tips on everything from decorating to exercising to manicuring to job hunting, and page after page of advertising.

You can't deny that they're pretty slick packages—and that's what Condé Nast is, too.

Headquarters in the "Condé Nast Building" aren't ultra-chic. But everything here seems carefully thought out and basically stylish. There's a common Condé Nast look to reception areas, offices and even staffers.

Each magazine's reception area has wall-to-wall carpeting, white walls, low tables with all the Condé Nast magazines on them, and modern plastic chairs. About the only distinguishing feature that lets you know which magazine you're actually at—besides the magazine logo behind the receptionist's desk—is the color of the chair cushions.

Walk past the reception area and into the editorial offices and it's less glamorous than you'd think, but still there's an attention to appearance. There are basic white walls enlivened with magazine pages, calendars and other pictures, basic white desks facing the walls, and basic white file cabinets against the walls. Usually there's more than one desk to an office—editors and editorial assistants work side by side here. As for the occupants of those crowded quarters, the specifics depend on the magazine. But it's safe to say that they are stylish, well groomed and, more often than not, female.

And when you're walking around here, whether you're in the more relaxed editorial offices or the more businesslike business offices, you get that Condé Nast feeling. It's a combination of business, class and style (with an emphasis on the latter). The magazines sell mystique, and the people here create it.

As one staffer summed it up, Condé Nast "could be termed a little old-fashioned—there is an effort to be gracious. That's the tone we wish to continue, a little grace and a little style. That goes along with the kinds of magazines we put out."

And it goes along with working here, too.

PEOPLE

"When you go up and down the elevators, you really can get a sense of who works here and who's visiting," said an advertising employee.

Ask anyone working here to describe the typical Condé Nast employee and "style" is the first word you hear. It's what one might expect of a company that owns four magazines specifically about fashion and five others equally concerned with a rather upscale lifestyle.

"It's important to dress the right way," an editor explained. "You don't walk around in a suit. Unless it's a fashionable, chic suit . . ."

Obviously, there's no such thing as basic blue pinstripes or gray flannel here. Condé Nast staffers are in the business of projecting an image to the public through magazine pages, and they follow suit (chicly and fashionably, of course). Employees say you can tell who works for which magazine just by looking at them. And it's the truth.

"At *Vogue*, they all look very chic and really well put together. At *Mademoiselle*, everyone's got a bit of a twist to the way they dress. Very stylish, with good taste—but more of a flair," a young woman explained. "*Glamour* is totally different, more conservative."

And staffers on the nonfashion magazines also seem to have qualities in line with the magazine's focus. *Self* staffers look healthy and peppy; *House & Garden* employees are quieter and aesthetically inclined, *Vanity Fair* folks are "resourceful and gutsy," and so on.

But no matter which magazine a Condé Nast person works for, he's a Condé Nast person first. As a four-year veteran explained, being a Condé Nast person means "being aware of culture, being involved in the arts to some degree—because fashion and architecture and art, all those things are culture."

There's another thing about Condé Nast people—whatever the magazine and whatever the position, staffers are described as "polite." In fact, you hear that so often, you start to wonder a bit—it sounds a little too good to be true. But form matters here. And a Condé Nast person knows that.

"Things are always done with image in mind, there's a right way to do things," an employee stated.

It's the Condé Nast way, of course.

JOBS

Jobs at Condé Nast are a lot like the jobs at any magazine— there's the business side and the editorial side. As far as business goes, we're focusing on the advertising sales people. As for editorial, when most people think of Condé Nast, they also think of fashion, so that's what we concentrated on. Especially since that's the glitzy editorial area to be in—sort of.

"It sounds so glamorous. Well, you know, it *is* glamorous. But it's also a lot of hard work," said one editor. "I think there are some people who didn't know what they were getting into."

People working here quickly see behind the glamour. Particularly **editorial assistants**. Sure, they're working right alongside a fashion editor on a flashy magazine; they're dealing with well-known photographers and models, designer clothes and celebrities. But it's not quite as wonderful as it sounds . . .

"My assistant is in charge of booking all of my appointments," a *Mademoiselle* editor explained. "When we have a shooting, we sit down together and I'll say get this person for hair and makeup. What else? Organizing and calling in all the clothes that need to be called in. Packing the suitcases, getting them to the shooting on time. Setting up. She just takes care of my schedule and works really closely with me."

So much for glamour. Staffers are quick to tell you that an editorial assistant position is *not* a secretarial job, but an apprenticeship, "a great learning ground." Yes, an editorial assistant can learn a great deal by observing an editor. But that also means she (or he—there are *some* males at Condé Nast) is stuck with a lot of dull clerical and nonclerical work. While actual job duties may vary from department to department, magazine to magazine, essentially an editorial assistant is there to make the editor's life easier. And that can mean anything from taking messages to making phone calls, ironing clothing, updating model files. And this nonsecretarial position also involves typing. It's a Condé Nast rule that assistants type, so type they do—some a little, others a lot.

It's not all handling phones and typing, however. Editorial assistants are present at the monthly editorial meetings that are held to determine what clothes and what fashion themes will appear in the magazine.

These meetings aren't dry affairs with a bunch of editors sitting around a table discussing possible stories and so on. First of all, meetings are held in rooms that look a lot like closets—complete with rows of shoes, piles of scarves and other accessories, and even jewelry. But it's all there for business reasons—a Condé Nast editorial meeting is like a mini-fashion show, complete with models, lines of clothing and commentary.

Condé Nast **fashion editors** act as reporter and buyer rolled into one. They're assigned a category of clothing (couture, American sportswear, designer sportswear, etc.) to cover. Periodically they go around to designers and manufacturers to view current lines and determine what would fit in the magazine. Then they call in the clothing to show it at an editorial meeting.

It's not just show and tell, though. Editors have to organize the clothing they've selected into a story. Usually a theme has been decided on earlier, so the editor has to show that her clothes fit that theme. "Standing up in these meetings is like being a lawyer, sometimes, defending a case." a *Vogue* editor said. "I have to get up there and *convince* the other editors."

That's the duty of a market editor at *Vogue*. Once the clothing and stories have been decided on, they're back out in the market. *Vogue* style and fashion editors take it from there, getting the story shot and so on. But at the other Condé Nast magazines, the fashion editor both covers the market *and* sets up the photographic shootings. That's where the dealing with top photographers and models comes in. And that's where the pressure mounts.

"It's really hectic," said one young woman. "There are days when you want to pull your hair out. The phones are ringing and a model has canceled on a booking and you have to get another one down. The photographer or the hair or makeup person is sick. Then someone calls in and the clothes haven't gotten there and you're sitting on a shooting waiting for the clothes to get there. It can be really crazy."

"I love it. I get off on it," she added. "You have to be able to like that."

And you have to be able to remain calm and organized no matter what crisis crops up. During a shooting, it's up to the editor to make sure everything's going smoothly. According to one staffer, most editors are assigned one major shooting a month; add to that possible reshoots and cover trys and it's a fairly busy job.

They're often dealing with strong egos, too. But editors here have to learn how to direct the shooting without ruffling any feathers. And they also learn to depend on their instincts.

According to former editorial assistants who've been promoted, moving ahead at Condé Nast is a combination of hard work, good timing and enthusiasm.

"It is important to have a sense of style, be attractively groomed, but there are other qualities that are more important," a *Vogue* editor said. "A sense of priorities, follow through, being quick, being good on the phone. All those things come first. Then a sense of style—an important secondary."

"I didn't say I could do it, I just showed I could," said an editor who worked her way up through the ranks.

Editorial assistants also have to be patient. Moves upward depend on jobs opening up. And that doesn't happen all the time. The usual wait is two to three years. According to a former assistant who paid her dues for a few years, "You don't get promoted really fast. It takes time. Sometimes you want to be able to do more."

But for all the headaches, long waits for pomotion and not always glamorous work, a lot of people maintain it's worth it. "I enjoy the prestige," a young woman said with a smile. "People are very impressed. And I can't say it doesn't make me feel good."

Just like the editorial staff, the **sales staff** gets the prestige of working for Condé Nast, plus the hard work. And entry-level sales reps, like editorial assistants, have to learn on the job.

"The first day when I came in," a successful advertising staffer recalled, "twelve magazines were dumped on my desk and they said, 'familiarize yourself with the magazines.' The next day a list of accounts was dumped on my desk and they said, 'Okay, now that you're familiar with everything, go ahead and sell.'"

Basically, Condé Nast advertising sales reps are responsible for their own advertiser categories—fashion, beauty, home furnishings, and so on. Staffers explain that each magazine has its own management style, its own way of doing things. But essentially, it's just plain old sales. And even though the Condé Nast magazine, are well known, it's not always an easy sell.

"Constantly people are saying, 'No, no, we don't want to advertise, we don't want your magazine,' " said a *Vogue* sales rep.

So the key is to keep plugging at it, to handle rejection gracefully and to keep picking up the phone. And a good way to find new leads is by going shopping.

"Very often, I'll go into Bloomingdale's and just run through the designer sportswear areas—see new resources, who they're featuring, who's hot, what's selling, what's not. That's just doing research, doing homework," a sales rep explained. "I can see who's been recently discovered, who may be smaller this year but a big advertiser in a few years."

LIFE
There is a down side to the glamour . . .

"You have to keep a strong head to survive, keep a bit of reality," said one woman. "There were times when I was an assistant, and I'd go on a shooting and be surrounded by beautiful models. You go home and get depressed. You think, 'Oh, I'm not thin enough, I'm not this enough or that enough.' "

"But then you have to really sit back and look at it and say, 'It's not the real world,' " she added. "It's a picture and the camera makes them look good—you have to keep reminding yourself of that, because it's not as if it goes away."

And Condé Nast employees aren't comparing themselves only to the unreal world of shootings. Most staffers here don't deny that there's competition in-house, too. They just have to learn to deal with it.

"Sure, you get frustrated," one staffer said cheerfully. "You say, 'Why didn't I get that shooting?' stuff like that. But basically everyone tries to help one another. And there are times when you get people who don't want to help you and you have little bouts with them, but it works itself out. It's not a dream world."

No, but it can be fun. Especially for people who enjoy clothes, fashion and style.

DOLLARS AND SENSE
This might be Condé Nast, but it's still publishing. And that means people aren't here for the money.

Editorial staffers are on a straight salary (which isn't that high) and sales staffers on salary plus commission—a commision based not on space sold, but on quota.

But if the money's not high, other things do make up for it. There are benefits and little perks that keep people going. Editorial staffers get to go on trips both in the United States and all over the world—depending on the market they cover and the shoots they set up. Plus, "You don't have to pay cover charges at clubs, that's another perk," an editorial staffer said happily. "You see a lot of movies for free. But then you start to realize that it you had a lot of money, you wouldn't worry about perks . . ."

GETTING IN—TRICKS OF THE TRADE

Forget the old stories about Condé Nast being a country club, that you have to be in the Social Register to get a job here. They aren't all that true. But that doesn't mean it's easy getting a job. Not by a long shot. Even if you *do* know someone.

"Even if your aunt knows somebody at *House & Garden*, that won't get you the job," a staffer said flatly. "Everybody has to be interviewed through personnel, no matter who they know."

According to staffers, personnel does the initial screening of job candidates, keeps an updated pool of possibilities, then passes the information along when editors and others ask for an assistant. A personnel staffer explained what helps people get that initial interview. "Remember that some human being is going to read your letter. If there's a touch of character or smarts or someone who seems special or interested or knowledgeable, not just a blah, blah, blah letter with six typos in it, we'll probably want to talk to that person."

And those who want to be editorial staffers should be prepared to take a typing test.

As for sales, Condé Nast is looking for the typical sales personality, plus that Condé Nast polish—"a pleasant aggressiveness," was how one employee termed it. Experience helps, but employees say it's not the primary focus. Enthusiasm, determination and dedication (as always) are. And one more thing. It helps to have an idea of which magazine you want to sell for. "If they come in and say, 'Well, I just want to work at Condé

Nast, it doesn't really matter where,' it doesn't do anything for me," a *Self* advertising manager commented.

But the bottom line for getting a job at Condé Nast—whether sales or editorial—is just fitting into the Condé Nast image.

THE BOTTOM LINE

Professional, polite, polished and yes, well-dressed.

TIME INC.

VITAL STATISTICS

- **locations:** New York (headquarters); offices and bureaus worldwide
- **revenues:** $3.06 billion (1984)
- **rank:** 1st (in magazine revenues)
- **employees:** 18,000

AS SEEN FROM THE OUTSIDE

> "1984 was Time Inc.'s best year ever."
>
> —from the Time Inc. 1984 annual report

So why are they changing? No one is really certain, but they are. Since its inception, Time Inc. has been known for its dedication to innovation, starting new business as well as absorbing losses, if need be. It all began in 1923, when the son of a missionary, Henry Luce, started a news magazine called *Time*. But he didn't stop there. Winning attention for its snappy writing style, Time grew quickly—up to a circulation of about 220,000. In 1930, *Fortune Magazine* was born; in 1936, Time bought *Life Magazine*. *Sports Illustrated* was launched in 1954, to a less-than-rousing reception. For about eleven years, *Sports Illustrated* lost money; but Luce kept it going, until it caught on in the late 1960s.

Time Inc. kept moving, starting *Money* and *People* in the 1970s. In 1978, Time revived *Life Magazine*, which had folded in the early 1970s, and bought the *Washington Star*. In 1980 it went into popular science publishing, launching *Discover*.

And that's not all Time has been doing since it was founded. Aside from the magazines, Time owns book publishers (Time-Life Books, Little, Brown & Co., the Book-of-the-Month Club, Oxmoor House); SAMI (Selling Areas-Marketing, Inc., which provides computerized reports of the movement of supermarket items); HBO and Cinemax, pay-cable TV stations; ATC (which builds and operates cable TV systems); and it owns interests in USA Network and Tri-Star Pictures.

And that's *still* not all. Time Inc. also has been involved in the creation of paper mills, and owns Southern Progress Corporation, which puts out lesser-known magazines like *Progressive Farmer* and *Southern Living*.

So that's what Time Inc. has been doing for the past few decades. But now there's change in the air. Time Inc. has reorganized itself, switching management of its Magazine Group to a separate team. And people are beginning to wonder what's going on. Some people think Time will sell off its less profitable video/cable holdings. Others talk about retrenching. And no one's talking about innovation any more.

Time management says it can't afford to be a risk-taker like Henry Luce. Its newest magazine, *Picture Week*, is due for a test marketing, and if it doesn't catch on quickly, it will be folded. Time is instituting cost cutting now, for the first time in its history. Management is talking about merger possibilities. It's buying properties, rather than starting them.

What's next? Only Time will tell. . . .

PEOPLE MAGAZINE

VITAL STATISTICS

- **locations:** New York (headquarters); 6 regional sales offices; nationwide news bureaus
- **revenues:** $233 million (1984 ad revenues)
- **rank:** 3rd best-selling weekly magazine
- **employees:** 385

AS SEEN FROM THE OUTSIDE

Everyone knows *People* magazine—even the people who *say* they don't read it (you know, the people who skim it in dentists' offices). It's a magazine that's virtually impossible to avoid. Which is just the way parent company, Time Inc., likes it.

Since *People* was launched in 1974, it's been talked about, criticized, laughed at and well-thumbed. It has also made money. A lot. And that makes the people at *People* real happy. No wonder they're celebrating people, like their ads say. People are making *People* pretty successful—to the tune of 22.7 million readers, over 4,000 advertising pages and $233 million in ad revenues in 1984.

Not bad for Time Inc.'s baby. But from the beginning, Time had a lot of expectations for the magazine. *People* was rolled out on March 3, 1974 with a bang. Time announced that the magazine would begin with a circulation of 1 million, then upped that figure to 1.25 million by 1975. The problem was that circulation at the start wasn't quite a million; it reportedly hovered around the 900,000 mark. But it didn't make much of a difference. People were taken with *People*; and advertisers began following suit. Eighteen months after *People* had been introduced, it was in the black.

Now that *People* isn't the new kid on the block, it's the magazine a lot of others are trying to copy. The *People* format—lots of pictures, a conversational style, and articles and "chatter" about stars and just plain folks—has spawned imitators. From the fresh-faced kid to the leader of the pack—and all by age 11. *People* has made its mark.

Like its primary audience—baby boomers—*People* is still coming on strong. There's talk of radio and cable television ventures and more. It's positioning itself as a key source of information on the baby-boomer market for advertisers and marketers (a stance helped by the fact that *People* publisher E. Christopher Meigher III, aged 39, just fits into that age bracket).

So that's *People*—young, brash, and on the move.

HEARD AT THE WATER COOLER— WHAT IT'S REALLY LIKE TO WORK HERE

If you like reading *People* magazine, you'll love working here. Even if you don't like reading *People*, you'll probably love it here. Simply put, *People* is a lot of fun.

Okay, so at *People* they're not changing the world. But they're not just covering Charo and Cher either. Despite popular beliefs, *People* isn't only gossip and flash. You've just got to get behind the glitz.

And that's just what you do at *People* headquarters. The only flashy item at the place is a neon sign behind the receptionist's desk. Walk past that and you're in college again—narrow halls, small rooms, the sounds of music and conversation and people. Young people and lots of them.

That dormlike atmosphere pervades the editorial area. Cluttered offices hold desks piled high with letters, notebooks and magazines. Walls are covered with just about anything—from rock star posters to cartoons to diagrams of the human body. It's a dream place for people who like distractions. Doors are always open, co-workers mingle in the halls, people chat through the walls—it's cheerful and chaotic.

Go to the business offices on another floor and it's not quite as loose. Here it's more buttoned up. Offices are neater, more corporate and crisper—and so are the occupants. This part of *People* doesn't interact too much with editorial (that old separation of church and state again) and the staff pays allegiance to Time Inc. more than to *People*.

Even so, wherever you go at *People* there's that touch of lightness and youth. One of the buttoned-down corporate staffers summed it up for them all. "It's a hard-working place, but we play hard, too."

PEOPLE

Ask *People* employees to describe the typical worker here and the first thing they'll say is *young*.

"It's the key difference between us and the other publications at Time Inc.," a young middle manager said. "*People* is only eleven years old, and the people here are between two and three times that."

"You're not fighting the old school here. There are still remnants of the old-boy network at *Time* Magazine, but not at *People*," added a young Time Inc. veteran.

They might not be fighting the old school, but they all seem to come from the *same* schools, namely Ivy League ones.

"I swear everyone here went to Harvard or Princeton." said one reporter. "I'm the only one who didn't."

But, prestige educations aside, staffers aren't all that similar. Your style depends on your job.

"The guys who handle the news are more conservative," explained a reporter. "But it would be out of place for me to watch Jimmy Cliff and Lou Reed record in a banker's suit."

One thing about the editorial staff: these people who write about glittering stars and celebrities are "*not* glamorous types," an editor stated. "In fact most people who work here are ordinary."

Ordinary? It really depends on how you look at it. "My editor walks into work in a sex, drugs and rock 'n' roll tee shirt," said one woman.

Try *that* at The *Wall Street Journal* . . .

JOBS

"To get in as a writer right out of college is virtually impossible," stressed a senior writer. "More people get in as reporters."

Sounds great, doesn't it? Fresh from school and you can land a reporting job at a top national publication. Well, it's not quite what it seems. Some job titles at *People* don't always mean what they appear to.

For example, *People* assistant editors actually do a staff writer's job; and while senior writer sounds like a lower job, it's one step above assistant editor. Correspondents out in the bureaus do much of the news-gathering. So what then does an entry-level *People* **reporter** do?

"A lot of fact-checking," a reporter said with a sigh. "And some reporters don't really do any actual story reporting."

Time Inc. believes in getting the facts straight. And they follow that corporate edict to the T at *People*. Even what might seem trivial gets checked and double-checked before the story is published. But sometimes something slips through, a reader sends in a letter and the reporter has to check on a fact once again—facts like *exactly* how tall Andy Taylor of Duran Duran is, which one reporter had to dig up.

No matter how trivial it all sounds, fact-checking isn't necessarily a dead end. Some reporters *do* get to do the real thing—interviews, stories, everything you'd expect a reporter to do.

"I'd say two-thirds of my time is spent fact-checking, the other third is reporting and writing or being on the phone trying to get stories together—a lot of dealing with press agents and that crap," a three-year reporter stated.

The key to getting a chance to do stories is initiative. Reporters here say there's flexibility in their jobs, that "it all depends on how you interpret what your job is. You can make of it what you want." So reporters push and let their editors know they're eager to begin reporting.

"A lot of us younger ones do stories," one reporter said. "I do. And luckily, since I'm here in the New York bureau, I can write them, too. I don't have to have somebody else write them."

Oh, yes. That's another thing about *People* magazine. Many correspondents don't write their stories; assistant editors and senior writers based in New York do. Correspondents get their assignments from New York, gather all the necessary information, do interviews and so on, then telex everything they've gotten to the editor or writer handling the story.

"The Los Angeles bureau hires entry level. And that's a great job," said a senior writer. "If you're looking for glamour, the glittery aspects of working for *People*, there's more there."

So what do non glamorous writers and editors do at *People*? "I get information from about fifty different reporters and I put it all together as a story," a writer explained. "For example, six to eight weeks ago, I sent wires to all the bureaus about this story I'm working on. I got about 150 files back from all over the place. Then I went over them with my editor and with the managing editor, decided what we actually wanted to include, and assigned correspondents to get more detailed information. Now I'm taking their files and compressing them into a story."

Magazine layouts are done before any stories are written, so staffers know exactly how long each story should be—to the word. Phew! No wonder one editorial staffer called *People* "the Cuisinart school of journalism."

"You've got so many people in on one story," she continued. "You've got the fact-checkers checking it, you've got the researcher rewriting it, you've got three editors rewriting it. You've got a million people with their hands on it."

What about the people who sell the advertising space? They're the ones who really keep the magazine on its feet. No matter how catchy the editorial content is, *People* wouldn't be *People* if the **advertising sales reps** (called advertising sales category managers) didn't sell all the ad space they do.

You'd think that sales reps here would have an easy job, since *People* is very popular entertainment, and *People* readers are the ones most advertisers want to reach. But . . .

"There is no such thing as an easy sell," said one young man. "We're paid to go the extra yard, to get the advertisers who don't read *People* or have a perception difficulty."

That's the tough part about being a *People* sales rep. The magazine is so successful in terms of advertising pages that most advertisers who want to be in *People* already are. As for the others, they think *People* isn't serious enough, that it's too frivolous a vehicle for their advertising.

"That's one of the hardest things to battle—their opinions," explained a sales category manager. "So you start gradually, encouraging them to take a different view, to put aside personal thoughts. You tell them that whether or not they read the magazine, there are 23 million Americans who do."

But it's not only headaches and convincing advertisers. One thing *People* sales reps love about working here is the degree of independence they have, which lets them feel like entrepreneurs.

"I don't have to do call reports," said one staffer. "It makes me feel like my sales category is my responsibility; this is *my* business. There's no one looking over my shoulder saying do this, do that. They treat you like an adult here."

LIFE

Life at *People* can be fraught with difficulties, not the least of which is keeping your sense of humor intact. That can be tough when you're faced with friends, family and colleagues who are convinced that *People* is pure gossip, a *National Enquirer* gone big time. And it's a problem that cuts across the business and editorial sides.

"You constantly have to defend the magazine to people who don't read it," one writer complained. "Everyone thinks of the trashy stories. We do a lot of serious stories, but a lot of people don't read that stuff."

But it can't be *that* bad doing those "trashy stories." Sure, everyone complains about them, but there are some *very* tangible benefits . . .

"The perks in this job are amazing—like Springsteen tickets that people camped out for seven days in D.C. to get," a reporter reported gleefully. "And we get them free!"

Sometimes it becomes an embarrassment of riches. "I throw out more records than I can keep," said a staffer in the music department. "I turn down more concerts than I can go to."

Yes, life at *People* can be awfully tough. . .

DOLLARS AND SENSE

It's not only free tickets, passes to new rock clubs or invitations to exclusive parties that keeps *People* employees happy. The money ain't bad either—on the high side by industry standards.

"I don't think anyone here has any complaints. Almost without a doubt, I'm outearning stockbrockers my age," a woman in her mid-twenties commented.

That's probably why "almost no one ever leaves. A very large number of people have been here since the magazine started."

That's the good news—the money's good, and the benefits are good. The bad news is that it takes a while to get ahead.

GETTING IN—TRICKS OF THE TRADE

So you went to high school with the hottest star around. Figure you'll write a story on him, send it to *People* and land a job, right?

Wrong.

"Suggest stories to us on people we don't know about," a senior writer offered. "Don't write us a letter suggesting we do a story on Michael Jackson. Come up with somebody unusual and different and you may very well get an assignment."

Hmm . . . someone like an Anglican priest who became a Methodist minister, and then converted to be an Orthodox rabbi? Don't laugh. It's that kind of "strange human interest story" that was the above senior writer's first assignment.

And don't be shocked if you don't immediately land a full-time job. Many people on the editorial staff began as interns, freelancers or part-timers. How did they do it?

"I know only one person who got in on the strength of an interview with personnel," said an editorial staffer. "It's really best to know someone."

And if you don't, don't give up hope. A business employee suggested that people "send their resumés directly to people who work here. Personnel? We hardly use it. You also could conceivably propose the ideal of being a summer intern to someone."

People who want to join the ad sales force are advised to be tenacious, aggressive and self-motivated. Anything else? "I think a marketing background helps immensely," said a successful sales manager. "And communications skills are a big plus. Take a good business writing class, or a presentation workshop."

But it isn't easy landing a job here. "There really aren't that many entry-level positions," one young woman said. But marketing and sales support are growing, so there may be possibilities there.

In short, to get a job at *People*, you have to be persistent, enthusiastic and optimistic. You also have to be just a little bit lucky.

Said a writer here, "Everybody who has a job here got it through a fluke."

THE BOTTOM LINE

The Ivy League meets popular culture.

SPORTS ILLUSTRATED

VITAL STATISTICS

- location: New York (headquarters)
- revenues: $230 million (advertising revenues)
- rank: 1st (in sports magazines)
- employees: 350+

AS SEEN FROM THE OUTSIDE

What do bathing suits and boxers have in common? *Sports Illustrated*, of course. The yearly bathing suit issue has become a byword. And so has *SI*'s consistently high ad revenues. Its Olympic Preview issue alone brought in $24 million, the highest ever for a single issue of a magazine. And 1984 saw *SI* break its own ad revenue record set in 1983, raking in over $230 million, which made it first among all U.S. newsweeklies.

So why does *Sports Illustrated* do so well? Because it's read by about 14 percent of all males in the United States. And why do so many males read it? Because since *Sports Illustrated* first came out in 1954, it's been noted as *the* comprehensive sports magazine.

Glossy color photographs, high-quality writing, in-depth sports coverage, special issues annually on baseball, football and The Year in Sports—and throw in a yearly touch of cheesecake, too—that's *Sports Illustrated*.

HEARD AT THE WATER COOLER—
WHAT IT'S REALLY LIKE TO WORK HERE

You don't have to be a sports nut or an ex-jock to like working at *Sports Illustrated*, but it certainly wouldn't hurt.

Even though *Sports Illustrated*'s offices are all over the place in the Time-Life Building, and many staffers move from magazine to magazine within Time Inc., there's still a *SI* kind of feeling.

We talked with people on the circulation, promotion, and editorial staffs. And while they have different perspectives on *SI* depending on their department, there do seem to be common bonds. There's a young atmosphere at *Sports Illustrated*, for one thing.

Circulation people tend to consider themselves more part of Time Inc. than *Sports Illustrated*. One reason for that could be that they work on the same floor as other Time Inc. circulation people. Offices there are basic—desk, computer, file cabinets, and so on. They could belong to anyone working for any magazine. But if you take a look at the promotional calendars or advertisements pinned up neatly on the walls, you get a clue. If you see Carol Alt in a skimpy bathing suit or the Refrigerator in full padding, then the office probably belongs to a *Sports Illustrated* staffer. Or rather, a Time Inc. staffer who works on Sports Illustrated.

Go down a few floors and you're in the promotion area. Part *SI*, part Time Inc., these offices have more personality than the circ offices. They're a little bigger, a little brighter, and a little less businesslike. You see more reminders of *Sports Illustrated*— sports posters, magazine covers, and so on. And there's more talk about sports going on here.

As for the editorial department, it's *Sports Illustrated* through and through. Wherever you look, there's something sports-oriented. Pennants, posters, a television set switched to a game— and young people all over the place. Offices aren't posh, they're comfortable. And there's a casualness about both the place and the people, as long as it's not deadline time. Then, it's fast talking and typing, phones ringing, and general pandemonium. But there's a Time Inc. twist even here . . .

"*SI*, Time Inc. in general, is corporate journalism," explained a staffer. "You don't have a newsroom, you have a little office. Everyone doesn't sit around, looking over their typewriters, blowing smoke at each other, and typing away. Everyone has his own little cubicle.

"It's a very different atmosphere that's not for everyone by any means."

But a lot of people like it.

PEOPLE
Sports Illustrated people *do* like sports. It might not be the most important part of their lives, but there's a definite interest there.

"I might not know everything there is to know about football," said one woman on the promotion staff, "but I know who the best players are and things like that."

But there's more to *SI* staffers than sports. Many staffers say Time Inc. has a "preppiness" to it. One staffer explained that it was more a matter of attitude than background. "Blustering people who come through cutting a wide swath and just being abrasively ambitious wouldn't fit in," she noted. "Let's face it a smoothness is going to make you more comfortable here. It isn't *necessarily* preppiness or Ivy League either. It's just a little bit of style. It's probably a corporate thing. Total nonsense, but it does exist."

Still, people aren't rigid and formal here—especially on the editorial side. Editorial employees are looser, more casual than the corporate employees. And they're a tight-knit group, particularly because they share a few things, not the least of which is an unusual schedule—a Thursday-through-Monday work week. "Two days a week when we come here, there's no one else around," commented a four-year vet. "So we'd *better* get along."

But there's more to being part of the *SI* editorial team than days off. "We've got people straight out of school and we've got people who worked for newspapers for ten years," summed up an employee. "But by and large, they're people who really enjoy journalism, who really enjoy sports."

Of course.

JOBS

The lowest level **editorial** position is reporter. Called a researcher at some other Time Inc. magazines, a *SI* reporter is responsible for accuracy in stories. When a story comes in from the field, reporters check all the facts in it, sometimes re-interview people to make sure things have been represented correctly, and work with the editors as the story is changed.

Then there's also sitting in on "color meetings" to help select pictures; participating in the layout meeting; helping with photo captions; essentially seeing the story through to its final galley form.

So why are they called reporters? Well, in addition to all the other duties, they do in fact report. Reporters here do both research-type reporting based on library work, phone calls, and surveys, and field reporting.

And that's *still* not all. "A number of reporters also do some writing, because it's the main entry-level position to the magazine for anyone who wants to get involved in the edit side of it," explained a young woman. "So a lot of the people who come here are aspiring writers."

These aspiring writers don't exactly write inspiring stuff—but they do get an opportunity to do "minor stories" and a variety of other things like the publisher's letter and occasional scouting reports or columns. In addition, there are a few parts of the magazine that are almost exclusively the reporters' domain: For the Record, ("which says 'compiled by' because it isn't the greatest writing in the world," commented an employee); and Football Week and Basketball Week, which are roundups of college games.

Since their main responsibility is fact-checking, however, reporters learn that "you're going to have to squeeze writing in on your spare time," as a staffer explained.

Those who do squeeze the writing in and prove their dedication and their talent may eventually move up through the ranks—first to writer/reporter, which one person described as "a half-step up. It's in the direction of becoming a writer. Like a halfway house. It's still under the research or reporting department, but 'officially,' given time, you're going to move." The next step up is to staff writer. After that, the sky's the limit. According to one young woman, about two thirds of *SI*'s editorial staff began as reporters here, starting with the managing editor on down.

But it's not that easy to move up. Time Inc. is known for notoriously slow promotion tracks. And to some extent, that's the case at *SI*. As one fast-tracker mentioned, reporters have to be patient. They can't come in expecting to be promoted in six months. "There's just no formula, no 'Come here, do this and you'll be a writer in two years.'

Still, the opportunities are good even if the titles aren't coming. I think reporters here at our magazine are doing more writing than ever." That doesn't mean they're getting the writer/reporter or full-fledged staff writer title. What it does mean is that they're getting to write more often.

In order to seize those opportunities, *SI* reporters have to be pretty flexible. While staffers say sports journalism is a little more predictable than other forms of journalism, "because most of the time you know when the major sports events are going to happen," that doesn't mean there aren't late-breaking developments, or last-minute additions. As one employee noted, "you never know when you're going to be assigned to go down to New Orleans on Thanksgiving, or be sent out to Houston at the drop of a hat to cover some game."

So staffers who want to get ahead have to learn to take the shifting schedules in stride. And they have to get used to high pressure and long hours too—15-hour days, working Saturday and Sunday. Add to that a healthy dose of competition among the aspiring writers and editors—the "future of the magazine" as a staffer termed the reporting department—and you can see that working at *SI* can be pretty intense.

"People are always saying, 'What a wonderful job! Sitting around and watching football games,' " an editorial employee said with a laugh. "Well, it's not quite like that, but it beats a lot of things.

"You've got the comforts of working for a large corporation without the whole executive rat race, but you've got a different, more creative, rat race."

Is it a whole different ball game for the *SI* employees who *are* part of the so-called executive rat race?

Well, first of all, it's much more corporate, more Time Inc. than *Sports Illustrated*. Said one young man, "There's no difference between working for *Sports Illustrated* or another Time Inc. magazine. My business is to produce subscriptions for *Sports Illustrated*."

But staffers say that the business of producing subscriptions for a magazine can be as creative as working in editorial. Essentially, **circulation** staffers are responsible for selling the magazine through television, direct mail, inserts, and so on. On one hand, they work with the creation of subscription campaign drives in their source field—whether it's coming up with a television campaign or a new direct-mail brochure—and oversee its production. That's the creative part.

On the other hand, circulation staffers work with budgets, analyze the results of their campaigns, keep track of the orders that are generated, and always try to make a profit. So no matter how creative the work may be, the bottom line is always the numbers.

As a source manager in television explained, "It's very quantifiable. You know which commercial works best, or which premium works best because you know how many orders this one brings in versus the others. It's all in the numbers."

BAs are usually hired as *assistant source managers*, handling special projects, billing, budgets, and other duties for a source manager. Staffers say there used to be a corporate training program, in which assistant source managers attended lunchtime seminars three or four times a week. Source managers and promotion staffers would give lectures that helped new hirees get a broad background in circulation. Word has it, however, that the training programs are either being dismantled or at least downplayed for the time being.

The next step up is *source manager*, the position in which MBAs usually begin, bypassing the initial assistant level. Source managers are responsible for subscription marketing activities within a specific source, such as TV. One young man described the position as being "literally a marketing manager. You create campaigns from start to finish, make sure the orders are coming in every week; you do all the analysis, all of the media buying." In addition, source managers coordinate activities among support groups like the promotion department, outside direct marketing agencies, outside advertising agencies, the cost management area, the Time telephone marketing area, the in-house agency. They also work with financial statements, drawing up the initial budget, doing quarterly and weekly estimates.

It's no wonder employees say that you have to like pressure to succeed here, that there's no such thing as a typical day when you're a source manager. "You just get used to being crazed," said one.

But the variety of duties and flexibility in following through is what staffers like about circulation work. They talk about the freedom they're given to work on their own, to do their own thing and innovate. "It's really managing your own business," one enthusiastic employee said. "I would never have thought four years ago as a junior in college that four years later I'd be running a ten-million-dollar business on my own. It's sort of mind-boggling to me, but it's a good feeling."

That kind of entrepreneurial feeling is shared by **promotion** staffers. They work hand in hand with advertising sales reps, develop presentations, write speeches and promotion copy, and produce television or radio spots. And, again, as in both the editorial and the circulation staffs, there's that feeling of being creative within a corporate atmosphere.

LIFE

Life at *Sports Illustrated* really depends on which department you work in. Circulation and promotion staffers seem to have a more corporate life. They all mention that they're friends with the other staffers, that the people they work with are great, that there's a real collaborative effort.

In editorial, team spirit is more intense. More often than not, life at *Sports Illustrated* is working for *Sports Illustrated*. Staffers here will tell you that "you've got to be willing to let your work rule your life sometimes." But there's more.

For one thing, there's that Thursday-through-Monday work week. "When people want to get a weekend house for the summer, you've got to get it with people you work with. Because who else is going to go in on a Tuesday/Wednesday beach house?"

And there are the long hours, described by one employee as a "seige thing that breeds team spirit." Plus the common interest in sports and in journalism. No wonder a four-year vet explained that it's very hard to leave. "Why? There's a comfortableness to it."

DOLLARS AND SENSE

When it comes to salaries and benefits, *SI* employees all are Time Inc. employees. Time Inc. pays the wages, gives benefits like profit-sharing, and keeps people happy.

"The salary is great, the benefits are great," raved a circulation staffer.

But the business side of magazines always pays decently. What about the editorial department? Well, they too are Time Inc. employees when pay day comes around. In fact, being a part of Time Inc. is one of the things that keeps many of them from job-hopping.

"Journalism isn't a very well-paying field," explained an editorial employee. "But, as journalism goes, it's not bad here. And the benefits are very good."

"Those benefits are hard to leave. You're going to stay and get vested. Then once you're vested, it's going to be something else."

GETTING IN—TRICKS OF THE TRADE

Getting into *Sports Illustrated*'s editorial department requires a combination of luck and timing. There simply aren't too many job openings. As always, experience will help, but it's not a necessity. Reporters are often hired directly from school.

Beyond that, "besides being intelligent and dedicated, people have got to be patient and have attention to detail and accuracy," explained a staffer on the interview circuit.

The key to landing a job in circulation? Ability with numbers. "When I was interviewing, I kept hearing, 'How are your numbers?' " said a recent hiree. But quantitative skills alone won't turn the trick. Those ubiquitous "people skills" are also a necessity.

Even with those skills, however, it's difficult to land a job. As in the editorial department, there aren't a wealth of job opportunities. But while editorial staffers are often hired through contact with the editorial department, getting a business job at *Sports Illustrated* means dealing with the Time Inc. personnel offices. And lately Time Inc. hasn't been hiring that many people in general.

That's why employees say you have to be persistent. A young woman who interviewed for one job but didn't get it was told "Stay in touch" by her interviewer. "I did and it paid off," she said. "And it was a blessing that I didn't get a job at Time Inc. at the beginning. Now I'm ready for it. It was good for me to go out and decide what I wanted to do."

Time Inc. likes people who know exactly what they want to do. So if you're interested in circulation and are lucky enough to land an interview either on campus or in the personnel office, don't say, "I just want to work for Time Inc. wherever you want." Say, "I want to be a source manager for *Sports Illustrated*."

THE BOTTOM LINE

Not for jocks only.

NEWSPAPERS

Forget all the nonsense about newspapering you see on television or in the movies. Gone are the "stop the presses" days. And chasing fire engines down city streets is a figment of some producer's imagination. This is a business. And it's run like a business.

Like most industries, the newspaper industry has a variety of staff functions like personnel, corporate relations, promotion, and so forth. But the two major sides to newspapers are advertising and editorial.

As with other industries dealing with news, there's the traditional "separation between church and state"—advertising people sell ad space and don't tamper with editorial content; editorial people write and edit stories and don't worry about pleasing advertising clients. Yet the two staffs are directly connected when it comes to generating profits.

Like magazines, most newspapers make their money in two different ways—through advertisers buying space in the paper and through readers buying the paper. Obviously, the more successful the paper is at attracting readers, the more money advertisers can be charged. And the higher the advertising "linage" (number of inches of advertisements), the more the paper can afford to pay its editorial staff. This means that the editorial content will be strong, which will attract more readers, and so on . . . So, even in the "Fourth Estate," money makes the business go round, just as much as hot breaking stories.

That's why the **advertising** side of newspapers is such an important part of the business. Essentially, advertising is broken into two main areas—classified and display advertising. More often than not, advertising salespeople in newspapers begin on the classified staff. A classified salesperson on a large paper usually sells a particular area of advertising—help-wanted, automotive, real estate, etc. Classified is generally acknowledged as the training ground for future display salespeople. It's the place where you learn selling techniques and the nuts-and-bolts of newspaper advertising.

Display is where the action (and money) is. Usually, advertising salespeople are assigned a distinct advertising category. Depending on the paper, display advertising may be broken into regional and national.

Being a newspaper advertising salesperson requires a combination of hustle, perseverance, and diplomacy. It's up to you to get new clients, maintain long-term clients, and keep both the newspaper and the clients happy. But that's not all. While it varies from paper to paper, advertising salespeople also are involved with layouts, checking proofs, and more. So advertising salespeople deal with the production or makeup department of a paper, too. That's all part of servicing the customer. The advertising salesperson had better make sure the client's ad is correct, is positioned properly and is running.

Many papers have advertising assistants, who work with a specific sales rep, handling the more mundane parts of the job—the proofreading, quoting rates, and so forth. Pay is usually low, in the teens or low twenties, and there's no commission paid, but it's usually great training. In many cases, an assistant will do everything a salesperson does except calling on customers.

Beyond that, there's no actual career path for advertising salespeople. While some people move into the administrative side of things, managing a staff of sales reps or running a regional office of a large paper, many others stay with their category because of the money. And that money isn't bad for established salespeople. Base salaries begin at about $20,000 on the larger daily papers, but advertising salespeople usually get commissions on the space they sell. The more clients they have, the more money they make. Not a bad arrangement for people who like to hustle.

Hustling is part of the **editorial** side of newspapers, too. The business of reporting is conducted under tremendous time pressures, and accuracy and cool professionalism are essential. Reporters also have to be able to maintain a distance between themselves and what they're covering. People simply can't get personal in this business. By the same token, they can't take anything personally either. As the old saying goes, reporters are only as good as their last story. They can be heroes one day and bums the next—so people with thin skins and easily hurt feelings had better steer clear. Add to those drawbacks long hours, relatively low pay, and heavy dues-paying and you've got the picture.

So why are so many people interested in becoming reporters? Well, there is glamour in newspapering. No matter whether it's a big city daily or a small town weekly, a reporter will rub elbows with and be courted by the power elite. Reporters are insiders to everything that happens. And that makes up for all the negatives.

So it's tough breaking in. There are a lot of people out there who would like to be Bob Woodwards and Carl Bernsteins. And most of them are in for a rude awakening. For one thing, people don't magically land a job on one of the prestige daily newspapers in this country. Far from it. There are dues to be paid first. Would-be hotshot reporters have to start small and work their way up.

And while even starting at the smaller papers isn't that easy, there are opportunities throughout the country. The United States has 1,688 dailies and over 7,000 weeklies. Of the dailies, 889 have a circulation of 25,000—and that's the kind of paper most beginning journalists start in.

Usually, new reporters begin on a small local daily or weekly and move later to larger circulation papers. With each move, they can hone their reporting skills and build their "clip file" of published stories.

Whatever the type of paper, reporting remains essentially the same. Most newspapers today want generalists who are great reporters and who can write well. Typically, reporting skills are more important than writing skills. That's because newspapers have editors who will clean up a decently written story. But these editors can't answer questions that a reporter didn't ask, and can't supply facts that were omitted in the story.

Reporters are assigned beats, their area of responsibility. A beat may be a town, a government body, an industry—any number of things. And it's up to the reporters to come up with stories on that beat. So they have to know everything that happened, is happening, and will happen on the beat.

Editors measure reporters by the way they search out a story (in many cases, on their own time). That's where "sourcing" comes in. Reporters meet as many people as possible connected with their specific area, and use these sources in their day-to-day work in tracking down and confirming stories.

Depending upon their beats, reporters are assigned to a specific desk—city, national, financial, foreign, and so forth—which is run by an editor. Those editors in turn report to a managing editor.

The career path in a newsroom largely depends on the individual. While some reporters would rather remain chasing down stories, others decide to move inside and start directing the show. The first move is to editor, working under a more senior editor. Then one may move up to the position of a desk editor, managing editor—perhaps eventually run the whole newspaper.

But it all boils down to dues-paying. College is the best place to begin. The college newspaper is a starting point, but even better is to land a part-time job on the local daily or weekly newspaper. While would-be big-time reporters may report only on what's happening at the college, these positions often lead to full-time employment in the summer. Many newspapers, including the prestige dailies, offer internships. Often, doing a solid job here can lead to full-time employment after graduation. But don't think an internship on a big daily is an automatic job offer.

As for pay, some smaller newspapers still start reporters at around $200 a week. The pay is better as you move to larger newspapers and you can go up to $30,000–$40,000 and even more in some cases. But let's face it. You can make more money in most other professions. So if you're out for the paycheck, this isn't the job for you. But if you have the curiosity and the reporting skills, and if you love the business, stick with it. After all, you'll know what's happening before anyone else. You reported it.

LOS ANGELES TIMES

VITAL STATISTICS

- **locations:** Los Angeles, CA; 12 domestic and 22 foreign bureaus
- **circulation:** 1,070,000
- **rank:** 4th in daily circulation; 1st in advertising linage
- **employees:** 10,000

AS SEEN FROM THE OUTSIDE

The *Los Angeles Times* boasts that it practices a "special kind of journalism," and it is known nationally for its long, in-depth articles and series. Industry-wide, it's known as a writer's paper. Most important, however, it's a very *successful* writer's paper. The cash generated by being tops in ad linage allows it to practice its own brand of journalism. Although there are a number of other papers in Southern California, the *Times* (as it refers to itself) looks at the *New York Times* and *Washington Post* as its real competition and prides itself on being a world-class newspaper.

The *Times* wasn't always this successful. Founded on December 4, 1881 by a couple of merchants, Nathan Cole, Jr. and Thomas Gardiner, the paper got into serious financial troubles and was purchased by Gen. Harrison Gray Otis. He used the paper to promote Los Angeles, and even to this day, the *Times* is part of the bedrock of the city's establishment.

Otis' son-in-law, Harry Chandler, assumed control in 1917, beginning a sixty-five-year span in which a Chandler was publisher. Several years ago, Otis Chandler handed the publisher's position to Tom Johnson, the paper's fifth publisher, who had started his career as a reporter. Chandler remains editor-in-chief and chairman of Times Mirror, which publishes the *Los Angeles Times*, papers in Dallas and Denver, and a number of magazines, and owns the Harry N. Abrams book publishing house.

The *Los Angeles Times* is clearly the crown jewel of the company. Covering Southern California from Santa Barbara in the north to the Mexican border in the south, the *Times* publishes what amounts to four different papers a day, with separate editions covering the L.A. metro area, San Fernando Valley, Orange County, and San Diego. Twice a week the paper publishes five sections covering smaller geographic areas of the city.

Each of these sections and editions has its own staff, both editorial and sales.

HEARD AT THE WATER COOLER— WHAT IT'S REALLY LIKE TO WORK HERE

Like Los Angeles and Southern California in general, the *Times* is big and spread out—it has all those different editions, downtown and zone offices, three printing plants, and over 10,000 employees.

And like the stereotype of Los Angeles and Southern California in general, there's something very easygoing about the *Times*. Sure, it's big, prestigious, and pressured. But it's laid back at the same time.

No wonder staffers here refer to the *Times* as a "velvet coffin." The jobs are comfortable, the pay is excellent, and you just sort of settle in for the long haul. People come to the *Times* and *stay*. That's why most *Times* employees are newspaper veterans. Even new hires usually have a few years experience under their belts. Face it, the *Times* can afford to be selective. There simply aren't that many people leaving.

And who can blame them? The *L.A. Times* is different from most other large newspapers. Sure, staffers talk about the long hours and deadline pressures. Those are givens in journalism. But the hustle-bustle, competitive push of the other papers seems far away—on another coast, maybe. (At another *Times*, maybe.)

"Perhaps we're a little too relaxed sometimes," said one employee. "This is a noncompetitive marketplace. Sometimes there isn't as much of a sense of urgency as there might be."

But they must be doing something right. Ad linage is high; editorial content is respected; and most employees seem terribly . . . well, comfortable . . . whether they're in advertising or editorial, out in the zone offices or downtown. Even the main offices downtown reflect a sort of ease. Advertising sales personnel work in somewhat old and crowded offices, with linoleum floors and metal wall partitions. The newsroom, on the other hand, was recently redone and is open, modern, quiet, and plush.

As a thirteen-year vet summed up the *Times*, "I enjoy the fact that it's a nontraditional place that does nonconventional things. The *L.A. Times* in its present incarnation has existed only since 1960, since Otis Chandler decided to make this a first-class newspaper. We don't have that tremendous weight of historical precedent weighing down on us."

That's why the *Times* focuses so much on writing. And that's also why it's an unconstrained, fresh, easygoing place to work.

PEOPLE

The *Times* prides itself on hiring the best. It's the big game in town, so it knows what it wants. But sometimes, working with the best takes some getting used to . . .

"In a situation like this, a lot of people are the best from wherever they came from," an editor said. "But here they're just another pretty face."

But that doesn't mean most *Times* editorial staffers have to watch their backs constantly. Yes, they have to work hard to be noticed and rewarded, but, no, they don't have to pull any political maneuvers.

"In relation to other newspapers I've been around, this is a remarkably noncompetitive place," noted an old hand. "I have very supportive relationships with the other editors."

On the sales side, it's a little different. "I think everyone wants to shine above the people they work with," said one salesman. "They have to do that if they're going to get ahead into the few management positions that open up."

Management positions don't open up very often, for one very good reason: the *Times's* "stability factor," as one manager termed it. While there are many young people working at the *Times*, there are also many veterans who've been with the paper twenty years or more.

As a result, people who work downtown tend to be older, with ten years' experience either at the *Times* or elsewhere, including some time in the zones. It also means that young staffers have to maintain a blend of aggressiveness and patience.

"You have to be willing to start at the bottom and work your way up," commented a young man, who explained that it took him ten years to get an advertising category he considered "decent."

"I ran into the vice president of marketing right after I got my most recent desk. He asked me how old I was, I said thirty-four, and he said, 'Well, you're a young man. You've got plenty of time . . .'"

But the fact that there are lots of long-time staffers doesn't mean the *Times* is stagnant. The same young man also noted that the sales staff has become more diverse lately. "The mold was, when I started, that a salesman was a tall, blond male. I was the second black hired. Over the last few years, it's changed pretty much. There are more females and minorities."

JOBS

Because it's so big, the *Times* has tremendous job opportunities. But like the freeway system, you have to know where to get on and how to get about—and you'd better have drive.

First off, the *Times* is considered the "big leagues," and as a result, very few people, if any, are hired right out of school. And like a big league club, the *Times* has its own farm system—the zones and regional editions. Working downtown at the main offices is the goal of many who start their careers in the satellite offices.

Secondly, for all the talk about being easygoing and laid back, working at the *Times* can be rather demanding. "This is not a nine-to-five job," an editor said. "Many people work a six-day week."

So new hirees at the *Times* learn that they have to pay their dues to get ahead, a combination of hard work, long hours, and starting out in the boonies. Then you can work your way downtown.

Each of the zone and suburban editions is run like a small, independent paper. The zones, which publish twice a week, don't have the same deadline pressures that the daily editions have. "We have our own beats, but we don't have to crank out two or three stories a day," a reporter noted. But that doesn't mean it's a breeze here.

"The hours can get long at times and sometimes assignments come up unexpectedly," said one female reporter working in a zone. "Those people who are interested in the profession have to really be prepared for the hours the job requires."

They also have to be prepared for sometimes less-than-fascinating beats. One young man in the zones said small community coverage, especially meetings, "can be long, boring, stupid." But *Times* reporters stick it out. They have to. Reporters are told to stay at the meetings until the bitter end—which can be 1:30 in the morning.

Those who stick it out, do a good job, and prove themselves may slowly work their way through the ranks. There's no preset course for that. It's largely a question of applying yourself and hoping you'll be noticed. "You have to be assertive, but it's not pivotal. And it doesn't hurt to be an editor's protégé," mentioned an editor.

In **editorial**, once you've made it downtown, you've arrived. Many of the people here are specialists on a certain beat, although there are a few generalists. One drawback on the editorial side, according to one staffer, is that "This is a very big place, and big places, for reasons of convenience, tend to type people. It's very hard, once the people above you have a certain impression of you, to overcome that. It happens very early."

But there are a lot of pluses to working here—especially for serious journalists who like both digging for a strong story and writing that story well. Time is given to write, and long features and in-depth news analyses are encouraged. That's all part of the "different kind of journalism," as one editor termed it, that the *Times* puts out.

"We place a much higher priority on news analysis, on sophisticated in-depth reporting," the editor went on. "We place a higher priority on writing quality, writing for writing's sake than other newspapers do. It's due to the fact that we have very good writers and we've developed an editing system and an editing attitude that encourages that."

He added that the emphasis on writing and the willingness to let people work on their own projects is the principal reason he likes working here—although that tolerance apparently has a few drawbacks.

"The same willingness to let you experiment with your dynamic forward-looking idea and let it go on and develop also means they tolerate the schmuck in the next desk who does something stupid for weeks on end. That can be sort of frustrating," he noted.

But, if you're a writer, the *Times* is *the* place. Editors go over copy closely, but "part of being a good editor is knowing when not to do something, when to leave it alone," commented an editor.

As a result, there "is no *L.A. Times* formula in the way there is a *Time* magazine story, or the way the *Wall Street Journal* will homogenize it. We don't do that. It's one of our distinguishing characteristics. Some people don't like that, it drives them to distraction," an employee stated.

"There are critics of the *L.A. Times* who say that it looks as if it's edited with a shovel. There are days when it probably looks like that. Take the *Wall Street Journal*—on their worst day, they look like lines of identical marching men, and on our worst day, we look like a lynch mob. It's a different approach."

The **advertising** side of the *L.A. Times* is similar to that of other newspapers, but again, there are special *L.A. Times* traits. As on the editorial side, there's a work-your-way-up system, and staffers pay their dues—either at another newspaper or a regional office.

"Most people who work downtown have come from either a zone office or another newspaper," one woman who works in display advertising said. "Even a lot of those people [from other papers] are usually started in one of our zone offices. Maybe they wouldn't stay there long, but they would start there."

Both display and classified advertising sales positions exist in the zones as well as downtown. Many times a person will start on classified and move over to display. "Although it's good training, classified ads is more of boot-camp type of training," a staffer commented.

The other training ground for would-be advertising salespeople is being a clerical trainee, assisting a display ad salesperson. It's one of the few positions at the *Times* filled by people straight from college. And despite the job title, clerks get an overview of the advertising sales business.

"I have a clerk who talks to a lot of my advertisers," said a saleswoman. "He writes a lot of orders, quotes a lot of rates. He'll even do layouts, corrections on ad proofs, and works with our makeup department. He does practically everything I do without going out and seeing the advertisers. It's good all-around training."

Display ad sales are broken into desks, like electronics, food, entertainment, and so on, and can be either regional or national. According to one staffer, it's one person per desk, which can be rather demanding.

"There's a great amount of independence and the responsibility is obviously greater," he said. "If anything goes wrong, you have no one but yourself to blame."

Because the *Times* is so well-established, sales reps here don't do much cold calling on clients. Most advertisers are established, so there's little need to solicit new business. But it's not always easy dealing with those long-time avertisers. In fact, perhaps the hardest part of a salesperson's job is battling with clients over position.

"That's what I don't like," an old hand said. "So much is based on where the ads must go, who they must be in front of. And some of the [clients'] personalities I don't like. Some people are real bastards." But salespeople have to be diplomats. Pleasing a client is part of their job. And people who know how to handle clients, responsibility, and pressure can eventually move up to bigger advertising categories or, finally, management. Actually, getting ahead here boils down to one key factor—attitude.

"The most important thing is to have a positive attitude, being willing to work hard and not shoving something off because it's not your job," said one salesperson. "It's looking to do one more thing than what you're asked to do."

Another sales employee reported that "it helps to have a sponsor. And patience is important, especially in an industry as conservative as newspapers."

"You have to wait, do a good job, and when the door opens, be able to step in."

LIFE

It really depends where you are. With such a large company, it's difficult to get to know a lot of people, especially with the spread-out nature of all the offices. One staffer noted that there's more socializing in the zones, since the staff members are a bit younger than those downtown.

But life in the zones is transitory. People are moving in and out, going from small zones to larger and eventually making it to downtown. There are some staffers, however, who are permanently assigned to the larger zones or regional editions. There are some constants to life at the *Times*, however, for all the sprawl. For one thing, there's the nonpolitical atmosphere.

"This isn't the kind of place where you can rise on office politics," cautioned an editor. "And you can't dress your way to success here," he added, noting the casual dress in the news-room.

As for the sales side? Sure, there's a little more competition than in editorial. But it seems to be good-natured. As one sales-man explained, "There's a lot of needling, to release pressure. Good support systems when a person is down, a lot of barbs, jabbing when things are going good."

But for all the apparent camaraderie, one staffer said, "The organization is not your family, thank god. It's not your friend down at the corner bar."

Yes, at the *Times*, you're allowed to lead your own life—with or without your fellow employees.

DOLLARS AND SENSE

Here's the velvet lining in that coffin—money. The *Times* pays very well, as even usually low-paid editorial types agree. And that's one of the big reasons people don't leave.

"Moving around means stepping down in class," said an editor, adding that in the newsroom, "most salaries are in the $40,000 to $60,000 range."

Pretty impressive, huh? But remember, those salaries are predicated on people coming in with at least five years experi-ence.

Sales is equally lucrative. "When I started in classified in 1980, I was making $450 a week," said a saleswoman. "When I left the classified department in December of 1984, I was making $1,000 a week. I was almost on straight commission basis and my ter-ritory was a high-volume territory. So when I went to display, I took a cut in pay, actually."

That's not as bad as it sounds. She added that she could make more bonus money each quarter in her territory. And that makes up for a lot. A sales rep can make up to 40 percent of his or her salary in a quarterly bonus.

So salespeople, too, aren't eager to leave the *Times*. As far as the L.A. area is concerned, the pay is tops, according to another sales staffer. "The problem is that we are the No. 1 paper in the country at what we do. There is no other competition in this market, so to make more money, I would have to leave this market or go into management. There is nowhere else to go."

GETTING IN—TRICKS OF THE TRADE

Want to work for the *L.A. Times*? There's a lot to do before you can land that job . . . like get a job somewhere else.

"First of all, you concern yourself with paying your dues. You have to learn your craft and learn as much about it as you can," advised one editor. "The *Times* almost never hires anyone out of college—it's so infrequent as to be a fluke. In the overwhelming number of cases, we hire people who have worked at other newspapers."

Those with a few years' experience under their belts generally get hired as writers in the zone sections or metro staff and work their way up from there. But experience alone won't guarantee you a spot on the *Times* editorial staff. Since the *L.A. Times* is one of the top papers in the country, resumés come pouring in to the employment section and employment supervisors.

So it helps to have an edge—which is something interning here can give you. An internship doesn't usually end up in a permanent job, but nevertheless it's a good way to make those all-important contacts and learn your craft.

As a human resources manager explained, "We watch someone work under deadline pressure. It gives the intern an invaluable learning experience, a chance to put his best foot forward and build a portfolio." And many times interns wind up at the *Times*, after they've gotten jobs with other papers.

On the advertising side, experience counts, too. "Most of the people who come to the *Times* worked at smaller papers and worked their way up to the big time," explained a salesperson. And while clerical trainee positions are usually filled by recent college grads, he added, "I haven't seen anyone come out of college and get directly into sales."

One advertising salesperson recommended having a marketing degree or a communications degree with emphasis in advertising or public relations.

But it always comes back to one thing: whether in editorial or advertising, the *Times* wants people who've already paid their dues.

THE BOTTOM LINE

Hard to get in, but even harder to leave.

NEW YORK TIMES

VITAL STATISTICS

- locations: New York (headquarters)
- revenues: $1.2 billion (1984, New York Times Co.)
- circulation: 1,010,000
- rank: 5th in daily circulation
- employees: 8,750 (New York Times Company total)
  700+ (NYT employees)

AS SEEN FROM THE OUTSIDE

The *Tuscaloosa News*, the *Daily Corinthian*, the *Daily World*, the *Houma Daily Courier*, and the *New York Times* have a lot in common—they're owned by the same company. The New York Times Company is more than just a newspaper, it's a diversified communications company that owns newspapers, magazines, television and radio stations, paper mill shares—and the *New York Times*.

The last paper gives the company its clout. The *New York Times* is the nation's premier daily newspaper, and one of the most influential newspapers in the world. A former secretary of state sits on the company's board; its top people revolve in and out of government; and it has received more Pulitzer Prizes than any other newspaper. It's a serious self-conscious newspaper—aware of its place in history and in world affairs.

The *Times* started out in 1851 as the *New York Daily Times* and, from the beginning, it had a serious objective tone. Some called it dull. By the 1890s, the public wasn't interested—circulation dropped to 9,000. That's when Adolph Ochs stepped in and started a family dynasty. Purchasing the paper for $75,000, he added a Sunday magazine and a slogan, "All the news that's fit to print." More reporters, book reviews and a lower price pushed up the Times's circulation—and influence. When the *Times* moved to Times Tower in Longacre Square, the city renamed it Times Square.

Today the *Times* is one block north, and Adolph Ochs's grandson, Arthur Ochs Sulzberger, is chairman and publisher. In the 1960s, strikes, tough unions and the rise of the suburbs (and suburban newspapers) took their toll on the *Times*, so Sulzberger changed the paper—and the company. The Times became more of a corporation, with marketing people, corporate planners, bureaucrats—and profits. It diversified into smaller city newspapers (28 at the last count), television (in Tennessee, Alabama and Arkansas), magazines (*Family Circle, Tennis, Golf Digest*), paper mills (partial ownership of three in Canada and one in Maine), radio (New York, Iowa, Illinois) and cable TV. The *Times* may be the flagship, but the company earns profits from many sources.

The paper has also changed since the 1960s. Under the leadership of executive editor Abe Rosenthal, new sections were added, including Weekend, Living, Home, Sports Monday, Business Day, Science Times, Careers, and Personal Investing. The *Times* went electronic, with video terminals and photo offsetting. It also went national, with five plants across the country receiving satellite transmissions beamed from the *Times* plant in New Jersey.

Although some newsroom staffers complained that the new sections adulterated the paper, they helped advertising revenues and circulation. One thing they didn't do was change the atmosphere. The newsroom still has a Byzantine air, particularly at higher levels. Factions compete for power and influence, while every day the *Times* reports the news.

HEARD AT THE WATER COOLER—
WHAT IT'S REALLY LIKE TO WORK HERE

When most people say they want to work for the *New York Times*, they're not thinking of the company, but the newspaper. So that's what we focused on.

There's a joke in the newspaper industry that all you get for working at the *New York Times* is fame and fortune. And that's pretty much the truth. You don't get coddled, you don't get to take it easy, you don't get patted on the back that often. And add to that the fact that you're working with other people who are just as talented, experienced, savvy and "special" as you think you are. So, sure, *Times* people have the prestige of working here. But they earn it—over and over again. It's not easy working for a prestigious newspaper.

There is one thing that's decidedly unprestigious about the

Times, though. Its headquarters is near seedy Times Square. You barely notice the large old-fashioned stone building, even though it has a large banner flapping outside; there's too much else to see (and watch out for)—*Times* trucks constantly pulling out of the garage, people milling around, taxis honking.

Walk inside the building and it's a *little* more glamorous, but not much more. Business offices are plain—file cabinets crammed with paper, tannish walls, word processing terminals and dark carpeting.

The newsroom is a little shabby. There are worn brown sofas on a worn brown carpet in the reception area, an occasional cigarette butt stubbed out on the floor, desks shoved together, video display terminals, newspapers and clips everywhere, and a lot of people on the phone, eating lunch, reading, talking or just hanging around. The busy newsroom of a major daily paper . . .

But this isn't just any major daily. It's the *Times*. And the people here don't forget that. As one business employee put it, "This is a place you can be proud of. In the morning, you open up the paper and you're glad to be working for it."

A newsroom employee echoed the thought. "It's kind of neat to be in a position to meet someone and they say, 'So, where do you work?' And you say, 'The *New York Times*.' And they put you a step above everybody else. It's a neat feeling. And it's hard to give that up."

"You pay for it though," she added. "You pay for it. Being on the fast track, you really pay your dues."

PEOPLE

At any publication, there's a distinction made by employees between business and editorial staffs. And the *Times* is no exception. But perhaps the distinctions are blurring.

"It's turning conservative here," said one five-year editorial vet. "You can see it. The wardrobes are like these yups—blue blazers and bow ties, oxford shirts, khaki pants. And half the people here are from Yale."

But looks aren't the key to *Times* newspeople. Attitude is. Like any journalists, they're serious about their work and the news, and, since this is the *Times*, they'll go to great lengths to succeed.

"There are people here for whom this is their whole life," an old hand said. "They spend sixteen out of twenty-four hours at the *Times* working."

Just working hard isn't enough, however. The people who make it at the *Times* also have to have talent, experience and plain old street smarts to survive.

"There are a hell of a lot of chiefs here," said a newsroom employee. "There's a definite sense of hierarchy. You know when you're a peon. They let you know."

So *Times* people learn how to play the game and stay afloat in a political environment pretty quickly. And, since this is a place where competition is high and famous bylines common, those younger people who *do* succeed here tend to band together.

"Among the younger reporters there very definitely is a camaraderie," a young reporter maintained. "A group of three of us came up as clerks, at the same time. We made it. We were very good friends then, and we still are."

But the main characteristic of *Times* people isn't social skill. It's dedication to their work and determination to succeed.

"If there's a will, there's a way," a young woman said. "And you've got to have a will and a determination to follow through on that will."

And that's how you become a true *Times* person . . .

JOBS

One thing every *Times* person knows—it wasn't easy landing that job. And it doesn't get easier.

People in the newsroom entry-level spots—**copy people** and **news clerks**—learn that at the very beginning. Even when they're just trying to get their foot in the door. It's tough breaking in. Even though this is the spot for people fresh from college, the *Times* expects them to have proven journalistic experience—on a college paper, a local newspaper or through an internship.

So what do these experienced people who beat the competition do? Well, the basic job responsibilities sound simple. Essentially, clerks and copy people do the newsroom grunt work—they answer phones, take messages for reporters, route copy and memos to the correct people. "You have to be familiar with reporters and you have to deal with story summaries," a young woman explained. "Sometimes a reporter will file part of a story and from that you'll write a summary. So when they have a meeting at 5:15, all the editors know what stories are going into their section."

News clerks work for a specific desk (such as foreign, metropolitan, sports, culture or national), while copy people work the floor, filling in for other clerks when necessary. According to employees, being a clerk is preferred to being a copy person ("there's a huge salary difference, the working hours are a lot better, and the respect is higher"), but both jobs involve a lot of pretty dull work.

One staffer described a typical night: "5:30, 6:00 you come in. You're on the floor . . . you start to run copy as copy comes in the wire—foreign copy to the foreign desk, national to the national desk, and so on. When you hear someone call "copy," you respond to it. You get clips for people, relieve clerks on their breaks, sit and answer phones. . . ."

If they're doing mainly clerical work, why do these people need prior experience? Because most of them are in the *Times* writing program, designed for aspiring reporters. And that means that the regular work is only half the job. As a supervisor explained, "This is an apprenticeship. By working as a clerk, employees understand how a news desk is run. And all the time, they're also writing for the paper—during their days and hours off. They're *expected* to write for the paper."

That's the clincher—no matter how many hours clerks and copy people put in, they'd better be producing stories as well. Somehow, they fit it in between the copy-running and the message-taking and everything else. And it had better be good, too. After ten months in the program, clerks submit their clips for evaluation to three editors and are told how they're doing, what they need to improve, and so forth. Six months later, the clerks submit clips to three other editors for evaluation, and its then that they find out what their chances are at the *Times*, whether they'll become reporter trainees, or whether they're not *Times* material.

So a lot rests on the quality of those stories. And clerks know they've got to hustle and write stories that will prove that they'll be good *Times* reporters.

"The trick is coming up with ideas that are good enough, that will make it into the paper," a reporter who worked his way up explained. "Anybody can write. The question is whether the story makes it in."

That isn't an easy task. It's up to each clerk to come up with his or her own story ideas, do the interviews and reporting and write the whole thing—all on off-time. That's why the *Times* tries to assign would-be reporters in the writing program to the night shift. The hours might not be great, but it's easier to get the reporting and interviews done during the day.

Once a story is complete, then comes another humbling experience—trying to convince an editor to run it.

"You have to be prepared to be treated as a nonentity," a staffer warned. "You might have felt special because your clips got you in and you got front page stories elsewhere. Then you get to the *Times* and it's like you have to peddle your stories like a shoe salesman."

Copy people here have to get used to paying those dues for a while—because they're probably not going to become reporters overnight. As one young newsroom staffer said, "The average wait is three to four years, and it's hard to keep that momentum." And during that period, you will not get a byline.

People who do keep up that momentum may make it to **reporter trainee**—a one-year position that leads, finally, to being a full-fledged *Times* **reporter**. Some employees maintain that the kind of desk a clerk is assigned to initially helps determine whether he'll make reporter. "They're really big on tradition here. They'll say, 'You come from the foreign desk, you have a decent chance of being a reporter.' National desk clerks haven't had much luck."

But the bottom line, naturally, is talent—in writing and reporting. One reporter cited the qualities that he felt marked potential *Times* reporters: "The tone and breadth of the stories that they write, and their ability to relate smaller incidents, individual news events to broader trends, be they political trends or changes in thinking. An ability to analyze very carefully, and an ability to draw parallels between various events and try to define what truly is a trend and what just looks like one."

Add to that an ability to determine what kinds of stories the *Times* and its readers are most interested in (according to one staffer, stories on public policy issues are a good bet) and you've got the ideal *Times* reporter.

Just like the clerks in the writing programs, reporters have to be self-starters and must possess the proverbial "nose for news." "By and large, I don't receive any instruction, or very light instruction, about what it is I should or should not write," a reporter said. "The news pushes you. Certain topics are 'on the news' as we say here—meaning that they're current and you have to cover them. They're happening now."

And reporters have to be on top of whatever is happening. Hours are long, and pressure is high—"It's learning how to write 1,200-word stories, starting at 4 in the afternoon and having them in at 6," one reporter commented.

"Two people could easily do my job," another reporter stated. "I have thirty phone calls a day to do. If I do a major piece, I have to travel a great deal. And almost every day, I have a working lunch."

The **corporate staffers** have a similar schedule. They're the people either working for the *New York Times* proper selling ad space, developing marketing ploys and doing market research, or working for the parent company, The New York Times Company. And one corporate staffer maintained that he and his coworkers "generally work later than the newspaper employees."

Corporate staffers get a different view of the *Times*; it's just one property among many that the corporation owns. Sure, it's the most prestigious, but there's other business to attend to.

"We're expanding nationally, we quite naturally dominate the New York market," one young man explained. The people who are helping that expansion are filling normal "corporate" jobs, in finance, personnel and marketing. And staffers say the latter is growing in importance. "A lot of the focus will be on marketing, since you have to distinguish your product," a finance employee explained. "I see the growth going into sales and marketing and finance remaining stable."

Like most publishing and communications companies, the Times is expanding outward—with a focus on purchasing papers and companies that dominate their market shares and bring in revenues. As usual, there's a hands-off attitude toward editorial. Business staffers care about the bottom line with Times papers, not the headlines.

There are fewer unionized shops in other cities, hence more control and more automation—and more profits for the company. The hottest new place for an aspiring Times Company business person? Santa Barbara—a long way from old Times Square.

LIFE

One thing that business, corporate and editorial staffs all seem to agree on is politics—that it's a big part of life at the *Times*.

"Politics is key," a corporate staffer said. "You have to learn when to ask, when not to ask."

Historically, the newsroom has been considered a hotbed of intrigue. And it doesn't seem to have changed. According to some staffers, this is because there's more of an allegiance to the different desks than to the newspaper itself. And each desk also has a status—foreign desk most prestigious, national next, metropolitan next. "It's very much little kingdoms," a staffer summed up. "And they all have their own little niches." It seems as though the newsroom has its own laws, customs and manners, separate from any place else.

But even while many staffers complain about low morale and high politicking, a lot of them learn to cope. And even more seem to learn how to play the game to their own advantage.

"It's not all that bad," one employee said cheerfully. "I have to admit that I got to where I am through politics. And I was very lucky because I did have a couple of people who did take me by the hand and say, 'Okay, we'll make sure you're okay. We'll protect you.' "

And there's another plus, besides making stronger allies. At the *Times*, you learn how to make it in the big bad world . . .

"I could be thrown into any corporate atmosphere and I know I could survive. Because I've survived here."

DOLLARS AND SENSE

The *Times* is a union shop—represented by the Newspaper Guild. Salaries aren't great, but they're not bad either. And it's up to the union to set the guidelines.

Money *is* low at the entry-level newsroom spots. But, while clerks and copy people complain about their poor salaries, they know that the experience they're getting and the credentials of working at the *Times* make up for it.

GETTING IN—TRICKS OF THE TRADE

It's not impossible to get a job here straight out of college, but you'd better stand out from the crowd.

One employee saw a memo one editor sent to another evaluating an applicant. "It basically said, 'So and so has competent clips, it seems that he can write, but it's nothing special.' And, of course you have to have something special to work at the *New York Times*."

What's that "something special?" No one's quite sure, but everyone admits that the *Times* can afford to be choosy. That's why entry-level people are expected to have pretty strong backgrounds. "They want to see something over and above. They want to see if you won an award. And if you *have* won an award in college for journalism, then it's have you taken a step to get published outside of the college environment," one recent hiree commented.

According to a supervisor, people who want to get into the writing program have to send in resumés plus about fifteen samples of newswriting—"hard news and feature stories," she stressed. "We don't even look at theater reviews, book reviews and so on."

And, even though the key is newswriting ability, you don't have to be a journalism major. An employee on the interview circuit explained that anything goes, from anthropology to Chinese history. A reporter recommended "staying away from journalism schools and doing the best liberal arts education you can get—with an emphasis on analytical thinking."

But another reporter who recently won a Pulitzer Prize came up with the most basic suggestion of all— "The most important advice is if you want to be a journalist is to be a journalist. It sounds trite but . . ."

It worked for him, and who can argue with a Pulitzer Prize winner?

THE BOTTOM LINE

Just like the paper—a lot of politics and a lot of prestige.

WALL STREET JOURNAL

VITAL STATISTICS

- **locations:** New York (headquarters); bureaus and offices worldwide
- **sales:** 1,990,000
- **rank:** 1st in daily circulation (1984)
- **employees:** 500+ news employees

AS SEEN FROM THE OUTSIDE

What is the largest daily newspaper in the U.S.? The *Wall Street Journal*. What is the premier business newspaper in the U.S.? The *Wall Street Journal*. What's the *Wall Street Journal*? No one really knows exactly, least of all the *Wall Street Journal* editors—except that it's a very successful blend of business news, stock market news and general interest stories; humorous at times, serious at times, and influential all the time.

Six million people read the *Journal* daily, 2 million of them subscribers, and these readers have an average net worth of $750,000, and $100,000 yearly income. It's the influential newspaper for influential people—a business newspaper with a dash of style and a huge measure of integrity. When Charles Henry Dow and Edward D. Jones started the paper in the basement of a soda pop shop on Wall Street back in 1882, they decided to cover the stock market with "uncompromising truth, good or bad." Later, under managing editor Bernard Kilgore, a new operating motto further guided the paper: "Economic news doesn't have to be dull."

And it isn't at the *Journal*. Part of this comes from Kilgore's emphasis on teamwork and in-depth stories. The *Journal* is famous for its front page columns 1, 4 and 6. These are the amusing, trendy, useful, unusual, interesting, in-depth stories on anything that an up-and-coming business person doesn't necessarily *need* to know, but wants to know anyway. Now there's a second section as well and the Second Front page, crammed with personal interest stories at the bottom left-hand corner; sandwiched in between is the heavy business news and stock market quotes—boring to anyone who hasn't made or lost a few thousand on the market (and not boring at all to those who have).

The newest managing editor, Norman Pearlstine, has promised even more changes designed to bring the *Journal* to the man on the street—maybe the guy who hasn't yet made his $750,000. He's expanded staff and news coverage, increased the use of graphs and charts and focused more on business-related foreign and entertainment news. The *Wall Street Journal* is already very international. It has two sister publications, the *Wall Street Journal/Europe* and the *Asian Wall Street Journal*, and about thirty staff correspondents in bases from London to Tokyo, providing in-depth foreign coverage. And it can draw on all the resources its parent company, Dow Jones, has to offer.

The *Wall Street Journal* is the best known newspaper of publishing giant Dow Jones & Company, Inc., which also owns *Barron's* magazine, Dow Jones News/Retrieval, Dow Jones News Services, National Business Employment Weekly, Ottaway Newspapers, newsprint mills, and assorted joint ventures including AP/Dow Jones. And like its flagship publication, Dow Jones takes the pursuit of excellence seriously. It was ranked No. 1 for two years running in *Fortune* magazine's survey of corporate reputations—the most admired company in publishing and the third most admired company overall. Nice guys sometimes finish first—or third.

HEARD AT THE WATER COOLER—
WHAT IT'S REALLY LIKE TO WORK HERE

The *Wall Street Journal* isn't quite what you'd expect from a leading daily newspaper. There's no large, crowded newsroom with the incessant ring of phones and clacking of teletype machines; no frenzied reporters running in waving wire copy, yelling about the big breaking story.

But, then again, the *Journal* isn't just any leading daily. It's a conservative business paper, first and foremost. That's what it stresses editorially and that's the prevailing mood here. In fact, the *Wall Street Journal* really seems more businesslike than many of the businesses it covers. There's an air of seriousness, of corporate concentration, that hits you when you first walk in. And it's very quiet.

The one thing that reminds you that this is indeed a newspaper is the Dow Jones Financial News Service wire clacking by the receptionist's desk. But beyond that, you'd swear you were at any company—perhaps one just a little down at the heels. Officers here aren't shabby, but they're far from posh. White walls, tan carpeting and zero decoration.

Journal reporters work in a series of cubicles—compartment after compartment after compartment—instead of a large open newsroom. Occasionally a reporter will emerge from a cubbyhole to hand in a story to the copydesk or go out on an appointment. The copydesks and page one editorial area do have more of a typical newsroom feel—desks pushed together, old-fashioned manual typewriters and editors in shirt sleeves blue-penciling copy. But that's about as "Front Page" as it gets here.

As a reporter described working at the *Journal*, "This is not a fun place. The work you do here can be fun and exciting, and I love my job. But it's a very serious place to work."

PEOPLE

Forget all the clichés about heavy drinking, chain-smoking, hard-boiled newspaper types. None of them apply to the *Journal*. The people here are dead serious about their work, not their image.

"You don't have a lot of flashy types here," a young woman commented. "They aren't flamboyant or colorful people. You have some very sharp people, very bright people—but this is not *People* magazine. Or even *Newsweek* magazine."

"We have gotten a little more buttoned-down over the last ten years," an old hand said. "But there are still a lot of eccentrics."

That really depends on how you define eccentric. Here, it's completely work-related. It means going to all ends to get a great story. Like one young woman who did a feature on street musicians. In order to really get a feel for it, she played her violin on the street for a week—and wasn't even fazed when a business source stopped and watched her in astonishment. Needless to say, her editor loved the story.

Add to that work focus the compartmentalized layout and what you have is a group of committed journalists who simply don't hang around that much. But that makes it easier to concentrate on business with a capital B. And that's what *Journal* people do best.

JOBS

Just like the bulk of the stories in the *Journal*, jobs here are serious business.

"The people really expect an awful lot from you," said a news editor with six years at the *Journal*. "You almost have to devote yourself to this place when you first get here."

That devotion can be tough to muster at times. Especially when you've just been hired as a **reporter** and you're stuck doing "spot news"—the short filler stories that are two inches long and run from earnings reports to press releases to announcements.

"Spot news is the KP of the *Wall Street Journal*," one reporter said. "And no matter how prestigious or how important a reporter you are when you come here, you do it."

There is life after spot news. But it doesn't get easier.

"Usually they throw more at you than you can take. That's what I do," affirmed an editor. "I have given people more than they probably should be able to handle and I see how much they can take."

New reporters are given "beats" to cover. In the larger bureaus, like New York or Washington, beats are an industry or group of related industries. In the smaller bureaus, they're companies. "You can specialize in a couple of companies," a reporter explained, "but since it's a smaller bureau, one day you could be covering Coca-Cola, the next day, the Bank of Georgia."

Usually the beats are established ones, so it's a question of reading past story clips and going through files of names that your predecessor has left behind. And, after that, "you start writing stories," an eight-year vet said. "That's the only way to learn about it. There are no courses, no nothing else."

It's not *quite* that cut and dried. There is something called "sourcing"—meeting people in the industry you're covering, from PR people to company executives and chairmen to Wall Street analysts who follow the industry. And then the stories start falling into place or the reporter starts digging or (usually) both.

There's still more to being a reporter here, though. If they can fit in the time, reporters do page one stories—the longer, in-depth features that everyone likes doing. Not that it's a simple task.

"There have been days when I've been working on a major story and I might not get a good page—one page—done in a day," an editor said with a sigh.

Why? "At the *Journal*, you don't print everything you know," she continued. "There's a great density to the writing that is much more difficult than when you can do an information downpour."

That's why so much writing, rewriting and general hard labor go into the six to nine pages that make up a page one story. Quality counts, not quantity.

And that applies to everyone at the *Journal*—from editors on down to **interns**. They're treated like new hirees, first doing the "most picayune of stories" in spot news, then getting an editor assigned to them who will discuss feature story ideas for the front page or Second Front.

"They'll let you jump right into things here," a reporter said, "and if you survive it, you can work at the *Wall Street Journal!*"

The *Journal* loves hiring interns, since they've already got a feel for the place and know the routine. The key is being a good intern—one as devoted to the work as any regular staff member.

The bad interns care more about how many stories they can file, not how good they are. "They really don't care if you rewrite their story; they just want to get on to the next thing, so they can get six bylines or ten bylines or something like that—which may help them get a job someplace else," said a news editor.

They wouldn't fit in here, because this is another story. Hard work and serious journalism. One reporter summed up his typical work day:

"Have some coffee, probably make some calls to check on stuff that's developing, then you talk to people. I'm working on some stories on the side so I'm setting up interviews, talk to other reporters . . ."

And, if there's time, he might get a story done.

LIFE

"Most people here do their work and go home," summed up a reporter. No, there isn't a lot of socializing or hanging out at the *Journal*.

"Mostly it's your little group, the guy you work with most in the industry most related to yours," a young woman said. "Everyone else sticks to his own little group. So it's compartmentalized. And within those compartments, people talk to one another."

But the *Journal* is also a friendly place, with little backstabbing or supercompetitiveness. A meritocracy is how most people describe it. And management's focus on merit is probably why politics aren't so apparent here.

There's a premium on protocol and courtesy, too. *Journal* employees are careful not to step on anybody's toes or snatch stories away from each other.

"Poaching is a famous word here," one reporter said. "No one likes poaching at the *Wall Street Journal.* As long as you work cooperatively with everyone and don't try to screw people, I think you do okay."

And apparently that system works, because most people seem to think their co-workers are okay—and that the *Journal* is pretty okay, too.

"There's incredibly good morale here for a newspaper and for how large it is and for how much pressure there is," said one editor.

DOLLARS AND SENSE

"If you have a trust fund, you could work here," a young reporter said with a chuckle.

Working at the *Journal* won't make you rich. But money isn't a key concern among *Journal* staffers. The pay might be low (even by industry standards), but the prestige is high. It's a trade-off, and most people here would rather forfeit the big bucks—at least for now.

Still, one never knows. As one reporter put it:

"One thing you see here which is always an incentive, is that Warren Phillips, who is chairman of this company, was once a reporter. And he now makes about a million dollars a year!"

See. There's always hope.

GETTING IN—TRICKS OF THE TRADE

"If you're really serious about getting in here, start pursuing an internship," advised a four-year staffer. "Don't think you're going to get out of college and just walk in."

That's the standard suggestion most people come up with for would-be *Journal* employees. Interning here is one of the best ways to break in. And it's not too tough to become an intern—you need a good academic record, a lot of enthusiasm and an interest in journalism. One reporter suggested applying to the local *Journal* bureaus for internships, since bureau chiefs tend to hire interns from their state.

As for those out of college already? It gets a bit more difficult.

"Ideally we're looking for someone with three to four years experience on a daily paper and a good stack of clips—not just in terms of quantity, but in terms of reporting quality," a high-ranking editor offered.

"Writing is secondary," he went on, "because we have a page one department and Second Front department and they're all veterans at converting prose to good prose. But you can't fix bad reporting."

That's why most staffers here stress the need for clips that show reporting skills—not hard news stories about murders or fires, but in-depth stories or a series.

"Some scoops or some features that show, not that you're a great stylist, but that you thought about another dimension to a story; features that show a little bit more thinking than that you got eight puns in a row or eight great phrases," was a news editor's summation. "It isn't so much the cleverness of the writing, it's the clarity and depth."

One final tip—don't give up if you think you've got what it takes. One reporter sent a letter in, promptly received a typical "sorry, we have no openings, but you can talk with us anyway" reply, and was hired two weeks later.

THE BOTTOM LINE

Quite simply, a great place to work.

PUBLIC RELATIONS

Public relations people are *information* specialists, seeking to put out the good word on a client's company, product or idea; and counseling the client on how to maintain good (and profitable) relations with the public.

But what do public relations people actually do? It all depends. And that's the best part of this fast-growing, wide-open field. Information, public relations, counseling and consulting are all nice vague terms with a lot of leeway. Some PR people are specialists in one type or product or field; some are great at one type of PR skill; most are generalists. It's the perfect field for bright liberal arts as well as science majors; former journalists as well as high school yearbook editors. All you need is intelligence, determination and a gift of the gab.

When people think of PR, Hollywood usually comes to mind. But the biggest employer of public relations specialists is the Federal Government. Every time a rocket is launched, a country is invaded or a new government program is announced, Uncle Sam's PR people are ready to explain to the taxpayers how their hard-earned dollars are being spent. Typically, the Federal Government uses terms such as press officer and information specialist. But it's still PR.

Besides the Federal Government, state and local governments as well as nonprofit agencies and organizations employ PR people to keep them in the public eye and to keep those donations or tax dollars rolling in. In Washington, trade associations and lobbying groups are the largest employers of PR people; elsewhere, it's museums and charities. But the big bucks in PR are found in the private sector.

Large corporations employ in-house public relations specialists—usually in the corporate communications department or press relations sector. Speeches, press releases on exciting new products (and what new product isn't exciting?), annual reports, public appearances, company newsletters—all are handled by the hardworking company PR people. Usually with a little help from their friends at the PR agencies.

Public relations agencies employ many of the best and the brightest of the 200,000 PR people in the U.S., and range in size from Burson Marsteller's 3,000 employees to small one- or two-man shops, "boutiques" as industry people call them. The big agencies try to touch on all aspects of the field and, because of this, are the best way to learn everything. And remember, good PR people know everything (or at least they act that way).

PR people have to have something upstairs because the agency has nothing else to sell but its people. It sells their PR skills and talents to outside clients. The agency makes its money by charging hourly fees or receiving retainers from its clients, or from a combination of the two. It earns its money by solving problems or helping to meet corporate PR needs.

It's that focus that makes job distinctions in PR a bit blurred. Everyone is really doing the same thing. As PR staffers move up through the agency's hierarchy, responsibility grows, but the job remains essentially the same—servicing a client or clients.

In order to do this, most agencies are divided into account groups, each having its own staff of account people at various levels—assistant account executive, account executive, senior account executive, account supervisor and group supervisor. The titles may vary a bit from agency to agency, but the responsibilities are much the same. At each level, a person does everything and anything for an account—from writing annual reports and speeches to calling media contacts and trying to place a story. And the higher up the ladder, the more accounts and responsibility, so the more delegation of work to lower-level account group members.

Since the job duties are so similar, it's which of the five basic categories of public reations that a person is in that makes all the difference . . .

Employee Relations, or keeping the employees happy. An agency may help write an employee handbook for a company, try to figure out morale problems and solutions, or even establish a corporate identity.

Community Relations involves the people outside the corporation as well. An agency may help its client's image through public affairs projects—marathons, races, fairs, open houses—activities where the neighborhood is involved with the company. Or it may be decided that the community is nationwide or even worldwide. For example, during the Olympics, Burson Marsteller organized a cross-country torch relay—an activity that publicized the profitable Olympics Games *and* Burson client AT&T's involvement as corporate sponsor. Good PR—and a lot of money and public recognition for the client.

Customer Relations gets to the nitty-gritty of PR work. PR people research consumer trends. Do American consumers want that new brand of purple soap?

Sales and Marketing takes that soap where it belongs—to the consumer. Here, PR people hold sales presentations and get publicity for the product. A hot new soap hits town! And everyone wants it! How do they do it? Usually through two tried-and-true PR tools that are as old as the business itself—the pitch letter and the news release. The pitch letter is just that—a factual, usually peppy letter that tries to arouse interest in the product through a sales pitch. The news release is the descriptive part—it's written like a news article and explains what the product is, who's introducing it, etc. What the agency tries to do is get someone in the news media interested in the client's product who will write or use a story on it as part of the day's news. Getting purple soap on TV is easy enough—the hard part comes when a PR person has to publicize ball bearings or snow shovels.

Financial Public Relations is a very important part of PR, especially because so many Americans buy, hold or sell stock. This is Wall Street public relations—writing annual and quarterly reports, handling shareholder meetings, working on proxy votes and takeover bids and generally dealing with crises. During large mergers and stockholder battles, most corporations employ public relations people in addition to investment bankers and lawyers to convince others to hold, buy or sell the stock—depending on what the client wants.

So PR is not just fast talk. It's a lot of hard work. Most of this work is done in large cities where the big corporations and big spenders are. But PR people don't get too much of that money, at least not at first. Starting salaries at a big-name PR agency usually range from $15,000 to $20,000; a bit more if you're coming on as a specialist. Mid-level employees earn $30,000 to $50,000. The recommended route for big money? Work hard and get promoted to upper management quickly; work hard and leave the agency for another higher job at another shop; or leave and start a one-man agency. Then all the money goes to you.

But first—learn PR. The trick to getting hired is to think PR before you do PR. At school, join clubs, write magazine or newspaper articles and show these interests and activities on your resumé. And when job hunting, don't just paper the town with mailed resumés. Get contacts, call on agencies in person. Don't be a nag, but be persistent. Persistence counts in PR. Know an agency's clients before you are interviewed and have ideas about what you'd suggest for each of those accounts. Volunteer a day or a week of free work for an agency—show your stuff and you'll get hired. And take *marketing* courses. Most people at agencies are lukewarm about public relations degrees, but all are hot on marketing. PR is just another form of selling, and marketing courses can tell you how.

A final word from PR pros—read and research. Not just the business, but the world. Who knows to whom and where you'll be pitching that new soap? Join a PR association, talk to PR people and read the newspaper from front to back. PR people may not be Boy Scouts, but they like the motto: Be prepared!

BURSON MARSTELLER

VITAL STATISTICS

- locations: New York (headquarters); Atlanta; Charlotte; Chicago; Cleveland; Denver; Houston; Los Angeles; Nashville; Pittsburgh; San Francisco; Silicon Valley; Tampa; Washington DC; 28 international offices
- revenues: $84,258,000 (1984 fee income)
- rank: 1st
- employees: 1,210

AS SEEN FROM THE OUTSIDE

> We have floated hamburgers across the bay in Hong Kong, driven down the main street of Knoxville in a stage coach and raced the world's fastest vehicle across the salt flats of Utah.
>
> —from a Burson Marsteller marketing pamphlet

And that was on a dull day! Growth, change and new ideas are the name of the game at top-ranked Burson Marsteller, growing at a zippy 30 percent a year.

Way back in 1983, Burson passed Hill & Knowlton as the No. 1 PR agency in billings, and it's still going and growing strong. Burson helped Johnson & Johnson regain the market for Tylenol after a nationwide poisoning scare, and assisted Coke in its top-secret effort to introduce the new Coke (code-named Project Kansas). And when the clamor began for the old formula Coke, Burson was there.

But it's not all fun and games at Burson. Burson is at the cutting edge of the "new public relations"—an attempt by its practitioners to redefine and expand the role of public relations in the corporate arena. Part of this involves breaking into new markets, such as Burson's leading role in the fast-growing medical marketing area. More important, though, it means answering a question that troubles us all in this ever-changing world—where do I fit in?

Burson thinks it has found the answer with Synergenics, which is a comprehensive program that finds and explains the meaning behind the bottom line for Burson's corporate clients.

Typically, Burson also did research on itself—and came up with its own "Visions and Values" statement, a one-page corporate motto and creed. Summed up, it really just means the company is dedicated to growth—both of business and of its employees.

Burson Marsteller's own growth has been helped by Young & Rubicam (the world's largest ad agency), which purchased Burson recently. So far, the Burson–Y&R relationship has been good, maybe because both are committed to the same thing—comprehensive communications services for their clients. That's the corporate way of saying "we do everything." And at Burson, they mean it.

HEARD AT THE WATER COOLER— WHAT IT'S REALLY LIKE TO WORK HERE

Burson Marsteller is a dream come true for workaholics. Even though the company is No. 1, it's still trying harder. And trying harder at Burson doesn't only mean working around the clock— it means total commitment to the power and the glory of the company.

There's a religious zeal in the air, a driven intensity in the halls about the Burson way of doing business. Employees aren't so much trained here as indoctrinated. They're constantly reminded to keep growing, stretching and moving.

It's a lot like an aerobics class. Even the Visions and Values statement mentions the "high threshold of pain" intrinsic to Burson. "No pain, no gain" is more than a jock's slogan here; it's a way of life.

This single-minded attention to business is evident even in the physical environment. Interior decoration means that each office has a framed or lucite-encased copy of the Visions and Values statement prominently displayed. That—plus a bulletin board covered with memos, newspaper clippings and daily reminders— is usually about as decorative as it gets. And while the company emphasizes growing, there are few plants on the premises. Presumably everyone is too busy "growing new clients, growing employees and growing existing business" to bother with a green thumb.

There's no time to stop and smell the flowers here anyway. But no one cares. The halls are imbued with the sweet smell of success—or is that something else?

"When I first started working here, I was told it was a sweat-shop," explained a cool, crisp vice president. "But that has neg-ative connotations. Sure, you work hard, but it's up to you. And I like to sweat . . ."

PEOPLE

A client service manager with four years at Burson summed up her co-workers: "When you look at Burson collectively, you see this incredible being that has this perverted workaholic tend-ency—and I mean that in a complimentary way."

When you look at Burson individually, you see a collection of "Burson persons." They're the people who are able to put up with the frantic pace, the long hours and the constant change.

A Burson person is a self-starting, energetic, logical thinker with good writing skills and a massive dose of ambition who won't take no for an answer. And while the people here are friendly enough, their overriding characteristic is a desire for success. Professional skills count, not social ones. At Burson Marsteller, it's better to make money than friends.

That's not to say it's a shark tank here. Since there's usually enough to go around—raises, promotions and, most definitely, work—people do get along. They hang out with their co-workers and talk. But what do they talk about? Work, of course. And as for the team spirit employees point to, that's tied right in to work, too.

"In this unit, it's real collegial," said a young woman recently promoted to vice president. "Usually several people are working late and everyone orders out pizza."

Ask other employees about their co-workers and you hear a description of a personnel manager's ideal employee: "People here are real turned on by challenges," said one account exec-utive. "The young people here are real go-getters," added a young go-getter.

When asked to describe the typical Burson employee, a client service manager said, "You've got to be achievement oriented. Whenever you get a promotion, you say, 'Great. Now let's see what I can do to get my next promotion.'"

Spoken like a true Burson person.

JOBS

Burson persons might sound like an android species of workers concocted by a mad scientist/CEO, but actually they're not. It's more of an evolutionary process. Those who can take the Burson madness prosper; those who can't were probably never hired in the first place.

Maybe that's why firings are so uncommon here. Since the company "pushes up" employees as it grows, management makes sure the people they hire are worth it. But occasionally there's a slipup, and someone is hired who *isn't* drooling over the chance to work harder than he'd ever worked before. These pseudo-Burson persons are quickly found out and fired, usually before six months have passed. How are they so readily detected early on in their Burson career?

"We load people up when they come in. We give them as much as they can handle," said a senior VP and unit manager. "You find out very quickly if they can handle real responsibility."

Those who do handle the pressure stay and get more work. They also get promotions fairly quickly. But some say that the movement upward isn't what it seems to be. According to a former employee, new lower-level jobs were created as Burson began to grow. These jobs were intended to accommodate the rapid influx of new employees. Management was able to bring people in at lower levels, pay them less, and after keeping them there only about a year, promote them to the next step—which was the old lowest level. "So then the person working there thinks, 'Oh, I'm moving up.'"

That may be the case, but it doesn't seem to bother most people. That's probably because the focus at Burson isn't on titles as much as it is on units. In fact, most people credit the unit they're in for their promotions.

While Burson is primarily divided into three sections (corporate services, marketing services and communications services), the key structures are the groups within them. These business groups, usually referred to by the name of the unit manager in charge, are responsible for specific accounts or parts of accounts.

These groups, with a hierarchy from top to bottom of unit manager (usually a senior vice president), client service manager, account supervisor, account executive, assistant account executive and account representative, are the front line at Burson. There are also the Burson specialists—the bookworms of PR who know more than you might ever want to know about subjects dear to their client's hearts—fun things like issues and trends in recombinant DNA research.

And for difficult problems, Burson has its own SWAT teams—sixty people who travel around the world, armed with skilled patter to pitch for new business accounts and PR know-how to come up with brilliant PR solutions.

But for all the titles, units and divisions, Burson people, outside of certain specialty areas, do pretty much the same thing. And that's PR the Burson way—growing and maintaining clients through expertise, flexibility and, above all, energy.

LIFE

Work. That's all people ever seem to talk about at Burson. Ask them about their outside interests and they'll tell you about that hot new Merrrill Lynch program they're working on. Maybe that's why so many Burson people marry each other. Who else would want to put up with hearing all about that hot new Merrill Lynch program?

"I met my wife here, which is not totally uncommon. This is a real live singles bar. You'd be amazed at how many people met their spouses here," said a client service manager.

But those that are married to *non*–Burson persons joke about problems that come up. "There *is* a lot of pressure and there *are* times when I wish I could be home and spend a little more time with my wife. You know, get reacquainted . . ." an account supervisor dreamed out loud.

On the whole, though, everyone is willing to put up with the lack of time to spend relaxing and having fun. Fun can be had on the job. Some of the parties Burson gives for clients are "fit for heads of state," maintained a unit manager. And you might get to meet some pretty important people like Henry Kissinger, Philip Habib or Frank Sinatra.

But then again, you might not. As an account supervisor explained, "I went to a Merrill Lynch meeting, instead of going to the press briefing with Diana Ross." That's life in the fast lane.

DOLLARS AND SENSE

First the good news. Employees are paid quite well at Burson. But . . .

"Are they paid in relation to their work? No. In relation to their work, they're grossly underpaid," a former employee stated.

All that means is that people work very hard here. And raises *do* come frequently to those who prove themselves.

"I've never had to ask for a raise," said a snappily dressed senior VP. "If you're good, it comes. And it's always been more than I've anticipated."

Money aside, beginning employees also get two weeks vacation, five free days a year and unlimited personal days. And time off for good behavior . . .

GETTING IN —TRICKS OF THE TRADE

Everyone interviewed says that Burson is looking for people just like them. Yes, it helps to have a healthy ego when it comes to becoming a Burson person.

Perhaps they need it. At Burson, there is no training program. You're thrown right in to learn on the job. The specialized seminars and workshops are for employees who've been here a while and who've been recommended by their managers.

And how do you become one of those overachievers? First, sharpen your pencils. When you interview for a job at Burson, you're usually given a writing test—several pages in which you're asked to edit phrases down to one word; write a press release on a given subject; and take a speech and write a press release from it.

Beyond that, the types of preparation can vary greatly. As one hot-shot unit manager on the interview circuit put it, "We love people who don't know quite what they want to do for a living. We *don't* like people who have taken four years of public relations in college."

Other than that, there are few prerequisites for getting hired. Burson is big on hiring young people, fresh from college, with little formal work experience. It's attitude that counts more than anything; Burson will supply the needed experience swiftly.

In short, what Burson is really after is a pushy, well-educated, liberal arts or business major who's recently graduated. Oh, yes. One more thing. You also should be work-oriented. Now, isn't that an understatement . . .

THE BOTTOM LINE

Blood, Sweat and Visions and Values.

CARL BYOIR

VITAL STATISTICS

- **locations:** New York (headquarters); Atlanta; Boston; Chicago; Dallas; Houston; Los Angeles; Philadelphia; San Francisco; Washington DC; London; Frankfurt; Australia; 30 international affiliates; 26 domestic/Canadian affiliates
- **sales:** $30,950,469 (1984 net fee income)
- **rank:** 3rd
- **employees:** 573

AS SEEN FROM THE OUTSIDE

When the Statue of Liberty needed a facelift, Carl Byoir was called in to plan and publicize the fund-raising effort. It was a natural match for an agency whose founder got his start rallying Americans to fight the Kaiser in World War I.

In between those two public interest campaigns, Byoir has come a long way—to No. 3 in the nation. But there's a big difference between No. 3 and No. 1 and 2, both of which are more than double Carl Byoir's size in income and number of employees. Carl Byoir is big—but it's still small enough to be personal and cozy.

That's not to say it's a laid-back place. Byoir is No. 1 in Silver Anvils—awards given by the Public Relations Society of America for outstanding performance—and that means a lot of hard work.

Carl Byoir started the tradition during World War I when he was lured away from a job with the circulation department of *Cosmopolitan* magazine (no, not Helen Gurley Brown's Cosmo) to join the first organized government public communications program. His energetic interest in all aspects of this newly emerging field eventually made him one of the grand old men of public relations. He started his own agency after the war, concentrating on the more enjoyable aspects of life. Byoir's first accounts were travel and tourism, and the agency helped make Cuba, Miami and Miami Beach the major tourist attractions of the times. It's still a Byoir speciality, although Cuba has been dropped and the Bahamas and Alaska have been added.

Along the way, Carl Byoir itself has changed. In the old days, the agency consisted of a small team of eccentric yet dignified former journalists—pros who knew the business. People still talk of these men in glowing terms, although pride in the new Byoir is also rampant. Byoir was one of the first major U.S. corporations to promote a woman to upper management, and by all accounts Executive VP Muriel Fox earned those promotions. Byoir was also among the first PR agencies to merge with an advertising agency—Foote, Cone & Belding purchased Carl Byoir Inc. in 1978 in what has been described as a happy, separate-but-equal marriage.

So being No. 3 is pretty good. Big enough to handle all aspects of public relations, and small enough to know all the people doing all the talking—and winning those Silver Anvils.

HEARD AT THE WATER COOLER— WHAT IT'S REALLY LIKE TO WORK HERE

At Carl Byoir, everyone seems glad that they're No. 3. They get to be big fish in a little pond that way. Well, make that a medium-size pond. Because that's what Byoir really is—king of the mid-size agencies. Byoir is medium, middle and average in size, attitudes and feel.

It's middle of the road, middle ground, middle and medium everything. And in the fast-paced, frenetic, slick PR business, Byoir manages to preserve a sense of Middle (there's that word again) America.

The offices are not flashy or showy, but they're not shabby or cheesy either. Walls are a soothing medium rose color. The reception area is comfortably utilitarian. And the major decoration at Byoir headquarters—a display of the agency's Silver Anvil awards—is underplayed.

Actually, everything at Byoir seems ultra-normal. Nothing in excess, everything in moderation, should be its motto. So what does that make Carl Byoir? Just what it seems to be. "The medium-size agency," as an a/e said. "Not too big, not too small."

PEOPLE

Just like the agency, the people at Byoir are middle-ground types. Stereotypical PR people with big egos and a fast line of patter wouldn't fit here. At Byoir, there are no hyped-up overachievers, just good, strong achievers; people are aggressive, but not *too* aggressive. Sticking to the norm is everybody's overriding characteristic.

"The people who work here are unpretentious in a sense," explained a recent hiree who put in time at a larger PR shop. "I don't think there's room for people who put on airs."

That's the real key to Byoir employees' personalities.

"I was kind of scared at first," a young woman admitted. "I was thinking it's a big company, I'm going to be anonymous. But it's not the case at all. Everyone says hello to you. My first week, it was 'How are you doing?' and 'How's everything?' and 'Can I show you where something is?' That just amazed me."

This leads to a comfortable feeling, "from the chairman down to the guy in the mailroom," as one a/e put it. "If I wanted to talk with senior management, it wouldn't be one of those worship situations where I'd have to go in a cold sweat."

There's an easygoing, we're-in-this-together attitude that most Byoir workers share. "One Friday afternoon, the guys in accounting opened up some beers," a young man remembered. "And I saw the Chief Financial Officer having a beer with everyone else. You never would have seen that at other PR agencies."

JOBS
Again, size makes all the difference . . .

"We're helped by the fact that we're smaller. People are encouraged to do their own thing," explained an a/e. "There's an effort to promote people's careers, and that includes the secretarial level on up. We truly try to promote people out of secretarial positions."

He's telling the truth. Secretaries at Byoir have a life beyond typing and filing if they want it. That's why a lot of the secretaries here hold degrees and use their jobs to get a foot in the door.

"I started as a secretary and literally learned my way up," a fresh-faced woman who climbed the corporate ladder said. "I learned the ropes from the ground floor up doing a lot of research. I've had four titles since then—basically, someone took a chance."

But it's not all altruism. Since Byoir isn't huge, but its client list is growing, it needs its employees to do a lot and do it well. That's why low-level account people are given quite a bit of responsibility early on. Unlike other agencies, the assistant account executive spot here isn't a glorified gofer. It's much more.

"My first Friday, I was here till 9:30," an assistant said. "When I came on, they put me on four accounts—it was 'Glad you're here, get to work.' You learn by doing, so the more you do, the more you'll learn."

It *is* largely learn as you go at Byoir. There's little in the way of formal orientation. They do have a training program for junior account people, called simply "The Byoir Training Program," that consists of hour-and-a-half luncheon meetings for new employees, with lectures from media representatives and Byoir people explaining the trade. Beyond that, you're on your own.

There's another thing that Byoir people like about their jobs. As at other agencies, people are assigned account groups, but unlike other agencies, these groups don't necessarily work with only one sort of account. "There's a wide variety in every group—from Reader's Digest to Crafted with Pride to Bermuda," one a/e said.

It's exciting then, but it's hard work. As a young woman recently graduated from college put it, "For 21 years, you've never worked a full day. You know how to study for finals and write term papers. This is different. This is a term paper every day."

LIFE
This is one PR agency where there really is very little competition between co-workers or departments. That's not to say everyone's a saint here. There's a very good reason why you don't see back-biting and malicious gossip here. Byoir is too small, there aren't enough people, so there aren't enough hours in the day.

"I think people are so busy that it's as much as they can do to do their own thing and have it go well," commented an earnest account exec. "There's not two hours of down time to figure out how you can screw the group head across the hall."

Maybe that lack of competitive aggression is why life here seems so stable. Sure, people put in long hours, but there's a team spirit to compensate.

"To me, this is fun pressure," said a five-year Byoir vet. "At the peak of it, all of us will sit down and just start laughing."

And while people complain about the long hours, they're really not *that* bad. Somehow, people manage to "take time to converse and laugh and get a little zany," said a senior a/e.

Just a *little* zany though. Doing things like hanging out after work for a quick drink. "And it's not uncommon for someone to crack open a few beers. If people are working at six, six thirty, you'll see someone go out and get a six of Bud and a pizza."

Six? Six thirty? Well, some people may stay longer than that, but, at Byoir, long hours can still mean you're home by seven.

DOLLARS AND SENSE
Yet another area where Byoir is middle of the road all the way—salaries are average, benefits average, everything is average.

GETTING IN—TRICKS OF THE TRADE

You don't need a PR background to get into Carl Byoir. As a matter of fact, you really don't need a background in anything. They'll hire you right out of school if they think you're the right type. And what type is that?

"When I'm looking to hire anybody, I see them as a blank slate, as a good piece of clay to mold," a vice president said. "I'm looking for someone smart, quick, eager to learn, with enough of an ego to think well of him or herself, but also who knows that he or she doesn't know anything. What I'm looking for is someone I can teach."

But you can't just walk in and appear malleable to get a job. One problem an account executive noted was an over-concentration of business-oriented types. "You get people who know all about market shares," he complained, "but who can't write their way out of a paper bag."

So, to nip that in the bud, Byoir gives interviewees a writing test—about an hour long, with a part on copyediting to check for grammar and punctuation, and sections in which you're asked to write a radio spot, two or three press releases and part of a booklet.

In short, Byoir is after your basic, average person with writing skills.

"What I really want to see," an account manager said, "is enthusiasm and, you know, the normal things. But maybe a little bit of cockiness is refreshing."

So, if you want a job at Byoir, be normal—but not *too* normal.

THE BOTTOM LINE

Stick to the middle and you can't go wrong.

HILL & KNOWLTON

VITAL STATISTICS

- **locations:** New York (headquarters); Atlanta; Austin; Boston; Chicago; Dallas; Denver; Detroit; Fort Worth; Houston; Los Angeles; Minneapolis; Pittsburgh; Portland; St. Louis; San Antonio; San Francisco; San Jose; Seattle; Tampa; Washington DC; 35 international offices
- **sales:** $69.4 million net income
- **rank:** 2nd
- **employees:** 1,210

AS SEEN FROM THE OUTSIDE

Hill & Knowlton is No. 2 in the public relations business and it shows. The offices are less slick than those of No. 1 Burson Marsteller, people are more conservative, and the zip and zest is missing here. Hill & Knowlton, or H&K, prides itself on its quieter business-oriented approach to PR. Glitz is out, at least for now.

Maybe that's because H&K has a past, a tradition, in an industry where last year is ancient history. Founded in 1927 by newspaper man John Hill to help gruff, inarticulate manufacturing titans sound like human beings, it was for years the biggest and best agency. And John Hill himself spent fifty years making certain of that. Then, in 1978, Hill & Knowlton was purchased by J. Walter Thompson, an enormous, low-keyed ad agency, which encouraged H&K to become even more buttoned down and bottom line.

Luckily, Hill & Knowlton is at its profitable best on buttoned-down Wall Street—where sharks wear pinstripes and big companies swallow small companies and small companies borrow money and buy big ones. This is the billion-dollar corporate takeover game—the real life "Dallas" and "Dynasty." It's also an H&K speciality. The agency represented Wall Street wheeler-dealer T. Boone Pickens, it fought in the Bendix–Martin Marietta battle and the Gulf & Western takeover of Prentice-Hall. On Wall Street, H&K is still No. 1—the seasoned old warrior, where experience and street smarts count and million-dollar billings are earned.

Other millions are earned more gently overseas. The government of Indonesia pays H&K a million-dollar retainer to make sure we all know and appreciate Indonesia's contribution to the world. And H&K is America's PR expert on China, with a new office in downtown Beijing, and earnest researchers earnestly researching the world's largest market.

From Wall Street to the Great Wall, H&K means business.

HEARD AT THE WATER COOLER— WHAT IT'S REALLY LIKE TO WORK HERE

At Hill & Knowlton, public relations is almost a dirty word. Everyone seems to go to great lengths to avoid it.

Employees are quick to say that they're not publicists, press agents or publicity people. They're *counselors*. And the agency provides its clients with such exotic fare as "destination marketing," "interview, speech and confrontation training," "corporate design and corporate identity analysis," and "legislative and regulatory monitoring and analysis."

Departments have names like "communications task force" and "financial relations special situations section." You feel as if you're at the Defense Department and you talk as if you're there, too. At H&K, you don't delegate work, you "deploy" people to help. And acronyms abound—new employees are confronted with LOOP, the Loosely Organized Orientation Program, and PETU, the Professional Employee Training Unit.

When H&K employees aren't acting like brigadier generals, they're behaving like bankers. Who can blame them? H&K is an uptown facsimile of the Wall Street firms they represent. Walls are dollar green, boardroom blue or plain white, and decorations are kept to a minimum. No distractions here. The place bespeaks business, serious business.

"Even though no public relations agency is really 9 to 5, this *is* the 9 to 5 agency," said a young VP who had worked at four other PR shops.

But then what would you expect from a public relations agency that pretends it isn't one?

PEOPLE

In one word, H&K employees are corporate. More descriptively they're traditional. However you slice it, it comes up blue pin-stripes.

They don't have much of a choice. H&K takes its reputation for serious business pretty seriously. Since it offers "corporate identity services," it's awfully aware of its own corporate identity, which is, of course, conservative.

Listen to what happened to one woman (recently made a VP) at her first job review after six months at the company. Figure they'd talk about her job performance, right? Nope. Try tights . . .

"I used to wear the same blue suit, but with bright-colored tights. And I was told, quite frankly, 'If you really want to get ahead here, I wouldn't wear those tights. I'm talking no red, no yellow, no blue . . .' "

Sound advice. Look around you at H&K and you see Brooks Brothers suits, red club print ties and oxford shirts.

At H&K there's a heavy concentration of people who have been at the company only a few years and a lot of people who have been here more than twenty years. No one in the middle. But it doesn't make much of a difference: both young and old look alike, act alike and think alike. As one recent hiree put it, "We're all here because of who we are."

Beautiful. And who they are is corporate.

JOBS

So what does a person who refuses to admit he's a PR person do? PR, of course. Or rather, in H&K terms, financial counseling, destination marketing, and crisis communicating.

As at other PR firms, most people here are account managers in some sense of the term. They begin as assistant account execs, move up to account exec, then account supervisor or VP. A nice conservative hierarchy for a nice conservative company—except that H&K gets a little psychedelic when it comes to organization. Blue pinstripe suits, blue chip clients, and an organizational structure modeled on a sixties commune.

How does an H&K account manager get a job done? "I deploy one or two other people. They're also working on their other accounts for other account managers. Simultaneously, I might be working with the director of the division on other accounts.

So theoretically I'm the account manager, but in point of fact, she might be the account manager and I'm more of the implementational person on that account," said an earnest account supervisor in the financial relations section.

Well, that explains everything.

But the job gets done—and maybe this organizational "flexibility," as H&K puts it, is the reason. It encourages personal responsibility. People are assigned accounts, but everyone is expected to help out everyone else as well, and there is no one way to do anything. "H&K can be very frustrating to people who want formal, set, immutable lines of responsibility," a financial counselor stated. "People who don't feel comfortable with that kind of flexibility can find themselves caught in a meat grinder." At Hill & Knowlton, they throw you the ball, you take it and—walk, sedately.

The one department most people want to work in is Financial Relations and Investor Relations. This is where the glamour jobs are at H&K. Account managers here "deal at the boardroom level" with the financial companies everyone knows, handling the big mergers and the stockholders. Financial counselors write annual and quarterly reports for their clients, come up with clever speeches for CEOs and, yes, counsel. These are the people who figure out ways to handle news that could reflect badly on a major finance company, such as E.F. Hutton, and who manage to convince their client that telling bad news quickly and completely is often the best step. It's a department for thoughtful thinkers and quick action-takers—account managers themselves find ways to work in their field of expertise, whether it's proxy fights, new stock offerings or sticky business.

Marketing is the other top department at H&K, and a lot of the people who don't want to get their hands dirty working with financial matters choose to work here. It's happier, peppier and bouncier. Marketing handles sports, medical, travel, food and liquor accounts and arranges publicity, trade shows, special events and press releases on all topics. It makes certain that the American public realizes that a new cookie is coming to town.

"I am a media planner, I am an account person, I am a copywriter—I sing, I dance," said a bubbly marketing account exec. And she'd better be all those things. In marketing, you do it all.

But there are those people who would rather do one thing and do that well. And that's why H&K invented the Crisis Communications Task Force. This is the verbal artillery of H&K, where speeches, press releases and copy originate—where an account manager from another department can call on a specialist. Unfortunately, according to the staffers here, this doesn't happen often enough. "They leave you alone in my department," said one writer. "*Real* alone." The writers blame the profit-center-based system at H&K, maintaining that the other departments are jealous of their clients and want to protect their turf.

Perhaps because the Crisis Communications Task Force is so often left alone, the mood here is somewhat different than in the rest of H&K. Thoughtful intellectualism reigns in the quiet offices dominated by brooding Xerox word processors. In these offices, people—most of whom proudly boast of their lack of PR experience—worry about whether they're selling out, as they make excuses for their long stay here.

But most H&K employees don't need excuses.

LIFE

The big plus about life at H&K is that everyone has one—a personal life, that is. That's a rarity in the high-powered, fast-paced PR world where serving a client at 10:30 on a Saturday night isn't far-fetched.

But H&K, true to its roots, upholds traditional values—simple values like having friends and spending some time at home.

"Why did I choose H&K? I wanted to stay married," a young woman answered with a chuckle. "I prefer to work here, even though I could make more at Burson. They want blood out of a stone there."

Here there's more time to enjoy things, even the day-to-day business. Everyone raves about the variety the loosely structured jobs offer and the different aspects of the work—from the ridiculous to the sublime.

One young man, at H&K for three years, still remembers his first plum assignment, publicizing a road company of Sesame Street. "What a range of possibilities! It's so fun. You get to spend the day with Bert and Ernie."

Then there's the other side.

"My client was the American Innerspring Mattress Association," a writer said with a grimace. "I had to do a brochure about innerspring mattresses, why they're great. This guy had amassed mounds of information. He thought this was fascinating. And that's when you think, 'God, this business is horrible.' "

DOLLARS AND SENSE

In keeping with its middle-of-the-road, conservative image, H&K is a bit conservative when it comes to salaries. Salaries aren't bad—neither very low nor very high. Entry-level positions at H&K start at fairly low pay. But usually you don't have to wait that long for raises. "I am encouraged by the money," said an account person. "Particularly in marketing there's a lot of money to be made." And there's more. Even recent hirees get to travel, and they enjoy that. Bonuses for exceptional work aren't unusual. And promotions, while not fast in coming, do come to those who wait. But, as at most large companies, the best way to make a good salary and reach a higher level is to leave and come back again.

GETTING IN—TRICKS OF THE TRADE

Before you get a job at Hill & Knowlton, you have to have a job—any job. It doesn't matter what kind of experience you've had, as long as it's been for one or two years.

"It's a bureaucratic thing," explained a VP who interviews for the marketing department. "They've hired PETU's with two years' experience as telephone operators at AT&T."

They've hired what?? PETU's? PETU, remember, is the snappy way H&K refers to its "professional employee training unit"— the closest thing to an entry-level position here. Problem is it's tough to get. First, you submit a resumé; then, if you pass muster, you go to two interviews; then there's the writing test; then a meeting with the president, an executive VP and an account supervisor. Out of hundreds of applicants, only four or five are finally admitted into the PETU program. Then it's sixteen months being taught the ropes of public relations. A PETU spends four months in four different departments, learning most facets of the company.

"I'm really working as an account person a lot. It's not like we're xeroxing and doing media lists all the time. The purpose of it is for us to be able to go right into handling an account," a PETU told us.

But after sixteen months doing a little account work and a

little scut work for low pay, there are not guarantees about where you'll go or what you'll be doing.

And for older, non-PETU types? "It was my specialty in food and nutrition that got me in the door—I had something to offer," explained a successful applicant.

The story then at H&K—be conseravtive and traditional, also different—but not too different.

THE BOTTOM LINE

You don't have to be a public relations person to work in public relations.

impressive $9,000 to $16,000. And the pay scale doesn't exactly skyrocket higher up. Full-fledged editors make between $30,000 and $60,000. That kind of money is the norm at even the larger publishing houses—on both editorial and noneditorial sides.

But about 68,000 people in the United States don't seem to mind the low salaries. That's roughly the number of employees at book publishers. And most of them *aren't* on the editoral side of publishing. About 25 percent are on the marketing and publicity staffs, 50 percent on administration and support staffs, 10 percent in production and 15 percent in editorial.

But whether they're dealing with textbook sales, subsidiary rights, promotion or plain old editing, employees tend to share a common bond—they're all book lovers.

The job most people think of when they think of breaking into publishing is that of **editorial assistant** (average salary range $9,000–$16,000). It's considered an apprenticeship spot, allowing would-be editors to see what editors actually do. Job duties vary from house to house and editor to editor, but one thing is certain—editorial assistants might be there to learn, but they're also there to do grunt work. Addressing envelopes, typing editors' correspondence, taking messages—all that fun stuff is part of being an editorial assistant. Those who show initiative and work with a willing editor may get the opportunity to read and evaluate unsolicited manuscripts and even work on acquiring manuscripts on their own.

Most editorial assistants don't stay in their jobs too long. As one industry insider noted, "If an editorial assistant is in his job more than two years, he's a flunky." The problem is there often aren't a lot of higher job openings. So many editorial assistants, once a couple of years have passed and there are no assistant or associate editor spots open at their house, move to another publisher, hoping to get a higher salary and a higher job.

The next step up on the editorial side of publishing is to **assistant** or **associate editor** (average salary range $17,000–$27,000). Assistant and associate editors work on acquiring and editing books. The key to being successful at this stage of the game is compiling a strong "list" of books you've worked on, and developing relationships with agents and authors. In some houses, assistant and associate editors are also assigned books to work

Still, in today's sales-driven publishing environment, the stress on profitable acquisitions.

PUBLISHERS

There's a lot of talk lately about how much the publishi[ng] [in]dustry is changing—becoming more businesslike, more b[ottom-]line oriented. Hot commercial properties are getting a[ll the] press; bids in excess of a million dollars aren't unusual an[ymore.] And while most publishers still seek books of literary [merit,] practically none of them will turn up their noses at poten[tial best-]selling potboilers nowadays.

Despite all the talk, however, publishing really hasn't [changed] that much. Maybe it's not the "gentleman's profession" [it once was,] *the* industry for wealthy, educated intellectuals who di[dn't want] to get their hands dirty mucking around with mone[y. But it's] not typical big business either.

First of all, it's not really that big. The publishin[g industry] generates about $7.6 billion a year. A large chunk of [that (about] $5.7 billion) comes from reference and textbook sa[les; the rest] from the sale of trade books—the industry's term [for general] interest books, fiction and nonfiction, hardcover and [paperback.]

Secondly, for all the attention paid to the big selli[ng books,] the hot money-makers, even the most unabashedl[y commercial] publishing houses still talk about literary quality. [As the pre-]vailing argument goes, publishing the flashy best[sellers enables] a house also to publish the not-so-profitable "litera[ry" books—] poetry, first novels and so on. So while publishing [is becoming] more and more bottom-line oriented, there rem[ains a bit of] the old days.

That's apparent when you take a look at ave[rage editorial] salaries. You don't have to be rich to work in a p[ublishing house,] but it sure would help. Editorial assistants bri[ng]

The next level is that of **editor** (average salary range $30,000–$60,000): These are the people with more clout. Many of them have hopped from publisher to publisher, have a strong list of books under their belt, and contacts galore. They work more on acquisitions and negotiating with agents and authors. Some editors with strong track records get their own "imprints"—and basically act as publisher of a book list with its own budget and imprint name. **Copyeditors** and **proof readers** (average salary range $15,000–$25,000) do the line work on manuscripts and galley proofs. They're responsible for checking grammar, spelling, usage and style as a book passes from manuscript stage to finished book.

Subsidiary rights staffers work with agents and/or authors in selling a book's subsidiary rights—to book clubs, paperback houses, magazines, foreign publishers, and others. It's currently a growing field in publishing, and one that's considered a great place to break in. Sub-rights assistants (whose salary wage is $15,000–$20,000) move up to become directors, and often get input into acquisitions and advance payment decisions.

The people who get the books into the bookstores are the **sales representatives** (average salary range $18,000–$25,000 plus commission). Sales reps are assigned a region, and they travel from bookstore to bookstore in that region. It is up to them to convince retail booksellers to buy a particular book, and they also have to push for prominent display of the book. To a great extent, they're told which books to push when they go out on their sales trips, based on the printing runs the publisher is planning. Sales reps are usually the ones who know what the market wants, since they're in constant touch with their clients. Successful sales reps may become sales managers, with the basic responsibility of managing the sales staff.

Publicists and publicity directors are the people who try to get media attention for a book. They're the ones who arrange talk-show circuits for authors, newspaper and magazine interviews, lecture tours, book parties, and anything else that will generate excitement, notice and sales. Their average salary range is, for a publicist $15,000–$24,000; for a director $28,000–$50,000.

Advertising directors place ads in the media and in some houses that use an in-house ad agency, are in charge of the creation of advertisements for books. Their average salary range is $25,000–$50,000.

Production managers oversee the actual manufacturing of a book, from manuscript on. They give estimates of production costs, set production schedules, and coordinate the work of design and editorial staffs, as well as of outside suppliers (primarily compositors and printers). Working closely with the production manager is the **managing editor**. It's the managing editor's responsibility to make sure that editors, copyeditors and production editors (who check galleys, proofs, camera copy, etc.) are informed, in synch, and sticking to the production schedule. The average salary range for these positions is $18,000–$30,000.

The **production staff**, as one might guess, actually produces the book. An art director works on the look of the book—jacket, typeface, size, layout and general design—and supervises an art staff. At large publishing houses, there's a traffic manager who coordinates the flow of production, keeps track of where a project stands in the production schedule, and generally makes sure that book production is going as smoothly and as on schedule as possible. Production directors supervise the production department, set production budgets and handle contracting for typesetting, paper, printing and so forth.

HARPER & ROW

VITAL STATISTICS

- **location:** New York (headquarters), San Francisco
- **revenues:** $181 million
- **rank:** 3rd (1984 BP Reports, trade publishing)
- **employees:** 1,800

AS SEEN FROM THE OUTSIDE

It was a solid but dull beginning. The first book printed by Harper's was an English translation of the Latin author Seneca: *Seneca's Morals by Way of an Abstract. To which is added, a discourse under the title of an afterthought.* Not the zippiest title nor the zippiest author—even for a Roman. That was in 1817, when two struggling brothers set up a print shop in New York. John and James Harper were later joined by two more brothers, Fletcher and Wesley, and began publishing English fiction and selected American authors. But that first book set the tone for most of the books they published—informative, interesting, and on the right side of morality.

And most were on the right side of the balance sheet as well. Harper's grew quickly. The brothers realized that publicity, and selling books in series, added to the bottom line, as did bringing serious literature to the book-hungry American public. They published American classics such as Richard Henry Dana's *Two Years Before the Mast* and J. R. Wyss's *The Swiss Family Robinson.* There were a few duds as well, most notably *Moby-Dick*, which had "unpromising" sales.

But no matter. With two brothers, five sons, and four magazines (*Harper's Bazaar*, *Harper's Magazine*, *Harper's Weekly*, and *Harper's New Monthly Magazine*), Harper Brothers became the largest publishing house in the world. Then came the third generation of Harper Brothers, and bankruptcy. Propped up by J. P. Morgan, Sr. with substantial loans, the house slowly rebuilt itself, but without a Harper at the helm. It became known for serious nonfiction and religious books, an identity that remains today. But there were some exceptions. Along the way, it established James Thurber and E. B. White with the best-selling *Is Sex Necessary?* A bit different from Seneca, but Harper's said yes and published the book.

It also said yes and in 1962 merged with Row, Peterson & Co., becoming Harper & Row. Today, Harper & Row is a leading publisher of just about everything—college textbooks, professional books, general trade books, and children's books. Its subsidiaries and imprints include Basic Books, Barnes & Noble Books, Ballinger's, and J. P. Lippincott. It's big, but far from the biggest. And unlike most other major publishers, it is not part of a conglomerate (half the shareholders are employees).

Some outside the house consider it just a little bit behind the times—less glitzy than other houses, less prominent, and less high-paying to authors. In fact, Harper's has recently advanced a great deal of money to several authors, and has revamped its paperback publishing program. Potential bestsellers—maybe. And also informative, interesting, and on the right side of morality.

HEARD AT THE WATER COOLER— WHAT IT'S REALLY LIKE TO WORK HERE

There are publishing houses that still cling to the old "gentleman's industry" ways and publishing houses that have embraced the new slick, sales-oriented approach. And then there's Harper & Row—squarely in the middle.

It's part old-fashioned, laid back, and serious, part new-fangled, aggressive, and hard-charging. So whether you define a "good" book in terms of literary quality or in terms of profits, you'll probably feel at home at Harper's.

Insiders say the traditional picture of Harper's—"one of the more important houses, but not one of the more exciting places"—is changing. So is it exciting now? Well, yes, it's spending more money, acquiring more hot properties, and moving more into fiction. But the atmosphere is revved up in a relaxed way. It's that middle ground again.

When you first see the Harper & Row building, you figure it's just another modern skyscraper like all the others in New York. But, when you look up, you see that this "skyscraper" isn't a towering structure. In fact, it's pretty short—a nice medium-scale building that's professional but never overwhelming. And that's what it's like inside, too. Exposed bricks, tile floors, modern lines, display cases filled with books, white walls with primary colors for accents—it looks successful and accessible at the same time.

Offices here are a lot like offices at any publishing house, complete with bookshelf-lined walls and desks covered with books, manuscripts, and papers. These offices aren't showcases by any means; they're too lived-in looking for that. But who cares? They make you feel comfortable.

Staffers make you feel that way, too. Sure, this *is* a company and people *do* want to make money here. But no one seems hyper about it. By the same token, they're not running around talking about Russian poetry and generally acting super-intellectual either. People look, sound, and act easy-going—there's a dash of savvy commercialism along with a dash of literary intellectualism.

"As far as giving Harper's an atmosphere, it's really hard to do," summed up an editor. "It's old-fashioned in a way without being sleepy. But on the other hand, it's not as glossy as Simon & Schuster, for example."

So what is its character? "It's something that nobody quite knows in publishing," he added. "Everybody says, 'What's Harper's doing? What are you people supposed to be?' "

Well, what Harper's is doing is changing—a bit. And what is it supposed to be? Well, a little businesslike and a little bookish.

PEOPLE

Harper staffers say their co-workers are like most people in publishing. "They're a well-educated group of people for the most part, who tend to be eccentric, who tend to have a lot of interests," an editor summarized.

Like staffers at any publishing house, most Harper's employees are committed book lovers. While they constantly complain about the low pay they get, they also say it's worth it because they "believe in books . . . we're making a contribution to the world," as a marketing employee stated.

But Harper's employees don't get holier-than-thou about their noble quest. They simply don't seem to be self-promoters. "Harper's is pretty easy-going," commented a trade editor. "It's not uptight."

JOBS

"We don't do cat books, we don't do dirty joke books," said one staffer. "Harper & Row has a certain image of quality, of doing serious, important works. I actually feel good about our image. Especially in the trade world, when you see so many loony publications coming out."

But all that corporate belief in quality doesn't mean Harper's isn't interested in making money. Sure, it puts out poetry and first novels and "literary works." But like the rest of the publishing industry, Harper's is becoming more and more aware of the bottom line. Along with everybody else, it's discovered that businesslike isn't bad—and that new attitude affects the jobs here.

It has especially affected the **trade department**. Long known for "strong nonfiction and political science," Harper's is changing. "Everybody seems to be noticing the fact that we are spending more money and we're buying these big paperbacks," one editor noted. "We're really coming on a lot stronger than we used to."

"We have a broad range of types of editors here," explained a staffer. "It's pretty much laissez faire—they hire people to do what they like to do."

And what do they like to do? "Just a little bit of everything," said one editor. "I really don't want to be a specialist or anything. I still suppose I want to be a literary editor, and that's what I enjoy doing most—good fiction or serious nonfiction, a few cookbooks on the side, some history . . ."

Sounds like the good old days, doesn't it? But editors can't do only those "small books" that they love so much.

"It's the economics of publishing now—it's probably a cynical thing to say—I do want to keep doing the small books that I like, but I can't afford to do them on an exclusive basis. So I do try to find a few commercial books every year to carry my weight at the publishing house."

So these easy-going, bookish editors have to run around and make sure people know them. They are usually so busy lunching, dinner-ing, cocktail-ing, and just generally selling and taking care of business that nowadays they don't have as much time for their basic responsibility—editing.

"The pen to paper work is all done at home these days—unless you can sneak an hour or two in the office," one editor said with a wistful smile. Harper's does its best to make it possible for editors to sneak that hour or two in. The trade department is flexible where hours are concerned, something that staffers applaud.

Editors will tell you that that there's more to their job than long hours, acquiring books, and selling themselves. They also have to be amateur psychologists to a degree, soothing and reassuring their authors.

"You basically have to be very selfless. Let's put it that way," said one editor, explaining about 1 A.M. calls from nervous writers. "When I first started acquiring a lot of books, I would just go home feeling hollow, because you have to spend your whole day giving."

But most editors take it—especially since they sweated it out as editorial assistants to get where they are today. And the drawbacks of being a young editor seem easier to stomach than those facing editorial assistants.

"Most editorial assistants I know fall into a six-month slump," explained one young man who lived through it. "I know I did. Because it's after those six months that you start hearing about your friends making so much more money and starting to get promoted. And you're just sitting there doing typing and filing and xeroxing, thinking, 'I went to an Ivy League school for this. I can't believe it. What are my parents going to say?' "

Moving up the ladder in the editorial department is notoriously slow throughout the industry. As one editor noted, "It's really not till your mid- to late thirties when people say, 'All right, you're a real editor now. You've made it.' " So Harper's tries to encourage young people to stay through that long climb. Staffers say management feels strongly about promoting from within and supporting young employees in general.

And promotion is the name of the game when you're at the lower levels. One employee mentioned that editorial assistants who haven't moved up after two years are really "flunkies." So even at easy-going Harper's, editorial assistants had better bite the bullet, put up with the tedious work, and keep learning anything and everything they can about being an editor.

This high attrition rate and slow promotion track is one reason noneditorial staffers choose to be on the **business** side of publishing. And for many, that choice was purely a fluke.

"I graduated from college, moved to New York, said I wanted to be in the publishing business and, of course, I'll be an editor.

What else is there?" a business manager reminisced. But the job she was offered at another major house was in subsidiary rights. "I said, 'Fine, I'll take it. But what is it?' " Well, she found out, like many others, that working on the business side of publishing wasn't half bad. "I was learning an incredible amount and it was exciting. And I stayed in rights. There seemed to be more room for me, more directions in which to go."

That's something a lot of business staffers say. Not only are there various entry-level spots in noneditorial departments like advertising, marketing, publicity, and promotion, there are also a lot of opportunities. Especially since Harper's and other major houses are now focusing more on business than ever before.

"The marketing side of publishing is great for people who aren't total book freaks," said a marketing employee. "People who want to be in the business world, but who won't sell their soul to sell something they don't believe in."

In the **college book** area, no one worries about selling any-thing—because here, books aren't sold, they're "adopted." Unlike those in the rest of the company, people in college books aren't talking about changes. This is traditionally a division that "brings stability to the company," as one staffer noted.

But that doesn't mean it's sleepy or moribund here. Especially for the people in the lower level jobs—the sales reps. They're out on the road, talking with professors and trying to convince them to buy, or rather, adopt, Harper's books. And that can be pretty difficult for someone who's not that long out of college himself.

"Imagine going to a college campus at twenty-three years old, knocking on the door of a professor in math or computer science, and you've been told it's your responsibility to sell him a book," mused a man who worked his way up through the ranks. "You're standing outside the door and you know he's a well-known scholar. And you have to have a cogent conversation with him, be liked, and do what you're paid for. It's a demanding task."

It certainly sounds like it. But that sales rep position is often the first step to moving up into higher positions. After about three years have passed, many sales reps move on—either into the marketing and sales management side, or the editorial side.

As far as editorial responsibilities go in this division, it's a little different from working in trade. Developmental editors usually work with large introductory books—the type that students in a freshman Introduction to Psychology course have to read. And there are the regular editors—who go out and acquire books, and see the book through to completion. College Division editors will often come up with an idea, seek out a prominent professor to write the book, hire technical reviewers to read and critique it, and then work with the sales and marketing people to get the book out to college campuses. "It's essentially following the book from soup to nuts," an editor explained. "In a sense, what I'm doing is product management—acquiring, developing and selling books." And the process for each book is a long one—usually two to three years.

LIFE

Life at Harper's mirrors the company itself—it's easygoing. Yes, people work hard here, put in their long hours, and have to adjust to a new sales-driven mentality. But they don't let it get to them. And they aren't becoming head-to-head competitors either.

Yes, Harper's is still big on good old-fashioned team spirit. "Compared to some other houses, Harper's is pretty close," said a trade editor. There's an emphasis on people getting together and working together. And that kind of thing has become institutionalized. In the trade division there are weekly editorial meetings and frequent editorial lunches. Management has also created a more intimate atmosphere by setting up "editorial teams or interest groups" of two to three editors who share a common interest and brainstorm about book ideas.

So most people feel a homeyness and accessibility about working here. As one marketing staffer summed up, "It's a large company but not a huge corporation. It's sort of in between. It's big enough to have all the security you get from a major corporation, but not so big that you get lost."

DOLLARS AND SENSE

This is publishing, right? And everyone will tell you that no one gets rich in publishing. Harper's is no exception to that rule. That's why people warn would-be publishing staffers to consider the practical side. As an editor commented, "For the most part, you're restricted to New York, and living on a publishing salary in New York is next to impossible. At $13,000 a year, you're going to be living in a studio apartment with six others like yourself."

But Harper's is unionized, and nonmanagement employees belong to a United Auto Workers local. That doesn't mean they make cars here on the side. It *does* mean that benefits and salaries are regulated, however. And that's something quite a few employees like. According to one staffer, nonmanagement employees are grouped according to title. And when an entry-level person moves up to another grouping—say from secretary to secretary/ assistant—he or she comes out of it with a 10 percent raise. Vacancies are posted internally for five days before being advertised outside.

Harper's also has a fairly liberal tuition reimbursement program, and it pays dues for professional organizations. But this is not the real reason for being here.

What is? That's not a tough question. One employee answered it for everyone. "Even though the pay is less, I'm here because I believe in books."

GETTING IN—TRICKS OF THE TRADE

So you want to work in publishing?

One editor voiced a litany of warnings. "The advice I usually give to people is, don't get into publishing unless you're very serious about doing it. Because the pay is bad, the hours are long, the number of people who are promoted compared to the number of people who start out is very small, there's a high attrition rate, you wind up doing a lot of work at home, it's hard to have a private life as an editor . . ."

But there are a lot of people out there who are very serious indeed about working in publishing generally, and at Harper & Row specifically. And there are a few ways to make it easier to get your foot in the door.

Naturally, an English Lit major is the most common background for editorial assistants. Would-be trade editors are advised to contact Harper's editors directly. One editor explained that it's fine to register with personnel also, but "most editorial jobs tend to be filled by word of mouth." He suggests getting to know editors, even if it's just through a letter. "And agents tend to know about a lot of jobs," he added. "That's also a good place to do informational interviews."

As for getting into the business side? It's pretty much the same thing—a combination of luck, good academic background, and timing. A business employee mentioned that business degrees are not necessary, but "a business degree does help you make larger steps faster." And computer skills can help—especially since Harper reportedly is planning to institute a company-wide information system.

College sales is looking for people with some experience, "seasoned people with some experience in selling." But it doesn't have to be only books. According to a College Division employee, any sales background is a plus. And even working in the college bookstore "would give people an edge, since it's an indication of their interest in the field." He also recommends talking with professors and college bookstore people about textbook publishing, since they deal with so many different publishers. "They'll give you a good impression of each company. They're opinionated, so they'll tell the truth."

A final comment about getting into Harper's—it's not easy, but it's worth a strong try. As Harper's has changed, it has become "a good place to be for young people. The publisher especially feels very strongly about supporting and promoting them." And, we hope, hiring them.

THE BOTTOM LINE

Middle-of-the-road doesn't mean stuck-in-the-mud.

RANDOM HOUSE

VITAL STATISTICS

- location: New York
- revenues: $300+ million (1984 net sales)
- rank: 1st (1984 BP Reports, trade publishing)
- employees: 1,600

AS SEEN FROM THE OUTSIDE

It's called the house that Bennett Cerf built—which he did in 1925. But it's not 1925 any more. And Bennett's house looks as if it's in for a bit of a remodeling job.

Long known as the quiet publishing giant that emphasized quality literature, Random House is changing. It's still rather quiet, it's still a giant, but it's getting a little louder and a little bigger. And that's not all—while many of Random House's imprints are still publishing "important" books, other imprints are coming out with more commercial books of dubious literary quality.

Actually, Random House is a lot like its logo—a funny house that's part cottage, part mansion, a little of this and a little of that. Random House imprints are a diverse group—including Alfred A. Knopf (one of the top literary imprints in the country); Vintage (trade paperbacks); Pantheon; Ballantine/Del Rey/Fawcett (mass market paperbacks); Villard; Random House (the flagship imprint) as well as the newly acquired Times Books, and textbook, educational and reference divisions.

It all started when Bennett Cerf and his friend Donald Klopfer scraped together $215,000 and bought the Modern Library line (112 book titles) from Horace Liveright in 1925. By 1927, they decided to start publishing contemporary authors, choosing the books "at random." The rest, as they say, is publishing history.

Random House began growing, adding prestigious authors and buying prestigious smaller imprints, until it in turn was swallowed up by a larger firm in 1966—when a whale called RCA bought it for $38 million. The marriage was doomed from the beginning. Big bureaucratic RCA simply wasn't run the same way as relaxed Random House, and both partners were relieved when, in 1980, S. I. Newhouse paid about $65 million for the company. Random House welcomed his "leave well enough alone" management style. And, true to form, he did just that—left the company alone to do its own thing.

But now, Random House's "own thing" was beginning to change. It had acquired mass-market paperback publisher Ballantine in its RCA days, and later added Fawcett (bought from CBS) and Del Rey to that division. And since apparently that still wasn't quite commercial enough, in 1983, Random House started a new imprint, Villard Books, which focuses more on flash and glitz than on heavy-hitting literature.

A lot of people in publishing are speculating where Random House is headed now. Chairman and CEO Robert Bernstein is keeping one eye on the past and one on the future. People like Robert Gottlieb, head of Knopf, maintain Random House's old reputation for non-bottom-line-focused literature. And new-comer Howard Kaminsky, hired in 1984 to head the Random House trade division, represents a newer approach. He's not rocking the boat, as many had expected, and he's keeping the elite list. But he's also gunning for a more commercial, promotion-oriented look.

Now Random House is everything it was *and* a lot of new things. Apparently, at this house, there's always room for more.

HEARD AT THE WATER COOLER— WHAT IT'S REALLY LIKE TO WORK HERE

Random House is the ideal place for people who never wanted to leave their exclusive and highly prestigious college. Working here is a lot like staying within those ivy-covered walls. It's scholarly, low-key, intellectual and terribly respectable. Here they make money the old-fashioned way—genteelly.

Sure, like the other publishing houses, Random House is moving away from the old "gentlemen's industry" image to plain ole big business. But here it's happening a bit more slowly. And that's the way employees seem to like it.

There's a relaxed pace at Random House, a cerebral "think before you act" spirit that makes you forget you're at a big company. And the surroundings are just as uncorporate. Most of the Random House floors are like an English Lit department headquarters at a large campus: comfortable chairs and couches that appear well-used; wood-paneled walls; manila envelopes lying on the floor beside the receptionists' desks; and, naturally, books everywhere—in the glass showcases flanking the reception desks, filling the tall shelves in editorial offices, piled in boxes along the hallways. Textbooks, gardening manuals, newest works by best-selling but literary authors, every kind of book imaginable is displayed in sloppy yet proper academic settings.

But that's not the whole Random House look. Ballantine especially appears a bit less intellectual and library-ish and a bit more in synch with modern, profit-oriented thinking. Here it is sleek gray walls, a streamlined reception area and a general high-gloss atmosphere. Here the books are more along the lines of Bonnie Prudden's newest exercises, even though they publish John Updike and other literary Random and Knopf authors in paperback. Still, it's Random House—old-fashioned even when it tries to be flashy.

A publishing company is what it prints and, in Random House's case, that's mostly heavy-hitters in some sense of the word. As one editorial staffer said, "Each house has its own persona and, of course, Random House has a very elite one. There's a sense of history about it, if you look at the list."

PEOPLE

Random House employees say there's no real Random House persona. It really depends on the division you're in.

Ballantine has "a very young feel, a real sense of energy," according to an editor. "People here are a little crazy, they have different ideas, they're open to different fads, styles, whatever."

The Trade Book division people are more preppie than punk and somewhat sedate. Maybe that's because even the lower-level people "have had previous experience or gone through the Radcliffe publishing program or have a Masters—they're generally older," as a staffer put it.

The College Textbook division employees are academics who don't follow fads or fashions and look as if they just walked off campus. And Knopf is known throughout the company as the place for literary, laid-back intellectual types.

So that makes Random House employees a diverse bunch, huh?

Well, to a degree.

"We like liberal arts graduates, people who have intellectual curiosity, we like Phi Beta Kappas," said an ex-Yalie in the textbook division.

"A lot of people from Yale, a lot of people from Smith, Radcliffe, Wellesley, that sort of thing," a trade book staffer said.

Summed up a Ballantine editor, "I think they definitely look for an Ivy League education."

No fooling.

JOBS

So what happens to the English Lit majors from Harvard who land entry-level jobs at Random House, all set to start reading literary masterpieces by promising young novelists?

They quit dreaming and start working. There's one key thing they do when they first start here and that's type. "I'm not kidding. That's what I did for six months—practiced my typing," said an editor who moved up through the ranks. "My boss wouldn't even look at me if I didn't type sixty words a minute."

And there's more . . .

"The title is editorial assistant, but you're really a secretary to an editor," said a current editorial assistant. "You might type letters, you have to do correspondence and answer phones, and, depending on the editor, very often you have to do things like get coffee, call a taxi, make restaurant reservations."

What fun. So that's what a pricey education can get you.

But that's really the worst of it. There's a lot more to being an **editorial assistant** than clerical work. At least if you want it that way. For all of Random House's apparent laid-back atmosphere, aggressiveness is rewarded here. So editorial assistants who want to make it make sure that they're noticed, particularly by trying to initiate their own projects and acquiring books themselves.

"What you have to do is basically put yourself on the line," a young woman explained. "You have to get up your nerve and you have to call agencies, preferably agencies that have young agents. You simply call them and say you're interested in acquiring a certain type of book."

Editorial assistants here say it's vital that you stand out from the crowd and show your stuff. The next step up is **assistant**

editor, and since that's usually filled in-house, assistants try their hardest to prove that they're learning the publishing business and can handle a promotion. To some extent, it's luck of the draw—if an assistant and editor click, the assistant gets the opportunity to do less of the clerical and more of the editorial work. Still, the bottom line is tooting one's own horn—and as quickly as possible.

"In the first six months, you have to come up with something," stressed an open-faced woman. "You either have to be involved in a big book—in other words, working closely on a book with your editor—or you have to bring up a project. Otherwise, they'll lose faith."

Since it sometimes takes a while to make an acquisition, some editorial assistants get noticed by performing even the more menial tasks well—like reading and evaluating manuscripts.

"A very good way to distinguish yourself is by giving very good reader's reports, instead of saying things like 'this book stinks,' " an assistant said with a laugh.

But even when editorial assistants do all the right things, they don't get promoted all that quickly here. As one young man said, "People don't leave Knopf, they die." That's about what it's like at all the Random House divisions. Sometimes that's difficult to take. So people have to learn to be both aggressive *and* patient.

"If you're a college graduate and you have ambition, it's very difficult to stay in a clerical position for two years, two and a half years," one woman said.

Difficult but not impossible. That's the normal stay for editorial assistants here. If they're not promoted in-house by that point, they'll usually move to another house. Those who do make the jump up the ladder have to continue proving themselves. As assistant editors, even at genteel Random House, there's tremendous pressure to sign new books.

"That takes a certain kind of person," said one of Knopf's top editors, describing young Random House editors. "You have to be sort of a go-getter. You have to be sort of brash, you have to build contacts. It's a lot of socializing and selling yourself to agents and saying, 'I'm the hottest thing at Knopf.' "

"I loathe that sort of thing," she continued with a sigh. "I would never have been able to make it today."

But working at Random House doesn't have to mean working in the newly go-getting editorial environment. There are also the traditionally go-getting fields—ones that many staffers say are too often overlooked by job seekers.

"There are a lot of jobs in publishing, a lot of interesting *other* jobs," a young editor pointed out. "Subsidiary rights, publicity, promotion—they're all very exciting."

Yes, many people do think it's exciting to be involved with books in a different way, a step away from the cerebral and a step toward hype. But remember, this is Random House. So even in the fields where you'd think hype belongs, there's still that dash of gentility.

A marketing manager explained that what drew him to Random House in the first place was his "tremendous amount of respect" for the company. "They knew their stuff," he continued. "There was less bullshit, less flash—it was solidly rooted."

But still, staffers in **advertising and marketing** are there to sell. According to one staffer, there is a Random House way to sell, one in keeping with its image—"it's the right way to pursue sales. We're heavily influenced by service, having the sales reps very involved."

According to most staffers, a great number of people begin in the field as reps, then move into higher positions—in some cases, even to the editorial side. "As far as college textbook publishing is concerned," one man stated, "editorial or management—it's almost a requirement to have come up through sales. In order to be a good editor of textbooks, you should have sold textbooks. That's how you know the market."

It's similarly stated on the marketing side. "Being in the field gives you an education," said one young man. "You're learning how it works in the field. And that's what stays with you."

So what's it like being a sales rep for Random House? A lot like being a sales rep at the other big publishing houses—you're on the road, traveling within your region, trying to sell books. "It's a relatively young sales force," one staffer said, describing the trade book reps. "They've got incredible experience for their years. We're very aggressive. It's just that we don't shriek."

"We've never confused being aggressive and being respectful."

LIFE
People at Random House don't rave about the life here, but they don't complain either.

"I worked at other publishing houses," one editor said. "And the people were cliqueish, they were basically unhappy. Here people are pretty happy by and large."

"All around, I feel it's pretty friendly," an editorial assistant concurred. "A lot of us go out to lunch frequently, talk shop talk."

That about sums up the social side of things. The work itself is what people like about working here.

"It's just exciting to see a book take off," a Knopf staffer said. "To see something financially rewarded when it's meritorious, not because it's junk."

There's one of the keys to working here—the quality list. People here know they're working for a respected company, so they're pleased. Add to that the relaxed, comfortable management style and it's a pretty nice place to work.

"There's a free and easy style," summed up an old hand. "We don't have endless meetings. We don't decide things by committee. It's just a lot of fun. And we don't take ourselves too seriously."

That attitude fosters a camaraderie among employees, particularly on the lower levels.

"The editorial assistants sit in this room and have lunch every day and shoot the breeze," a Ballantine editor said. "They laugh and giggle and tell horror stories about what their bosses did to them."

And since this is one of the largest publishing houses, there's a little glamour to life here too . . .

"You meet interesting people, prestigious authors. It's sort of a kick to go home and tell someone I met Isaac Asimov, James Michener or someone else," an editorial employee commented.

It's not all highbrow though. "We signed Raquel Welch's newest book. And it's fun to meet Raquel and go out to lunch with her," said a soft-spoken young woman.

See, even nonintellectuals can find something here.

DOLLARS AND SENSE

As for the financial side of working at Random House, "one likes to think it's good for the soul—the starving young dilettante or whatever," as an editorial assistant said.

Couldn't have summed it up better. Publishing doesn't pay well and Random House is no exception to that rule. Top authors can live like kings. And their editors? Well . . .

"Knopf is known for its 'Knopf kids' right now—the under thirty novelists who are doing very well," a Knopf staffer said. "As to working for such a company and being young? It's a feather in your cap—'cause you're certainly not getting money for it."

Those who stick it out find Random House rather generous— after promotions and subsequent raises. Another plus is Random House's benefits program. According to one staffer "the benefits director talks about it in the sense that if you're making $20,000, the benefits are so good you may as well consider yourself making $25,000." "But," he added, "having benefits and having ready cash are two different things."

GETTING IN—TRICKS OF THE TRADE

The best way to get a job at Random House is the old "have a contact in the company who'll tell you about job openings and recommend you for them" route. As you'd expect, personnel is flooded with resumés. That's why "it's hard to break the ice. You're very lucky if you get in on a resumé," as an editorial assistant stated.

And if you're thinking about being clever, bypassing personnel and sending your resumé to a specific editor, you're not as smart as you think. Why? Well, guess who opens the mail? The editoral assistant, of course. That means your wonderful resumé is either filed away or sent up to personnel. So much for ingenuity. Still, most people do recommend sending resumés to both editors and personnel.

As for those lucky souls who either know someone here or managed to get a reply to their cold mailing—the first thing to do is bone up on your typing.

"They screen you in personnel," a young woman explained. "And they make you take a typing test. It's really demeaning, but you take it. And you should type at least sixty words a minute."

Once applicants prove that their typing skills are up to par, it's on to more esoteric things—a meeting with an editor and, often, a manuscript to take home and evaluate. People who've been hired here recommend getting that manuscript read and the reader's report written as quickly as possible, a day or two at the outside. And the report should be brief—half a page maximum. One more thing. Criticize away, but "be as respectful as possible," cautioned a staffer. Of course. Remember they're all gentlemen and gentlewomen here.

So what's the best way to break into Random House? In short, there are a few basic attributes that can make the difference between you and a thousand other publishing hopefuls: strong typing, enthusiasm, previous experience in publishing, attendance at one of the publishing programs like Radcliffe's, U. of Denver's, etc., and, don't forget, an Ivy League diploma. After all, when in Rome . . .

THE BOTTOM LINE

A haven for English Lit majors.

SIMON & SCHUSTER

VITAL STATISTICS

- location: New York
- revenues: $300 + million (1984 net sales)
- rank: 2nd (1984 BP Reports, trade publishing)
- employees: 2,000

AS SEEN FROM THE OUTSIDE

Simon & Schuster (S&S) started out in the fast lane. Three months after Richard L. Simon and M. Lincoln Schuster began S&S with $3,000 and no authors, they contracted a crossword puzzle book and sold over a million copies. That was Dick Simon's aunt's idea. Two years later, they published a little-known author named Will Durant, called his book *The Story of Philosophy*, and made the bestseller lists in 1927. That was Max Schuster's idea.

Along the way, S&S earned an image as a publishing company with a knack for marketing. It was one of the first to use coupon advertising in books, one of the first to use full-page print ads, and one of the first to use odd pricing (only $4.95!). Those were Dick Simon's ideas. The older, more intellectual book publishers sniffed, but the founders kept pushing and publishing to near top of the stack. They were publishing "good" authors like P. G. Wodehouse, S. J. Perelman and, more recently, Graham Greene, and a lot of "commercial" authors whose books sold well.

S&S is the unabashedly commercial book publisher, and it's become more so since 1975. That was the year the unabashedly bottom-line conglomerate Gulf & Western Industries, Inc. acquired the company. Richard E. Snyder became president, and along with editor-in-chief Michael Korda, oversaw its growth from a $40 million to a $300 million company. Recently, G&W bought another big book publisher, Prentice-Hall, and in 1985 reorganized everything under an umbrella company called G&W Publishing and Information Group, headed by Snyder. S&S remains the cornerstone—along with its Pocket Book division and Linden, Summit, Poseiden and other imprints.

HEARD AT THE WATER COOLER—
WHAT IT'S REALLY LIKE TO WORK HERE

Like books? Like business? Have we got a publishing company for you . . . Simon & Schuster is the king of the new-fangled, you-don't-have-to-be-ashamed-of-making-a-profit publishing companies. And it shows.

S&S has moved beyond the old "gentlemen's industry" feel. Sure, some noncorporate, intellectual literary types roam around here. This is, after all, a publishing house and books are its business. But here it's big business. And that's the heart and soul of S&S.

Walk through the S&S floors and you'll feel as if you're at any large company—and one that's doing very well. Sleek reception areas, dark walls and a general air of corporate prosperity are everywhere. Only the inevitable displays of books tell you that this is indeed a publishing company. And one to be reckoned with, too—no unknown titles by promising authors around; here it's blockbusters ranging from the not-so-literary (Jackie Collins's newest steamy novel) to the more literary but best-selling (Larry McMurtrey's western epic).

It's fitting that books are usually referred to as "packages" here, because *everything* looks packaged—like a glossy photograph of an office. Even the editors' offices aren't the usual sloppy academic ones you see at other publishers. Here there's always a polished look to them—whether it's the carefully placed book jackets pinned to a bulletin board or the neat rows of books on the ubiquitous bookshelves.

S&S is just as slick as the books it produces—and that means it's *very* slick. Especially when it comes to running a business.

As one staffer put it, "This is definitely a real Martin Marietta type corporation. It's not good-old-boy publishing by a mile."

No, but it works—and in a very big way.

PEOPLE

Wheeler-dealers who also like literature would feel perfectly at home here. It's that blend of bookishness and business savvy that most S&S people seem to have—with emphasis on the latter.

"A hot-shot business school person who thought, 'Gee, I'm interested in books and marketing concepts . . .' That's the kind of person who would really take off here," an earnest young man said. "Not somebody who had visions of Nobel Laureates dancing through his head."

That's not to say S&S doesn't have its share of nonbusiness creative types—especially in the Simon & Schuster imprints. "Here it's a very casual, easy feel. There are a lot of artsy-fartsy people, some loose clothing," explained a recent hiree at a top imprint. "You see plenty of people who are very casual, laid back, relaxed and easy."

S&S imprint people tend to be a little different from the people on the fourteen floor—where S&S trade is located. There, they can't afford to be too relaxed and easy. Simon & Schuster is a hard-driving, power-driven place and you've got to be pretty strong to succeed.

Said one young woman, "There's tremendous competition within the trade department. You've got to be tough to last there."

And that's not all you have to be. S&S people have a certain something . . . "There's a lot of style and image at Simon & Schuster," one staffer said. "You have to have an act."

But an act isn't enough, either. "You've still got to play the game up there," she continued. "You can be as stylish and imagey as you want, but if you don't have a Jackie Collins or a Jane Fonda . . ."

You figure out some way to get them. S&S people just won't give up. That's why they manage to thrive in a competitive atmosphere and that's how they succeed. And, without a doubt, S&S people can take it.

JOBS

Okay, so S&S isn't the most relaxing place to work. "It is very aggressive, very power-oriented," said an editorial employee.

That's true. And because of that, it's also great training ground. As one long-time staffer said of a friend who put in half a year at S&S after years at another publishing company, "She says she learned more in her six months at Simon & Schuster than she did in twelve years at Doubleday."

That might be a bit of an exaggeration, but the fact remains—Simon & Schuster is a tough place to work. Those who can take it, however, end up with a strong publishing background, and a lot of business savvy.

How tough is it? Here's how an employee sees the S&S philosophy toward editors: "Whip them into a frenzy so that they're performing just outrageously well; then, just when it's time for them to be rewarded, kick them in the back of their knees. It sounds ruthless, but that's the way it is. I see people who are incredibly successful running scared. It might be a psychological thing—not being comfortable with success and having to always prove themselves. But I also see it as the Simon & Schuster mentality."

Phew! Guess that's why S&S produces so many overachievers.

Even **editorial assistants** learn quickly to be as aggressive as possible. As in most publishing houses, editorial assistants are encouraged to begin acquiring books as soon as possible. But here, editorial assistants are working in a pretty high-powered environment.

"Half of the editors upstairs were heads of houses," a young editor explained. "There are so many stars up there."

That makes it a bit more difficult for editorial assistants or young associate editors and editors to get noticed. Still, many do. "I do see some young editorial assistants who are now associate editors," one employee said of the trade division. "I see their names on ed board minutes and see that they're bringing in projects."

Editorial assistants seem to have it easier in the S&S imprints. Imprints are smaller, so the competition is lessened, making the atmosphere a bit more relaxed. "I feel extremely lucky to be here," one assistant said. "Friends of mine who are editorial assistants don't describe the same kind of rapport I have with my bosses. They seem to do a hell of a lot more grunt work—filing things, counting things, stapling things. And they seem to have a less close relationship with the editor they work for."

Lower-level employees who can hitch their wagon to a more established person usually move ahead more readily. Lucky editorial assistants work under an editor who helps push them ahead. And that's what most lower-level employees hope for.

Even with sponsorship, though, it isn't easy to become an **editor**. "You have to have ideas, you have to believe in them and you have to push," an editorial assistant stated. "Nobody gives you anything."

"You really have to have somebody on your side in sales, promotion and publicity," one young man said. "So when you have a book that you want to make into a best seller, you go to them and collect favors."

To succeed at S&S, you'd better do that well. This is a company that's highly numbers-oriented and used to a high profit margin. S&S books are expected to sell well. "Break even, that's the least they'll accept," one employee stated. Some people find that up-setting—"How can you invest in an author who's going to grow"— but all admit it works. "You're guaranteed better distribution," explained an editor. And that means authors, editors and S&S make money.

Possible acquisitions are discussed at an editorial meeting. General business is discussed, then editors present the book proposals (called "hand-to's") that they're interested in. The acquisitions committee (three higher-level people) then meets, discusses the hand-to's, decides which to pursue, and officially announces its decisions.

As one might expect, that decision is based to a great degree on the saleability of the book. That's not to say S&S goes only for commercial ideas. Many editors here work with so-called "important books," those that have obvious literary quality. And when the numbers look right, and the book isn't just one more potboiler, then everyone's happy.

While the company is profit-oriented, the staffers are, without a doubt, true book people. As one young woman described it, when an important literary work is acquired, "there's a certain kind of excitement. I see how excited the sales force gets when you give them something good, when you give them something important."

So that's what it's like having a job at Simon & Schuster—a lot of work, a lot of competition, some headaches and some plea-sures. And, of course, the business of making books.

"The first thing you have to realize is that this is a business," stressed an editorial assistant. "And that's the way it's run."

LIFE
The size of S&S is the common aspect of life here. It's so big, it's sometimes difficult to meet people.

"You work with terrific people and never meet them," said one editor with a laugh.

"The way I've found kindred spirits is through people outside, saying, 'Oh, so-and-so has just gone over there. Make sure you go meet her.' You do feel isolated sometimes."

Life at S&S depends to a great extent on the division a person is in. A recently hired imprint employee described the fate of an editorial assistant in one of the bigger S&S divisions: "It's less personal. You can just sit at your desk and no one talks to you all day." As for working in the imprints—people feel somewhat isolated from the rest of the company, but believe that gives them more flexibility and freedom. One editorial assistant described it as being "kind of like Yugoslavia." But, in the imprints, staffers say it's easier to develop strong relationships with *all* co-workers—peers and bosses.

There is one factor to life at S&S that cuts across divisions. As with many publishing companies, lower-level employees tend to stick together. "There is some unifying property in the fact that we're all kind of poor," an editorial assistant said with a smile.

DOLLARS AND SENSE

S&S might operate like a typical corporation, but it's still publishing, right? And the salaries definitely mirror that fact. They're average by industry standards, which makes them typically low by any other industry's standards. Starting salaries here tend to be a cool $11,500 to $13,000, which is probably why Dick Snyder reportedly joked that Simon & Schuster should buy an apartment building in New York just for editorial assistants to live in.

But, since S&S hasn't done that, most editorial assistants just have to get used to being broke a lot of the time. One young woman summed up the situation: "I earn $12,000 a year before taxes; I take home $186 a week. I live in a tiny little space and it breaks me. I don't ever have an extra penny to my name. That's why I think you've got to really want publishing."

GETTING IN—TRICKS OF THE TRADE

"Know somebody and bring money!" That's what an editorial assistant recommends. And she's not far from the truth. It's never easy to break into publishing and it's even more difficult to get into a hot-shot company like Simon & Schuster.

But Simon & Schuster does its best to encourage new blood. It sponsors a Simon & Schuster scholarship for college students. The three winners each receive a $6,000 cash award to go toward his or her senior year in school as well as a guaranteed salaried position at S&S for one year. As one winner explained, people are selected on the basis of their GPA and their submitted essay—

basically an autobiographical piece explaining why you're interested in publishing, why you're interested in winning the scholarship and so forth.

Beyond that, S&S staffers recommend the usual—try to meet people inside the company who'll help you get your foot in the door, flood the market with resumés both to personnel and to individual editors, and just keep trying.

THE BOTTOM LINE

Not for wimps, but for hotshots.

RETAILING

Fashion plates who don't like to get their hands dirty or break a carefully manicured nail had better steer clear of retailing. Sure, retail executives get to work in classy department stores. But it's a far cry from shopping in one. This is a hands-on, fast-paced, hard-driving business. It's tough work, so that's what the people in it have to be—tough.

Apparently there are a lot of people in the United States who fit that description—about 5.5 million to be precise. That's the number of employees in department or specialty stores that sell clothing, home furnishings and all those other things consumers love to buy. Roughly 166,000 of those employees are the retail executives, serving in either administrative, merchandising or operational capacities.

The usual way to become a retail executive is to go through one of the many management training programs offered by department stores. First, the good news about these programs— no specialized background is required. While it helps to have some retail experience (even being a part-time salesperson can help), that's about the only preference the stores have. Retailing is an industry where business majors are *not* preferred over liberal arts majors. Most stores hire a cross-section of people with a variety of backgrounds, from art history to plain history to, yes, merchandising.

Okay, now the bad news. The money in retailing isn't that great. In fact, starting salaries in retailing are lower than those in many other industries. An executive trainee can make from $14,000 to $21,000. Salaries do fluctuate according to geographics (stores in the large metropolitan areas, especially New York and Los Ange-

les, pay higher), but no matter how you slice it, an entry-level retailing position isn't going to make you rich. People who stick it
out find their financial situation improving dramatically. Retailing middle managers are paid *higher* than people at a similar level
in other industries, with salaries of $30,000 and up (*way* up, de-
pending on the store you're with and the responsibilities you have)
being the norm for recently promoted buyers at major department stores. And to make matters even better, there's not too long
a wait to reach those middle-management spots—usually two to
four years. So while you might starve at the beginning, you can
make up for it sooner than you might expect.

The most popular career in retailing is in **merchandising**,
which involves the management of departments and the buying
of merchandise. The majority of stores offer the same career
path in merchandising:

The typical entry-level position for college grads is **executive
trainee**. This position involves classroom training in merchandise
math, consumer profiling, forecasting, buying concepts, presentation and advertising, and business writing, combined with
or followed by hands-on work on the selling floor, assisting a
department manager. Training programs usually last from three
to nine months.

Trainees then become **assistant department managers**, working in a specific department under a department manager, with
responsibilities including inventory control, stock maintenance
and merchandise presentation. Hours are long and pressure is
high. This is when some people start to wonder why they wanted
to be in retailing in the first place. Assistant department managers
spend much of their time dealing primarily with the stock—
unpacking it, getting it out on the floor, moving it from rack to
rack and making sure it looks good. The usual length of time
people spend as assistant department managers is from six to
nine months.

Next, it's on to **assistant buyer**. Assistant buyers work with a
buyer in a department's buying office, doing a number of different things: tracking sales by classification and by store; checking on merchandise markdowns; informing department managers about price changes; clerical work; writing reports for the
divisional merchandise managers on the department's sales; determining trends in the sales; dealing with vendors about shipping dates and more; seeing vendors in the market or in the

office with the buyer; and "shopping the competition" (checking out the merchandise in other stores). It's a very numbers-oriented position, and assistant buyers are there to learn what it is a buyer does. By observing their buyers, assistant buyers begin to see how the buyer makes decisions on what to buy based on the customer profile; how to buy on a margin; how to determine prices and factor in for markdowns and so on. This is the spot in which many people realize that retailing isn't necessarily as creative as they thought. In a buying office, they learn that it's business and numbers that count—and their own taste has little to do with determining what merchandise to sell. Most assistant buyers stay in their positions for a year to a year and a half.

Then it's back to the selling floor as a **department manager**. Department managers are responsible for an area of a store— anything from a tiny space selling small leather goods and sunglasses to a large area selling designer sportswear. And what they're *really* responsible for is the profit that square footage generates. They determine where merchandise is displayed, what's on the mannequins or in the showcases, what's coming in, and when and what's selling and why. And if that's not enough fun, department managers also get to work with the executive trainees (which they were only a year or so ago). Being a department manager means being on your feet most of the day, dealing with sales and stock people and unionized receiving people and a lot more general down-and-dirty stuff. If no one's around to unpack the 300 dresses that came in just before closing, department managers will hang around or come in extra early and do it themselves. This is a high-energy sport, perfect for go-getters with strong legs.

Finally, it becomes the job most people think of when they think of retailing—the **buyer**. Buyers get the chance to spend millions of dollars shopping. But it's not as simple or glamorous as it sounds. Buying isn't based only on taste and instinct (although that helps). It takes a shrewd analytical business head to determine what's selling, what's not, and what *will* sell in the future. Buyers "go to market" (which means they go to wholesalers and place orders) and have vendors visit them to show goods. They might have the opportunity to shop foreign markets if their merchandise category warrants it. In addition, they're the ones who determine when to mark down an item and the amount to mark it down. And they often decide what items in their department should be advertised. Centralized buyers in the larger store chains buy for the flagship store and the branches, so they have to know the type of customer for each store, then buy the appropriate merchandise and allocate it for maximum profitability. And profitability is most definitely the key. While the department manager is responsible for the profits of a selling area, the buyer is *really* responsible for the profits, since she's the one who bought the merchandise in the first place. And how can they tell if merchandise will sell? It's a combination of knowledge about the customer, creativity, the ability to predict trends and a huge amount of luck.

Some people remain buyers all their lives, because they like being right on top of the merchandise. Others move into senior management positions and become Divisional Merchandise Managers (in charge of a merchandise division and the corresponding buyers and department managers), Group Merchandise Managers and on up.

For those who are strictly interested in **store management** as opposed to merchandising proper, the path is similar. Some stores offer separate managerial career paths—executive trainee, department manager, group manager, divisional group manager, assistant store manager, store manager, then group vice president. At other stores, you follow the merchandising career path, become an assistant buyer, then department manager, and advance on the store management side from there. It's often up to the individual.

Retailing also offers careers in **operations**, which is more concerned with the operational side of retailing as opposed to the merchandising side. Operations staffers may be responsible for receiving and ticketing merchandise, overseeing the warehouses, customer service and security, managing the sales and stock people (scheduling, training etc.), and a variety of other support fields. Operations was long considered the nonglamorous side of retailing, a poor cousin to merchandising, but that's changing. More and more stores are offering executive training in operations, salaries comparable to merchandising ones, and a more visible position. And many people now believe that operations training is perfect for moving into store management at an upper level or opening their own store.

That's retailing—a lot of hard work, a lot of long hours, but (apparently) worth it to many.

BLOOMINGDALE'S

VITAL STATISTICS

- **locations:** New York (flagship store); 14 branch stores
- **revenues:** $903 million (1984 volume)
- **rank:** N/A
- **employees:** 4,000

AS SEEN FROM THE OUTSIDE

If hoop skirts were still the rage, Bloomingdale's wouldn't be *the* innovative, trendy and fun department store, and American shopping wouldn't be the art form it is today.

But even back in the 1870s, the Bloomingdale brothers saw the future: hoop skirts were out. So they closed their father's hoop skirt factory and opened their "great East Side bazaar" in the then dull Upper East Side of New York. It's not dull now.

As New York grew, so did the store, and so did its image—up from slightly stodgy to highly trendy. Bloomingdale's today is a pace-setting store, and a slick advertiser and promoter. It was a leader in giving a boutique look to its departments, and the first to give designers like Ralph Lauren, Perry Ellis, Halston, Calvin Klein and Yves St. Laurent their own shops inside the store. And Bloomingdale's "country promotions" are world famous—an annual event highlighting the culture and merchandise of a particular nation. First Italy in 1960, then France, and in 1986 the best of exotic India. Exotic foods are also a Bloomie's specialty—gourmet foods and wares from around the world. Why travel? Just go to Bloomingdale's.

Bloomingdale's is owned by Federated Department Stores, Inc., the largest department store operator in the U.S. Along with Bloomie's, it owns some of the biggest and the best in American merchandising, including Burdine's, I. Magnin, Bullocks and Abraham & Straus (A&S). Federated was famous for its hands-off management—letting the individual stores pretty much do their own thing. Then a few problems and a new chairman changed that a bit, and some of the less profitable stores had some management changes. But for Bloomingdale's, the largest department store division, things couldn't be better. Already a regional power, with thirteen stores on the East Coast, Bloomie's is moving west. It's in Dallas, and new stores in Chicago and another in Florida are planned. And California is a major market for Bloomingdale's catalogue division.

So the excitement continues . . .

HEARD AT THE WATER COOLER— WHAT IT'S REALLY LIKE TO WORK HERE

Bloomingdale's slogan—"like no other store in the world"—isn't telling the whole truth.

Bloomingdale's really is like every other store in the world. Only more so. And that's what makes it different. It's a hundred stores rolled into one—flashy and brassy, trendy and conservative, offbeat and proper at the same time. Bloomingdale's is retailing at its biggest and brashest. It's retailing to the nth degree.

Most people see only the selling floors at Bloomie's. And it is difficult to see beyond them. Each floor is a modern bazaar, filled with merchandise, shiny fixtures and gleaming glass cases. There's something for everyone; everything a person doesn't need but has to have.

But there's a Bloomingdale's behind the hustle and bustle of the selling floor. Ask for directions to one of the corporate offices or centralized buying offices that are housed in the flagship store, and you're told something like this: "Go downstairs to the lower level, walk across lingerie to the other side of the store. Go through men's designer clothes to the corner. We're behind Ralph Lauren suits."

The offices that make Bloomingdale's a shopper's paradise are decidedly nonflashy. Here it's the business of retailing, not the glamour. Small offices, desks piled with paper, calculators and notebooks, phones ringing . . . The one thing these offices have in common with the selling floor is energy. No matter where you are at Bloomingdale's, you can't escape that feeling.

As one young man summed it up, "I decided to come here because of the excitement. The excitement is *definitely* here."

PEOPLE

The typical Bloomingdale's person is super-chic, intimidatingly slick, a trendy fashion plate on the cutting edge of everything that's new and modern, right?

Wrong.

"I was not what I would have figured to be the Bloomingdale's person," a soft-spoken young woman said, in describing her initial job interview. "I mean, I had on a navy blue conservative suit."

Heavens, how typically corporate! But that's actually the case at Bloomie's. These people might be in the fashion business, but they're business people first and foremost. And retailing isn't that easy. So the varied people who work here have a few things in common—they're an aggressive, self-confident, highly capable bunch. They have to be.

"I think you need a tough shell," a department manager explained. "Sometimes in this business, people get so crazy, they forget to be nice. People do yell at you. They expect things of you—and if you don't get them done, it's not Mom and Dad saying "Oh, it's okay. Next time."

At Bloomingdale's there's never a next time. Work comes before socializing here, and, while people are friendly, the emphasis is squarely on the fast-paced business. As one merchandiser described the Bloomingdale's person, it's "not someone who has to be intellectually brilliant, but someone who is able to size up a situation and deal with it. And think on their feet, *definitely*."

That's the key to the Bloomingdale's personality. Nothing to do with style, appearance or even social skills, but everything to do with coping in a hectic environment.

"You have to be able to keep your cool," an earnest young man summed up. "If you can't keep your cool and act in a very professional manner, you're not going to survive."

And Bloomie's staffers are, without a doubt, survivors.

JOBS

Tough, but worth it. That's how most employees here describe their jobs, whether in merchandising or operations. Responsibilities, duties and career paths are different, but they've got something in common—hard work and lots of it.

The people who start out on the **merchandising** side, fresh from college as executive trainees, don't sit back and let themselves be trained. Far from it. From day one, they're plunged into the hubbub.

"The classes really are secondary," a woman who had completed the training program stated. "Bloomingdale's believes you learn by doing."

And how! In addition to the classes, executive trainees work with a department manager on the selling floor. They learn there and then that working for Bloomie's isn't too glamorous.

"You're dealing with unionized stock people and salespeople who have been there forever and have seen a lot of executive trainees come and go," one staffer explained. "You're put in the position to be in charge of them. It's tough because they think, 'Who are you? Who's this little snippet coming in and saying that she can tell me what to do when I've been here forty years?' "

But trainees stick it out for three months, then start working their way up the ladder—assistant department manager, assistant buyer, department manager, associate buyer, buyer, all the way up to vice president. One thing many trainees like about the Bloomingdale's merchandising hierarchy is the balance between management and buying. In the first year or two, a recently hired employee gets a chance to experience both sides of the business.

An assistant department manager works on the selling floor with the department manager "doing absolutely everything. Nothing is too high or too low." From untangling bikinis for four months as one young woman did, to working on merchandise presentation, to inventory control. After that, it's work in one of the centralized buying offices as an assistant buyer where, as an assistant buyer said with a grin, "the phone rings from 8:30 in the morning to 6:30 at night nonstop. It's crazy."

Then, back out on the selling floor as a department manager in one of the stores for more hands-on work, dealing directly with the merchandise and the customers. And while it's often grueling, staffers love the pace.

"You'll come in at 7 o'clock," a department manager explained, "even though you don't have to be there until 9. You get this loyalty to the floor presentation. You almost get addicted."

It's a healthy addiction, however. While mangement explains to new hirees that there is a time frame of usual lengths of stay in the various positions, employees say it's up to the individual. Show dedication, energy and, above all, enthusiasm, and you'll move ahead.

The pace is the same on the **operations** side. At Bloomie's, there's more of an emphasis on the operations career path for college graduates. The path goes from entry-level assistant division superintendent to division superintendent (DS), service manager, assistant floor superintendent, floor superintendent and on up to upper management. The primary responsibility is handling the selling floor proper (not the merchandise)—sales staff, security, customer service, receiving goods, anything operational.

A young man described the entry-level position this way: "When I first came in, I had never been here before. Suddenly I had sixty sales-people I had to schedule, I had to take care of customer complaints, just basically run the floor. It's tremendous. At a young age—I was 21—you're thrown right in."

As operations people move up, their job duties remain basically the same, but they handle a larger area. It's no longer just a department they work with, it's a few departments or a few floors. And it's not only a sales and stock staff they supervise; they begin working wth executives, also. The normal length of stay as a DS is a year to a year and a half, and for operations assistant or service manager, another year. "I was service manager for a year and I was ready to move," a two-year vet said. "Being on the selling floor for 18 months is a *long* time. Every single day to be out there talking to customers and salespeople; to come in every day and be standing on your feet—it can really take its toll on you."

As an assistant floor superintendent or floor superintendent, you're off the selling floor and in an office, but the pace doesn't let up.

"It doesn't get easier, but it gets different," an assistant floor superintendent said.

No, it most certainly doesn't get easier. "I deal with a lot of the larger management people in the store," a floor super said. "They want something done right now, I have a customer yelling at me, all five lines on the phone are ringing, there's a salesperson yelling and there's a customer in the manager's office for me. That's a normal day. And I wouldn't be here if I didn't like it."

And that's the case with most Bloomingdale's employees. It's hard work, but they'll do it. Are they crazy? Maybe. But they certainly seem happy.

LIFE

Naturally, life at Bloomingdale's is busy. And it revolves around work. Ask an employee what he likes best about working here and he'll say the work. Ask what he likes least and it's—you've got it—the work.

"Just to watch that merchandise blow out of a store is very excting," an operations staffer said. "To watch them open a new floor, to go to an Italian society promotion party and fraternize with all these people you read about in the society pages—it's so exciting!"

Okay, so that's the glamorous side. There's a down side too.

"It's frustrating at times," a young woman confessed. "You have very practical problems that you have to solve and everything should have been done yesterday. You're never completely done and there's always a million things to do. You make a list every morning and you go home at night, and you're adding more than you're taking off of it."

And that wicked pace increases around Christmastime. Like any retailer, Bloomingdale's is busiest from Thanksgiving to New Year's. So the people who've been working hard all year *really* hit their stride in November.

"It's six days a week, two to three nights—9 to 9. You work every Saturday," said one staffer of the holiday season schedule. "It's very, very hectic but you get used to it. Your body adjusts. Your social life becomes nothing, you send your laundry out because you don't have the time to do it. You really need dedication."

Now, that's an understatement . . .

DOLLARS AND SENSE

Here's where the hard work pays off. Bloomie's pays above the fairly low industry standards. So the salaries might not be great, but they're better than those of many other retailers.

"They offered me more than any of my friends had been offered in the retailing industry," a staffer maintained. "About $4,000 more."

But if you're not careful, that money can slip through your fingers easily—all because of one of the perks. As an assistant buyer explains, "There's an employee discount for everyone who works in the store. But it's a dangerous perk, unfortunatey."

GETTING IN—TRICKS OF THE TRADE

As you can imagine, Bloomingdale's is looking for take-charge types.

"We're looking for someone who is very willing to accept a large amount of responsibility early on. And somebody who's calm," a middle manager said. "If they see someone who's nervous and a little edgy, who'd say, 'My God, that's a lot of responsibility for someone who's just starting,' they'd stay away from that."

"Being able to focus on more than one thing is a definite requirement," an operations staffer added. "You have to be able to do seventy-five things at once."

Okay, so Bloomingdale's is after a hyperactive, capable doer, and preferably one who knows the business. "It's imperative that you have worked in the industry before," a young woman asserted. "*Especially* as a salesperson. That's been a big help to me."

All right. Take that as a warning. If you love hard work and think you can take anything that's thrown at you, Bloomingdale's might be the place for you.

THE BOTTOM LINE

Like no other work in the world.

NEIMAN-MARCUS

VITAL STATISTICS

- locations: Dallas (headquarters); 22 branch stores
- revenues: $620 million (1984 volume)
- rank: N/A
- employees: 3,850

AS SEEN FROM THE OUTSIDE

As usual, Stanley Marcus said it first. Or better. The son of one of the founders of this famous department store, he gave the world the philosophy and history of this artistic, exciting and very profitable department store chain in three best-selling books. As if running Neiman-Marcus weren't enough . . .

Now his son, Richard Marcus, is in charge, and the legend continues and grows. The legend? Neiman-Marcus Fortnights—lavish extravaganzas highlighting the fashion, merchandise and culture of different countries. And Neiman-Marcus's catalogues, and the Christmas book—with unusual His and Hers gifts (the first was a pair of Beechcraft airplanes). And the Neiman-Marcus look—the stores are spacious, airy and beautiful, designed by famous architects.

But most important, fine merchandise and superb customer service. Neiman-Marcus salespeople keep a clientele book, detailing past purchases and the future needs of customers. Old-fashioned courtesy and knowledgeable salespeople are common in all Neiman-Marcus stores. And the merchandise is top of the line; something for the person who has everything, and a lot for the rest of us as well.

Neiman-Marcus first opened in downtown Dallas in the early 1900s, a joint venture of Herbert Marcus, Sr., Carrie Marcus Neiman and her husband, A.L. Neiman. Bringing styles to a still somewhat rough-and-ready Dallas, it flourished under the twin operating goals of personal service and a sense of space. When Carrie Neiman divorced her husband, the Marcus family purchased Mr. Neiman's interest, and ran the store in their own very personal way. Carrie Marcus Neiman gave the store its chic NM style, while Stanley Marcus promoted, advertised and guided the company in its initial expansion into the major Texas cities.

By 1968, Neiman-Marcus had become a nationally famous small chain, and attracted the eyes (or tentacles) of retailing giant Carter Hawley Hale, a multibillion-dollar operator of department stores based in Los Angeles. Carter Hawley Hale purchased Neiman, but left things alone, enabling Neiman-Marcus to expand into a nationwide chain. Today, Neiman-Marcus operates in nine states (and Washington, D.C.) with twenty-one stores—and a Marcus is still at the helm, striving for "hassle-free shopping" and "a sense of euphoria." Chairman Richard Marcus is as enthusiastic about retailing as his father before him—making Neiman-Marcus a very special place.

HEARD AT THE WATER COOLER—
WHAT IT'S REALLY LIKE TO WORK HERE

Neiman-Marcus is "Dallas" and "Dynasty" rolled into one. Dallas? That's where Neiman's flagship store is. Dynasty? Well, you could call the Marcus family one. Both shows are about rich people; the kind who would shop at Neiman-Marcus. But that's not really it. The main similarity is a simple one—"Dallas" and "Dynasty" are pure entertainment. So is Neiman-Marcus. Neiman-Marcus isn't just any old retailer. It has "an aura," "a mystique," a "romanticism," to use a few terms employees mention.

So what's the big deal? Well, Neiman-Marcus has created the ultimate shopping experience; it's retailing as a pure (and often expensive) kick, merchandising plus a heavy dose of culture and the arts. Shoppers love it and so do the employees.

Walk into any Neiman-Marcus store and you'll notice the focus on artistic creativity. Management goes to all ends to make their stores different—sometimes to the tune of several million dollars *over* budget. Like the time they built a store in San Francisco and decided to build around an old stained-glass window rather than demolish it. That's probably why one employee said, "There's an appreciation for aesthetics here that goes beyond sound business practices."

And aesthetics don't stop at the selling floor. Flashy displays and gala events aside, Neiman-Marcus taste extends everywhere—even to the centralized buying offices. Housed at the Dallas flagship store, these offices aren't the typical retailing office tucked away behind the scenes. Not at Neiman's. Here, they cover the top two floors and they seem miles away from the commotion downstairs. A cool mauve and gray color scheme, carpeting, clean lines, little clutter, computer terminals, even windows for some—the buying offices are sleek, modern and terribly deceiving.

Why? Because the people in those offices are typical retailing go-getters. Well, maybe not completely typical. This is Neiman-Marcus, remember, so the workers here have that special Neiman-Marcus attitude. Some say it's part of the Texas heritage; others say it's part of the Marcus dynasty influence. But whatever it is, it's all part of that Neiman-Marcus brand of show business.

As one young woman put it, "Neiman-Marcus is in entertainment. That's what this business is all about and Neiman's is one of the best at doing that—entertaining the customer."

PEOPLE

Neiman-Marcus people have all the attributes most retailing people have—they're aggressive, ambitious and hard-working. But there's more—Neiman-Marcus people are as distinct as Neiman-Marcus itself. In fact, the people who work here are a lot like the stores.

First, the special look. "It's a matter of sophistication," an assistant buyer said in describing the typical Neiman-Marcus person. "Everybody in my training class has some type of sophistication about them."

That's the truth. Since Neiman-Marcus is so big on creativity, employees are, too. "There's nobody here who wears a blue suit, a white shirt and a red tie," an eight-year vet asserted.

But Neiman's does have *some* rules about clothing—while it promotes a distinct, personal look, "on the sales floor, there are certain stipulations," explained a buyer. "Silly things like pantyhose and underwear."

Sounds pretty logical, actually. But Neiman-Marcus people aren't just clothes nuts.

The main thing that makes Neiman-Marcus employees what they are is what distinguishes Neiman-Marcus stores—a focus on creativity and culture. "I could talk about the arts to over 50 percent of the people working here and they would know *everything* that's happening culturally in the Dallas area," a young man said.

So what's the typical Neiman-Marcus employee? A buyer summed it up: "Someone who enjoys the arts, who likes to go to the theater, who likes rock bands. You've just got to have an interest in life."

And Neiman's people do.

JOBS

The one area Neiman-Marcus *doesn't* seem that creative in is jobs. People here follow the same **merchandising** career path that most other stores have—the basic executive trainee, assistant buyer, department manager, buyer and so on.

But even though it all *looks* the same, there are certain little Neiman-Marcus touches. Starting in the executive training classes, where trainees quickly learn just how much attention Neiman-Marcus pays to detail.

"The training class is spectacular," raved an assistant buyer. "We learn everything—all about textiles, how to do alterations, every single aspect of the business."

Alterations? In classes for executives? "Sometimes we're sitting in there bored to tears," she admitted. "But it's going to help us in the long run. They're trying to give us a taste of everything."

That's an understatement. Trainees take two full days of classes each week for ten weeks. In addition to learning about fabrics and alterations, they learn retailing inside and out—retail math, management, personnel and more. And as if the learning itself isn't enough, these trainees get tested, too—six exams and a final. Not to mention their main project—a case study, in which the trainees are given a true retailing problem to solve. They're assigned other people in the class to work with and—here's the kicker—they're given the assignment the night before it's due. No wonder one former trainee who survived the course said, "It was tough. I had responsibility in the office *and* responsibility to pass the training class before I could even stay here."

Oh, yes. While new hirees are taking these classes, they're *also* serving a three-week stint as an assistant to a department manager, then taking rotating assignments in different buyers' offices. And one more very important item—people who don't pass the training class do *not* have a job at Neiman's.

And for those who *do* stick it out? Then, the real fun begins, kind of.

"Unfortunately, when you're first learning the business, you do a lot of crunching of numbers. It's a lot of tedious paperwork," a buyer commented.

Even though the buying offices all use computers, the paperwork still mounts up. "This business has so much paperwork, I'm going crazy," said an assistant buyer. "We've got so many different reports, telling what color is selling, which style is selling, which class is selling—everything."

There *is* a positive side to it. As an aggressive young man said, "There are some 22-year-olds here who are managing a $10-million business. Granted, it's the paperwork they're doing, but still, that is no small potatoes."

Neither is the work. "You're constantly being pulled in three to twenty different directions," said a young woman. "The phone's ringing, your divisional wants you, the buyer wants you . . ."

If you're lucky enough and outspoken enough, you will be doing more than clerical work. Neiman-Marcus employees learn that the way to get ahead is to be honest and ask for the work.

"There are times when I stop my buyer and say, 'I want to do that. I want to learn how to do that, because when you're in New York, I'll need to know.' And she appreciates that."

It shouldn't be difficult for the lower-level Neiman employees to be that frank. One thing Neiman/Marcus stresses to new hirees is "be sure you like the people you work with, be sure you can work with your peers and enjoy your work."

And most people here seem to enjoy their work—even when it *is* the more grueling assistant buyer duties. At every level, employees are encouraged to have fun with what they're doing. In some cases, it isn't too difficult. The Neiman emphasis on customer service, shopping as entertainment and creativity makes all the grunt work worthwhile.

One of Neiman's premier buyers summed it up for all of them: "I could never stay here if I felt I was just buying clothes for rich people. I go beyond that to color, and fabric. It's an art form. Maybe you've conned yourself into thinking that, but you do. You just find the magic of it."

LIFE

Neiman-Marcus makes it easy for people to get ultra-involved in their work—on or off the job. For example, a buyer explained some of the ways Neiman-Marcus people figure out what to buy—"What's new at the art museums? What's the latest video on MTV? It sounds silly, but it all fits. This summer, all I've seen are crop tops because of Madonna's little belly . . . Just keeping your eyes open. That's the personal stuff you do outside of work. It's my life now."

And a department manager explained the excitement in setting up a new department—"We are creating a department from nothing. It's wild. It's visual applied arts, like the theater. It's actually a production."

It's that kind of attitude that keeps everyone going.

"You're always thinking of new ways of merchandising, new ways of getting the customer's eye," said a young woman. "It *is* the entertainment business. The actor and the audience—and the audience is right there. It's an adventure working here."

And a time-consuming one, too.

DOLLARS AND SENSE

Salaries here are nothing to complain about, but nothing to write home about either.

As for promotion opportunities, there's an "unofficial official" length of stay at each of the merchandising job levels. (One to one and a half years as an assistant buyer, one and a half to two years as a department manager, two to three years as a buyer, and so on, like most stores.)

That career path is one of the few things employees complain about. "We lose a lot of good people because they get bored at those levels," asserted a fast-moving department manager. "Personally, I could not be an assistant buyer for one to two years. It's that old traditional notion—you've got to pay your dues."

But it's not cast in stone. Some people who come in with strong background experience do move faster. And one employee said she's seeing a change. "More and more, it's getting tailored to the individual."

GETTING IN—TRICKS OF THE TRADE

"If you love people and love things and get enjoyment out of seeing people get enjoyment, retailing is for you and Neiman/Marcus is for you," gushed a recent hiree. "But it's quite a thing to get into this program."

That's the truth. Even if you like the arts, go to the theater and art museums a lot, and you love quality merchandise, you need a few more things to break in.

First, and most important, you've got to have experience. "When I looked at the bios of everyone in my training class, they all had experience," said an assistant buyer.

And even though Neiman's prides itself on its professional salespeople, selling is not necessarily the best experience to have. "Get good concentrated experience," one young woman suggested. "Managerial experience if possible. It's hard but it's worth it."

And how. Staffers here explain that a lot of people don't make it into the training program; they're told to go get experience and try again.

What else? On the practical side—"Math skills are real important," said one buyer. "If you don't like math, forget it. I mean it. Forget it!"

Another thing that helps you stand out from the crowd is computer skills. Said an assistant buyer, "I would never have thought I'd be glad I had a concentration of computer courses, but here it's important to be familiar with the computer, not intimidated by it."

But remember, there's that Neiman reputation you've got to be aware of. And if you want a job here, you've got to believe in it. As one of the top buyers in the store said, 'I get ill when I see people come here who don't fit in. There's a magic to working here other than jumping from merchandising position to merchandising position. It takes a real curiosity, a real creativity."

And, as always, creativity is the last word at Neiman's.

THE BOTTOM LINE

Retailing, Texas style—y'all come down now, heah?

TELEVISION

"So much is written about the networks. I think, oddly enough, news divisions are more concerned about leaks than the White House is."

That's what an employee of one of the networks said. And he's got a point. In 1985, TV news shows aired a lot of stories about television: Capital Cities merging with ABC; Ted Turner trying to take over CBS; Senator Jesse Helms trying to take over CBS; GE buying RCA, which owns NBC; Dan Rather and other CBS News staffers discussing a purchase of CBS News; and so on.

But all the uncertainty and all the transitions aren't keeping people from wanting to break into television. And who can blame them? Working in TV can be exciting, exhilarating, and glamorous. It can also be exhausting, backbreaking, and boring. But 110,000 people think it's worth it. That's the approximate number working in television.

Essentially, television can be broken into three main units—Entertainment, News, and Sports—and television jobs can be broken into three major groups—business (people in sales, affiliate relations, or programming), production (people involved in the actual work of producing news, sports, or entertainment shows), and engineering/technical (people operating the technical equipment—tape editors, camera people, electronic news gathering crews, studio personnel). We're going to be focusing on television news.

Until recently, news was a profit-eater, and time was given over to news only because of the FCC rules and the prestige value. But with the popularity of shows like CBS's "60 Minutes" and ABC's "Nightline," and the birth of Ted Turner's 24-hour

Cable News Network, news has become more of a money-maker.

While sports and news are distinct departments, usually the operation and jobs are similar.

The typical entry-level position in news is that of **desk assistant** (starting salary $12,000–$15,000). This is the grunt job in any newsroom. Usually, desk assistants answer phones, take messages, pull wire copy, and act as gofers. **Production assistants** or **associates** (starting salary $13,000–$20,000) work more on the production aspects of the show, helping out producers and associate producers. While at most networks this is a step up from a desk assistant position, the work is still generally menial. PAs may type rundowns of the show, pull and screen file tape for reporters and producers, work with tape editors in putting together footage for a story, and so on.

Another lower level news job is that of **researcher** (starting salary $13,000–$24,000). Researchers do such work on stories or shows as fact-checking, getting background information, finding interview subjects, and setting up interviews.

Above the entry-level positions is that of **news writer** (average starting salary $25,000–$50,000). News writers write introductions, or "leads," to "packages" (reporter's stories on tape) for the anchors, and rewrite wire stories. They work closely with news editors (average salary $30,000–$60,000), who work on the production desk, editing copy for air.

Associate producers (starting salary $25,000–$35,000) are more involved with the production of pieces for air. Depending on the show, they may generate story ideas, work with tape editors in cutting pieces for air, write when necessary, and generally assist the producer.

Producers (average salary $40,000–$100,000) on a nightly news show develop the lineup of stories and are responsible for all stories appearing on that show. They usually come up with angles on the stories, determine where in the show stories will appear, how long each story will run, etc. Producers on documentaries or other news specials are more involved with the development of a show idea and seeing that idea through to completion, with responsibility for every phase of the project from on-air talent to editing to budget. There are different kinds of producers, also, depending on the station or network. Field producers work in the field with an electronic news gathering crew, usually on complex stories or on stories that are not assigned to a reporter, making sure they get the shots necessary, and so on; studio producers work in the studio with the director. On some shows, producers are responsible for specific segments (there may be a style producer, a sports producer, etc.).

On the nonproduction side of news, staffers may be on the assignment desk as **assignment editors** ($25,000–$50,000), assigning camera crews to stories, keeping tabs on those crews, listening to police scanners for possible breaking stories, and generally keeping the news-gathering process running smoothly. Assisted by assistant assignment editors and desk assistants, they basically pull together news for the nightly show, assign crews and reporters to stories, then brief the producer when he or she comes in.

Directors and **associate directors** ($35,000–$100,000) work in the studio, directing the studio and technical staff. The director tells studio camera people what to do, tells the technical director which tape machine or which camera will be on air, cues tapes, and essentially keeps all the elements of the broadcast moving. The AD assists the director by doing such things as counting down tape, tracking the length of pieces, informing the director what's coming next, how long commercial breaks are, and so on. Specialized positions in the control room include that of **technical director**, who works on the board, essentially pushing buttons that control what appears on screen. An **audio** person controls the audio levels of the microphones on set; a **video** person controls the video quality in terms of color and balance. A **Chyron operator** operates a character generator, typing in the supers (titles) that will be used on show and calling them up at the director's cue. Near the top of the heap in a news operation are the **executive producer** and **managing editor**, who have overall responsibility for the news show. Then at the top there is the **news director**, who is ultimately responsible for the entire operation.

And there's more: the entire technical staff, the graphics staff, headed by an art director, and others.

Most jobs in news are unionized. And most unions cover different areas. Technicians have a union, nonmanagerial production people and writers have a union, directors and associate directors have a union. Just about everybody seems to have a union. And it's the union that determines pay scales, job levels, overtime rules, and so on. Typically, the technicians' union is the strongest at a network or station.

Working in news means long hours, periods of near frenzy, and absolute dedication. TV News is a twenty-four-hour a day, seven-day a week job. When a big story breaks, no matter where you are and what you're doing, you're expected to show up at that newsroom, prepared to work your fingers to the bone.

And that's what most news staffers do. They might complain about having no life outside of news, but that's really the way most like it. News people are news people—and that means news is their life.

ABC

VITAL STATISTICS

- **locations:** New York (headquarters); affiliates and stations nationwide, including VHF stations (New York, Chicago, Detroit, Los Angeles, San Francisco)
- **revenues:** $3.70 billion (1984); $3.30 billion (1984 broadcast revenues)
- **rank:** 3rd (in network ratings 1985) 3rd (in evening news ratings 1985)
- **employees:** 1,400

AS SEEN FROM THE OUTSIDE

ABC has long had the reputation of being the scrappy underdog, the perennial No. 3 of the big (3) networks. Then came "Happy Days," "Mork and Mindy," "Three's Company," "Charlie's Angels," "World News Tonight," and "Nightline," and No. 3 became No. 1. Only for a while, though.

Because then came NBC and the "Bill Cosby Show," "Miami Vice," and "Hill Street Blues." And the old No. 3 went back to being No. 3. But this too should be only for a while, or so Capital Cities Communications hopes.

Capital Cities? They're the folks who merged with ABC in January 1986, paying over $3.5 billion under the merger agreement. It's a case of a small fish swallowing a whale, actually. Not that Cap Cities is tiny. Not counting ABC's holdings, Cap Cities owns and operates seven television stations and six AM and six FM radio stations. That's the broadcasting side of things. There's also the publishing: Cap Cities puts out ten daily newspapers, twenty-seven weekly newspapers, and has a Specialized Publication Group that includes such heavy weights as Fairchild Publications (home of *Women's Wear Daily*). Then there's the cable television division, with interests in fifty-four cable TV systems. And all those holdings add up to roughly $939.7 million in 1984 revenues.

That's certainly not peanuts. But look at the broadcasting company that got swallowed. In the same time period, ABC racked up about $3.7 billion in revenues. As for holdings, well, there's the ABC Broadcast Group, which includes ABC Television Network (distribution and sales for Entertainment, News, and Sports to 212 affiliate stations); five ABC-owned television stations; five AM and seven FM radio stations; seven satellite-delivered radio networks to about 1,800 affiliates; and ABC Motion Pictures. And then there's ABC Publishing, which is split into ten operating units; and ABC Video Enterprises (ABC/VE), which owns ESPN, Lifetime (held jointly with the Hearst Corporation and Cable Health Network) and Arts & Entertainment Network (held jointly with the Hearst Corporation and RCA).

Add the two communications companies together and you've got quite a large alliance. So large that the FCC gave ABC and Capital Cities eighteen months to sell seven ABC-owned radio stations, three Capital Cities-owned radio stations, two Cap Cities TV stations, and two New Jersey newspapers. It all gets rather confusing . . .

And that's what people at ABC are discovering. With the announcement of the merger and the consequent complexities, not to mention lagging ratings and a less-than-stellar advertising performance, about 350 ABC staffers were laid off. And fear of further layoffs is still in the air. Capital Cities has a reputation as a frugal company. And some of ABC's holdings aren't all that profitable, such as the motion picture and cable programming units.

As for the network itself, word has it that if Capital Cities maintains a hands-off attitude, all will be well. Let the Cap Cities people work with the ABC owned-and-operated stations; that's where their expertise is. But ABC wants to be No. 1 again. That means strong programming, popular TV shows, and money.

Cost-cutting simply won't do where ABC, the network, is concerned. And it's getting tired of being No. 3 again.

HEARD AT THE WATER COOLER—
WHAT IT'S REALLY LIKE TO WORK HERE

ABC is big, it's young, it's brassy, and it's a little confused lately.

"I came here and I thought, 'This is great. A network—it's stable, secure, never changing. There's only three of them. What could happen?' " said a young woman. "Who would buy a network?"

Capital Cities would, for one. So ABC isn't *quite* as brassy and self-assured as it used to be. A lot of staffers are holding their breaths, wondering what it's going to be like under Cap Cities. Some are worrying about layoffs and cost-cutting; others are cautiously optimistic. And everyone seems to be taking a "wait and see" stance.

But there are some aspects of ABC that probably won't change all that much, despite all the rumbles. For one thing, ABC is an awfully big place. And it has a reputation for being a scrappy, young upstart.

How big is it? Well, it's so big that staffers say they don't know what most of their co-workers are doing. And no wonder. They're all working in different buildings. Corporate employees are in a dark, tall skyscraper just up the street from CBS. News staffers work among messier, paper-filled offices, bustling, crowded newsrooms, and mazes of editing and control rooms in other buildings farther uptown. Not to mention all the bureaus and what not. For all the size, though, there's a similar feel. There's a youthful attitude everywhere, and a lot of young people working here.

And they're all over the place. Especially in news. That's one part of ABC where energy is an absolute necessity. People are always running around, shows and stories are changed at the last minute, and air time is never far away. Like most news organizations, it's chaotic, crazed, and pressured. But staffers seem to thrive on that.

Sure, it's bureaucratic here, and, yes, staffers are always complaining. But when the chips are down, they'll stick with ABC, merger or no merger. It's network television and that means it's one of the big guys.

As one staffer said, "I don't know exactly what it's going to be like after the merger, but it's always going to be ABC."

And that means it's going to be young, energetic, and sassy.

PEOPLE

"It's very young," commented one news employee. "I remember walking on the 'Nightline' floor and I couldn't believe all these young people running around and doing so much."

That's the overwhelming characteristic of ABC News—and of

ABC generally. But it doesn't mean everyone's alike. Corporate staffers are typically corporate since "it's a typical big company on that side." And people in news are "inquisitive, curious . . . Very bright, but not head-in-the-cloud intellectuals."

But that's not all by any means. At a big network, it's not enough to be smart and ask questions. People have to be pretty aggressive to survive. To get ahead, they have to be even *more* aggressive. And a lot of ABC news staffers are hell-bent on success.

There is a downside to working with a lot of people who are just as bright, go-getting and ambitious as you are, however. "There's a constant attitude of 'I can outdo you,'" a staffer commented. "Like, 'you're not in at 8 and staying till 12, and I am. If you're not working 12 hours a day, I can outdo you. If you haven't read all the newspapers yet, I read them all before 10 A.M.'" And so on . . .

But for all that, even a cynical staffer who's planning to quit says ABC News staffers are fun to work with. They're all pretty much in the same boat, after all—they're on the young side working in a high-pressure business and trying to get ahead. So having a sense of humor keeps them sane.

"There's a lot of joking," said a young woman. "Totally irreverent humor about everything."

But when air time comes around, it doesn't make any difference how bright or ambitious or funny you are. It's simply a matter of getting your work done as quickly as possible. There's just no time for anything else.

"It's really phenomenal. When a lot of pressure is on, you see people pulling together," explained a young woman who's seen many shows changed at the last minute. "When it's over, people say, 'It's amazing that we got all this done.' But somehow it always gets done."

JOBS

"I've met and spoken with people here who know so little about this company," explained a public relations staffer. "We all work for the same company, our jobs are interrelated in that we're all working toward something for ABC—but when it comes to the day-to-day things . . ."

When it comes to the day-to-day things, no one quite knows what everybody else is doing. Big networks aren't streamlined.

There are so many jobs, so many departments, and so many different aspects of broadcasting that staffers say it's impossible to understand exactly what ABC is all about.

And it doesn't get any simpler even if you look at only one division. Take **News**, for example. ABC News people don't merely say, "I work for ABC News." That's too easy. Instead, it's, "I work for 'World News Tonight' or 'Nightline' or 'Close-up' " And they're not just news staffers—they're technicians or production people or support staffers. And technicians may be tape editors or film editors or camera people or ENG crew members; production people may be field producers or studio producers or some other kind of producers; support staffers may be publicists or budget coordinators or unit managers . . .

And that's not even taking the unions into account. Like most news operations, ABC is unionized. There's a union for technical people, another one for nontechnical, even the Directors Guild for directors. It's no wonder no one knows anybody else's job.

"One of the disadvantages to working for a network—everything is very fragmented," a news employee commented. "People have a very specific detailed job description and do only one thing."

That's why many people say you can get more diverse experience working at an affiliate or a local station. But there is a payoff to working at ABC in your very specific position, as one young woman explained. "Working at a local station is probably better for developing the skills you need to be a great reporter or great producer or something. But in terms of being successful, if you have the chance to work at a network—even in an entry-level job—I think you should take it."

Being at ABC might not be the best professional learning ground, but it's network TV. That means prestige, good contacts, and an impressive credit on your resumé. And that explains why so many people compete for the less-than-exciting lower level jobs.

How do they prove they're ABC material? "You sort of have to be willing to do anything," explained a young woman. "It's a combination of being bright on one hand and not smug about doing whatever needs to be done on the other hand. I mean, there are Columbia Journalism School graduates who are desk assistants and they're answering phones, taking messages, thing like that. You just can't think your work is beneath you."

Even though in the entry-level desk assistant position, it usually is. Desk assistants do all the grunt work. It's essentially a gofer job, although duties vary from show to show.

"It's not an enjoyable job," remarked a staffer, "but it's a great way to break in."

Once they have made it in, DAs have to learn to do anything and everything and keep pushing for promotions. And push they do.

"Around here, there's an attitude that if you stay in a job for longer than a year or so, you're making a big mistake, you won't make it," explained a producer.

DAs who do make it usually move up to become researchers, production assistants, or production associates. According to one staffer, a DA at ABC News in New York who becomes a production assistant is tracked to an eventual director's position, whereas a production associate is tracked to a producer's spot.

Whatever position news staffers land in, there's one constant. News is never predictable; stories, even entire shows, may change at the last minute. So staffers have to realize that, no matter how hard they've worked on a piece, there's always the chance it won't make air.

"You plan a piece, plan a shoot, and put everything you have into it," explained a young woman. "Then it gets dumped. It's hard not say, 'I just won't work as hard next time.' You have to learn to say it doesn't matter. You have to think, 'I'm going to kill myself and put 100 percent into this even though it might never be aired.'"

It's a little different for people on the **support services** staff. Yes, they deal with the unpredictable nature of news, but more important, they deal with the unpredictable nature of news *people*.

"One thing we have to deal with is personalities. And it's a love-hate relationship between our department and other departments," said a young man in news administration. "As far as they're concerned, they're all journalists. They do yell . . ."

According to a staffer who handles the financial end of news operations, "support services is the easiest thing to get into." Essentially, the support services staff does budgeting, estimating, and other financial duties for a particular program or unit. The career path here is very clear-cut—entry-level people begin as budget coordinator, move up to program budget controller, then senior controller, and finally manager. And the hours are fairly long. Said one employee, "Nine to fivers don't fit in. It requires more than that—say 7:30 to 6:30. And you work at least every other weekend."

But there are a few plusses to being apart from the hands-on news work. One manager explained that support services gives you the most flexibility to move ahead. "I could go to the corporate side, to systems . . ." Is he going to move? "There are still opportunities here."

Once you've passed the entry-level stages, you might travel. Since news happens all over the place and ABC News people are where the news happens, ABC News controllers go overseas to deal with the money matters and supervise the actual financial transactions—such as cashing checks, exchanging money, paying local crews. It's really like being a local banker. And that can be a real trip.

One young man mentioned that he spent time in England, Switzerland, Nigeria, and France. Plus, he added, "I spent three weeks in Beirut. I was scared going in, scared going out." So, even being in the financial side of ABC News can be exciting.

On the **corporate** side, the ABC Broadcast group has people in jobs like corporate communications, public relations, special projects, and so forth. Many corporate staffers started in entry-level spots and moved up. On ABC's corporate side, who you know counts. And being a secretary to someone important is a decent start in the right direction.

"You have to work your way up," a former secretary, now a manager, stated. "You come in as a typist, a secretary, or a page. And you get a sense of people, how the company is run."

And staffers say it's not that difficult to stay enthusiastic—even when they're doing the most menial of jobs. After all, they're doing that work for ABC.

LIFE
Yet again, life at ABC depends on where you are at ABC. Corporate life is corporate life and news life is news life.

On the corporate side, people talk a lot about team spirit. "There's a great esprit de corps," said a young woman. "Maybe it's from ABC struggling for so many years."

In the news, some people mention the glitzier aspects—working alongside media celebrities or calling some VIP to set up an interview. "You're walking down the hall with Peter Jennings or someone else and it's pretty exciting," said a news employee. "But the glamour part of it wears off very fast. You really can't function if you're spellbound."

People work long hours and odd schedules, and they live the news. One news employee described her co-workers as "an incredibly insular, tightly knit group."

But it's not all hunky-dory. It's a *competitive* tightly knit group so "a good knowledge of politicking helps, for better or for worse," noted a staffer. "If you know the right place to be, the right people . . ."

Well, it just makes life a little simpler.

DOLLARS AND SENSE

All around, rather good. Salaries are "competitive," and unionized new employees get the stuff that union contracts are made of—overtime, holiday pay, golden time (double time and a half), and so forth.

One benefit that many employees appreciate is a liberal tuition reimbursement program. "I've taken part in the education assistance program," said one staffer, "and now I'm going through law school."

That's a good move. As the merger nears, the more skills and credentials an ABC employee has nowdays, the better. As a staffer noted, "These are no longer fat times. They're more concerned with the bottom line now."

And, along those lines, many employees mention that the promotion rate has slowed a bit. "Now, whenever a position is vacated, that position has to be rejustified," explained a long-term employee.

GETTING IN—TRICKS OF THE TRADE

This is network television, right? Good luck!

"In the five years that I've been here, I'd say in four and a half of them we've been in some type of job freeze or another," an employee said with a rueful smile. That's how it is with networks, espeicaly lately, in the new "let's go out and buy us a network" corporate world. But people do make it in, despite all the difficulties.

People in the corporate part of ABC say it's best to take any job offered you. That gets your foot in the door. "And try some of the avenues less traveled," suggested a successful young woman who worked her way up. "You should really try to contact people in the company. Try different areas—not just news."

What about news, though? It's a little different. For one thing, "It's not that easy to start as a secretary and move up," said a former secretary who moved up. "It's much more common to be a desk assistant and work your way up through the ranks."

And that's not easy. Staffers say it's really a fluke to break into news—although contacts help make that fluke more possible. Persistence is really the key. Establish contacts with whomever possible, send in letters, and check out the internships.

And another tip that might help make the difference between you and a thousand other applicants: take college courses that will help with your understanding of news. "Take government courses, political science, and follow current events," one producer advised.

THE BOTTOM LINE

Still brassy.

CBS

- locations: New York (headquarters)
- revenues: $4.92 billion (1984 total); $2.72 billion (1984 broadcast revenues)
- rank: 2nd (network ratings 1985); 1st (evening news ratings 1985)
- employees: 30,500

AS SEEN FROM THE OUTSIDE

CBS is the communications company that everyone is communicating about. And that makes CBS a little nervous.

First came the Westmoreland case, when the former general in Vietnam accused the company of unfair reporting. Then came Senator Jesse Helms with his concerns that CBS was too liberal. And then Ted Turner of TBS in Atlanta decided to have a go at buying the company. CBS fought off these attacks successfully, but expensively.

During Ted Turner's attempted takeover, CBS took on a lot of debt—buying back stock and fending off the raiders. That hurt, and according to some reports, CBS has offered early retirement to as many as two thousand employees from all sectors of the company—from cleaning women in Georgia to mid-level managers in New York. To the company's credit, the early retirement program is comprehensive and earnestly tries to offer the best to those unfortunate people. But that hasn't kept some people from being nervous and some feathers from being ruffled.

Things got even more sticky in late 1985 when 74 staffers were let go from CBS News. Traditionally, the News department was considered the crown jewel of CBS Broadcasting, CBS's heart and soul. So when cost-cutting and staff cutbacks struck there, the atmosphere became a bit strained. It culminated in another "attempted takeover" of sorts, when CBS News employees, including "60 Minutes" producer Don Hewitt, anchorman Dan Rather, Morley Safer, Mike Wallace and Diane Sawyer, offered to buy CBS News from CBS. Needless to say, they were turned down. But the impact of their apparent dissatisfaction has lingered.

So CBS has come through the storms, but a lot of debt and a lot of fear have made the giant network just a bit flighty . . . And now they're battening down the hatches—electing Lawrence Tisch to the board (initially invited as a measure against an unfriendly takeover), and cutting down on some of their diversified holdings—selling their interest in Tri-Star Pictures, trying to sell their toy business, and leaving the computer software business. Why all the moves?

First and foremost, CBS wants to remain CBS. Like Gaul, it's divided into three parts. CBS Broadcast Group is the nuts and bolts of the company, its primary identity. It includes Television Network and Stations divisions, Sports, News, Radio, Operations, and CBS's productions division. Number two is the CBS Records Group, and number three, the ailing CBS Publishing Group. And all of this makes CBS, Inc. one of the largest diversified communications companies in the world.

For a while, though, CBS wanted to be something more, and along the way bought such diverse things as the New York Yankees, a riding toy company and a musical instrument company. But at CBS, tradition is always around the corner, and tradition said that CBS is a *communications* company, not a diversified conglomerate. So the communications stayed. The ballplayers and electric guitars went.

The tradition began in 1927, when the United Independent Broadcasters Incorporated began a network of sixteen independent radio stations. But the *real* CBS tradition began one year later, whenWilliam S. Paley became president of the struggling sixteen and renamed it the Columbia Broadcasting System, Inc. Network radio propelled CBS into TV, first with an experimental station in New York called WZXAB, then WCBS in 1941. All along the way, supersalesman and television visionary Paley was at the helm—making CBS No. 1 in television news and general programming.

But Paley's two hats of salesman and visionary have created an ambivalence that still characterizes the company. Traditional and deeply concerned with quality, CBS prides itself on programs such as "60 Minutes," "Face the Nation," and "M*A*S*H." But tradition doesn't pay the programming bills—advertisers do. So

CBS helped to start the trend to mass-market popular programming with the daytime soaps, and more important, the not-so-high-quality shows like "The Beverly Hillbillies."

Jed Clampett and his Beverly Hills kinfolk aside, CBS is seen as *the* quality-conscious programmer, particularly in its News division. CBS news gathering began in 1933; by World War II it was big time. CBS invented the news roundup, with Edward R. Murrow and William Shirer contributing on-the-spot analyses and viewpoints on the German invasion of Europe. Then, of course, came Walter Cronkite (who now sits on the board of directors) and an image of CBS that it still tries to maintain, that of integrity, decency, and a large dose of self-restraint.

And at CBS, you'd better not forget that.

HEARD AT THE WATER COOLER— WHAT IT'S REALLY LIKE TO WORK HERE

CBS is a lot like any other network—more big business than show business. The only difference is that CBS has a pretty famous past to counter the pretty shaky present. And it's not about to let anyone forget it—least of all the corporate employees.

Maybe that's why there's such a cautious, restrained air at corporate headquarters, affectionately(?) called Black Rock. The looming black monolith has doors that reach the ceilings, a careful color scheme of cheery colors like black, gray, white, and purple, and hundreds of people working in hundreds of jobs, dedicated to preserving the CBS tradition of integrity and honesty on the one hand, and money for the corporate coffers on the other.

But that's the corporate side of CBS. It's by no means the whole picture. While the corporate side runs the show, the News and Sports staff put on a show. Those are two of the most popular departments at any TV station, and it's the case with CBS, too.

CBS Sports is in Black Rock, but in terms of feel, it's a whole other ball game. Even the offices look different—light wood instead of somber colors, posters of sports stars instead of Bill Paley, and a general mood of hustle, bustle, and cheerfulness. It's called the "toy department" by staffers and that's the prevailing mood here—fun and games, even though the fun is hard work and the games are the ones they're trying to get on the air.

There's even more energy at CBS News. Housed in the CBS

Broadcast Center, a converted dairy with labyrinths of halls, tiny offices, editing rooms, and crowded newsrooms/studios, the News department never sleeps. It's across town from Black Rock and worlds apart in terms of atmosphere. People run back and forth, clutching wire copy, recently edited tape, or lunch (if they can fit it in). Constant movement, high energy, and suppressed hysteria are the norm here. There's always a show to put on and never enough time in the day.

But, still, Sports and News do share something with the restrained CBS headquarters. There's one thing they've all got in common, and that's CBS.

As one Sports staffer summed it up for them all, "You're aware of the fifty-nine years of mission and pride that we all have in CBS, because of Bill Paley and what CBS stands for—from Edward R. Murrow and Cronkite on the news side to Jack Benny and 'I Love Lucy.' "

And that's the way it is. (And, presumably, that's the way it always will be if CBS has anything to say about it.)

PEOPLE
"We have a stiff, kind of reserved, 'we'll think about it before we say anything' attitude," a young woman said, describing the CBS corporate staff.

Right on target. CBS corporate types are all those things and more. They work for a big corporation, they're proud to be part of that corporation, and by God, they're not going to rock the boat. They're like a Central Casting call for the perfect employee—neat, clean, loyal, reverent, careful, smart.

Especially smart. Black Rock is big on brains and it shows. Here you can overhear a secretary discussing Christopher Lasch and his theories on narcissism; "the powers that be pride themselves on intellect and chide each other for not knowing William Blake backward and forward," as one manager maintained. There's even a professor-in-residence program, providing an on-premises office for visiting professors who conduct seminars for employees' enrichment. It's all rather impressive.

Still, it's not just eggheads.

"You don't have to be a brain surgeon," said a Sports employee. "But the people who make it here are pretty shrewd. There are a lot of egos in this business. You've got to be pretty clever to work around that."

"We always called ourselves 'the kids,' " a fresh-faced production person said. "Someone said it was like a fraternity. You're all in the same boat, you've all been thrown into this high-powered place working with people you've seen on television."

Some of those TV personalities aren't too bad. According to a News staffer, "Dan Rather insists on knowing everyone's name all the way down to the guy who comes in and does the trash. Some of that spills into the main newsroom."

But social skills aren't the key for CBS employees. Survival skills are. "If you're lackadaisical in any way at an entry-level job, you can hang it up," a news assistant stated. "You have to be hungry."

JOBS

At CBS, it's not the job that counts, it's the place—CBS, of course. "The Tiffany of the networks," as a news employee termed it. And even though the image may be just a bit tarnished lately, it still keeps staffers, especially the new ones, intimidated.

"The first impression I had was 'I can't believe I'm actually at CBS,' " a young man explained. "You're just so proud of yourself, so happy to be here that you're kind of in awe."

That CBS mystique gets 'em every time. Why else would young, seemingly sane people put up with "self-inflicted torture," as a news staffer said, being "a slave for a few years," as another employee added? Why, because they get to be part of CBS. And that's a big deal as far as they're concerned.

Unfortunately, so is the work.

"You get there the first day and say, 'God, what have I done?' " remembers one staffer. "This stuff's flying all over the place, people are talking to you in code—but you just have to survive."

That's something entry-level personnel in **News** learn quickly. Straight out of school or from a smaller local station, they're thrust right into the thick of a busy network newsroom and they're expected to perform.

Surviving as an entry-level news assistant or desk assistant (DA) means putting up with a lot of grunt work, a minimum of glory, and long hours. No matter what a person's background is, "you're asked to roll wire copy, to change paper on the wire machines; you're at the beck and call of correspondents who may have had a hard day and start bitching at you, and you can't turn around and say, 'I graduated from Brown. You can't talk to me like that,' " summed up a man who went through all that.

That less than glamorous job description is probably why news staffers say being a desk assistant is a "humbling experience." But this *is* CBS, so those who can make the best of it.

"You can throw your arms up in the air at the end of the day and say, 'Screw it. This is too much for me,' " a young staffer explained. "But also, if you get all those pitch reels out and you see your pictures on the 'Evening News,' you can say, 'I did that,' and it's like scoring a touchdown."

That kind of enthusiasm keeps these people going, combined with long-range planning. "You realize that the reason you're working at that entry-level job is to do something more rewarding at a later date. You keep a level head, keep it in perspective and remember where you are," advised a recently promoted assignment editor.

But that doesn't guarantee easy promotions. Competition is tough here and everyone knows that. People say it's rare to rise through the ranks at the Broadcast Center, although it does sometimes happen. The general rule of thumb, though, is to start here as a DA, move to an affiliate for a higher job, then come back to the madness.

It's a little less intense in **Sports**, but it's still a ton of work. Entry level people here can come in as production secretaries, who answer phones, type, and do general gofer work. As in the News department, it's up to the individual to stand out from the crowd and get noticed. Translation—people learn to be political.

"The idea is, once you're in, to establish connections," a Sports employee explained. "With no exaggeration, I could literally still be sitting at my desk, answering phones all the time and typing."

Shrewd people figure out who to work for and they slowly move up the ladder—to researcher and broadcast associate. Five to six people usually are chosen for the Broadcast Associate program, and they go on all the shoots, operate the *Chyron* machine (which stores the titles that will be used on a show), make plane reservations for correspondents, and more. It's described as serving like a second assistant producer, and it's where most entry-level folks hope to land.

It's not all gravy though, by any means. Expecially from September to December when the NFL, the NBA, and the NHL seasons are on, not to mention the baseball playoffs and World Series.

"They [broadcast associates] leave Thursday, they take a late shuttle home Sunday, they come in Monday. From Monday to Wednesday, they're preparing their stuff. They might take off half a day so they don't go nuts, and on Thursday, they're back on a plane," a Sports employee rattled off. "And they go to glamorous places like Cleveland and Detroit and Buffalo . . ."

So that's what it's like working for a hotshot network? Well, as one employee put it, "When you first get here, you *really* have to have a desire to stay in television, to stick this out."

You've got it . . .

LIFE
As one might suspect, life at CBS is no picnic especially lately. And especially for non-corporate staffers.

"You stay in the same room for ten hours a day," a news employee explained. "Sometimes I'm envious of people working for other companies. . . . But you have to turn it around and make it a challenge."

That's it. Work hard and keep your head low . . .

DOLLARS AND SENSE
Money is rather low here at the starting News and Sports positions, which makes it about average for a television network.

"Pretty much when you start, you make about fifty dollars a day," a sports employee said. "If you work only five days, that's $250 before taxes. That's why people *will* work six days. To get the extra money."

"If you start complaining about the pay, you shouldn't be doing this," one News staffer said. "I consider this my graduate program, my last year of school and, hey, I'm getting paid for it. It's like being an artist. You're going to be poor for a while."

But only for a while. One thing CBS is very strong about is promoting from within. As one Sports employee in upper management said, "I'm not the only one here who's moved along. That's a first priority here—to find somebody on the floor who can take the next step. There's a great deal of effort given to moving people along at CBS."

You've just got to hang in . . .

GETTING IN—TRICKS OF THE TRADE

Well, it's not impossible to get a job at either CBS Sports or News, but it's close to it. Especially since the News department began laying off people in late 1985. Still, it can't hurt to try.

As far as News goes, the key is perseverance. Experience is most *definitely* preferred, but people who push and keep pushing can eventually break through the barriers. The best bet is knowing somebody, anybody. And one News staffer even suggests coming in person to the Broadcast Center lobby and letting yourself loose. "Jump right in and say, 'Hey, I'm here and I'm willing to work.'"

News staffers also advise getting into the newsroom by working for radio first. That's where a lot of the big-time newsmen started out (and where many still work). Breaking in through radio gets you into the newsroom (TV and radio share space) and can get you into a TV job.

A VP in the Sports department on the interview circuit recommends "being keenly interested and aware of what the job really represents. I look for a genuine spark, someone who's prepared to sacrifice, who's challenged by opportunity." He also suggests applicants know the difference between a touchdown and a field goal . . .

Who knows? If you've got that CBS spirit—a combination of enthusiasm, dedication, devotion, and a large dose of humility and staying power—you too may be able to say, as one young man did, "If you had told me when I was in college that I'd be working in CBS Sports, I would have said, 'Are you nuts? I'll be working at some cable station in Pennsylvania doing the pig farming reports. If I'm lucky.'"

But he was luckier and at CBS. Miracles do happen.

THE BOTTOM LINE

A few rough years, but it's still CBS.

CNN

VITAL STATISTICS

- **locations:** Atlanta (headquarters); 8 domestic bureaus; 9 foreign bureaus
- **revenues:** $88.5 million (1984—including CNN Headline News)
- **rank:** 1st (in cable news programming)
- **employees:** N/A

AS SEEN FROM THE OUTSIDE

It wasn't a bad idea: a twenty-four-hour news network. More news, more stories, more live coverage. News when the networks were airing "I Love Lucy" reruns—and news when they were airing news. And it's worked.

A lot of people laughed when Ted Turner launched CNN, but then again, a lot of people laughed when he said he'd win the America's Cup. But he won.

CNN's pioneering days are over now, but its future is still far from certain. Whose future is? A few years back, there were reports that CBS and NBC were interested in buying CNN. And last year, when Ted Turner tried to take over CBS, CNN could have been merged or sold. One thing is certain, though: CNN is growing. In 1985, CNN opened a Nairobi bureau, debuted twenty-four-hour transmission in Mexico, hit its highest rating, and began live twenty-four-hour transmission to Europe.

Not bad for six years in the business. CNN began on June 1, 1980 with a 1.7 million subscriber base. Today it reaches 34 million households, in all fifty states and a good bit of the rest of the world. A few years ago it was losing money; today it's in the black. And there are three CNNs now. In addition to the station, there's CNN Radio and CNN Headline News (syndicated)—a fast-paced news program that runs in quick half-hour cycles.

CNN now has eighteen news bureaus in the major U.S. and world cities, and some of the best live coverage in the business.

Less glitz, more information, and few media stars. But a lot of news.

HEARD AT THE WATER COOLER— WHAT IT'S REALLY LIKE TO WORK HERE

It's tough enough managing to stay sane working on a basic network newscast. Long hours of work go into that hour-long show. Now imagine multiplying that one-hour show by twenty-four and what have you got? A lot more work. But add to that smaller staffs, smaller budgets, smaller salaries, and less of a history. Sounds like sheer madness, right? Well, that's CNN.

CNN is everything you'd expect a twenty-four-hour-a-day, seven-day-a-week news operation to be. It's frenetic, exhausting, and exciting. Phones are always ringing, people are always running around, and there's always a crisis going on. No wonder most people here are super-energetic. They couldn't survive otherwise.

And probably because the network has been operating for only a few years, there's still a pioneer atmosphere in the air here, a "we might have less than the big guys, but we can take them on" attitude. Add to that a refreshing, non-hype, open atmosphere that's far from the media slickness of those big guys, and you find yourself pulling for CNN. And that's what makes CNN a pretty special place.

According to one man who's been with CNN since it began, "There's none other like CBS, ABC, or NBC. And there's none other like CNN, believe me. It's a unique bird altogether."

Added another old hand, "Working here *has* got a flavor. To say that it's a constant challenge is putting it mildly."

PEOPLE
So what kind of people would put up with the lunacy? First off, they're tough and enthusiastic. How else could they manage to take the pace?

"It's so easy to let the grind get to you," confessed one young woman. "But we're all good at keeping on our toes, keeping a sense of humor, and keeping our energy up."

CNN staffers are also pretty young. Wherever you go at CNN, you run into young people holding a variety of positions. TBS (the parent company) should stand not for Turner Broadcasting Systems, they say, but Turner Broadcasting *School*.

"There's more youth at CNN. I know my cohorts at the other three networks are older," an assistant bureau chief stated. "When I'm in the field and I see our youth against their maturity, I kind of chuckle to myself, because they've been doing it for ten years, fifteen years. And my guys have been doing it for three years."

What other characteristics do these people have that enables them to put up with the work? Well, like most TV news people, they're news nuts, they're dedicated, they've got a lot of energy—and they try to keep cool when the pressure mounts.

"One of the things that's always made the work do-able," explained a bureau chief, "is that there isn't an attitude problem on the part of people. People we've hired have always been 'Let's pull it together, let's get it on the air' types."

Yes, CNN people are good old-fashioned team workers, a personnel department's dream. That's not necessarily because they're abnormally friendly. Here, people *have* to be part of the CNN team. Who else works those crazy hours and makes a minimal salary? Still, there is something beyond that . . .

"Obviously, cynicism pervades throughout the television news business," a bureau chief said. "But people on CNN tend to be less cynical about things. You see people at other stations and they've got some type of attitude problem. CNN people by and large—although there are some notable exceptions—don't have that attitude problem."

"It's a very humorous place," added one noncynical director. "I won't go as far as to say it's fun—it's *almost* fun."

JOBS

In brief, jobs at CNN mean long hours, hard work, little money, and almost no glamour.

One young woman who was working for WTBS but wanted to be at CNN was warned by the staffers. "I kept calling downstairs to CNN and everybody told me CNN is not a fun place to work; it's a grind; it's twenty-four hours a day, and it's monotonous; it's overly challenging; the money isn't necessarily all that great. You're probably better off at TBS."

Well, she didn't listen to the voices of doom. And, now that she's been there a few years, what does she think about it? "I'm just thrilled to pieces to work here. Even with some of the worst working conditions . . .'"

That's the way most CNN staffers seem to feel. They know it's not perfect, but they really don't care that much. Especially the lower-level people. They're the ones who get the real grunt work, the lowest pay, and the strangest schedules. But they're at CNN to learn broadcasting and they'll take whatever is necessary to learn.

Many people praise CNN for its training. It's big on hiring entry-level people and it's easier to get experience here than at the networks. Entry-level video journalists, or VJs, work in a variety of jobs that teach them virtually every facet of broadcasting.

"You get a good overview of our business," one woman stated. "If you want to be an operations person, a technical person, a writer, a correspondent, or whatever, you can have a good idea of what your options are."

The program is an unusual one in the industry, mainly because, unlike other TV stations or networks, most bureaus of CNN aren't unionized, which means entry-level people can do anything and everything, even jobs of a technical nature, without having first to break into a union.

So what do VJs do? "They run camera, they floor direct, they run teleprompter," explained one staffer. "The first thing they do is tape evaluation—that's where you evaluate three-quarter-inch tape, decide if it's usable or should be thrown away. And that is a very boring position. But that's the first thing they do."

After VJs have worked on the floor for a while, they move into three-quarter-inch tape playback for the on-air shows, then to "ripping" (pulling and distributing) scripts. And then they decide which route they want to take—whether to pursue a technical career and move to audio operator, technical director, and eventually director, or a production career and move to become an editor, a writer, and finally producer.

On the technical side, the step after ripping scripts is working in the preproduction control room—dubbing tapes, playing tapes, or helping to put effects on packages. Then it's on to the on-air control room, running audio.

"And, eventually, if you're good enough, you go to Master Control. And after Master Control, you become a technical director. Meanwhile, you've been there all your life," said one former VJ ironically.

But that's really not the case. The key thing people like about the VJ program, and about CNN in general, is the relatively short amount of time it takes to get ahead. One young woman moved from VJ to director in five years.

"CNN has always been very careful to try to promote from within," said a young man who zoomed through the ranks. "At other places, you do a good job and you get a raise. Here, you do a good job and you get a promotion."

Still, some people maintain that the fast track at CNN has slowed down a bit since the early days. "There isn't as much movement," explained a veteran employee. "You are a VJ much longer now. I was a VJ for only a couple of months, but now you're a VJ for six months to a year."

That's really not that long a time in the grand scheme of the television industry. Still, it gets wearing. VJs are running around like crazy, doing all the things no one else would like to do, and at hours that might end at 2 A.M., or even begin at 2 A.M.

"All it takes is a little patience," a director advised. "Anybody at CNN will tell you that the first year is the hardest. And after the first year things start getting a little bit easier. It may feel like they're using you and taking advantage of you, but you have to use CNN as well, as your place to learn everything you can about television. At CNN, you can touch anything you want, unless it's on the air."

Once CNN employees have that foundation, it's time to move up. As at any place, the key to moving ahead is showing initiative, ability, and enthusiasm.

"The great thing about CNN is that they will give you the opportunity if they think you can handle it," said one staffer. "It's not like one of the entrenched networks where there's a definite procedure to follow to make any sort of move and you're looking at years and years and years. If you've got the ability, here they're willing to let you do it."

Sounds wonderful, right? Well, yes, CNN does give people opportunities, but, no, it's not quite as easy as it sounds. Showing you can handle a new job sometimes means going above and beyond the regular call of duty—way above and far beyond. Like the staffer quoted above. He's a success here, all right; but he "got lucky" and made people notice him while he was a VJ by staying after his shift was over (two o'clock in the morning) and writing for the overnight anchor. No sleep and no pay. But eventually it paid off.

One young woman who's got a plum on-air job managed to get it by working the gruesome overnight shift for free—and that while she held another job. You hear a lot of stories about people forging ahead like that here and you wonder how they manage. Because no matter what the job title, working at CNN is far from sweetness and light.

"There's a lot of pressure, of course," a five-year vet said. "Because the pay is so low, the people who you have working here don't have any experience, or very little experience. Many times as a director, I'll have the supervising producer getting really angry because of some mistakes going on. And I have to stand up for this person who's making the mistakes."

A bureau chief explained how difficult it sometimes is to cover a major story with a small staff. "Other stations have half a dozen correspondents they can rotate through; we have two. So it means a heck of a lot more work, a lot longer hours."

"And we need more pieces," he continued, "because we're a twenty-four-hour news network. We don't have one newscast a day, we have essentially twenty newscasts a day, and we need fresh material and new stuff on the air all the time."

There are other things that make CNN different from the networks. "No one comes with a limousine and picks *me* up like they do with every other morning anchor at the networks," a young anchor said. "We don't have the luxury—but, then again, we have the excitement."

Is it enough? Well . . . "Frankly," she added with a laugh, "A limousine *would* help."

LIFE

Life at CNN isn't quite as down and dirty as it was in the beginning. Back then, staffers were scrambling to get everything together—and often with few resources.

"I tell the story about how the day I started, they handed me a manila folder with two resumés in it—that was the foreign desk," a high-level woman explained.

And the pace hasn't slackened much. "We're always tap dancing as fast as we can," one young woman stated.

As for those people who do get fed up with the CNN pace and go to the networks or local stations? "They get bored," one staffer baldly asserted. "It's not that they don't have enough to do, they just don't do as much as they did here. Here you're busy practically all the time. Your day goes by pretty quickly. But, of course, the pay is always better at other places and that's what entices people to go elsewhere. And any place else you go, you're not going to have to work overnight."

And overnights are, without a doubt, a real part of life at a twenty-four-hour network.

DOLLARS AND SENSE
Not that good. Money is one of the chief complaints among CNN staffers.

"I started out as a VJ and I was paid minimum wage, $3.25 an hour," a staffer said. "Now the pay is a little bit better, it's still very low, though."

That's the truth. Most people here make less money than people in similar jobs at the networks. But it's not the end of the world. CNN staffers seem to weigh the low salaries against the opportunities they can get, and they realize there's a trade-off. "For me, it's tremendous," a young bureau chief raved. "I'm running a bureau, we're doing things that I think are good pieces of journalism, and so it's worth it to me. Maybe I don't make as much money right at this moment and maybe I won't down the road, but I wouldn't trade this time for anything."

GETTING IN—TRICKS OF THE TRADE

So you think you can take it? Figure the low pay, the long hours, and the general craziness are worth it? Join the club. There are a lot of people out there who want to work for CNN.

"It's hard to get in," said a VP. "There's a lot of competition now. But once you are in, you get some of the best journalism training in the world."

CNN is still bullish on hiring entry-level people, but they definitely prefer entry-level people with some experience.

"While there are certain people who are naturally talented who would probably make it if they just knew animal husbandry, they certainly do prefer people with some journalism background," a woman with a variety of news experience said.

Working at a college station, majoring in journalism, doing internships—all are highly recommended by CNN staffers. The Washington bureau has a sophisticated internship program that involves classes in broadcasting and rotating assignments every six months. And according to the assistant bureau chief there, they've hired eighteen of those interns as full-time staffers now. What does it take? "Our interns are creative, imaginative. They've got to have a willingness to put up with the work, no matter what bullshit you have to do and what hours you have to work." Those hours are a bit trying, with shifts from 5 A.M. to 1 P.M. and 1 P.M. to 11 P.M. But the interns who make it get jobs.

As for getting into the VJ program? The people who tend to make it are "the ones who hustle and the ones who have some talent," a young go-getter said.

"Travel as much as you can," advised one old hand. "Take an interest in issues, know world events, know the capitals of the world. I want somebody who says, 'I really don't know what I want to do, as long as it's in a newsroom.' "

THE BOTTOM LINE

It's not CBS but the opportunities are greater.

ABOUT THE AUTHORS

ROSS PETRAS speaks two foreign languages fluently and is a confirmed capitalist. After graduating from Brown University with a major in international relations and economics, he worked at a major metropolitan bank, switched to the United States Department of State and served overseas as a Foreign Service Officer. Upon returning to the States, he did an about-face to work in film. But he's now happily settled into writing and planning a business.

KATHRYN PETRAS, a graduate of New York University, has tried her hand at many different jobs in various industries—public relations, television and retailing full-time, almost everything else part-time, freelance or temping. She enjoys organizing offices, fixing computers and reading detective novels. After sampling different careers and industries, she's decided to create her own.